Women, Families, and Communities

Readings in American History

Volume One: To 1877

Women, Families, and Communities

Readings in American History

Volume One: To 1877

Nancy A. Hewitt
University of South Florida

SCOTT, FORESMAN/LITTLE, BROWN HIGHER EDUCATION
A Division of Scott, Foresman and Company
Glenview, Illinois   London, England

To my brother Will and in memory of Tom.

Credits

Cover: *War Spirit at Home*, 1866, by Lilly Martin Spencer. Collection of The Newark Museum, New Jersey, Purchase 1944 Wallace M. Scudder Bequest.

Additional acknowledgments for the copyrighted materials not credited on the page where they appear are listed in the Credits section on page 247. This section is to be considered a legal extension of the copyright page.

Library of Congress Cataloging-in-Publication Data

Women, families, and communities: readings in American history /
   [edited by] Nancy A. Hewitt.
         p.   cm.
   Includes bibliographies.
   Contents: v. 1 To 1877--v. 2. Since 1865.
   ISBN 0-673-18859-0 (v. 1) ISBN 0-673-18860-4 (v. 2)
   1. Women--United States--History. 2. United States--Social
conditions. I. Hewitt, Nancy A.
HQ1410.W646 1990b
305.4'0973-dc20   89-36113
                                                              CIP

      99   8 7

PREFACE

Good research and good teaching go hand in hand. *Women, Families, and Communities: Readings in American History* grows directly out of the connection between these two activities in my own work. As a student of women's history—and more specifically of women's activism and women's work in Rochester, New York, and Tampa, Florida—I have traced the ways that ordinary mothers, wives, and daughters contributed to the development of their families and communities. At the same time, as a teacher of introductory American history, I have focused on the ways that the major events in our nation's past—wars, elections, depressions, and technological revolutions—shaped and were shaped by the lives and actions of common women and men.

The articles collected here provide an introduction for students and instructors to the rich historical literature on women, families, and communities as well as a means for integrating the insights of this research into the story of North America's past. Traditionally focused on political, economic, and intellectual developments, U.S. history survey texts now include material on social relationships and popular culture and on the lives of women, workers, minorities, and immigrants. Still, it is difficult in a textbook or in lectures to cover both the broad sweep of American history and the particular experiences and actions of a wide array of historical actors. By combining the readings from this anthology with texts, lectures, and other monographs, students will learn how ordinary individuals, like themselves, participated in the shaping of America's past.

What is clear in looking at the table of contents to this volume and to works on social history in general is the diversity of American experiences. Though it is impossible to capture this diversity in a single collection, it is possible to encourage students to think about the range and richness of the American past. How did Native Americans respond to European colonization? How did Africans respond to slavery? How did the experience and meaning of industrialization, World War I, or the Great Depression differ by region, race, class, ethnic background, and gender? How and when did groups generally viewed as oppressed—Native Americans, African Americans, workers, women, immigrants—find the means to organize and protest on their own behalf? Each of these questions and the many others raised by the authors of the articles included here challenge us to see how everyday life and the "great events" of history intersect.

It is precisely at such intersections that women's historians most often are struck by the impossibility of separating women's experiences from those of men. In teaching American history, many of us have now integrated research on female activists and female workers into the larger stories of social reform and industrial development. Even if we focus on seemingly more masculine historical endeavors such as war, we quickly see how the activities and experiences of women and men are intertwined. We cannot fully understand the causes of wars, their short-term consequences or long-term significance, the means by which one side wins and the other loses, or even the particular strategies and tactics employed, without examining women's as well as men's participation.

In the earliest wars studied in an American history survey course—the French and Indian War, the Revolutionary War, the Civil War—the boundaries between the battlefield and the home front were blurred and always changing. During such conflicts, though women and men were expected to carry out different tasks, either sex might find itself called upon to nurse, cook, sew, spy, or fight. In later periods, when North Americans fought their wars overseas— in Cuba, the Philippines, Europe, and Asia—women's and men's roles were more distinct. Still, as men left for training camp and foreign combat, women expanded their activities on the home front to encompass many traditionally male jobs within the family, community, industries, government, and professions. Moreover, whatever the location or duration of battles, family and community members found their normal relations disrupted and transformed—sometimes temporarily, sometimes forever.

Developing links between women's history and history that has traditionally emphasized men and masculine activities is one of the goals of this work. Thus, the readings included here, most of which were written by women's historians, were selected because they chronicle local as well as national history, social as well as political and economic development, and women's as well as men's experiences and actions.

These articles provide case studies of individuals, families, and communities which illustrate broader historical themes. The introductions to each of the chronological parts, the headnotes to each of the articles, and the Suggested Readings and Questions for Study and Review at the end of each article place the individual essays in a wider context. At the same time, this material suggests how larger historical developments were themselves shaped by the events that occurred in particular families and communities. For each article, the first three study and review questions require students to relate the material presented to major issues of the time period and to other articles in the reader. The last question asks students to think about how the particular reading relates to other historical events and eras, thus pushing them to consider long-term continuities and changes in the American experience.

As researchers, scholars generally approach history as a complex process in which a wide range of individuals, experiences, and institutions come into play. As teachers, we often find it difficult to convey such complexities to our students. This volume is an attempt to introduce into the survey course more of the process of studying history. By asking students to connect political events with social forces, great affairs of state with common occurrences such as birth, marriage, housework, childrearing, sex, sharecropping, and washing clothes, we can help them understand what was involved in forming, sustaining, and transforming the people, families, and communities that built our nation.

Accompanying this collection is an Instructor's Resource Manual which provides detailed outlines for syllabi, coordinates the readings included here with chapters in a number of leading survey textbooks, and offers suggestions for in-class projects, library assignments, and further readings. In addition, the Instructor's Resource Manual includes sample questions for multiple choice, essay, and take-home exams.

ACKNOWLEDGMENTS

Good books owe much to good editors. I am deeply indebted to Larry Malley of Duke University Press who introduced me to the editors at Scott, Foresman/Little, Brown, and to Charlotte Iglarsh, Bruce Borland, and especially Barbara Muller and Betty Slack, who guided this project from conception to completion. I would also like to thank Julie Howell, Julie Hotchkiss, and Catherine Skintik. My colleagues and friends in the Department of History at the University of South Florida have contributed more than they know through their constant reminders of the intimate connection between excellence in teaching and research. I owe a special thanks to my newest coworkers, Giovanna Benadusi and Fraser Ottanelli, who at a critical moment provided me with a safe haven as well as strong coffee and encouraging comments. I also greatly appreciate the support of my department and university along with that of the College of Social and Behavioral Sciences and the United Faculty of Florida for providing me with the sabbatical that allowed me to complete this work.

For the contributors to this volume, my warmest regards for your generosity and assistance, especially Sarah Deutsch, Lori Ginzberg, Jacquelyn Hall, Joanne Meyerowitz, and Ruth Milkman, whose efforts went well beyond the call of sisterhood. To those whose research on women, families, and communities inspired my own, and especially to William Chafe who reinvigorated my commitment to local studies, my deepest thanks.

I am grateful also to the following, who read this volume before publication and offered many insightful, helpful, and encouraging suggestions: Robert Abzug, University of Texas at Austin; Jim Cobb, University of Alabama; Sarah J. Deutsch, Massachusetts Institute of Technology; Margaret Goodart, California State University at Sacramento; George C. Rable, Anderson College; Marilyn Rhinehart, North Harris Community College; Ingrid W. Scobie, Texas Women's University; and Kathryn Kish Sklar, State University of New York at Binghamton.

My most long-standing debt is owed to those special teachers whose eloquence and encouragement inspired me to pursue this career—Mendel Dick, Robert Smith, Susan Stuard, and Drew Faust—and to my fellow teaching assistants at Penn—Steven Zdatny, Marcus Rediker, and Andrew Feffer—with whom I shared my first forays into the classroom. My students in American history and women's history courses at the University of South Florida also deserve acknowledgment for keeping me informed, in ways both subtle and direct, of the effectiveness of my approach to teaching.

Steven Lawson has sustained me in this project from the beginning. His trenchant comments, timely infusions of humor, and masterful editing, along with his willingness to supervise an amazing array of household crises as I finished the manuscript, were only the most visible expressions of his support. These pages are dedicated to my brothers, Will and Tom, who gave me my first sense of how intertwined family and community could be. To them, to my parents, and to all those women, families, and communities who have shaped my own history, my deepest appreciation and affection.

Nancy A. Hewitt
University of South Florida

CONTENTS

Introduction   xv

Part One   Peopling the New World   1

One. Suzanne Lebsock   6
**"'No Obey': Indian, European, and African Women in
Seventeenth-Century Virginia"**

Two. Lyle Koehler   21
**"The Salem Village Cataclysm: Origins and Impact of a
Witch-hunt"**

Three. Anne Firor Scott   38
**"Sisters, Wives, and Mothers: Self-Portraits of Three
Eighteenth-Century Women"**

Part Two   Birth of a Nation   59

Four. Linda K. Kerber   61
**"Politicizing the Household: Sacrifice and Survival
During the American Revolution"**

Five. Catherine M. Scholten   78
**"'On the Importance of the Obstetrick Art': Changing
Customs of Childbirth in America, 1760-1825"**

Six. Paul E. Johnson   90
**"The Modernization of Greenleaf and Abigail Patch:
Land, Family, and Marginality in the New Republic"**

Part Three   Remaking Society   105

Seven. Thomas Dublin   110
**"Building a Community of Labor: Women, Work, and
Protest in Lowell"**

Eight. Caroll Smith-Rosenberg   124
**"Beauty, the Beast, and the Militant Woman: Sex Roles
and Sexual Standards in Jacksonian America"**

Nine. Nancy A. Hewitt   139
"Women's Antislavery Activism in Rochester,
New York"

Part Four   Expansion and Division   155

Ten. Theda Perdue   159
"Domesticating the Natives: Southern Indians and the
Cult of True Womanhood"

Eleven. Deborah G. White   171
"Female Slaves: Sex Roles and Social Status in the
Antebellum Plantation South"

Twelve. John Mack Faragher   181
"The Midwestern Farm Family at Midcentury"

Part Five   Civil War and Reconstruction   197

Thirteen. Lori D. Ginzberg   202
"A Passion for Efficiency: The Work of the United
States Sanitary Commission"

Fourteen. Jacqueline Jones   217
"Freed Women? The Civil War and Reconstruction"

Appendix

Ruth Milkman   235
"A Statistical Portrait"

Credits   247

Women, Families, and Communities

Readings in American History

Volume One: To 1877

Introduction

History has a dual meaning: It refers both to the events of the past and to interpretations of those events. The events that make up American history involved all kinds of people and took place in every type of setting. Rich, middling, and poor; white, brown, and black; native-born and immigrant; young and old; female and male; in cities and on farms; in metropolitan centers and in small villages; in long-settled communities and on the move; North and South; East and West; all Americans shaped the nation's history. Indians, blacks, and Hispanics as well as Europeans populated the North American continent; immigrant and farm families as well as "first families" produced its citizens; workers and grass roots activists as well as entrepreneurs and political leaders shaped its development.

Yet for a long time, scholars' interpretations of the past concentrated on Western Europeans and their American-born descendants, especially the men who served as business, political, or military leaders. These figures received far more attention than any other group, often more than all other groups combined. Such interpretations directed our eyes to a narrow segment of the continent's rich history. Like viewfinders at the Grand Canyon, they focused our gaze on the most spectacular peaks and valleys but failed to reveal the more mundane materials and processes that helped forge these vistas.

Historians are less like viewfinders than photographers. They actively select the angle of vision and the subject that they think will best reflect or illuminate a particular moment. A photographer covering a presidential campaign rally may stand in the crowd, but he or she will use a telephoto lens to zoom in on the candidate. In the morning paper, then, one will see only blurred, background images of the women and men who will vote in the election but a detailed, larger-than-life portrait of the man or woman who seeks to represent them. If we think of history textbooks as providing snapshots of significant moments in America's past, then this volume is an attempt to bring the blurred backgrounds into focus; indeed, to bring those background figures momentarily to the forefront.

To do so, we can draw on the voluminous work produced in the last two decades by social historians. Social history emphasizes the experiences of common women and men, allowing us to hear the voices of those rendered "inarticulate" by traditional interpretations. Viewing the past as a dynamic process in which all Americans participated, these scholars have revealed the ways that native Americans, African-Americans, immigrants, workers, and women shaped their worlds and our history.

Social historians have been especially concerned to discover the ways that those with only limited resources influenced the course of economic, social, and political development. By focusing on individual forms of resistance to exploitation (such as a slave feigning illness or purposely setting a slow pace of work) as well as collective acts of protest (such as boycotts, demonstrations, and organized social movements), social historians have illuminated an entirely new historical terrain. This terrain is one on which ordinary women and men, regardless of their wealth, status, or formal political power, become active agents of change, affecting critical historical developments.

To uncover the activities and ideas of less powerful groups, social historians often search out evidence on individual families and communities as a means of exploring the occurrences of everyday life. These events are then placed beside those we conventionally think of as important in America's past to illuminate the relations between ordinary people and extraordinary events. The present volume will draw on this rich body of research to bring these background figures into focus.

The purpose of focusing on more common people and their daily routines, of moving apparently peripheral figures to center stage, is not simply to replace one angle of vision with another. While we are examining seemingly unremarkable women and men in their families and communities, we will often discover their remarkable qualities—courage, persistence, strength, ingenuity. We will find that common folk performed uncommon feats when social upheaval, economic crisis, wartime mobilization, or personal necessity demanded that they do so. Yet at the same time, we will find women and men prevented from acting in their own interests or those of their neighbors by poverty, prejudice, and other disabling factors.

This volume, then, will examine how ordinary people both shaped and were shaped by the persons and events traditionally considered central to the nation's development. Ultimately, a new vision of our history will appear, one that brings into simultaneous focus national events and leaders and ordinary people in local communities. In this way, relationships between common folk in their everyday lives (people like most of you reading this book) and individual leaders of states, armies, corporations, and social movements will be made clearer.

Photographs are not only selective images of persons and events. They are also often idealized versions, simple images that reflect complex realities. The portrait of a former slave holding a white child (facing page) can carry many captions, none of which will fully capture the intimate and ambiguous relations between black women and their white charges. The look in this unnamed woman's eyes may be resignation or defiance. Her employment as a nanny after the Civil War may be a sign of new opportunities or renewed bondage. The baby may grow up to be a member of the Ku Klux Klan or a founder of the National Association for the Advancement of Colored People.

We all develop images of the kinds of people who make up the population—of women and men, blacks and whites, workers and bosses, rural Southerners and cosmopolitan Northerners. Our perceptions range from accurate to stereotypical to fanciful. These images emerge from newspapers, television, schoolrooms, novels, films, advertising, community and family attitudes, and a host of other sources. In past centuries, sermons, paintings, magazines, lectures, traveling museums, cartoons, folktales, and songs were even more important in shaping Americans' views of the world around them and, perhaps more markedly, of people and places far distant. Such images, regardless of their accuracy, affected the ways that any one group of Americans responded to others—Europeans to native Americans, whites to blacks, country folk to city dwellers, Southerners to Northerners, women to men.

Depictions of women, family, and community have changed dramatically over the years, but in each era dominant images have provided ideals to be either emulated or defied. Indian princesses, Salem witches, hardy pioneers, black nannies, Victorian ladies, flamboyant flappers, wartime riveters, happy homemakers, women's libbers—each presented a portrait with which or against which women were measured and measured themselves. Since most such figures were based on a single class or race of women, it is only by examining a variety of individuals from a range of families and communities that we can begin to understand how such ideal types arose and what their effects were on women and men of particular times and places.

Family and community are also idealized notions. Leading commentators from every generation of American citizens have lamented the decline of the "traditional" family and the loss of the "close-knit" community. Puritan clergy and born-again Christians, female moral reformers of the mid-nineteenth century and political candidates of the late twentieth, eighteenth-century diarists and contemporary documentarians have all bemoaned the failure of real-life families and communities to live up to the models we carry in our minds. We should not let the similarity of these laments obscure real differences in the changing forms of family and community life over time and across region, race, ethnicity, and class.

Yet commonalities in these laments can tell us something important about people's shared desire for a sense of place and of belonging, regardless of how big or developed or powerful the nation as a whole becomes. Again, only by examining a variety of settings and situations over the course of American history can we begin to understand the multiple forms family and community have taken and their effects on regional, racial, ethnic, and class relations and on national development.

Among social historians, women's historians have devoted particular attention to these dimensions of our American heritage: common folk, daily life, dominant cultural symbols and images, definitions of family and community, popular forms of protest, and differences in each of these rooted in race, class, ethnicity, and region. Women's historians, focusing initially on the differences in women's and men's experiences in the past, have asked new questions, have introduced new sources, have offered new interpretations of the roles that women played in America, and have suggested new ways of marking major transitions and turning points in our nation's history.

Emerging from the women's movement of the 1960s and 1970s, these scholars have applied the feminist rubric—"the personal is political"—to examinations of history. Thus, they focus on the relations between public and private spheres, home and work, domesticity and politics. They consider whether changes in household technology and birth control methods might be as important as presidential elections and wars in determining how to divide American history into meaningful units of study. To probe these and other issues, researchers examine diaries and letters, census data and wills, sermons and novels, clothing and advertisements, and other artifacts left by those whose words and actions were not purposely recorded for posterity.

This research provides portraits of women as mothers, daughters, and wives; as servants, slaves, and free women; as wage earners, housewives, and volunteers; as immigrants, migrants, and settlers; and the whole range of roles that formed the female half of society. Some scholars focus on notable women—Abigail Adams, Elizabeth Cady Stanton, Ida B. Wells, Eleanor Roosevelt, Rosa Parks—demonstrating their right to be set alongside their male counterparts in the pantheon of American heroes. Others study all-female organizations and institutions—women's colleges and prisons, suffrage associations, literary societies, or single-sex reform groups—arguing for women's vital contributions to every phase of the nation's development. Some examine women's work, in and outside the family, and analyze its contributions to farming, commerce, slavery, industry, and the ever expanding service sector. Many follow the lives of ordinary women, as individuals and in groups, from birth to death, seeking to understand the parameters of female lives and how they have changed over time and place.

Yet researchers are not interested only in looking at women in relation to other women, as important as that dimension of our history is. Rather, they also want to study women in relation to men, to communities, and to the larger society. From this dual perspective—women's own experiences as women and their relationships with men—women's historians have begun rewriting American history to reflect the contributions and activities of the whole population. In doing so, they introduce gender—the cultural prescriptions and social roles assigned to individuals on the basis of their sex—as a critical category of analysis.

This volume highlights the work of those who analyze women in the context of their families and communities. In such studies, the new scholarship on women is integrated with that on men, and the lives of native-born white women and men are set beside those of native Americans, African-Americans, and immigrants. The particular communities examined here cover various regions of the country and include members of a wide range of races, classes, and ethnic groups. Using gender as a key category of analysis, each study illuminates some important aspect of our nation's development. Collectively, these readings reveal the changing nature of women's and men's roles and of family and community across the course of American history and analyze how these changes shaped and were shaped by larger social, economic, and political forces.

The articles in this book will provide evidence that can be used in combination with information from other readings, lectures, and discussions to draw a new portrait of our national past. Imagine for a moment what American history would look like if viewed for the first time through the lens of a video camera held by a woman standing in her local community. Imagine the Pocahontas legend if it had been recorded and embellished by Indian women rather than English men. Think for a moment of the way Sherman's March to the Sea during the Civil War would have been portrayed by a house slave in Atlanta. How might the the breaking waves of the Atlantic Ocean or the overland trail to the west have been seen by a young wife with a child in tow and another on the way? Consider what a document listing the advantages of technological progress might contain if it were compiled by a Lowell mill worker in the 1840s or the owner of a new wringer washer in the 1920s. Contemplate what Pearl Harbor meant to a black domestic servant in Texas or a Japanese-American girl completing her senior year of high school. Speculate on the way organized black women in Montgomery, Alabama, would remember Martin Luther King, Jr., whom they had to persuade to lead the city's bus boycott in 1955.

How might these portraits of the past vary if in each situation the woman recording or recalling the moment was replaced by her brother? How would they differ if history were recorded not from the perspective of their family and community, but from yours? By combining the rich documentation of ordinary women's and men's lives collected by social historians with traditional interpretations of significant events and with our own understanding of how change occurs, we can begin to focus on a more complete picture of the past. This picture brings into view diverse groups of Americans and a wide range of issues, individuals, and events. If we could make it move, we would have something like a videotape of the past, perhaps the closest we could come to making the events of history and our interpretations of them converge. Even then, however, we might not agree with another person's idea of American history, for each person's view of historical events is unique. That uniqueness reflects in part America's heritage of diversity.

From the moment when native Americans, Europeans, and Africans first encountered one another in the New World, diversity characterized the continents development. In the present, diversity—and the creativity and conflict it nurtures—continues to define our nation. Differences in race and region, ethnicity and class, wealth and power, sex and social status shaped our nation's history as they shape our lives, our culture, our economy, and our government. By capturing that half of history which occurred in local communities, among ordinary families, composed of common women and men, we reveal this diversity and thus more fully illuminate both the past and the present. The readings in this book will remined us that everyone—presidents, generals, corporate leaders, students, wage earners, and house-wives—is a creator of history.

Suggested Readings

Nancy F. Cott and Elizabeth H. Pleck, eds., *A Heritage of Her Own: Toward a New Social History of American Women* (1979).

Sara Evans, *"Born for Liberty": Women in American History* (1989).

Jean E. Friedman, William G. Shade, and Mary Jane Cappazzoli, eds., *Our American Sisters: Women in American Life and Thought* (4th ed., 1987).

Michael Gordon, ed., *The American Family in Social-Historical Perspective* (3rd ed., 1983).

Carol Groneman and Mary Beth Norton, eds., *"To Toil the Livelong Day": America's Women at Work, 1780-1980* (1987).

Carol Hymowitz and Michaele Weisman, *A History of Women in America* (1978).

Jacqueline Jones, *Labor of Love, Labor of Sorrow: Black Women, Work and the Family, from Slavery to the Present* (1986).

Linda K. Kerber and Jane DeHart-Mathews, eds., *Women's America: Refocusing the Past* (2nd ed., 1987).

Mary Beth Norton, ed., *Major Problems in American Women's History* (1989).

Mary P. Ryan, *Womanhood in America: From Colonial Times to the Present* (3rd ed., 1983).

Susan Ware, ed., *Modern American Women: A Documentary History* (1989).

Nancy Woloch, *Women and the American Experience* (1984).

PART ONE

Peopling the New World

In the early 1600s, three peoples met on the North American mainland. The first group, long settled, initially welcomed the newcomers, seeing opportunities for trade and perhaps for domination. The second, recently arrived from Europe, found survival difficult and the transplantation of life-style and values even more problematic. The third, forcibly removed from African homelands, struggled to adjust to the new environment and to the intense labors demanded by white masters.

None of these groups were homogeneous, however. Among native Americans, differences in the size, location, and economic base of tribes assured not only separation but conflict, which might be intensified or eased upon contact with the new arrivals. Though clearly differentiating themselves from Indians, Europeans migrated from different regions for diverse reasons and established distinct political, religious, and social patterns in northern and southern colonies. Africans, too, emerged from different regions and, especially during their first years in the New World, faced a variety of legal and laboring conditions.

In addition to these distinctions, each group was divided by sex. Differences in the roles of women and men were probably most noticeable in the area of work, though the sexual division of labor varied significantly both within and among the three groups. Several of the largest and most powerful Indian tribes—such as the Iroquois and the Cherokee—assigned women to agricultural labor and men to hunting and war. The importance of women's economic contribution was recognized by their inclusion in religious ceremonies, in tribal government, and in negotiations over war and trade. Suzanne Lebsock demonstrates the range of women's activities among Virginia Indians, comparing their access to resources and power with that of their European and African counterparts. She shows how differences in the roles of women in each society contributed to misunderstandings and hostilities among the three peoples, despite the efforts of Pocahontas and others to promote peaceful coexistence.

From the beginning, women played a vital role in the settlement and colonization of the New World. Queen Isabella of Spain sponsored Christopher Columbus' first voyage to America in 1492. In the drawing here, Columbus is reporting to the Queen and her husband, King Ferdinand, the details of his discovery.

The number of native Americans declined in the 1600s as European diseases and weapons provided formidable foes. In the same period, the number of African women in the colonies remained relatively small. White owners preferred men as laborers and gave little thought to buying female slaves for any purpose other than reproduction.

Only European woman and their colonial-born descendants multiplied rapidly. Despite alarmingly high death rates in the southern colonies, particularly among infants and among women in labor, the white population surged through a combination of immigration and high birth rates. Bearing an average of eight to nine children, women who survived their childbearing years contributed mightily to peopling the New World with their own kind.

Though white women soon outnumbered Indian and African women, they were far fewer in number than white men. The shortage of European women and workers in the early years of settlement and the death of husbands (who were often several years older than their wives) offered a number of opportunities to healthy, enterprising women. Through brewing, baking, innkeeping, sewing, midwifery, shopkeeping, printing, and a variety of other skilled trades and petty enterprises, some female migrants gained a degree of financial autonomy they would not have attained in Europe. Margaret Brent, already a wealthy woman when she arrived in Maryland in 1638, managed plantations, sued (successfully) in court, acted as a business agent for others, and served as executrix for the estate of Lord Calvert, Maryland's governor. Demonstrating the status that few women could obtain, she nonetheless was denied the political rights that a man of her property and stature would have enjoyed.

Most early immigrants, male or female, faced considerably harsher circumstances. Large numbers of women and men reached the colonies by means of indentured servitude, which involved four to seven years' bound labor in exchange for passage to the New World. Engaged in long years of arduous toil, housed in cramped quarters, provided with minimal food and clothing, offered little privacy, and sometimes subjected to severe punishments, colonial servants hoped only to survive their indenture so they could take advantage of the opportunities that awaited. For female servants, sexual exploitation and premarital pregnancy posed additional hazards to the path to freedom. Though courts were sometimes sympathetic to women abused by masters, most servants who found themselves pregnant had their children taken away and their contracts extended to forestall such behavior in the future.

Premarital pregnancy and other punishable offenses were probably as prevalent in Puritan New England as in other regions of the New World. Despite the Puritans' desire to set a righteous example for the rest of the world, sexual and social turmoil characterized Massachusetts Bay from its earliest years. Women, moreover, were often at the center of such controversies. In part, this was because female sexual misconduct was starkly visible when manifested as pregnancy or a child born out of wedlock. In addition, all women, as daughters of Eve, were considered more innately evil than men and more firmly ruled by their passions. Recognizing and accepting female sexuality as long as it was contained within marital bonds, Puritan leaders were nevertheless eager to find in unbridled female lust both the cause and consequence of social disorder.

The wave of heretical teaching that washed over Massachusetts Bay in the 1630s, especially those offered by Anne Hutchinson, gave Puritan leaders an opportunity to voice these fears under the guise of protecting the colony. Convinced that female intellect was a contradiction in terms, Governor John Winthrop characterized Hutchinson as "a woman of fine and haughty carriage, of a nimble wit and active spirit, and a very voluble tongue, more bold than a man, though in understanding and judgement, inferiour to many women." Upon her banishment from the settlement, Reverend John Cotton articulated the presumed links between religious heresy and sexual deviance. He admonished her, "though I have not herd, nayther do I thinke, you have bine unfaythful to your Husband in his Marriage Covenant, yet that will follow upon it."

Lyle Koehler traces these same attitudes and responses to assertive or otherwise unusual women into late seventeenth-century Salem. In that village, social and political upheaval converged with economic and sexual tensions to fuel the colonies' most tragic witch-hunt.

By the beginning of the next century, war and economic change replaced religious and sexual tensions as the most powerful shapers of colonial life. By 1750, in long-settled regions, women and workers were no longer scarce, Indians were no longer a threat to colonists' safety, and heretics were no longer a disruptive force in the colonies. Still, economic development and population growth coincided to nurture new regional and class divisions aggravated by war. Throughout the century, war—in all its forms—transformed the landscape of the New World, until by the beginning of the Revolution few traces were left of that world in which red, white, and black vied for power.

Wars between Indians and Europeans were overshadowed during most of the eighteenth century by conflicts between European competitors on both sides of the ocean. The French and Indian War (in Europe known as the Seven Years' War) found Europeans and Indians on both sides of the battle line. The resulting victory for Britain and its allies then unleashed an array of forces that culminated in colonial revolt and western expansion. Yet even before its political consequences were realized, the economic disruption wrought by this and earlier wars was widely felt. Though serving as an economic boost to merchants, shipbuilders, and provisioners, and temporarily to artisans and seamen, wars also drove up prices, left large numbers of widows and orphans in their wake, and induced seaboard cities to establish poorhouses. Between 1740 and 1755, for example, the number of poor people needing assistance in Philadelphia grew ten times faster than the population at large. In Boston, a spinning factory was opened in 1748 in response to the large numbers of women left without support by earlier conflicts between the English, the French, and the Indians. The French and Indian War simply multiplied these problems.

Even those in more affluent circumstances found their lives disrupted by war. Anne Firor Scott uses the diaries and letters of three women from prominent families to paint a portrait of eighteenth-century womanhood. She shows both how the opportunities afforded women and men differed across time, place, and class and how common crises—childbirth, death, widowhood, and war—shaped most women's lives in the period, whatever their region or class.

These self-portraits reveal the domination of the New World by Europeans who pushed Indians and Africans to the geographical and economic margins of settlement. In another sense, they represent class domination, focusing on families whose life-styles set the tone for colonial society. Here, however, the comparison of Jane Mecom's existence with that of her brother Benjamin Franklin illustrates the potential chasm between women's and men's choices and chances in life even among the fortunate. Finally, the portraits reflect the broad spectrum of colonial womanhood, lived largely within the confines of domesticity—though here and there an escape hatch opened into some wider world. These women, like their counterparts throughout the colonies, contributed their physical and intellectual labor as workers and mothers to people the New World, one of the few tasks shared by native American, African, and European women.

Suggested Readings

Gary B. Nash, *Red, White and Black: The Peopling of Early America* (1974).

Laurel Thatcher Ulrich, *Good Wives: Image and Reality in the Lives of Women in Northern New England, 1650–1750* (1982).

John Demos, *A Little Commonwealth: Family Life in Plymouth Colony* (1970).

Daniel Blake Smith, *Inside the Great House: Planter Family Life in Eighteenth-Century Chesapeake Society* (1980).

ONE

"No Obey": Indian, European, and African Women in Seventeenth-Century Virginia

Suzanne Lebsock

Pocahontas—Indian princess, savior of Captain John Smith, wife of tobacco entrepreneur John Rolfe—has long been a symbol of the peaceful co-existence of native American and European peoples in the New World. One might easily conclude from the popular legend that the only role women played in Jamestown was that of saving handsome colonists from hostile natives. Yet Indian, English, and African women all filled diverse roles in their native villages; and all were called upon to expand their activities under the pressures of colonization.

Among some Chesapeake tribes, women traditionally held positions of political and social prominence. Thus, despite Pocahontas's choices, few Indian women were likely to be lured away from their countrymen by undernourished, pale, quarrelsome, and seemingly inept Englishmen. Pocahontas's fate—she died of a fever while visiting England in 1617—probably did not encourage other young tribeswomen to follow her lead.

For English and African residents of Jamestown, simple survival far outweighed every other concern in the first decades of settlement. African women and men struggled to survive the passage to America. Once there, most found themselves literally worked to death, regardless of sex or age.

English women came to America as indentured servants or free wives. Either way, life in the colonies took a heavy toll on them. Though the shortage of European females in Virginia villages did increase their value and allow some to gain wealth and status through marriage, even good marriages could not save women from frequent childbearing, backbreaking labor, and early death.

Lebsock's study of Indian, African, and European women in colonial Virginia demonstrates that women in all three groups began the seventeenth century under difficult but fluid conditions that placed great physical burdens on most women but also promised wealth and power to a few. She documents the variety and range of women's contributions to political, social, and economic development in their communities, illuminating the diversity in women's and men's roles that characterized American society in its earliest years. Yet she also shows how the English "established dominion over Virginia" just as "English men were establishing increasingly effective dominion over women."

Both in the early years of settlement and later in the century, Indian, European, and African women had different types and degrees of access to political and religious authority and to land and other economic resources. These distinctions were reflected in the three groups' different, often conflicting, assumptions about the proper role of women and led to miscommunications among Indians, Europeans, and Africans over land, labor, trade, and war. In succeeding articles, we trace continuities and changes in women's and men's roles across class, race, region, and time.

Whereas these later articles assume the dominance of Europeans in the New World, Lebsock captures that moment when their hold was far more fragile. Then the New World was still filled with rich possibilities as well as fearful dangers for women and men of all races.

In the early seventeenth century, people from three parts of the world converged in the land the English named Virginia. In 1600 all Virginians were Indians. Before long their claim to the land was challenged by the colonizing English, who needed laborers to work the land they took from the Indians, and who were willing to fill the bill by buying slaves, people forcibly imported from Africa.

In all three groups, of course, there were women. Reconstructing their lives is a delicate and at times frustrating enterprise, for the evidence is thin, and we are dependent on whatever the English—and English men at that—saw fit to write down. But it appears that not one of the three groups had what we think of as "traditional" sex roles. In Indian Virginia, for example, and in much of West Africa, women were the farmers. Among the English, meanwhile, ideas about the proper roles of women were often undermined by the fluid conditions of life and death in the New World.

By 1700 the English had established dominion over Virginia, and English men were establishing increasingly effective dominion over women. But none of this was a foregone conclusion in 1607. In the beginning, almost anything seemed possible. From the writings of early English chroniclers, we learn of two powerful Indian women. One was Pocahontas, who, as legend had it, saved John Smith's head in 1607. The other was the queen of the Appamatuck, who had received an English exploring party a few months earlier. "She is a fatt lustie manly woman," wrote one of the admiring explorers. The queen wore a crown and jewelry of copper; she presented a "stayed Countenance"; "she would permitt none to stand or sitt neere her." In other words, she reinforced her authority as rulers often did and in ways that Englishmen readily understood—by regal dress, by a dignified bearing, and by keeping her distance.

In the Indian's own language, this formidable woman was a *werowance*, the highest authority in her tribe. Among Virginia Indians, for women to hold such positions was not unusual, and the English, fresh from the reign of Elizabeth I (1558–1603), knew a queen when they saw one. What was more difficult for them to grasp was the importance of Indian women in the texture of everyday life.

At that time more than twenty thousand Indians lived in what came to be called Virginia. There were more than forty different tribes, and while each had its particular territory and tradition, the tribes were clustered in three language groups. South of the James River were the Iroquoian-speaking tribes, the Nottoway and Meherrin. In the Piedmont lived a number of Siouan speakers. About these groups we unfortunately know little. Most numerous and by far the best known were the Algonquian-speaking tribes of the Tidewater region, among them the Appamatuck, Chickahominy, Mattaponi, Nansemond, Pamunkey, and Rappahannock. Long sharing a common language, many of these tribes had recently become political allies as well. Powhatan, the werowance of the Pamunkey, had inherited control of six tribes, and by the early seventeenth century he had wrestled two dozen other Algonquian tribes into a confederacy—some would say kingdom. The English, for their part, were impressed with the "terrible and tyrannous" Powhatan, just as he intended them to be.

So centralized a political structure could not have been built without a sound economy, and the economy was based on the work of

In many native American populations, both men and women performed agricultural labor, but their tasks were divided by sex. Men, using wooden-handled hoes made of fishbones, prepared the ground and loosened the soil. Women then dug the holes and planted the seeds. This sixteenth-century engraving is by Jacques Le Moyne.

women. Women were the farmers in a society in which farming was the central occupation. "Their victuall," as John Smith put it, "is their chiefest riches." Corn was the single most important product in the Virginia economy. During the growing season, the Indians drew together in towns of from ten to one hundred houses. Between the houses and sometimes on the town's edge were the fields, where women planted corn and beans together in the same hills (this way the cornstalks doubled as bean-poles and the land stayed fertile longer). They also grew peas, sunflowers, and several kinds of squash.

The Virginia soil was generous with wild fruits, berries, acorns, hickory nuts, and wal-nuts, and the gathering of these foods fell to the women. So did all of the food processing and preparation. The making of clothing was women's work, too. This meant, among other things, dressing skins and making thread "very even and readily" by rolling bark, grass, or the sinews of animals between hand and thigh; the thread was good for fishing nets as well as for sewing. Pots were usually made by women. So were baskets; and the weaving of mats was a major industry, for these were used both as furniture and as siding for houses. The women also had to carry the wood, keep the fire alive, and "beare all kindes of burthens," including their babies, on their backs.

As for housework, there was little to do, for Indian houses were very simple—one room, furnished mainly with mats and skins. Made of bark or mats stretched over bent poles, the houses were snug and smokey, as fires burned along the center axis of the floor and the smoke was allowed to find its way out through a hole in the ceiling. It is not clear who built the houses in the summer villages. In winter, however, when the villagers separated into smaller groups and hiked to their hunting grounds, the women were once again in charge:

> In that time when they goe a Huntinge the weomen goes to a place apoynted before, to build houses for ther husbands to lie in att night carienge matts with them to couer ther houses with all, and as the men goes further a huntinge the woemen goes before to make houses, always carrienge ther mattes with them.

And what did the men do? One observer summed it up in a single sentence: "The men fish, hunt, fowle, goe to the warrs, make the weeres [fishtraps], botes, and such like manly exercises and all laboures abroad." The men, in short, hunted, fished, fought, and made the implements they needed for each activity. They also cleared the grounds for fields, though since they used the slash-and-burn method, this was not especially laborious; they cleared away small trees and underbrush by burning, while larger trees were stripped of their bark and allowed to die.

Since the English regarded hunting as sport and not as work, they quickly concluded that Indian men were lazy, that the women were drudges, and that the unequal division of labor between the sexes was proof of the general inferiority of Indian civilization. The English were wrong, for men did make substantial contributions to the Indian diet, even though the work of women was more essential to the material welfare of their people. English men and Indian men, meanwhile, had more in common than the English knew, both "scorning to be seene in any woman like exercise." The Indians and the English had differing ideas about what was properly masculine and what was feminine, but men of both groups assigned their own activities more prestige than the activities of women.

For all that, authority in Indian society did not belong to men alone. Succession among Virginia Indians was matrilineal: Political power was inherited through the mother rather than the father, and females were eligible to become rulers. John Smith explained how it worked with Powhatan: "His kingdome descendeth not to his sonnes nor children." Instead, Powhatan's position would pass first to his brothers, then to his sisters, "and after them to the heires male and female of the eldest sister; but never to the heires of the males."

Our knowledge of family life and family structure is otherwise confined to a few intriguing scraps of information; on the whole, the English chroniclers were much sharper observers of politics and the economy than they were of families. Sexual attitudes were somewhat different from those of the English, at least to the extent that women (whose individual status within the tribe is not clear) were sometimes offered as bedfellows for visiting male dignitaries. Some relatively wealthy men had more than one wife, and divorce was permissible. Parents were said to love their children "verie dearly." Mothers gave birth with no crying out, whereupon English men concluded that for Indian women childbirth was not painful.

Would that we knew more. What we do know, however, adds up to an impressive record of female influence in Indian Virginia. And this is the significance of the Pocahontas story. Pocahontas was a girl with sparkle. Her name, according to the English, translated as "Little Wanton"; we might say playful, mischievous, frisky. She was about twelve in 1607 when John Smith made his first appearance in the immediate domain of her father, Powhatan. Uncertain of Smith's intentions, Powhatan's warriors killed two of Smith's men and took Smith himself prisoner. After three weeks of captivity and feasting, Smith was led to a large stone and made to lay down his head. The warriors raised their clubs as though "to beate oute his braines." Suddenly, Pocahontas sprang forth, the clubs were stayed, and John Smith was spared.

Or so Smith told it. The authenticity of this story has been challenged many times, partly because in John Smith's earliest recountings of his exploits the Pocahontas episode does not appear at all, and partly because the dusky-princess-rescues-bold-adventurer theme was commonplace in European culture long before Smith set foot in Virginia. He could easily have borrowed it. On the other hand, it could have happened. In Indian warfare, women, children, and werowances were almost always spared. While male warriors were sometimes tortured and often killed, they, too, could be spared and adopted into the victorious tribe. Here the judges were women. Given women's importance as breadwinners and in the kinship structure, their deciding if and when a new person was needed made eminent sense. So Pocahontas could have saved John Smith after all. What Smith experienced, although he did not know it, may have been a ritual of mock execution and adoption.

As time went on, of course, Pocahontas was the one who was adopted by the English. After John Smith's release, Pocahontas continued to live up to her name; she was spotted turning cartwheels through Jamestown, for instance. Her story took a more serious turn in 1613, when she was taken hostage by Samuel Argall, who hoped to use Pocahontas to gain bargaining power with the Indians. While living under English authority, Pocahontas met John Rolfe, who would one day achieve fame as the primary promoter of tobacco culture. They were married in 1614 and had one son. In 1616 they sailed for England, where Pocahontas was received as both a curiosity and a celebrity; early in 1617 she was presented to James I and Queen Anne. A few months later, just as she was preparing to return to Virginia, Pocahontas died. She was no more than twenty-two years old.

For a long time no one took much notice of her story. Then some 150 years after her death, Pocahontas took hold of the American imagination as no other woman has. She was brought to life on stage, in verse, and in the pages of novels and of countless children's books. Her name was given to people, places, and an astonishing variety of things, from tobacco and quack medicines to cotton mills and coal mines. As powerful legends usually do, the Pocahontas story had several symbolic meanings. But there is no doubt that the national romance with Pocahontas helped to soothe the troubled conscience of white America. Pocahontas had rescued one colonizer and had married another. She professed the Christian religion and was baptized "Rebecca." She learned to speak the English language, sat for her portrait in English costume, and met her death on English soil. Symbolically, Pocahontas put an Indian stamp of approval on white people, white culture, and white conquest.

We could opt for a different symbol. The queen of the Appamatuck—the "fatt lustie manly woman" the English encountered in 1607—thought it all very interesting when the first explorers appeared. She looked the visitors over, fed them, and asked them to shoot their guns, "whereat she shewed not neere the like feare as Arahatec [the werowance of the Arrohateck tribe] though he be a goodly man." The following year, when the English were desperate for food, she supplied them with corn. By 1611, however, she was alarmed. Launching an aggressive policy of expansion, the English began carving out plantations on her tribal territory. The queen of the Appamatuck decided to resist. She began by inviting fourteen colonists to a party. When the men arrived, they were ambushed and every one was killed. Reprisal was immediate. An English detachment attacked her town, burned it, and killed everyone they could find, including women and children. The queen herself was shot, probably fatally, as she tried to escape.

Or we could take for our symbol the queen of the Paspahegh tribe. In 1610, the English governor engaged Powhatan in negotiations over the return of some Englishmen who had run off to join the Indians. Frustrated by Powhatan's "disdaynefull Answers," the governor ordered punitive raids on nearby tribes. The

English marched on the Paspahegh's chief town, killed several people, torched the houses, cut down the corn, and took the queen prisoner along with her children. Returning to Jamestown by boat, some of the soldiers complained about the sparing of the children. This situation was resolved by throwing the children in the river and "shoteinge owtt their Braynes in the water." On hearing further complaints about the sparing of the mother, the commander decided against burning and instead had her led away and stabbed to death.

This was unspeakable brutality, even for a brutal age. After Pocahontas married John Rolfe, an uneasy peace was established for a few years, but the basic pattern was already in place. Regardless of the Indian's strategy—be it aloofness, cooperation, or armed resistance—the determination of the English to take Indian land for soil-depleting tobacco crops was paramount. The brutality escalated. Under the leadership of Opechancanough, the Powhatan Confederacy made a concerted effort to expel the English in 1622; this time women and children were not spared, and nearly 350 colonists were killed. The English reeled from the blow—and retaliated with extraordinary force. Somehow, after many years, Opechancanough's allies regrouped, and they struck again in 1644. By this time the English were far stronger, and their counterattack demolished the Powhatan Confederacy. In a treaty of 1646 the surviving Indians were placed on reservations and promised protection in exchange for their help in fending off outlying tribes. Still, for the Indians there was no real safety. Whites were divided on Indian policy, and in 1676 the followers of renegade Nathaniel Bacon, Jr., made war on Indians of every description. A new treaty was signed in 1677, but in the meantime the Indians had suffered another bitter disaster. Killed in battle, wasted by disease, driven out and starved out, the Indian population of Virginia by 1700 was perhaps one-tenth of what it had been a century before.

Among the survivors was Cockacoeske, the queen of the Pamunkey. In the treaty of 1677 all the subscribing tribes pledged their allegiance to her as well as to the English king. And as a probable reward for her loyalty during Bacon's Rebellion, the government presented her with gifts including a dazzling silver badge. The English, it seems, were still willing to accept female political authority when they encountered it.

✳

Virginia was named for a female ruler, of course, and the point was not lost on Virginia Ferrar. In 1650 Ferrar wrote to Lady Berkeley, the wife of Virginia's governor, offering encouraging words and a novel interpretation of history. Women, she claimed, deserved the credit for Europe's discovery of the New World. First there was Queen Isabella of Spain, "to the Eternall honour of her Sexe . . . (though laughed at by all the wise Conceited Courtiers)" sent Christopher Columbus on his famous voyage of 1492. Then Elizabeth I of England ordered the "planting" of a colony in North America, "giving it as she was a Virgin Queene the Happy and Glorious name of Virginia." Next, Ferrar suggested, the governor's lady herself might continue the "Heroyicke Interprize" by funding an expedition to find a route to the East Indies.

For Virginia Ferrar and many historians after her, heroism was found in exploration and conquest. For the women who helped colonize Virginia, there was heroism in survival. Wherever they came from—the British Isles, the West Indies, Africa—Virginia's new women faced a rugged existence. Thanks to Indian women, the colonists after a few years learned how to grow enough food to support themselves. Then in 1614 they began marketing the crop that would sustain their colony and run their lives. This was tobacco, of course, the seeds imported from the West Indies and the cultivation techniques once again borrowed from the Virginia Indians. Profits were high, at times spectacular, and so an entire society dedicated itself to putting more land in tobacco.

For the women life was not easy. The death rate was appalling. Living conditions were crude, and all but the wealthiest could expect a lifetime of hard labor. Yet, if a woman lived long enough, she could sometimes experience a surprising degree of personal freedom. If she began as a slave, she might become free. If she started as a servant, she might become a planter. If she were a member of a wealthy family, she might become a politician. In the rough-and-ready world of the seventeenth century, almost anything might happen.

The gentlemen of the General Assembly had their moments of insight. "In a newe plantation," they declared in 1619, "it is not knowen whether man or woman be the most necessary." Believing that a permanent colony would not be established until the planters settled down and raised families, influential men had for some time tried to bring more women to Virginia. Decisions on who would come to America, however, were not made by legislators alone. Instead, they were made by hundreds of individuals, among them planters who decided that in the short run, on their particular plantations, men were the most necessary. The result was an extremely unbalanced sex ratio. Among blacks there were at least three men for every two women. Among whites, men outnumbered women by three or four to one.

The Virginia Company, chartered in 1606 to finance and oversee colonization, resolved to send shiploads of "Maydens," young English women who would dare an ocean voyage and marriage to a stranger on the other side. In her novel *To Have and to Hold*, Mary Johnston later imagined the commotion when the first group of maids arrived in Jamestown. "I saw young men, panting, seize hand or arm and strive to pull toward them some reluctant fair; others snatched kisses, or fell on their knees and began speeches out of Euphues; others commenced an inventory of their possessions—acres, to-bacco, servants, household plenishing. All was hubbub, protestation, frightened cries, and hysterical laughter." The narrator drew closer and heard some bargaining: "Says Phyllis, 'Any poultry?'"

Corydon: A matter of twelve hens and twa cocks.

Phyllis: A cow?

Corydon: Twa.

Phyllis: How much tobacco?

Corydon: Three acres, hinny, though I dinna drink the weed mysel'. I'm a Stewart, woman, an' the King's puir cousin.

Phyllis: What household plenishing?

Corydon: Ane large bed, ane flock bed, ane trundle bed, ane chest, ane trunk, ane leather cairpet, sax cawfskin chairs an' two-three rush, five pair o' sheets an' auchteen dowlas napkins, sax alchemy spunes—

Phyllis: I'll take you.

The legend of early Virginia was somehow brightened by the tales of this strange marriage market, although the Virginia Company in truth sent out only about 140 maids. Other English women made the crossing in ones and twos, sailing with their husbands or following husbands who had ventured over earlier. The vast majority of women colonists, however, were unfree laborers. Some, though their numbers were small in the first half of the seventeenth century, were slaves brought by force from different parts of Africa (and from Africa via the West Indies). About 80 percent of all English immigrants, meanwhile, were indentured servants. These people owed from four to seven years of faithful labor to whoever paid their passage from England. Until their time was up, they were not free to marry at all.

The new arrivals, single or married, bound or free, could expect rude beginnings. If, like the fictional Phyllis, her new household really

Realizing that women and families were essential for the successful colonization of the New World, the Virginia Company arranged to send shiploads of young Englishwomen to the new colonies. In this idealized depiction, the hardy young "Maydens" have just arrived at the marriage market at Jamestown. In truth, most women colonists came to America as indentured servants or as slaves.

contained five pairs of sheets, she would be doing very well indeed. The newcomer would need only a few seconds to size up her surroundings. From the outside the typical Virginia farmhouse looked (and was) small, and it probably needed patching. The inside could be inspected in three or four glances. This was a one-room house, measuring perhaps twenty-five by sixteen feet. It was a story and a half high and probably had a loft where children and servants slept. Otherwise one space had to suffice for every indoor purpose.

Except for its enormous fireplace, it was something like an Indian house, and like an Indian house, it was sparsely furnished. Standard equipment for a house owned by a middling planter was one feather bed (not to say a bedstead), a chest for storage, a cooking pot, a mortar and pestle for pounding corn, an axe, some knives, a few wooden dishes, some odd spoons, and containers for storing crops. Stools and benches were not standard, although some households had them, nor were tables, forks, sheets, skillets, lamps, or candles. Occasionally, some bright and beautiful object would light up a Virginia household, and some of the most prosperous planters lived in higher style. But the typical planter stuck to ruthless utility. If furnishings were spartan and houses leaked and leaned and all but tumbled down, no matter. The money was in tobacco, and the planter who wanted to succeed invested every spare shilling in laborers.

That, of course, is what brought most women to Virginia. Indentured servitude was the system that connected young English people in need of work to planters in need of workers. In the England of the middle seventeenth century, finding a place in life could be difficult. The population was exploding, wages were falling, and unemployment was acute. Looking for something better, the resourceful left villages for towns, towns for cities, and some of them took a chance on Virginia.

They were in for a few surprises. Servitude was no lark in England, but it was harsher still in Virginia. Masters were required by law to provide adequate food and clothing (including a send-off of three barrels of corn and a new suit of clothes when the servant's time was up), and they were instructed to keep punishments reasonable. The economic interest of masters, however, dictated squeezing their servants to the limit. By the same token, the interest of servants lay in resisting. This could be dangerous, though, because the master literally had the whip hand. Court records are rife with testimony concerning life-threatening punishments. One young woman was "sore beaten and her body full of sores and holes." Another was beaten "liken a dogge." More than one was killed in the course of a whipping.

Sexual abuse was an added hazard. According to law, an indentured servant who became pregnant was obliged to serve her master an additional two years. Not until 1662 did the House of Burgesses respond to the logic of the situation: The old law encouraged masters to sexually exploit their own servants or to stand by while someone else did the exploiting. The new law of 1662 stipulated that the pregnant servant would still serve two more years, but she would serve them under a new master.

Another surprise was that some women servants were set to work in the fields. A popular ballad called "The Trappan'd Maiden: Or, the Distressed Damsel" made the point:

I have play'd my part both at Plow and Cart,
  In the Land of Virginny, O;
Billets from the Wood upon my back they
  load,
When that I am weary, weary, weary, weary
  O.

Through ballads and by other means, the rumors about the nature of women's work in Virginia reached England. Because proper English women were not supposed to do heavy field work, this posed a problem for Virginia's promoters. A pamphlet of 1656 offered a neat resolution to the problem: The only English women "put into the ground," it was explained, were those "wenches" who were "nasty, beastly, and . . . aukward."

It was not as though women needed work in the fields to keep them busy. Slaves, servants, mistresses, and daughters carried out all the day-to-day never-done tasks that made life possible. Every day they ground corn by hand and made it into soup or bread. If their children had milk, it was because the women tended cows. If there was butter or cheese, it was because the women made them from the milk. If there were eggs, it was because the women raised chickens. If there was meat, it was because the women had butchered it, preserved it, and boiled it. If there were vegetables, it was because the women gardened. If there was cider or beer, the women brewed it. While cloth was mainly imported, women did all the sewing, washing, and mending, major chores in a time when work meant sweat and when most people had few changes of clothing. If someone fell ill, women did the nursing; in large households someone was probably sick all of the time. And if the family prospered, chances were that the master would acquire a new male indentured servant. The women, as a result, acquired another bundle of laundry, another person to be nursed through inevitable illness, and another hearty appetite.

If the woman was married, she was likely to be pregnant, breastfeeding, or looking after a young child. This was a duty and a labor of love. It was also a major economic contribution as surely as growing tobacco or corn. The planters' primary economic problem in the seventeenth century was the shortage of labor. Anyone who brought children into the world, therefore, and nurtured them until they grew into productive adulthood, made direct and essential contributions to Virginia's economic development.

Rearing a child to adulthood, however, was often out of the parents' power. Death was simply everywhere. It came, as we have seen, from wars between colonists and Indians. It came much more often from disease, from what the colonists called "fluxes," "agues," and "fevers"; we would say typhoid, dysentery, smallpox, and malaria. A child born in Virginia had only a fifty-fifty chance of living to see adulthood. About a quarter of all babies died before they reached their first birthday.

Adults were vulnerable, too. Although experiences varied a great deal from one person to the next, we can reconstruct the life of a typical white woman. She was twenty when she arrived in Virginia as an indentured servant. If she lived through her term of service (her chances were not especially good), she would marry almost as soon as she was free. She was now about twenty-five, and she would begin bearing children, one every two years, as was commonly the case in societies without benefit of birth control. Two of her children would die in childhood. Whether she would live to see any of her children grown was doubtful. After seven years of marriage her husband (who was older) would die, and she would follow in a few years.

Some additional statistics (again, these are for whites) help us appreciate the disruption that death wrought in Virginia families. Only one marriage in three lasted as long as ten years. From the perspective of the children, losing a parent was the normal experience. By the time they reached the age of nine, half of the children had already lost one or both parents. Virginia was a land of widows, widowers, bachelors, and above all, orphans.

As a consequence, families hardly ever matched the English ideal. A family, in English theory, consisted of a father, a mother, their children, and servants. In Virginia practice, few children were raised exclusively by their own parents, and many people found themselves raising other people's children. Families were suddenly bereft, then just as suddenly recombined into new households as surviving parents remarried, each bringing with them the children, stepchildren, orphans, servants, and slaves from their previous households. The shape of the family, therefore, was complex, unpredictable, and always changing.

Virginia practice also challenged English views concerning the proper lines of authority within the family, and this was a major step forward for women. In theory, English families were "patriarchal." That is, the husband and father was responsible for the welfare and good behavior of the entire household; he ruled, and everyone else—wife, child, and servant—owed him unquestioning, uncomplaining obedience.

Virginians may have believed in patriarchal authority with all their hearts, but conditions in the New World at times made enforcement difficult. The patriarchs simply did not live long enough. In marrying, for example, young people often made their own decisions; they could hardly ask permission of fathers who were back in England or long since dead. Fathers often realized that their families might have to get along without protectors. Accordingly, the terms of men's wills tended to be generous, more so than in England. Virginia daughters stood a good chance of inheriting land, and Virginia wives were very often given larger legacies than the law required. What is more, the Virginia wife was usually named her husband's executrix—the pivotal person who controlled the property until it was finally handed over to the heirs.

Add in the sex ratio, and the result was a formula for considerable upward mobility among women. Because women were dramatically outnumbered, they could often "marry up." A former servant might marry a property owner, and if she outlived him, she might assume control of the property. She might marry still better a second or third time around.

If she was anything like Sarah Harrison of Surry County, she would have a strong sense of her own bargaining power. When Harrison was married to James Blair in 1687, the wedding ceremony began like any other. Presently, however, the minister intoned the standard question: Did Sarah promise to obey her husband? "No obey," said Sarah. The minister repeated the question. "No obey," said Sarah again. The minister tried yet again. "No obey," said Sarah, one more time. The minister was checked, and the ceremony went on, no obey.

Virginia had its share of Sarah Harrisons, women who were strong willed or rowdy or powerful, women who made their influence felt not only in families but in local communities and in the colony. Nothing in English law or thought encouraged their participation in public affairs. The prevailing idea, in fact, was that women were inferior to men in every way—in physical strength, in reasoning ability, in their capacity to withstand moral temptations—and thus was justified the exclusion of women from voting and holding public office. Yet officeholding was only one way to exert influence. In the seventeenth century Virginia women explored some fascinating alternatives.

The obstacles to female participation in public affairs were formidable. Women were not allowed to vote, to serve on juries, or to hold office in either government or church. This in turn meant that women were seldom drawn out of their immediate neighborhoods for court days and militia musters. Women ordinarily could not read, either. Church was as far as they could expect to go. Consequently, for most women the known world was isolated and small. It was perhaps five miles across and populated mainly by family and a few neighbors.

Within that small world, the challenge for women and men together was to forge some sense of community. In England and in Africa, most people lived in villages. In Virginia, Indians excepted, most people lived on scattered farms; thus for people to form bonds with their neighbors was especially important. Here the Sunday church service was central. So were weddings and funerals, and when a woman went into labor, she was attended by other women from the neighborhood. Women also served their communities by taking in orphans, paupers, and those who were physically and mentally disabled. In a time when there were no orphanages, almshouses, hospitals, or old people's homes, people in need were taken care of in households. Local authorities recognized this care as a community responsibility; the families who provided it were accordingly compensated by the taxpayers.

Since many of the surviving records for the seventeenth century are court records, we know more about the negative means of maintaining community. Enter the stocks, the whipping post, and the ducking stool—the instruments of public humiliation. Inflicting pain and shame was a practical means of controlling troublemakers in a society with no jails to speak of and with no police force. Transgressors were expected to confess and to beg forgiveness. In the process they reaffirmed the neighborhood's notions about what was right and what was wrong.

Cases of fornication and adultery—the crimes that most frequently involved women—showed how the system worked. Virginians did not as a rule prosecute those who engaged in premarital sex; probably a third of Virginia brides were already pregnant at the wedding. Nonmarital sex was another matter altogether, a violation of good order and, if a child was born to the offenders, a possible drain on the local welfare funds. Among the lawful penalties were whippings and fines. A third penalty required each offender to appear in church, draped in a white sheet and holding a white wand. Standing on a stool in front of the congregation, the offender was then expected to apologize.

Like other systems this one did not work every time. Edith Tooker of Lower Norfolk was brought before her congregation in 1641 for the "foul crime of fornication." On being instructed to say she was sorry, she instead proceeded to "cut and mangle the sheet wherein she did penance." The court was not amused;

"a most obstinate and graceless person," the clerk muttered. Tooker was resentenced to twenty lashes and, two Sundays hence, to another try at the sheet treatment.

Tooker was getting to be a regular. In an earlier case the court had compelled her to apologize for slander, the other crime frequently perpetrated by women. In early Virginia most information circulated by word of mouth, and personal reputation was extremely important. (Imagine your marriage prospects, your employment credentials, or your credit rating being established by rumor.) Virginia was also a place in which bawdy joking was a way of life. It was therefore a thin line between conversation and slander, and legal actions were legion. In Northampton County, Goodwife Williams called John Dennis a "knave and base knave" and had the satisfaction of seeing him put into stocks for calling her "a whore and a base whore" in return. Edward Drew sued Joane Butler for calling his wife a "common Cunted hoare." Ann Fowler of Lower Norfolk was sentenced to twenty lashes and a public apology after she said, in reference to a high public official no less, "Let Capt. Thorougood Kiss my arse."

By 1662 the House of Burgesses was so vexed by the "brabling" women that a new law was passed; each county was required to build a ducking stool to quiet female scandalmongers. (Besides making the offender look ridiculous, the ducking stool held her under water until she spluttered out an apology.) This was testimony to the power of the spoken word. The power to wreck a reputation or to ignite conflict in a community—this was well within the reach of women, and some of them used it to even scores, to intimidate neighbors, or merely to show that they could not be pushed around. At the same time "gossip" could be a force for good. A man who beat his wife, a woman who whipped her servant, might both behave better when they found out their neighbors were talking about them.

Witchcraft demonstrated some of the same dynamics. A witch was someone who used supernatural powers to bring harm to someone else. Everyone believed that witchcraft was real, because it accounted for evil and suffering in a world where scientific explanations were not yet available. In 1671 in Northumberland, for example, Edward Cole's "people all fell sick and much of his cattle dyed." We would look for a germ or virus. Edward Cole suspected witchcraft.

That he accused a woman was no coincidence. In the witch traditions of Europe and Great Britain (Virginia's Indians and Africans probably had their own traditions, but we do not know the details), alleged witches were almost always female. Women, especially the old and poor, were easy scapegoats. For centuries, moreover, women had been stereotyped in the image of Eve—passionate, lusty, and easily seduced by the devil, the culprit who presumably gave witches their magical powers. Actually, a woman who was otherwise powerless might find her only leverage in behaving as though she might be a witch; that way neighbors who feared a bewitching would be likely to treat her with more care.

Or they might take her to court. Virginia seems to have had the dubious honor of hosting the first witch trial in British North America: Joan Wright of Surry was accused (and released) in 1626. No one was ever executed for witchcraft in Virginia, however, and the most famous case on record suggests that the authorities tended to proceed with caution. In 1698 and at several times thereafter, Grace Sherwood was accused of bewitching various neighbors. In the investigations that followed, a gallows-happy set of justices could have found sufficient evidence to convict. A panel of matrons found "'two things like titts'" on her body, the extra nipples with which witches supposedly suckled the devil. Later, Sherwood was bound and thrown in the river to test whether she would sink or float; the spot in Virginia Beach is still called Witch Duck Point. She floated—more evidence of her guilt.

But Grace Sherwood was not condemned. Possibly, Virginia communities were too fragile to withstand the potentially explosive impact of witchcraft convictions. In the Sherwood case the local population was apparently badly divided; when two subsequent panels of matrons were summoned to give evidence, they refused to appear. Were they deliberately protesting the proceedings?

They may have been, for seventeenth-century women did launch into political battles when the occasion arose, and high-born women were involved at the highest levels. Margaret Brent arrived in Virginia around 1651. She lived out her days quietly on a Westmoreland plantation she named "Peace," a welcome change after a career in Maryland that had been anything but peaceful. Brent had served as the executrix of Maryland's governor, she had headed off a mutiny of hungry soldiers, and she had asked for the vote—the first woman in America to do so. In fact, she asked for two votes in the Maryland assembly, one as executrix and one in her own right. When she was denied, she lodged a protest against all the assembly's further actions.

Margaret Brent would probably have recognized kindred spirits in the women who were caught up in the turmoil of Bacon's Rebellion. Civil war broke out in Virginia in 1676. Indian policy precipitated the trouble; believing themselves too vulnerable to Indian attacks, planters on the frontier found a leader in Nathaniel Bacon and began making war on peaceful Indians. When Governor William Berkeley tried to stop them, Bacon's followers rebelled against their government, burning Jamestown and pillaging the plantations of Berkeley's supporters. Luckily for the forces of the governor, Bacon died in the fall of 1676 and the rebellion fizzled soon after.

While Bacon's Rebellion was apparently set in motion by men, women were quickly em-broiled, too. One of the most important histories of the rebellion was written on the scene by a woman. Anne Cotton apologized for writing "too wordishly," but her *Account of Our Late Troubles in Virginia* was in fact an eloquent summary—and it earns her the distinction of having been Virginia's first woman historian. On the side of the rebels were several fiery women. One of them was Sarah Drummond, whose husband was executed for his role in the rebellion. Sarah herself was said to be "a notorious & wicked rebel, in inciting & incouraging the people to the late rebellion: persuading the soldiers to persist therein, telling them they need not fear the king, nor any force out of England, no more than a broken straw."

In this she was mistaken, for Lady Frances Berkeley soon returned from England with a thousand redcoats and orders to crush the rebels. Lady Berkeley was the wife of the governor and well connected at court. When the rebellion flared, the governor dispatched her to England to act as his representative. On returning to Virginia, she continued her vigorous defense of her husband's actions, and after he died in 1677, she harassed his successor unmercifully. She was joined by several influential men who met at her home, Green Spring, to plot strategy; they were collectively known as the Green Spring faction. Eventually Lady Berkeley married the governor of North Carolina (her third governor), but they lived at Green Spring and she remained a force in Virginia politics until her death in the 1690s.

From the widow who served as executrix of a small planter's will to the adventures of a Sarah Drummond or a Frances Berkeley, women in seventeenth-century Virginia frequently assumed positions of power, authority, or trust. There was a catch, however. No matter how well these women performed, their achievements did not undermine the prevailing belief in the natural inferiority or women. Instead, these active women were thought of as exceptions, as honorary men; ideas about women as a group changed not at all.

As the century drew to a close, these ideas were expressed and given new strength by two developments. First was the founding of William and Mary in 1693. The college was for men only and would remain so for 226 years. Then in 1699 a new law spelled out who in Virginia could vote and who could not. While custom prevented women from voting everywhere, Virginia was the only colony to say explicitly that women could not vote. It was the beginning of a long tradition of legislative conservatism on issues affecting women.

As the seventeenth century gave way to the eighteenth, then, some doors began to close on women. For black women, unfortunately, this was nothing new. Their turning point seems to have come in the 1660s. Before then Africans in Virginia had at least a slim chance of becoming free people, and those who were slaves had work routines not very different from those of English indentured servants. But from 1662 on, Virginia lawmakers made a series of momentous decisions: One law after another made slavery more rigid, more degrading, and more difficult to escape.

So far as anyone knows, the first blacks arrived in Virginia in 1619. It is certain that they were brought by force. Less is known about their status over time—whether they remained slaves who were kept in bondage all their lives, or whether they became indentured servants who went free after a few years. Since there was no slavery in England, white Virginians had no fixed ideas about what they should do with their new laborers from Africa. We do know that among the relatively small numbers of Africans who came to Virginia in the early years, a few did achieve freedom.

An outstanding example was the family of Anthony and Mary Johnson of Northampton County. "'Antonio a Negro'" and "'Mary a Negro Woman'" arrived in separate ships in 1621 and 1622. They met when they were put to work on the same plantation; Mary was the only woman on the place. How they got free is not known, but at some point they married, and their family

life proved to be a miracle of good health. They raised four children, and Mary and Anthony both lived to see grandchildren. Economically they did well. When the entire family moved to Maryland in the 1660s, Anthony sold a 250-acre plantation. Their grown son John owned a 450-acre plantation.

The Johnson family was surely not exempt from racial prejudice. Long before the English had laid eyes on actual Africans, they associated blackness with evil, and they made up their minds that darker-skinned peoples were inferior beings. English prejudice must have weighed on the Johnsons and all other black Virginians.

Still, there was a time in Virginia's early history when race relations were fluid, possibilities were open, and blacks and whites of the same class could expect roughly similar treatment. The best evidence of this comes from the courts' reactions to affairs of the heart. Black couples and interracial couples who were found guilty of adultery or fornication took the same punishments as white couples; in 1649 William Watts (white) and Mary (a "negro Woman" servant) found themselves "standing in a white sheete with a white Rodd in theire hands in the Chapell." Blacks and whites who actually married each other—and there were several documented cases of this—were left in peace.

But not for long. At midcentury the black population was still small—perhaps 500 people in a total population of about 14,000—and the great majority of bound laborers were still English servants. By century's end Virginia was fast making its fateful transition to slave labor. There were thousands of blacks in Virginia by 1700 (between 6,000 and 10,000, it is thought, in a total population of 63,000), and for every new indentured servant imported from England, four black slaves arrived from Africa or the Caribbean.

The legal system was ready for them. From 1662 to 1705 the assembly passed a series of laws that together defined the essential character of slavery and race relations in Virginia. It was a chilling list. Who was a slave? Any child born of a slave mother, the law answered (1662). Indians, too, could be made slaves (1682). Could a slave ever become a free person? Hardly ever, the law answered. An owner who wanted to free a slave would have to pay to send the freed slave out of the colony (1691). In 1723 the law was revised; henceforth a slave could be freed only by special act of the assembly. Could a white person marry a black or an Indian? No, and any white who tried was to be banished from the colony (1691). Could a slave own property? No, a slave *was* property, and any livestock belonging to slaves was to be confiscated and sold (1705). How could a slave be lawfully disciplined? If in the course of punishing a slave, the owner or overseer killed the slave, it was legal (1699). A runaway slave who resisted arrest was to be killed on the spot (1680).

A slave who was merely unruly could legally have fingers or toes cut off (1705).

The law, fortunately, was not the only influence on the lives of slaves. As we shall see, slaves themselves continually invented ways of exerting influence on their owners, on the system, and on one another. Yet it is important to appreciate the law's full power. By 1700 the typical black Virginia woman was "chattel"— property—and as such she could be bought, sold, mortgaged, or swapped, or even gambled away in a card game. She would remain property all of her life, and so would her children, who could be taken away from her at any time. She could try to protest, but she did so knowing that her owner had life-and-death power over her. These were among the basic facts of life under slavery, and they would remain in force for more than a century and a half.

Questions for Study and Review

1. How might differences in women's roles among Indians and Europeans have affected negotiations between the two groups over land, trade, and war?

2. In what ways did English women and men share a common experience of settlement, and in what ways did their experiences differ?

3. How was the status of Africans transformed between 1619 and 1700 and why?

4. Given what you know about present-day roles of women in each of the three groups studied by Lebsock, what might contemporary women in these three groups learn by examining their counterparts in the seventeenth century?

Suggested Readings

Julia Cherry Spruill, *Women's Life and Work in the Southern Colonies* (1938).

Rayna Green, "The Pocahontas Perplex: The Image of Indian Women in American Culture," *Massachusetts Review* (Autumn 1975).

Lois Green Carr and Lorena S. Walsh, "The Planter's Wife: The Experience of White Women in Seventeenth Century Maryland," *William and Mary Quarterly* (October 1977).

James Axtell, *The Invasion Within: The Contest of Cultures in Colonial North America* (1985).

Alan Kulikoff, "The Beginnings of the Afro-American Family in Maryland," in Michael Gordon, ed., *The American Family in Social-Historical Perspective* (1978).

TWO

The Salem Village Cataclysm: Origins and Impact of a Witch-hunt

Lyle Koehler

In late seventeenth-century Massachusetts, Puritan women and men were no longer confronted by powerful Indian societies, nor were they as dependent as their Virginia counterparts on African labor. Nonetheless, Indian attacks on frontier villages and the religious practices of Caribbean slaves fed the fears of English settlers and thereby contributed to one of the most shocking incidents in colonial history—the Salem witch-hunt. Within fifty years of the founding of Plymouth, social and economic tensions began to plague the colony. Internal dissent—over religion, land, and politics—combined with external threats—from Indians, the Dutch, and the French—to disrupt the early vision of a "'city on a hill' that would stand as a beacon of righteousness for the rest of the Christian world."

Women were often at the center, symbolically and literally, of these upheavals. Heretic Anne Hutchinson, Quaker martyr Mary Dyer, and the Salem women hanged as witches were some of the most visible manifestations of Massachusetts's spiritual decline and earthly disarray. Both the accusers and those accused of witchcraft in Salem were predominantly female. The two groups of women reflected the deep economic and political cleavages and the social and sexual tensions that divided not only Salem but the colony as a whole.

The ever growing number of non-Puritan settlers, the expansion of commerce and shortage of good farm land, the migration of younger men, the resulting surplus of marriage-age daughters, and increasing numbers of poor folk and transients heightened anxieties among many settlers.

Koehler explores the question of why that anxiety was translated into a witch-hunt in Salem. He notes that the breakdown of family and community cohesion that became apparent in this now notorious village eventually spread throughout the colonies, and was accelerated in the next century by revolution, revivalism, and industrialization. Then, too, as Linda Kerber and Paul Johnson show in later readings, changes in women's lives were a good barometer of changes in society as a whole.

Only in Salem, however, did the barometer fail to reflect the prevailing social climate. Perhaps the recognition, when the hunt ended, that innocent women may have been put to death kept such outbursts of witch hysteria from invading other towns. Yet the contagion of witchcraft was as believable in the seventeenth century as the germ theory of disease is today. Diatribes against the social, moral, and sexual practices of witches were not unlike those hurled against AIDS victims in our own time. Perhaps the most intriguing point is that the witch-hunts in the colonies did not become more severe. In the larger historical context, this was a period of great turmoil, during which European nations burned tens of thousands of witches. It is significant that New World residents managed to contain their fears. This was most important for women, who were most likely to be the targets of accusations and executions. Koehler traces the horrors and the limits of the Salem witch-hunt, illuminating both the powers and perils it offered women.

Between 1689 and 1692 a large number of political, economic, and religious frustrations raised the already high anxiety level of Calvinist New England. The governments established in Massachusetts, Connecticut, Plymouth, and New Hampshire after Andros's expulsion suffered from a general inability to reassert political or religious order. Even though the King approved of these transitional governments, Puritans realized that they no longer determined their own futures. The Crown's reluctance to restore the old charter privileges soon convinced all but a few skeptics that the independence and relative isolation of earlier years had almost vanished. Many who believed the charters were New World Magna Cartas—valued symbols of the Biblical Commonwealths' continued viability—felt stripped of self-government, law, and religious purpose, not to mention humiliated and helpless before royal whim. Prone to see conspiracies everywhere, Calvinists worried about the disruptive effects of a "monstrous" Catholic plot involving Andros, James II, the Canadian French, and the Indians.

Distressed by the political factionalism of the 1680s, many Massachusetts Puritans expressed great concern over the nature, as well as the legitimacy, of the government installed after the little Glorious Revolution. The new governor, Simon Bradstreet, served ineffectually and sometimes suffered sharp attacks from an angry populace. The rural-based General Court, wishing to revive the charter and a sense of holy mission, opposed those merchants and

non-freemen who desired changes, including a new franchise law and more extensive guarantees of property. Anglicans (about 5 percent of the population) also pressed for liberty, because they feared a resumption of the charter would force them to move to New York, northern New Hampshire, or Maine.

Other sources of stress undermined Massachusetts's stability. Pirates, particularly French ones, roamed the New England coastline. The wheat blast continued to destroy a major portion of the annual grain crop. Smallpox, "burning and spotted Fevers, shaking Agues, dry Belly Acks, plagues of the Guts, and divers other sore distempers" killed more than 150 persons between February and June, 1690. Trade fell to a point where it was insufficient to sustain the colony's economy, debt came due without payment, and the poor, according to one observer, seemed "ready to eat up one another, or turn Levellers." Severe taxation, levied to cover the costs of Indian warfare, left the colony deep in debt, and an inflated paper currency forced farmers to receive payment for their scanty crops in money worth only 60 to 70 percent of its stated value. The outbreak of warfare with the French and Abnaki Indians caused the colonists to fear the disastrous effects of another bloody, financially debilitating conflict.

In such impoverishing times, a growing sense of materialism threatened the spiritual basis of the Bay Colony. Cotton Mather angrily stated in 1691, ". . . might I hold out a Turf of earth; and say, Here is the God of many a poor New-England man! A beelzebub indeed! a fine God, made of Dung!" Governor Bradstreet and the General Court proclaimed that laws had fallen into widespread disrespect, as people sinned in "Blasphemy, Cursing, Profane Swearing, Lying, Unlawful Gaming, Sabbath-breaking, Idleness, Drunkenness, Uncleanness, and all the Entice-

From "The Salem Village Cataclysm: Origins and Impact of a Witch Hunt, 1689–92," *A Search for Power: The "Weaker Sex" in Seventeenth-Century New England* by Lyle Koehler. Copyright © 1980 by The Board of Trustees of the University of Illinois. Reprinted by permission of the University of Illinois Press.

ments and Nurseries of such Impieties." Magistrates often hesitated to prosecute such offenders, or gave them very minor punishments.

The abuse of old moral values, property contention, illness, war, poor crop yields, pirates, and political disarray testified to the disruption of virtually all aspects of Puritan life. "In imminent danger of perishing" and feeling completely powerless before a God whose "Ax is laid to the Root of the trees," many Puritans reportedly imagined that the colony had been reduced to a Hobbesian state of nature, where only the strong would survive. The once-proud Commonwealth had become a chaotic "labyrinth of Miserys." Indeed, life's problems pressed in so profoundly that a tendency toward "self-murder" lay "fierce upon some unhappy people," threatening a veritable "epidemic" of suicide.

Like Massachusetts, Connecticut faced, after Andros's expulsion, a general political confusion. People were apprehensive about the King's hesitation in responding to three petitions for the restoration of charter privileges. Many feared that William might divide the colony between New York, with its Catholic governor, and Massachusetts. Still, Connecticut citizens possessed a good deal of independent spirit.

While Connecticut faced illness, economic distress, and political "discontents and murmurings," Puritans there did not feel quite the same degree of confusion as prevailed in Massachusetts; nor did they berate themselves with quite the same intensity. None of the Connecticut authorities would protest quite as bitterly as the Massachusetts Governor and Council, who in 1690 exclaimed, ". . . shall our Father spit in our faces and we not be ashamed!"

While Massachusetts [and] Connecticut struggled to avert disasters in one form or another, the settlers of Maine and New Hampshire had to confront the daily possibility of Indian warfare. Massachusetts leaders recalled Andros's troops from the northerly forts in 1689. Soon afterward, Indians overran two hundred miles of

coastline from the St. Croix to the Piscatauqua rivers, destroying seven forts and the towns of Pemaquid, New Harbor, New Dartmouth, Sagedehoc, North Yarmouth, Richmond's Island, and Saco. Warriors killed or captured over three hundred persons and caused property damage totalling £60,000 in 1689–90. Commercial fishing and the mast trade all but ceased. Some Maine residents stayed on, begging England for help; others moved to Salem and Boston, where they often received allotments of poor relief. In 1691, partly to provide for the protection of Maine, the Crown included that "province" with the Massachusetts charter.

While each New England colony (with the possible exception of Rhode Island) underwent severe distress between 1689 and 1692, the diverse sources of tension did not affect all geographical areas in similar or equally intense ways. Residents of Hampshire County, for example, had little sense of the turmoil enveloping much of eastern Massachusetts. Many Maine settlers, on the other hand, could become profoundly concerned only about the stinging effects of total warfare.

The sources of tension which the inhabitants of Essex County, Massachusetts, shared with Puritans elsewhere were numerous and somewhat diffuse, but nevertheless hard felt. Salem, the only "really significant merchantile center in the colony" other than Boston, had become cosmopolitan and wealthy—much to the chagrin of people in the more tradition-oriented, financially declining inland areas. The diminishing availability of land at communities like Andover, Topsfield, Ipswich, Wenham, and Salem Village often led to sharp conflict over land boundaries. Rural Puritans with decreasing acreages envied the material prosperity of Salem merchants with their "great houses," although that was not the only factor disconcerting many inland settlers. The Salem merchants, like their Boston counterparts, ignored the old laws against usury and excessive profit-taking. Agriculturalists, once protected by fair-price and fixed-wage laws, now were at the mercy of the international market. Moreover, the material products of trade, so readily apparent in the many Salem shops, threatened to push more spiritual concerns into oblivion. A flourishing commerce brought newcomers, novelty, and a spirit of individualism into an area desperate for stability and unity. Taverns, those symbols of the moral decay which so many Puritans felt was becoming altogether too common, proliferated, especially along roads connecting town centers to Salem.

Salem Villagers, in particular, experienced great political, economic and social strain. With no real power for the church, town government (Salem Village did not have official town status), or selectmen, all institutional authority had broken down by 1692. Lacking viable channels for the expression of their grievances, especially in these times of colony-wide political insecurity, the inhabitants had fallen into "uncomfortable divisions and contentions." According to one contemporary, "brother is against brother and neighbors against neighbors, all quarrelling and smiting one another." Villagers addressed their ministers in "scoffing" and "contemptuous tones." By 1689–90, 20 percent of all rated persons refused to pay the minister's salary, and that figure increased to 29 percent the following year. Many inhabitants of the eastern and southern portions of Salem Village had large landholdings and connections with Salem's merchant community, thereby cutting off possibilities for real estate expansion and reducing the influence of prominent village families like the Putnams.

The many problems confronting Salem Villagers in 1692 "encompassed some of the central issues of New England society in the late seventeenth century." Sources of tension included "the resistance of back-country farmers to the pressures of commercial capitalism and the social style that accompanied it; the breaking away of outlying areas from parent towns; difficulties between ministers and their congregations; the crowding of third-gen-

eration sons from family land; the shifting locus of authority within individual communities and society as a whole; the very quality of life in an unsettled age." Salem Villagers sought security, a place which "could offer shelter against sweeping social change and provide a setting where the Puritan social vision might yet be realized." In early 1692, quite suddenly, everything exploded.

The Salem Village witch mania began easily enough, when several young girls experimented with fortune-telling and read occult works. In late January 1692, these girls began creeping under chairs and into holes, uttering "foolish, ridiculous speeches," assuming odd postures, and, on occasion, writhing in agony. Their antics soon became full-fledged hysterical fits. Their tongues extended out to "a fearful length," like those of hanged persons; their necks cracked; blood "gushed plentifully out of their Mouths." A local physician named William Griggs, unable to explain the girls' behavior in medical terms, warned that it must be due to an "Evil hand." The fits quickly spread to other youngsters ranging in age from twelve to nineteen, as well as to married women like Ann Pope, Sarah Bibber, Ann Putnam, and "an Ancient Woman, named Goodall."

The afflicted girls initially charged Sarah Good, Sarah Osborne, and the minister's Indian slave Tituba* with practicing *maleficium* on them. Local magistrates served warrants on these designated witches, who faced a courtroom examination on March 1. Twenty days later, Deodat Lawson, an ex-Salem Village pastor visiting from Boston, delivered a rousing anti-witchcraft sermon after observing the convulsive fits of Mary Walcott and Abigail Williams. A week later, Samuel Parris called his congregation to search out the many devils in the church. Parris was an old-line Puritan—a man anxious about

---

* Author's Note: Other sources identify Tituba as being a Caribbean slave of Indian heritage.

The combination of political instability, economic woe, and social tensions that plagued seventeenth-century Salem found expression in the hysterical witch-hunt that swept the village. In fits of delirium that were taken as proof of witches' power and presence, adolescent girls leveled their accusations of witchcraft. In the beginning the accused were usually women considered eccentric, deviant, or disreputable, but as time went on any woman might be charged with witchcraft and brought before a tribunal for judgment. Here a courtroom of examiners searches an accused woman for the "devil's mark"—physical evidence of her pact with Satan.

his declining ministerial power, intensely suspicious of his neighbors, obsessed with thoughts of his own filthiness, and fearing the subversion of the Biblical Commonwealth.

The half-dozen afflicted girls had accused only three witches in February and four in March, but after the ministers' warnings no fewer than fifteen girls and women of Salem Village accused witches—at least twenty-five additional during April, and fifty-one in May. "Witch" Martha Corey warned the authorities in March, "We must not believe all these distracted children say," but prosecutions continued. More persons from areas outside Salem Village were

added to the list of accused witches—thirteen from Topsfield, most of whom had previously quarreled with the Putnam family over land boundaries; twelve others from Gloucester; thirteen from the port of Salem; and fifty-five from Andover, a locale torn by land stress. Twenty-eight different persons, including four Andover women, fell subject to hysterical attacks in five outlying towns. Altogether, these ostensibly bewitched persons denounced almost all of the 56 men and 148 women accused of practicing witchcraft in 1692–93. Not only were three-quarters of the accused persons females, but of the 56 men half were singled out only after a close female relative or a wife had been accused—a sort of guilt by association. The reverse pattern holds true for only one, or possibly three, of the remaining male witches. Thus the traditional notion of the witch as a specifically female type held true for most Essex County accusations—even during times of severe stress, when virtually anyone might suffice as a scapegoat.

Estimates of the actual number of witches at large ranged from 307 (by confessed witch William Barker) to 500 (Susannah Post, Thomas Maule). Sir William Phips, the newly appointed royal governor who arrived in May, soon established a Special Court of Oyer and Terminer to try the many recently imprisoned witches. This court included Salem magistrate John Hathorne, Sam Sewall, the stringent chief justice William Stoughton, Dorchester merchant John Richards, Salem physician Bartholomew Gedney, Cavalier Waitstill Winthrop, the wealthy Peter Sargent, and Nathaniel Saltonstall of Haverhill—all members of the coalition government, who in Roger Thompson's words, "were very much on trial themselves." Although Saltonstall soon disapproved of the proceedings, resigned, and was replaced by Salem magistrate Jonathan Corwin, the justices listened to testimony against witch after witch, usually presuming that the accused was guilty before the trial began. In court, the afflicted girls pointed to imaginary specters, and officials flailed away at such witches until the floor was "all covered" with invisible blood. As the frenzy escalated, ten persons broke out of prison to hide in other locales, and eight or ten more fled "upon rumor of being apprehended." One of these, sixteen-year-old Elizabeth Colson, outraced the Reading constable and his dog in a wild chase through thick bushes, while Philip English escaped a group of searchers by hiding behind a bag of clothing.

The Court of Oyer and Terminer sentenced Bridget Bishop to be hanged on June 10. Five more women followed her to the gallows on July 19, four men and a woman on August 19, and seven women and a man on September 22.

On September 16 the authorities ordered Giles Corey pressed to death under a pile of stones when he refused to plead. All these witches, Cotton Mather related, faced execution "impudently demanding of God, a Miraculous Vindication of their Innocency."

Faced with the awful possibility of their own deaths, other accused witches began propitiously confessing their wrongdoings. After the July 19 hangings, five accused Andover witches "made a most ample, surprising, amazing Confession, of all their Villanies and declared the Five newly Executed to have been of their Company." Such "witches" may have observed the immediate leniency extended to self-confessed offenders like Tituba and Sarah Churchill. In August and September fifty-five other "witches" confessed—many, if not all of them, under extreme duress.

Accused witches clogged the prisons of eastern Massachusetts, where they suffered from the biting cold of winter and sometimes from a lack of sufficient food. Often jailors held them in irons for long periods, to prevent them from afflicting their accusers by moving their bodies. The Salem jailor tied each of three boys neck and heels together "till the blood was ready to come out of their Noses" (and did, in fact, gush out of William Proctor's). Thirteen or fourteen accused witches at Ipswich prison petitioned the General Court for release on bail as winter approached, asserting they were "all most destroyed with soe long an imprisonment." By October six "witches," including Sarah Osborne, had died in jail. Two, Abigail Faulkner and Elizabeth Proctor, gave birth under such atrocious conditions.

Witchcraft accusations diminished during the summer (eight in June, seven in July), but after a council of eight ministers at Cambridge affirmed the reality of specter evidence on August 1, charges again boomed—twenty-five in August and twenty-seven in September, mostly from Andover. Throughout 1692 people intently scrutinized their neighbors' behavior, being especially watchful of those against whom they had some personal grievance. In court, "it was usual to hear evidence of matter foreign, and of perhaps Twenty or Thirty years standing, about over-setting Carts, the death of Cattle, unkindness to Relations, or unexpected Accidents befalling after some quarrel." The accusatory tone established in the trials helped activate animosities existing within families as well, with many parents therefore "believing their Children to be Witches, and many Husbands their Wives, etc."

For many people who were already struggling against spiritual, political, and economic deprivation, and against the force of late seventeenth century changes, making a witchcraft accusation expressed their anxiety while it reasserted a sense of their own potency. Accusations allowed the angry, the helpless, and sometimes the sensitive to fight the imagined malign powers that frustrated them by scapegoating suitable incarnations of evil. By testifying against a witch, they not only exposed but also conquered their own feelings of powerlessness in a changing world. By blaming witches, men and women attempted to reestablish some feeling of order, of control, when confronted by the discomforting effects of threats both external (e.g., Indians, political anarchy, urban materialism) and internal (e.g., the inability to achieve assurance of justification before God, or to understand, if assured, why God had chosen to "providentially" destroy a given animal or person).

The sixty-three men and twenty-one women who testified as corroborating witnesses against accused witches had much in common with the six males and thirty-seven females whose hysterical fits initiated proceedings. In specifically sex-role-defined ways, members of each sex responded to an apparent condition of helplessness. Men primarily appeared before the magistrates and, in typically straightforward fashion, gave accounts of the witches' *maleficium*; women usually made their accusations more circuitously, behind the cover of a fit. Men revealed their feeling of fear and impotence by describing how witches had pressed them into rigid immobility; bewitched women demonstrated dramatically, before the very eyes

of the justices, how that—and far worse—could happen.

Women, particularly those adolescents who experienced fits, used the witchcraft accusation as a viable form of self-expression in 1692–93. Burdened by the restrictive contingencies of the ideal feminine role, with its dictum (reinforced in church and school) that good girls must control their longings for material joy and submit to stronger adult authority figures, many young females probably felt a great deal of frustration as they searched for gaiety, attention, accomplishment, and individual autonomy. This was especially true considering the recent fits of the Goodwin children in Boston (1688), the occupational assertiveness of female innkeepers and school dames, and the patent examples of so many women who violated Puritan laws—all of which had an impact on the consciousness of developing adolescents.

After studying spirit possession and shamanism in primitive societies, I. M. Lewis concluded that accusatory fits are "thinly disguised protest movements directed against the dominant sex. They thus play a significant part in the sex-war in traditional societies and cultures where women lack more obvious and direct means of forwarding their aims. To a considerable extent, they protect women from the exactions of men and offer an effective vehicle for manipulating husbands and male relatives." Lewis's conclusion is equally applicable to Salem Village. There, in the paranoid atmosphere of 1692, girls used the fit—although not necessarily consciously— as a vehicle to invert the traditional social status hierarchy. Similarly, adult women, those perpetual children, expressed, through the fit, a need for excitement and dominion. For females, such assertion entailed, symbolically and on occasion literally, the elimination of the immediate oppressing force—the adult, the husband, or, in Mercy Short's case, the Indians. The bewitched parties, through their accusations, did help to eliminate authority figures—if not actual parents or husbands, whose destruction would be *too* discomforting or would deprive them of necessary support, then surely "representative" substitutions. A female figure suggestive of parental authority by her mature years, or one closely associated with a male of high position, was frequently chosen as a safer but still satisfactory surrogate. Later, as the afflicted girls achieved more self-confidence, they actually attacked men, including at least two ministers.

All of the afflicted women, most particularly the Salem Village girls, exercised fantastic power. The public watched spellbound while the girls contorted their bodies into unbelievable shapes. Magistrates hung on their every word, believing them even when the girls were caught in outright lies. At least one justice changed his opinion of a prominent friend after that man came under accusation. Accused witches hardly knew what to say, save to maintain their innocence, when confronted by the awesome spectacle of girls throwing themselves about the courtroom, pulling four-inch-long pins and broken knife blades out of their own flesh. Some accused witches even became confused as to their own complicity in such goings on. Anyone who criticized the court proceedings or the afflicted quickly fell under accusation as another witch, including even defecting members of the girl's own group.

As early as March 20 the afflicted proved they could also, on occasion, assume a more self-consciously assertive stance. When Deodat Lawson prepared to give a Sabbath lecture, eleven-year-old Abigail Williams shouted out, "Now stand up, and Name your Text." In the beginning of his sermon Goodwife Ann Pope told him, "Now there is enough of that," and after it was finished, Williams asserted, "It is a long Text." Twelve-year-old Anne Putnam shouted out that an invisible yellow bird, a witch's familiar, sat on Lawson's hat as it hung on a pin. In the afternoon sermon Williams again spoke up: "I know no Doctrine you had," she informed the minister, "If you did name one, I have forgot it." Such outspokenness

dumbfounded the congregation. Here three females had violated the biblical injunction against women speaking in church; furthermore, a little girl had criticized the minister. Obviously witches were to blame!

Not only had such females assumed the power to speak in church, and to designate men and women as witches; they also claimed the ability to vanquish supernatural creatures. They asserted that they could see and talk to the Devil, yet emerge unscathed from those encounters. Tituba, powerless both as servant and as woman, told imaginative tales of her own fearless contact with frightening spectral creatures—hairy upright men and great black dogs. Mercy Short, a fifteen-year-old Boston girl who two years before had watched while Indians cut down her frontier family, in her fits dared the Devil (interestingly enough, a man "of Tawny, or an Indian colour") to kill her: "Is my Life in Your Hands? No, if it had, You had killed me long before this Time!—What's that?—So you can!—Do it then if You can.—Poor Fool! . . . . What? Will you Burn all Boston and shall I be Burnt in that Fire?—No, tis not in Your Power." Although "Satan" was able to cause her much physical pain, she ultimately emerged victorious in the confrontation by relying upon the transcendent power of God. Always assertive while in her fits (although she did not blame witches for them), Mercy Short hardly hesitated to call one onlooker a fool when that person objected to singing a psalm which Mercy had requested.

Power and influence were not the only deep-seated impulses revealed by the fit. Filled with "repressed vitality, with all manner of cravings and urges for which village life afforded no outlet," the bewitched girls of Salem Village danced and sang for several hours at Job Tyler's house. Ephraim Foster's wife also danced at her home, and Martha Sprague sang for nearly an hour—both ostensibly under the influence of witchcraft. Mercy Short's torments sometimes "turned into Frolicks; and she became as extravagant as a Wild-Cat." Margaret

Rule laughed much and would drink nothing but rum in her fits. When Sarah Ingersoll accused one girl of lying about Goody Proctor's witchcraft, that girl placed this need for joy on an overtly conscious level by declaring simply, "they must have some sport."

Repressed sexuality also emerged as a theme in the behavior of some of the afflicted, in the charges levied, and in the confessions of "witches." In her fits Ann Pope suffered a "grievous torment in her Bowels as if they were torn out," which may have been a manifestation of her sexual fears, since the bowels were considered the seat of passion. Mary Warren, age twenty, believed that a spectral nineteen-year-old male witch sat on her stomach, and she sometimes crossed her legs together so tightly that "it was impossible for the strongest man ther to [uncross] them, without Breaking her Leggs." Such behavior is frequently observed in sexually repressed hysterical women. Margaret Rule reacted with obvious sensual appreciation when Cotton Mather rubbed her stomach to calm her, but she greeted a similar well-meaning effort by a female attendant with the words "don't you meddle with me." In her fits she loved being "brush'd" or "rub'd," as long as it was "in the right place." Sometimes she wished only men to view her afflictions; once "haveing hold of the hand of a Young-man, said to have been her Sweet-heart formerly, who was withdrawing; She pull'd him again into his Seat, saying he should not go to Night."

At times the sexual theme was even more explicit, although not as much as it often was in European witchcraft proceedings. One girl cried out that witch John Alden "sells powder and shot to the Indians and lies with Indian squaws and has Indian papooses." Two "witches," Bridget Bishop and Elizabeth Proctor, reportedly afflicted while dressed only in their shifts—by Puritan standards, a most seductive approach. "Witch" Rebecca Eames admitted giving the Devil her "soul & body"; then, in "horror of Conscience," she took a rope to hang herself and a razor to cut her throat "by Reason of her great sin in committing adultery." Mercy Wardwell, daughter of the hanged "witch" Samuel Wardwell, confessed to having sexual relations with Satan after "people told her yt she should Neuer hath such a Young Man who loved her." Abigail Hobbs also admitted giving herself "body and soul to the Old Boy."

In the increasingly secular world of the 1690s, Satan reputedly offered alluring temptations to Puritan women—"Carnal and Sensual Lusts," wine, "pretty handsome apparell," a horse to facilitate physical mobility, "a piece of money," "a pair of French fall shoes," "gold and many fine things." When asked how Satan had approached them, many confessed "witches" explained that they were "Discontent at their mean Condition in the World" and wished to sample the many joys he offered. They asserted that feasting, dancing, and jollity were the rule at witch meetings. Witches indulged in all those pleasures that good Puritans detested—the same pleasures that had gained so many adherents in these changing times. Regardless of whether they were sincere or merely prompted by the desire to escape execution, such confessions helped fuel both the spreading panic of the general community and the fervor of the most active accusers—not only because they *were* confessions, but also because their details echoed the same forbidden impulses with which their accusers, as well as many of the courtroom spectators, were grievously "afflicted."

The nine ringleaders of the Salem Village accusations included the daughter and niece of the minister, the daughter of a church deacon, and the wife and daughter of the parish clerk. Since material luxuries, expressions of vitality, and power impulses were not completely acceptable, especially to women who had grown up in very religious families, the psychosomatic pain experienced in fits, and the afflicted's obsession with imagining "Coffins, and bodies in shrouds" calling out for vengeance against their witch-murderers, manifested the accusing women's guilt at the unacceptability of their own disowned impulses. Caught between their training and their desires, there was no resolution, save in laying the blame for the latter on someone who by definition epitomized, in a fully malign way, those same impulses. Condemning the witch purged the self. Projecting the self into accusations of witchcraft helped religious women and envious adolescents to deal with the change in the female sex role which began occurring gradually after 1665. They were able to resist such change, while on another level giving explosive expression to it behind the fit's veil.

The choice of victims, many of them eccentrics, suggests that the bewitched females were most discomforted by those women who had acted upon their own inner needs to ignore or defy the ideal feminine sex role; i.e., those women who best illustrated the projected desires of the afflicted. Unable to be similarly assertive, the accusers turned instead to equally unfeminine, but disguised and purely destructive, aggression in punishing those nontraditional women.

Scapegoating witches did not always work for the individual accuser, as the shocking inhumanity of sending people to the gallows sometimes became too much for the afflicted girls to handle. Some initial accusers ceased to have fits or to denounce witches long before the frenzy abated. Mary Warren, after actively accusing a number of witches, suddenly began to charge that the "afflicted children did but dissemble." Immediately she was cried out upon as a witch, but in prison she continued to speak out against the proceedings. She explained, "when I was afflicted, I thought I saw the apparitions of a hundred persons," but then added that her head had been "distempered." In court, however, the other girls, Ann Pope, and John Indian attributed their violent fits to her, and under stringent cross-examination Mary Warren fell once again into fits. Imprisoned for a month, she finally retracted her criticism, admitted her own witchcraft, and once more began accusing others. Similarly, when Deliverance Hobbs wavered from her accusatory afflictions, the bewitched girls denounced her. She,

like Mary Warren, denied signing the Devil's book, but then, under the magistrates' relentless questioning, also admitted her witchcraft. Another of the girls, Sarah Churchill, fell under suspicion of practicing witchcraft, probably for the same reason. After her examination she cried and appeared "much troubled in spirit." She explained to Sarah Ingersoll that she had confessed her *maleficium* only "because they threatened her, and told her they would put her into the dungeon."

The line between witch and bewitched was dangerously thin, both on the psychological level and in terms of the social distribution of power which an accuser manipulated. Once a woman began having fits in which she declared herself afflicted by agents of Satan, she could afford no second thoughts, however sane and humane. Once she had "sold her soul"— that is, disavowed responsibility for her own deepest impulses—she could not recover it without sharing the fate of her accused victims, without becoming as powerless as they in the grip of the larger Puritan community.

Many of the alleged witches fell under suspicion not for any personal deviance, but because friction existed between families who contended over land. When some failed to secure satisfaction from the county courts or town meetings, they themselves, or women in their families, could easily accuse opponents of witchcraft in order to get even. In this respect, the 1692 outbreak represented a new departure in the history of seventeenth-century New England witchcraft. Previous witch-scapegoat accusations had been hurled at community eccentrics; in Essex County, however, because of the extreme level of anxiety prevailing, the witch's character in many instances became irrelevant. The Salem Village bewitched included at least three females who would have been privy to the antagonisms between the Putnams and their neighbors. The Putnams, a fairly well-to-do family with old roots, envied the prosperity of the *nouveau riche* Porters, who had close ties to Salem mercantile interests. Accusations followed, not of patriarch Israel Porter—perhaps because he was related by marriage to Judge John Hathorne—but of persons more distantly connected to the family. The bewitched girls charged Daniel Andrews, who was the husband of Sarah Porter, a schoolmaster, and ex-deputy to the General Court, the owner of a Salem apothecary shop, and one of the four wealthiest men in Salem Village. Another "witch," Philip English, a confederate of the Porters, owned an imposing house in Salem, fourteen town lots, and twenty sailing vessels. He fled with his wife, Mary, rather than appear before the Court of Oyer and Terminer. Andrews's brother-in-law George Jacobs, Jr., and Jacobs's wife and daughter faced prosecution, as did Andrews's tenant Peter Cloyse, his wife, and the wife of a servant in John Porter's household. Francis Nurse, the brother-in-law of Cloyse, had long antagonized the Putnams, by living on land which Nathaniel Putnam claimed and by his ties to Salem, where he had served as constable. Despite her reputation as a holy and God-fearing person, Nurse's wife, Rebecca, was hanged for practicing *maleficium*. Altogether, twelve of fourteen accused Salem Village witches lived in the eastern part of the village, near Salem, as did twenty-four of twenty-nine witch defenders, whereas thirty of thirty-two accusers lived in the west. The chart on pages 32–33 indicates the connections between twenty-three "witches" at Salem Village.

Because the Putnams had also become involved in land disputes with some inhabitants of Topsfield, the afflicted girls and the Putnams accused the most economically and politically important persons at Topsfield—those most able to injure the Putnam cause. Charges were filed against Isaac Easty, who was a selectman, tithingman, surveyor of highways, and member of many different town committees, as well as against his wife, Mary. The latter was hanged on September 22, two months after her sister Rebecca Nurse. Sarah Wilds, mother of the Topsfield town constable, was also hanged, on July 19.

While many witches served as scapegoat-victims of various men's land greed, others more clearly fitted the image of social deviants. Women who did not toe the ideal feminine line offered the afflicted females a superb opportunity to work out their own projected aggressions and needs for dominion—those unacceptable urges which the afflicted found desirable yet incompatible with their Puritan training. In what was probably an overstatement, Thomas Maule estimated that two-thirds of the accused were either guilty of rebellion against their parents (who included, in Puritan terms, husbands and magistrates) or of adultery. One, Sarah Osborne, had lived in a common law relationship with her "wild" Irish servant; another, Martha Corey, had given birth to a mulatto child. "Witch" Susannah Roots had earned a reputation as a "bad woman" who entertained company late at night.

Those women who had openly flouted the ideal role in the changing world of the late century received quick convictions. One of the first three persons accused, Sarah Good, was such a woman. Born into a wealthy family, she had been cheated out of her inheritance after her father's suicide in 1672. She married twice, both times to men who became debt ridden. By 1689 her second husband, William Good, had lost all of his land and seventeen head of cattle to his creditors. Too poor to own a house, he lived with Sarah and their infant daughter in neighbors' houses, barns, and sometimes open ditches. Turbulent and vitriolic, Sarah Good often scolded and "fell to muttering" when people extended charity to her. When one neighbor refused her lodging, she was not above setting his cattle loose. In court she answered the magistrates "in a very wicked spiteful manner, reflecting and retorting against the authorities with base and abusive words." After the minister Nicholas Noyes urged her to confess, since "she knew she was a witch," Sarah pulled no punches in lashing out, "you are a liar; I am no more a Witch than you are a Wizard; and if you take away my Life, God will give you Blood to drink." She died on July 19, protesting to the end.

Bridget Bishop, the first "witch" hanged, would not be dominated by her three husbands. She operated an unlicensed tavern where visitors congregated late at night to play the illegal game of shuffleboard, and she dressed provocatively—some of her contemporaries might say whorishly—in a red paragon bodice. Once she had driven an accusatory stranger off her porch with a spade. Like so many other alleged witches, she protested her innocence, asserting, "I know not what a witch is."

Martha Carrier, accused of no less than thirteen witchly murders at Andover, had actively disputed with neighbors over land, physically shaken up one twelve-year-old girl in church, and threatened a male opponent by saying that "She would hold his Nose close to the Grindstone as ever it was held since his Name was Abbot." Her interrogator asked at the witch trials, "What black man did you see?" She retorted, "I saw no black man but your own presence." She charged the magistrates with not listening to what she said, while they "shamefully" paid

Connections Between Various "Witches" at Salem Village

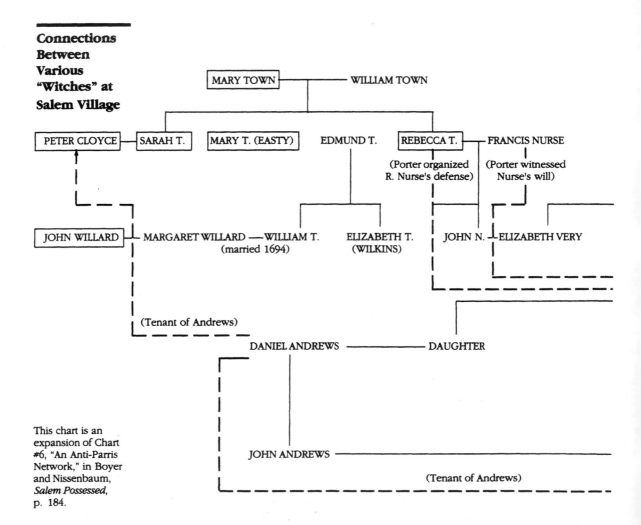

This chart is an expansion of Chart #6, "An Anti-Parris Network," in Boyer and Nissenbaum, *Salem Possessed,* p. 184.

attention to every little utterance of the bewitched girls. Cotton Mather, detesting her outspokenness, termed her "this rampant hag."

Despite the realizations that they faced a death sentence, most of the accused women refused to insure their own releases by concocting confessions. Instead, they "would neither in time of Examination, nor Trial, Confess any thing of what was laid to their Charge; some would not admit of any Minister to Pray with them, others refused to pray for themselves." Nineteen women died protesting their innocence, including five in prison. One of the hanged "witches," Mary Easty, knowing that she could not save her own life, wished to save those "that are going the same way with myself." She urged the Salem Court to examine carefully all confessing witches who accused others, for, she explained, they "have belyed themselves and others."

Those women who walked bravely to the gallows may have summoned strength from their religious faith, or from recognition of the integrity of their own personhood. Other women signed petitions supporting accused witches,

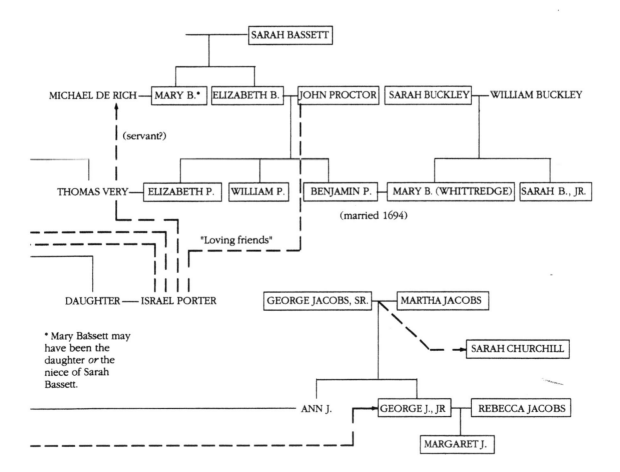

* Mary Bassett may have been the daughter *or* the niece of Sarah Bassett.

even though such petitioners should have been aware that the afflicted girls quickly accused their critics. Two Putnam opponents, Israel and Elizabeth Porter, headed a petition signed by sixteen other women and twenty-one men on behalf of Rebecca Nurse. Another thirteen men and seven of their wives requested leniency for the Proctors. At Salisbury fifty-eight women and fifty-seven men, neighbors of "witch" Mary Bradbury, asserted they had never head that Bradbury "ever had any difference or falleing oute wth any of her neighbors man woman or childe but was always, readie and willing to doe for them wt laye in her power night and day, though wth hazard of her health or other danger more." Twelve women and forty-one men of Andover also petitioned for the release of their accused neighbors. No one, however, argued on behalf of the nontraditional women accused.

During the trials, from time to time an occasional unaccused woman went so far as to attack the character of one or more of the afflicted. For example, Lydia Porter charged Goody Bibber with mischief-making and lying. Mary Phips, the wife of the governor, expressed her own disagreement by pardoning one convicted witch in the governor's absence, although she had no legal power to do so. Lady Phips, Lydia Porter, and the almost one hundred female petitioners, as well as many of the "witches," were acting assertively in varying degrees, reflecting and contributing to the style of the nontraditional woman.

As witchcraft accusations increased in numbers, protests also mounted, from men as well as from women. Husbands spoke up in defense of their wives. Ex-deputy Robert Pike told Justice Corwin that "diabolical visions, apparitions or representations" were "more commonly false and delusive then real." A Salem Quaker named Thomas Maule anonymously blasted the Puritans for murdering one another under the Devil's influence, and as early as June the Anabaptist William Milbourne protested to the General Court against the use of "bare specter

testimonie" to convict "persons of good fame and of unspotted reputations." A Boston merchant by the name of Thomas Brattle, in an October letter, penned a scathing criticism of the Salem proceedings. At about the same time Samuel Willard published a disapproving analysis of the arguments used against witches, in *Some Miscellany Observations on our Present Debates Respecting Witchcraft, In a Dialogue between S[alem] and B[oston]*. Cotton Mather had begun to doubt the reality of specter evidence, while other ministers raised objections to the proceedings. Two of them took occasion to preach the text, "they that are persecuted in one city, let them flee to another," and then counselled four "witches" to escape from prison.

The afflicted girls ultimately insured that the witchcraft proceedings would halt—by accusing the most prestigious members of Puritan society. The girls had first charged contentious, penniless Sarah Good, disreputable Sarah Osborne, and the exotic Barbadian Indian slave Tituba. Sensing their own power in the court's response, they subsequently broadened their attack by clamoring not only against low-status eccentrics, but also against virtuous women like Rebecca Nurse, and even against men. On May 31 attorney Thomas Newton would assert that they "spare no person of what quality so ever." By November the bewitched had charged the wives of critics Moody, Hale, and Dane, as well as several members of Boston's ruling elite. However, the authorities were reluctant to prosecute. Margaret Thatcher, the widow of Boston's wealthiest merchant and mother-in-law of Judge Jonathan Corwin, who presided at witchcraft trials, escaped apprehension, even though she was much complained about by the afflicted. So did Mary Phips, Samuel Willard, and Mistress Moody. The magistrates did issue a warrant for the arrest of a prominent merchant named Hezekiah Usher, but he received lodging in a private house and was then permitted to leave the colony.

Bostonians had less respect for the orders of the Salem Court than did the citizenry of any other area; their constables ignored warrants. Accused witches broke out of prison altogether too easily, suggesting complicity on the part of the jailer. In fact, the keeper had no apparent hesitancy about releasing one "witch" upon receipt of Lady Phips's pardon. Other Bostonians hid "witches" who had escaped from prison or fled apprehension.

The Salem Village girls who accused proper Bostonians quite possibly exploited the resentment of many rural Salem Villagers for those alien yet very powerful urbanites who often valued capital over land, commerce over husbandry, ornamentation over simplicity, and new ideas over old. The Putnams, in particular, facing diminishing land resources and declining status, had a good deal to resent; they listened with open ears while the girls accused nine prominent Bostonians and denounced Nathaniel Saltonstall, the Haverhill Councillor who had resigned his seat on the witch court.

The colony's economic and political leaders objected to the accusations levied against so many of their friends and wives. Quite probably their objections were crucial in bringing the frenzy to a halt. Robert Calef credited one prominent Bostonian with stopping proceedings at Andover by threatening to sue his accusers there in a £1,000 defamation action. Governor William Phips initially left all witchcraft affairs to the Court of Oyer and Terminer, but after returning to Boston from an expedition against the Maine Indians he found "many persons in a strange ferment of disatisfaction." Soon the royal governor forbade the issuance of any new literature on the subject, asked the Crown for counsel, and dissolved the Court of Oyer and Terminer. In the winter of 1692–93 Phips pardoned some convicted witches, caused some to be let out on bail, and "put the Judges upon considering a way to relieve others and prevent them from perishing in prison." The General Court on December 16, 1692, directed the newly created Superior Court to try the "witches" still in custody within Essex County. The Superior Court, meeting on January 3, 1692/3, acquitted forty-nine "witches" and convicted three. Deputy Governor Stoughton, the chief justice, ordered the execution of those three, as he had of other "witches," but Phips pardoned these and five other convicted persons. Stoughton, enraged, refused to sit on the bench of the next court at Charlestown. That body released all the accused persons tried before it.

Before the Superior Court met at Salem, the bewitched girls had ceased their afflictions. Perhaps by then they had realized that their reach exceeded their grasp. Perhaps they felt guilty over precipitating the deaths of twenty-five persons. Perhaps their power impulses had been satiated. (After all, for some time people as far away as Boston, Andover, and Gloucester had sought their advice in pointing out witches.) Perhaps they were drained by the physical and emotional strain which attended fits. Perhaps they felt purged, for a time, of their own unfeminine longings. For whatever reasons, they *had* had their day; now it seemed only appropriate that they return to their status as unobtrusive members of the Puritan community. Only in Boston did two girls, Mary Watkins and Margaret Rule, continue to have fits during 1693.

More than forty Massachusetts residents had suffered from hysterical fits in 1692 and 1693, accusing over two hundred persons of witchcraft. While Massachusetts was not the only colony to experience such an outbreak, the event in Connecticut, where for the first time in three decades the courts also began trying several "witches," ultimately produced a very different outcome. In late 1692 and early 1693, a seventeen-year-old French maidservant at Fairfield assumed the hysterical fit pattern of the Bay Colony's afflicted persons. Catherine Branch sometimes acted as one struck dumb, "put out her tong to a great extent," and experienced "a pinching & pricking at her breast." Like many at Salem Village, she sought the joys of "Singing, Laughing, Eating, [and] Rideing" in her fits. As she threw herself convulsively about, she complained of six different witches afflicting her. The accused included among their small numbers both the virtuous and the unholy. Mercy Disborough, the only one of these "witches" to receive the death sentence, had the worst reputation; she had tossed harsh words at many men in the community and had earned a general reputation as a witch before 1692. Elizabeth Clawson, on the other hand, never spoke threatening words. Believing in the motto "we must liue in pease," she often served as a mediator whenever her neighbors argued.

Unlike many Essex County inhabitants, those in Fairfield County had a more skeptical attitude about witchcraft. Some thought Catherine Branch "desembled." Abigail Wescott, her mistress, said none of the girl's accusations held any validity; she reportedly claimed that Branch "was such a Lying girl that not any boddy Could belieue one word what she said." Sarah Betts wished to treat the young woman's bewitchment through medicinal bloodletting, while Sarah Ketcham expressed disbelief that any witches at all existed in Fairfield. Men also objected to Branch's charges, and the special Court of Oyer and Terminer held at Fairfield on September 15, 1692, freed all the accused save Mercy Disborough; she received a death sentence, but later (in May 1693) the Connecticut General Assembly granted her a reprieve. On October 17, 1692, a meeting of Connecticut ministers held the water test to be "unlawfull and sinfill," rejected special evidence, considered "unusuall excresencies" or teats no proof of witchcraft, dismissed strange accidents as no evidence whatsoever, and expressed the view that Catherine Branch was deluded by the Devil. Two successive trials of "witches" resulted in acquittals. Like the Salem Village girls, Branch had made a play for power, but she could not convince her associates of the legitimacy of her claims.

Connecticut was not ripe for a witch hunt. A progressive ministry helped to undercut any accusatory zeal there. Although the colony's residents certainly experienced much tension between 1689 and 1692, their general anxiety level did not equal that of their Bay Colony neighbors. Political affairs were volatile, but the relative isolation and independence of towns defused the political turmoil. Land antagonisms, although emergent, had not reached serious proportions. The conflict between rural and urban lifestyles, so clear at Salem Village, was insignificant in this almost completely agrarian colony. The concern over moral decay was somewhat less extreme than in Massachusetts. Connecticut did not have to suffer the frightening effects of a witch hunt; instead, residents could cope with stress through less harsh actions, such as voting to catechize all "Bachelors and boys from eight years ould and upwards . . . once a fortnight on the Lords Daye in Ye meeting house."

The inhabitants of Maine, New Hampshire, and Plymouth had no concern about witches. In Maine, the Indian problem diverted attention from any occult concerns, while both the "red devils" and political factionalism had the same effect in New Hampshire. In both areas real enemies abounded, and neither had a history of witchcraft accusations. In Plymouth, the basic problem—a high tax rate—was alleviated through incorporation into the Bay Colony.

Only in eastern Massachusetts, with its intense and numerous frustrations, could a sustained witch hunt be mounted. There the reality of the nontraditional women loomed larger, helping to precipitate fits in powerless adolescents and religious Puritan wives, as well as aggravating the already established tendency to view unfeminine behavior as witchlike. Those independent-spirited women who faced prosecution as witches were victims of other, more conservative women's unconscious search for power.

Questions for Study and Review

1. What were the differences, and how might we explain them, between the treatment of women in seventeenth-century Virginia and Massachusetts?

2. What does Koehler's study of the witch trials reveal about economic developments in colonial Massachusetts and their different effects on women and men?

3. Since witchcraft trials were rare in the colonies and common in Europe, how might the uniqueness of the Salem episode reflect positively on American society?

4. In 1953 Arthur Miller wrote *The Crucible*, a play about the Salem witch trials that was intended to raise questions about the anticommunist "witch-hunts" of the McCarthy era. Compare the two situations.

Suggested Readings

Lyle Koehler, "The Case of the American Jezebels: Anne Hutchinson and Female Agitation during the Years of the Antinomian Turmoil, 1636–1640," *William and Mary Quarterly* (January 1974).

Philip J. Greven, *Four Generations: Population, Land, and Family in Colonial Andover, Massachusetts* (1970).

Carol Karlsen, *The Devil in the Shape of a Woman: Witchcraft in Colonial New England* (1987).

Stephen Boyer and Stephen Nissenbaum, *Salem Possessed: The Social Origins of Witchcraft* (1974).

Edmund S. Morgan, "The Puritans and Sex," *New England Quarterly* (December 1942).

THREE

Sisters, Wives, and Mothers: Self-Portraits of Three Eighteenth-Century Women

Anne Firor Scott

Most women's lives were not as dramatic as those of the small circle caught up in the Salem witch-hunt. Most women and men spent their days in the necessary but mundane tasks of providing for families, rearing children, and surviving personal and communal crises. The family was the center of life for these colonists. Women contributed to the family's well-being by assisting men in their labors, managing the household in their absence, and performing the bulk of domestic chores, which included everything from hauling water and planting gardens to making clothes, preparing food, and educating children.

Still, the tightness of family bonds did not mean that sisters, wives, and mothers shared fully in the same experiences as brothers, husbands, and fathers. For instance, while "death was an omnipresent reality" for all colonists, women of child-bearing age lived with a special sense of foreboding. War, which was also omnipresent in the eighteenth century, affected women and men differently as well. The French and Indian War, for example, called men away to battle, left women behind to fend for their families and themselves, and resulted in huge increases in the numbers of impoverished widows and children.

The experiences of three women Scott studies here—Jane Franklin Mecom, Elizabeth Sandwich Drinker, and Eliza Lucas Pinckney—cover a broad spectrum of colonial life. From Boston to South Carolina, of Quaker and Anglican faiths, members of artisan, entrepreneurial, and planter families, these women shared the ability to write and the desire to record their daily lives. It is true that their letters and diaries were saved in part because of the fame and fortune of their respective male relatives. Yet despite their renowned families, the three reveal much about the experiences of thousands of other women who waged unrecorded battles against childbirth, death, and the disruptions of war and who silently took comfort in good husbands, supportive brothers, and trusting fathers.

Boston-bred Jane Mecom, the sister of Benjamin Franklin, provides the most dramatic portrait of the contrasting opportunities available to eighteenth-century women and men. Her counterpart in Philadelphia, Elizabeth Drinker, garnered more of the advantages of an urban life-style alongside her male kin. Perhaps Drinker's Quaker faith, which emphasized equality among the sexes, had a beneficial effect. In the South, it was apparently the faith of a well-placed father, and his lack of a responsible son, that allowed Eliza Lucas to move among planters and entrepreneurs with ease. She demonstrated just how large was the opportunity for female enterprise under the right circumstances. Yet like Mecom and Drinker and most other colonial women, her life was still bordered and ordered by marriage, childbirth, widowhood, and war.

Through these three lives, Scott reveals both the particular hardships faced by women and the opportunities still open to them in a colonial world that was to be transformed by revolution.

Colonial history has so long been written in terms of high achievement, of political theory, of Founding Fathers, of economic development, of David-and-Goliath conflict that it is easy to forget how small a part such things played in most individual lives. Seen from the standpoint of ordinary people, the essential theme of the eighteenth-century experience was not so much achievement as the fragility and chanciness of life. Death was an omnipresent reality. Three children in one family die on a single day from epidemic disease; fathers are lost at sea; adolescents mysteriously waste away; mothers die in childbirth; yet life goes on to a constant underlying murmur of "God's sacred will be done." In these circumstances, how is the meaning of life perceived? What social structures do people build to sustain the spirit? What, in this context, become the central values? What is the texture of daily life?

The life histories of three colonial women give some clues.

The three women are Jane Franklin Mecom of Boston, Elizabeth Sandwich Drinker of Philadelphia, and Eliza Lucas Pinckney of Charleston. Taken together their lives cover nearly a century, from 1712 when the first was born to 1807 when the youngest died. Their experience encompassed three cultures—Puritan, Quaker, and plantation—and covered a broad spectrum of colonial social classes. The life of each is illuminating, each in a different way. All three loved to write, and each created a self-portrait—two in letters, one in a journal she kept from the time she was twenty-four until a few days before her death. Various depredations have washed out important parts of their life histories; and many things went unrecorded. Yet the documents which have survived bring us into the midst of daily experience and reveal, from time to time, their most deeply held cultural values.

Jane Franklin Mecom

Jane, youngest of Josiah Franklin's seventeen children, was born in 1712, six years after Benjamin. Because in later life she would become her brother's favorite correspondent, we know more about her than about any other women of her social class in eighteenth-century Boston.

She was eleven when Benjamin made his famous getaway, breaking his apprenticeship and embarking upon the legendary career which would make him the archetypal self-made American. In old age both looked back with favor upon their early childhood: "It was indeed a Lowly Dwelling we were brought up in but we were fed Plentifully, made comfortable with fire and cloathing, had sildom any contention among us, but all was Harmony: Especially betwen the Heads—and they were Universally Respected, & the most of the famely in good Reputation, this is still happier liveing than multituds Injoy."

Even allowing for the rosy glow the passage of time creates, the recollections of both brother and sister suggest that the parents were remarkable people, and that such education as children get at home, both had gotten. The things Jane Mecom singled out for recollection were central values all her life: a good reputation and the respect of the community. She always tried to "live respectable," and her fondest hope was that her children should do so.

At the age when her brother had run away to begin his climb to fame, Jane Franklin married a neighbor who was a saddler. Her brother sent a spinning wheel, an appropriate gift for a seventeenth child who could expect no dowry. The best efforts of both spouses

From "Self-Portraits: Three Women" by Anne Firor Scott. Reprinted by permission of the author.

would be required to keep up with a growing family, as—for a quarter of a century—every second year brought a new baby. Three died in infancy, but nine survived to be fed, clothed, and trained for self-support.

By the time we catch another glimpse of Jane Mecom she was already thirty, living in a house owned by her father, taking in lodgers, and caring for her aging parents. Her twelve-year-old son was learning the saddler's trade, and she was searching for appropriate apprenticeships for the younger ones. Between caring for parents, children, lodgers, and her husband's shop it is no wonder that the only written word of hers which survives from this period is a postscript to a letter her mother wrote to Benjamin. His letters to her began a pattern which would last a lifetime, as he spoke of sending "a few Things that may be of some Use perhaps in your Family."

His help was more than financial. Busy making his own way in Philadelphia, he took time to find an apprenticeship for his namesake, Benny Mecom, who gave some promise of talents similar to his own. There were problems "such as are commonly incident to boys of his years," although, Franklin added, "he has many good qualities, for which I love him." Diligence was not one of those qualities, and Jane Mecom was deeply concerned lest Benny never learn to work. He never did, at least not steadily, and would continue to cause his mother anxiety as long as he lived.

We get our next clear glimpse of Jane Mecom when she was fifty-one and entertaining her brother in her own house. While he was there, she enjoyed what would ever after be her measure of "suitable Conversation," and shone, however briefly, in the reflected glory of Dr. Franklin as Boston admirers paid court to him at her house. The fact that he chose to domicile himself with the Mecoms, rather than with the far more affluent and equally welcoming "cousen Williams," says

something about the quality of her conversation, or, perhaps, about his sensitivity to her feelings.

That interval of pleasure was brief. Four of the twelve Mecom children were already dead; now Sarah, at twenty-seven a "Dear and Worthy child," died, leaving a husband and four children who promptly moved into Jane Mecom's house. Within six months two of the four grandchildren were dead. She was still grieving for them when Edward Mecom, her husband of thirty-eight years, also died. She wrote one of the two comments about him to be found in any of her letters: "It pleased God to call my Husband out of this Troblesom world where he had Injoyed Little and suffered much by Sin & Sorrow." Two years later she lost her youngest and favorite, Polly, at eighteen: "Sorrows roll upon me like the waves of the sea. I am hardly allowed time to fetch my breath. I am broken with breach upon breach, and I have now, in the first flow of my grief, been almost ready to say 'What have I more?' But God forbid, that I should indulge that thought. . . . God is sovereign and I submit."

In 1766 she was fifty-five. Of five surviving children the oldest was thirty-four and the youngest twenty-one, but none was in a position to support a widowed mother. Two sons had been bred to the saddler's trade; one had died and the other gone to sea. Peter, a soap-boiler like his grandfather, showed signs of mental illness which would eventually incapacitate him, and the feckless Benjamin was not earning enough to support his own wife and children. Her son-in-law Flagg was an unskilled workman, hard put to take care of his two children. The one daughter who still lived with her was a melancholy and sickly young woman.

Jane Mecom's thoughts turned, therefore, to self-support. She continued to take in lodgers, and her brother sent from England a small stock of trading goods which arrived just as

Bostonians decided to boycott English goods in protest of the Stamp Act. Poverty, she concluded, "is Intailed on my famely."

She was acutely aware of her dependence on her brother's help. She tried to repay him with reports of life in Boston. "The whol conversation of this Place turns upon Politices and Riligous contryverces," she wrote, adding that her own sentiments were for peace. With his reply he sent her a set of his philosophical papers, which she proudly read.

Somehow in 1769 she contrived a trip to Philadelphia, where Franklin's wife and daughter found her "verey a greabel"—so much so that he was moved to suggest, from London, that she consider staying on permanently. But Boston was home, and back she went into the midst of the rising conflict with Great Britain.

Her brother, though thoroughly engrossed in the same conflict in London, took time to write Jane Mecom asking for detailed instructions as to the making of "crown soap," a family secret which he feared might be lost if it were not preserved for the next generation. Here at last was something she could do in return for all his help; her instructions were given in minute detail.

At about this time her letters began to grow longer and more revealing. Perhaps her visit to Deborah Franklin had reduced her awe of her famous brother; perhaps confidence in her own capacities was growing. Whatever the reason, she began to speak more freely, range more widely, and fill out—for us—the scanty self-portrait belatedly begun.

An admirer of Thomas Hutchinson and a lover of peace, Jane Mecom was no early patriot. By 1774, however, "Proflegate soulders," making trouble and harassing citizens on the streets of Boston, pushed her closer to the rebel position. The battle of Lexington finished what the soldiers had begun, as she locked her house, packed such goods as she could carry, and took refuge in Rhode Island.

In some ways the war changed her life for the better. Catherine Ray Greene, with whom she stayed at first, became her good friend. Her granddaughter, Jenny Flagg, married Elihu Greene, brother of General Nathanael Greene, a solid farmer, merchant, and entrepreneur. A man of his standing could well have demanded a dowry, but his willingness to marry Jenny for love marked a change in the hitherto unbroken stream of Mecom bad luck.

In the fall of 1774 Franklin came home after a decade in England, and not long after took his sister for a prolonged stay in Philadelphia. His wife, Deborah, had died, and Jane was able to be helpful to him until he went off to France. In two years General William Howe's decision to occupy Philadelphia sent her back to Rhode Island to her granddaughter's house, where she was "much Exposed & . . . under constant Apprehensions" that the British would invade.

Yet the British were not as troublesome to her as a personal crisis brought on by wartime inflation. The country woman who cared for her son Peter suddenly demanded more money for that service than Jane Mecom had or could see any way to get. Dependence on her brother was galling enough when he anticipated her needs; now she had to ask for help. Her spirits felt "so deprest" that she could scarcely write, but what else could she do?

The war had disrupted communication, and her letter was a long time reaching him. Meanwhile, relief came in a painful guise: Peter died. Accustomed as she was to accepting God's will, Jane Mecom reflected that Peter had been "no comfort to any won nor capable of injoying any Himself for many years." His death was a blessing.

But at the same time she had heard nothing for five months from her daughter Jane Collas in Boston and began to worry lest this last remaining child might be going the way of her brothers into insanity. Apologizing for burdening a busy and important man, she wrote her fears to Franklin: "It gives some Relief to un-bousom wons self to a dear friend as you have been & are to me."

Her daughter was, it turned out, physically rather than mentally ill, but sick or well she was never able to live up to her mother's standards of energy and enterprise. "You say you will endeavour to correct all your faults," Jane Mecom wrote in 1778 when Jane Collas was already in her thirties, and proceeded to out-line in some detail what those faults were: a tendency to look on the dark side of "God's Providence," an inclination to despair and to extravagance, laziness, and a lack of ingenuity in working to meet her material needs, an unseemly fondness for a great deal of com-pany. She also tended to lie abed late, which her mother found "a trouble to me on many accounts." To top it off, she aspired to gentility without the means to support her aspiration—a tendency Jane Mecom scorned whenever she encountered it.

Nine children had survived infancy, and none had fulfilled their mother's hopes. Most had died in early adulthood. Benjamin simply disappeared during the battle of Trenton, and no trace of him was ever found. Peter's tragic end has already been noted. The fate of her children pushed Jane Mecom to a rare moment of questioning God's will: "I think there was hardly Ever so Unfourtunate a Famely. I am not willing to think it is all owing to misconduct. I have had some children that seemed to being doing well till they were taken off by Death." But there was nothing to be done. One must accept these things or go mad.

In the late 1770s the long train of bereave-ment, displacement, and struggle abated for a while. Her granddaughter Jenny Greene, with whom she was living, was a most satisfactory young person whose conversation and atten-tion to her comfort she much appreciated, and whose husband she respected. Though there was no neighbor for two miles, many visitors

dropped in. She herself never left home unless someone sent a carriage (the Greenes owning none) since "I hant courage to ride a hors." She made and sent to Franklin several batches of crown soap, which he wanted for his friends in France, took care of Jenny Greene in her successive lyings-in, helped with the babies, supervised the household, and, from time to time, sold "some little matter" from the small store of goods she had brought from Boston in 1775. "My time seems to be filled up as the Famely I am in Increases fast," she wrote. She was sixty-eight and very energetic, though "as I grow older I wish for more Quiet and our Famely is more Incumbered as we have three children Born since I came & tho they give grat pleasure . . . yet the Noise of them is some-times troblesom." She knew "but little how the world goes Except seeing a Newspaper some times which contains Enough to give Pain but little satisfaction while we are in Armes against each other." In spite of the inflation and the losses the Greenes were suffering as many of their ships were captured, her life was pleas-anter than it had been since childhood. "I contineu very Easey and happy hear," she wrote in 1781, "have no more to trroble me than what is Incident to human Nature & cant be avoided any Place, I write now in my own litle chamber the window opening on won of the Pleasantest prospects in the country the Birds singing about me and nobod up in the house near me to Desturb me."

Life had taught Jane Mecom to be wary when things were going well. Ten months after that happy note her granddaughter died, giv-ing birth to the fourth child in four years, and at seventy Jane Mecom was suddenly again the female head of a household of young children who needed, she thought, "some person more lively and Patient to watch over them continu-aly"; but since there was no one else, she did it anyway. Fortunately she found them a comfort as she grieved for her beloved grandchild, a sacrifice to the age's custom of unbroken childbearing. She was too busy to pine, though the war had cut off her communication with Franklin for three years.

His first postwar letter included a "grat, very grat, Present," for which she thanked him extravagantly, adding that his generosity would enable her to live "at Ease in my old Age (after a life of Care Labour & Anxiety)."

By 1784 she was back in Boston, in a house long owned by her brother, where she was able to "live all ways Cleen and Look Decent." It was a great comfort. She had leisure to read and write, a minister she respected with whom to discuss theology and other things, the care and companionship of her granddaughter Jenny Mecom, the regular attention of her nephew-in-law Jonathan Williams. Her grandchildren and great-grandchildren were often a source of pride and pleasure.

One grandchild, Josiah Flagg, turned up in Philadelphia and, as she saw it, presumed upon his relationship to persuade Franklin to take him on as a secretary. He beseeched his grandmother to conceal the fact that he, Josiah, had once been a shoemaker, thus bringing down upon himself the scorn she reserved for false pride. She lectured him severely, betraying trepidation lest her demanding relatives threaten her warm relationship with her brother. Fortunately Josiah turned out to be an excellent penman and behaved well in the Franklin family.

With her brother back in Philadelphia, correspondence quickened. He was still concerned that someone in the family be trained to carry on the tradition of the crown soap. Might she teach the younger Jonathan Williams, or even Josiah Flagg, how to make it? She would think about it. She had thought earlier of teaching her son-in-law Peter Collas, whose difficulties in earning a living had become almost ludicrous. Whenever he took berth on a ship, it was promptly captured. But she had

decided that the soap required a man of "Peculiar Genius" and that Collas was not. Meanwhile she continued to make the soap herself, sending batch after batch to Franklin.

He felt the urge for some "cods cheeks and sounds," a favorite New England delicacy. She managed to acquire a keg to send him. She wished him well in the enterprise of the federal convention, and when the Constitution arrived in Boston she reported that while some quarrelsome spirits opposed it, those of "Superior Judgement" were going to support it.

She assured him that she followed his advice about taking exercise and walked even when a chaise was available, "but I am so weak I make but a Poor Figure in the Street." She had her chamber painted and papered against the day she might be confined to it.

Six more years of life remained to her. The new Constitution was inaugurated, George Washington took office, merchants and politicians concerned themselves with their own and the nation's prosperity, foreign conflicts flamed and threatened. Jane Mecom, for her part, worried about Benjamin Franklin's illness with "the stone" and prayed for his tranquility in the face of pain. Their correspondence ranged around topics mostly personal and family, and upon reflections on life as they had lived it. "I do not Pretend to writ about Politics," she said, "tho I Love to hear them."

Franklin's death in 1790 was a blow, but she was now seventy-eight herself and prepared to be philosophical about this, as she saw it, temporary separation from her best friend. In his will he provided for her, and when she died four years later this woman who had lived so frugally was able to leave an estate of a thousand pounds to Jane Collas (in trust—she still worried about her daughter's extravagance!) and to her fifteen grandchildren and great-grandchildren.

When the historians came to treat the years covered by her life, they dwelt on wars and politics, on the opening of land and trade and manufacture, on the economic development of a fertile wilderness, the rapid growth in population, the experiment in representative government.

That all these things shaped Jane Mecom's life experience there can be no doubt. Yet life as she perceived it was mostly made up of small events of which great events are composed: of twenty-one years of pregnancy and childbirth which, multiplied by millions of women, created the rapid population growth; of the hard struggle to "git a living" and to make sure her children were prepared to earn theirs; of the constant procession of death which was the hallmark of her time; of the belated prosperity and happiness which came to her in old age. What added up to a wilderness conquered, a new nation created, was often experienced by individuals as a very hard life somehow survived.

In chapter three of Virginia Woolf's *A Room of One's Own* there is a clever and moving fantasy: what if Shakespeare had had a sister as gifted as himself? The end of the fantasy is tragic, for Shakespeare's imaginary sister, born with a great gift, was so thwarted and hindered by the confines of "woman's place" that she killed herself. In Jane Mecom we have a real-life case, for of the sixteen siblings of Benjamin Franklin, she alone showed signs of talent and force of character similar to his. At the age of fifteen one ran off to Philadelphia and by a combination of wit, luck, and carefully cultivated ability to get ahead began his rise to the pinnacle among the Anglo-American intelligentsia. At the same age the other married a neighbor and in a month was pregnant. From that time forward her life was shaped almost entirely by the needs of other people. Like her brother she had a great capacity for growth, though the opportunity came to her late and was restricted by her constant burden of family responsibilities. The Revolution broadened her experience as it did his, yet she was almost never without children to care for, even in her seventies. Her letters showed a steady improvement in vigor of style and even in spelling. Her lively intelligence kept Franklin writing her even when he was very busy. Perhaps she had herself half in mind when she wrote in 1786: "Dr. Price thinks Thousands of Boyles Clarks and Newtons have Probably been lost to the world, and lived and died in Ignorance and meanness, mearly for want of being Placed in favourable Situations, and Injoying Proper Advantages, very few we know is able to beat thro all Impediments and Arive to any Grat Degre of superiority in Understanding."

The "impediments" in her own life had been many, some might have thought unsuperable, yet clearly by the age of eighty she had arrived at the "superiority of Understanding" which makes her letters a powerful chronicle of an eighteenth-century life.

Elizabeth Sandwich Drinker

Jane Mecom's life emerges full of interest from the most fragmentary records. Elizabeth Drinker, by contrast, left the most detailed record of any eighteenth-century American woman, one which provides an intimate view of daily life among the tight little community of Philadelphia Quakers of which she was a part.

Born Elizabeth Sandwich, of Irish inheritance, she was orphaned in her teens and lived with her sister in another Quaker family. In 1759 when she was twenty-four she began a laconic record of how she spent her time ("Went thrice to meeting; drank tea at Neighbor Callender's") which gradually grew into a regular journal wherein she recorded the details of her life and speculated a little upon them. The last entry was made a few days before her death in 1807.

As a child she had had the great good fortune to go to Anthony Benezet's school, and she knew French as well as English. To a solid basic education she brought an inquiring mind—science and medicine were particularly fascinating to her—and a touch of intellectual (though not religious) skepticism.

At twenty-six after a long courtship she married Henry Drinker, a widower her own age, who after an apprenticeship to a merchant firm, and the requisite trading voyage, had been taken into the company.

For thirteen months the journal lay untouched but for one minor entry, and by the time she began to keep it regularly again "my dear little Sal" had already joined the family. For the ensuing nineteen years pregnancies, miscarriages, births, deaths of four infants, and the weaning and raising of the other five formed the principal focus of her life. Henry, for his part, was on the way to becoming one of the busiest men in Philadelphia, constantly "from home" on business or on Quaker affairs, for his progress in business was paralleled by his gradual accumulation of responsibility in the world of the Friends.

As child after child was born and lived or died, the journal became in part a medical record. Capable of serving as midwife for her friends, Elizabeth Drinker could do little to ease her own difficult childbirths, "lingering and tedious," as she called them. She liked to nurse her babies, but was often forced for reasons of health to put them out to nurse. Though the family could afford the best doctors in Philadelphia, she was an independent-minded practitioner herself who often went contrary to their advice. When one of her sons fell out of a tree and broke a collarbone, she was pleased to find herself able to help the doctor set it. When newly acquired indentured servants (often under the age of ten) arrived with the itch and with lice and without small-pox inoculation, she undertook to deal with all of these problems. Her husband and children fell ill with astonishing frequency. Along the way she read weighty medical books and speculated, sometimes in conversation with

her good friend Benjamin Rush, about the cause and cure of various diseases.

The conflict with Great Britain marked a turning point in Elizabeth Drinker's development. Quakers tried to remain aloof, both for religious reasons and because those who were merchants had much to lose. One consequence was that in 1777 Henry Drinker and a number of others were arrested and taken off to prison in Winchester, Virginia. At forty-two Elizabeth Drinker was suddenly head of a household composed of her sister Mary, five children, and five indentured servants, and the British army was about to occupy Philadelphia. While she dutifully trusted that "it will please the Almighty to order all for the best," it was clear that she would have to lend Him a hand, and she prayed for resolution and fortitude.

There were daily challenges. Barrels of flour disappeared, and rumors of widespread looting sped through the town: "'Tis hardly safe to leave the door open," she noted; "I often feel afraid to go to bed." Henry's business affairs had to be attended to. One of her servants was first "very impertinent and saucy" and then ran away altogether with an audacious British soldier. Meeting the soldier on the street, Elizabeth Drinker confronted him, demanding that he pay for the servant's time. The British began commandeering blankets and other things. Horses were stolen; wood was scarce; other servants disappeared, to the point that "we have but 9 persons in our Family this winter; we have not had less than 13 or 14 for many years past."

As if they had overheard her, the British authorities arranged to enlarge the family again by quartering a certain Major Crammond, his two horses, two cows, and a Hessian stableboy in the Drinker household. The major kept the family awake with late dinner parties.

In the midst of the effort to keep the household fed, warmed, and healthy, she joined with other wives of incarcerated Friends to visit George Washington on behalf of their absent spouses. By some means which the journal does not make clear, release was arranged and she could thankfully turn back the headship of the household to H.D., as she always called him.

His return was quickly followed by the British evacuation. People who had been too friendly with the enemy were now turned out of their houses, their goods were confiscated, and a few, including some Quakers, were hanged. The Drinkers were understandably nervous, but only one member of the family, Henry Drinker's brother, ran directly afoul the American government. Still, the Americans were worse than the British in expropriating what they wanted (calling it taxation), and good furniture, pewter, blankets, and provisions were hauled off under their eyes. Servants continued to disappear, and they found themselves with only one. When news of Cornwallis's defeat arrived, Quakers who refused to illuminate their houses in celebration were subjected to a mob. Seventy panes of glass were broken in the Drinker's house.

By the time the treaty of peace was signed, she, like the new nation of which she was somewhat reluctantly a part, had reached a new stage of life. "I have often thought," she wrote in later years, ". . . that women who live to get over the time of Childbareing if other things are favourable to them, experience more comfort and satisfaction than at any other period of their lives." When that was written in 1797 she was certainly commenting upon her own life, which by our standards would not seem to have been precisely one of comfort, whatever it might have enjoyed of satisfaction. Though her last child had been born when she was forty-six, illness continued to be a major theme of the Drinker experience through the rest of her life.

Eleven pregnancies had left her own health uncertain at best; her son William had tuberculosis; H.D. was a constant victim of intestinal disorders and even more of the heroic treat-ment he received for them; one child had yellow fever and the whole family lived through three yellow fever epidemics; everyone sooner or later had malaria; in the household someone—husband, children, grandchildren, and servants—was always ill. Yet this seemed to interfere very little with the daily routine. Sick people entertained visitors along with the rest of the family, and people down with chills and fever one day were riding their horses off to the country the next.

Though she regularly worried about the ill health of her daughters, all three married and began at once to have children of their own. One daughter, the youngest, caused a family crisis by running away and marrying "out of meeting" a perfectly respectable young Friend whose only disability, apparently, was that he did not wear the plain dress. Henry Drinker took a hard line: no one was to visit the miscreant daughter. Elizabeth Drinker, after a few months, defied him, noting without contrition: "I feel best pleased I went." Henry finally relented, and Molly and her husband became part of the growing clan of sons and daughters and in-laws.

Elizabeth Drinker attended each of her daughters in childbirth, assisting the midwife and doctor. After a hard time with Sally's fourth, she recorded that she had slept only two of the preceding fifty hours and noted that she was "much fatigued, bones ache, flesh sore, Head giddy, etc. but we have at the same time much to be thankful for." Mother and child had both survived.

Two years later Molly and Sally were in labor at the same time. Sally's delivery was a very hard one; Molly's baby was stillborn. "The loss gives me great concern, not only being deprived of a sweet little grandson, but ye suffering of my poor Child, who lost, what may be called the reward of her labour . . . [and who] may pass through, if she lives, the same excruciating trouble a year the sooner for this loss." In 1799 Sally was in labor with her sixth child and very depressed. Elizabeth Drinker tried to cheer her, reminding her that she was now thirty-nine and this "might possibly be the last trial of this sort, if she could suckle her baby for 2 years to come, as she had several times done heretofore." It is odd that Elizabeth Drinker should have offered this particular argument, since she herself had twice become pregnant while nursing a baby, but it was standard advice from mothers to daughters in the eighteenth century. Neither she nor her daughters made any bones about their dislike of pregnancy and childbirth, though it seems in no way to have diminished their affection for the children themselves. Indeed, rather the contrary, since the burgeoning family was the center of Elizabeth Drinker's life. Children, in-laws, grandchildren moved in and out of the house daily and formed the subject for much of what she wrote. All her children lived nearby and visited each other as well as their parents constantly, sharing carriages, lending servants, sharing summer houses, exchanging children. In 1799 Eliza Downing, a granddaughter, came to spend the winter with Elizabeth and Henry Drinker. "I trust it will be for the child's good," her grandmother wrote, "[I] having no other little ones to attend to." She was much concerned to teach the young people "wisdom and prudence."

The Drinkers included servants in their conception of family—bound boys and girls or indentured adults. Often they came as children of seven or eight. Once there were three black boys under ten at the same time. Elizabeth Drinker gave them careful attention, mending their clothes and trying to teach them. "I have much to do for the little black boys; these small folk ought to be of service when they grow bigger, for they are very troublesome when young." Pretty bound girls were likely to flirt or, worse, get pregnant. One who had lived with them since she was ten gave birth to a mulatto baby, at the Drinker's expense. There followed much soul-searching as to what the

child's future should be, but it died before they could decide. Elizabeth Drinker, who had raised the mother, thought she was as good a servant as she ever had, but for this "vile propensity" for getting pregnant. She was hard put to understand how all her training in moral values had gone for naught.

There was no doubt in her mind that the "poorer sort" were different from herself, yet some of her former servants were close friends who came back often to visit. When one favorite servant came down with yellow fever, the family reluctantly decided to send her to the yellow fever hospital where, of course, she died. The matter weighed on Elizabeth Drinker's conscience.

She recognized that much of the comfort and satisfaction of her later life was because of Mary Sandwich, who never married, and who chose to care for household things, leaving her sister free to "amuse myself in reading and doing such work as I like best."

The natural world interested her greatly: insects, butterflies, turtles were brought for her inspection by children and grandchildren who knew of her curiosity about such things. Eclipses fascinated her. She speculated as to the causes of all sorts of natural events, and she loved to read about science.

Her reading, indeed, was prodigious. She felt constrained to note in her journal that it was not her sole occupation; but it was certainly an increasingly important part of her life as she grew older. She kept lists of books read, and they encompass most of what eighteenth-century Philadelphia had to offer. She read Mary Wollstonecraft's *Vindication of the Rights of Women* and noted that "in very many of her sentiments, she, as some of our friends say, *speaks my mind.*" Then she read William Godwin's memoir of Mary Wollstonecraft and modified her opinion: "I think her a prodigious fine writer, and should be charmed by some of her pieces if I had never heard of her character."

She read Tom Paine and abhorred what she took to be his dangerous principles. She took *Gargantua and Pantagruel* from the library and, after one quick look, hastily sent it back. She was equally shocked by Rousseau's *Confessions*. She read Swift, seven volumes of Sterne, tracts by Madame Roland, dozens of religious books, Plutarch's *Lives*, *The Letters of Lady Russell*, medical books, *The Whole Duty of Women* ("a pretty little book which I have read several times within forty years"), a book on logic, Mungo Park's *Travels in the Interior of Africa*, Edmund Burke, Maria Edgeworth, Wordsworth's *Lyrical Ballads*, Francis Bacon's *New Atlantis*, Paley's *Principles of Moral Philosophy*, and on and on.

While she read and wrote, children and grandchildren (by 1804 there were seventeen) moved steadily in and out; often twenty people came to dinner. Friends from other towns arrived for the Yearly Meeting and lodged with the Drinkers. Henry continued to be the busiest man in Philadelphia, and she remarked that if good works would take a person to heaven he would certainly get there. William, so careful of his health, was her companion for walks and talks. She was not in the best of health herself but was "seldom Idle." She took snuff and taught her grandchildren. Nancy's husband had an urge to move to "ye back woods," and she dreaded the thought. Every year she took stock on the first of January and was surprised to find herself still alive. More and more she enjoyed solitude, which had been disagreeable to her when she was young.

Her son Henry went off to India on one of the Drinker ships and wrote home about seeing a widow burned on her husband's funeral pyre. An old black woman came to call who had been her slave fifty years before, when she and her sister were orphaned, and whom they had sold. Not long after they had been conscience-stricken and tried to buy the child back, but the new owner refused. He had freed black Judey in his will, and now here she sat in the kitchen telling her life story. Elizabeth Drinker observed and reflected on the life around her.

Friend after friend died. The last pages of the journal recorded an endless succession of deaths and funerals, accompanied by the small sense of triumph that oneself was still alive. Sally's death at forty-six bore heavily on her spirit. I have had nine children, she mused, and now my first, third, fifth, seventh, and ninth are all dead.

She fell and bruised herself, and the doctors wanted to bleed her, "which I would not comply with." Old age had brought the courage to resist their violent treatments, of which she had long been rightly skeptical. On the eighteenth of November in 1807 she noted in her journal that the weather was clear and cold, and the moon was out. One grandson dropped in; she sent William to make the rounds of all the family dwellings. He came back to report that, but for one toothache, all were in good health. With her world thus in as good order as it could be, Elizabeth Drinker died.

The newspaper spoke of her remarkable personal beauty, her superior education, her journal, and her goodness. Perhaps it was, as she was fond of saying of obituaries of her friends, a "just character." She had lived seventy-two years. Born in a prosperous colony when no more than three-quarters of a million people lived in all British North America, she died a citizen of a nation of nearly seven million. Her own town had grown remarkably in those years, had been the scene of the Declaration of Independence, the Constitutional Convention, and the early years of the new government. James and Drinker, her husband's firm, had exemplified in microcosm much of the mercantile history of the colony and the new nation. Her son who sailed off to India and her son-in-law with a yen for the backwoods were both part of much larger movements.

Yet for Elizabeth Drinker, observant, thoughtful, well-read person that she was, life almost began and ended with family, work, and religion. From the day Sally was born until the day she herself died, she was deeply concerned with the welfare, first of children, then of grandchildren. They were part of her daily experience, even when they were grown and settled in their own houses. She was never without a child in her house and never ceased trying to teach them the ways of righteousness as she saw them. She abhorred idleness and made sure that her journal noted this fact lest some future reader think she spent all her time reading books! And, like Jane Mecom, she believed the Almighty knew what He was about.

Eliza Lucas Pinckney

Born almost midway between Jane Mecom and Elizabeth Drinker, in the West Indies, daughter of an army officer whose family had owned land in South Carolina (or just "Carolina," as the family invariably referred to it) and Antigua for three generations, Eliza Lucas came from more favored circumstances than either of the others. The contrast between Jane Mecom's rough-hewn prose and phonetic spelling, and her equally rough-hewn handwriting, and the elegant language, copperplate penmanship, and ritual formality of Eliza Lucas's early letters is remarkable. While Jane Mecom's friends and relatives included people in almost the whole range of the social scale, and Elizabeth Drinker belonged to the solid middle class, with Eliza Lucas we move at once to the top of the scale and stay there.

There had been money to send her "home" to England for a careful education, and, when she was seventeen, her father had settled her, along with her mother and her younger sister, on one of his plantations in Carolina while he carried on his duties as governor of Antigua.

In contrast to the other two, we can see Eliza Lucas clearly in her youth, and an astonishing young person she was. As vigorous and enterprising as the young Franklin or the young Jefferson, she began at once to administer the

work of three plantations. For five years she taught the three R's to her sister and the slave children, experimented with new plants, dealt daily with overseers and factors, wrote long letters on business matters to her father and his business associates, taught herself law and used her knowledge to help her neighbors who could not afford a proper lawyer, and read so much in Locke, Boyle, Plutarch, Virgil, and Malebranche that an old lady in the neighborhood prophesied that she would damage her brain.

A touch of humor and of self-deprecation was all that saved her from being unbearably didactic when she wrote to her younger brothers or younger friends. With older people—especially her much admired father—she was witty and straightforward.

Given her talents and wide-ranging interests, it was no wonder that she found the run of young men dull. "As to the other sex," she wrote, "I don't trouble my head about them. I take all they say to be words . . . or to show their own bright parts in the art of speechmaking." Her father proposed two possible candidates for her hand. She thanked him but declined both suggestions, saying of one "that the riches of Peru and Chili if he had put them together could not purchase a sufficient esteem for him to make him my husband." She hoped her father would agree that she should remain single for a few years.

So she continued happily as his agent, writing dozens of letters, dealing with the factor and with the agent in England, supervising planting, instructing overseers, paying debts, and contracting new ones. "By rising early," said this female Poor Richard, "I get through a great deal of business." It was an understatement.

The social life of Charleston appealed to her less than the work of the plantation. "I own," she wrote, "that I love the vigitable world extremely." Loving it meant study, experiment, and constant attention. The most visible consequence of her love affair with vegetables was

Ruins of the Pinckney mansion. Although she shared with Jane Mecom and Elizabeth Drinker—along with most other women—the experiences of marriage, childbirth, mothering, and grandmothering, Eliza Lucas Pinckney also managed affairs and handled responsibilities beyond the traditional expectations of women. Widowed at age thirty-five, she oversaw all the details of running her large and complex plantation while also supervising and attending to the upbringing and education of her children.

the development of indigo as a major export crop for South Carolina. At her father's suggestion she began to plant indigo seeds, and when, after several failures, a crop was achieved, she worked with servants he had sent from Antigua to refine the process by which it was prepared as a dye.

A true exemplar of the Enlightenment, she believed religion and right reason could coexist and said that "the soports of the Xtian religion" enabled her to view life's hazards with equanimity. She endeavored to resign herself to events as they came, since "there is an all Wise Being that orders Events, who knows what is best for us," and she believed in subduing the passions to reason.

Migraine headaches hardly slowed her down. It occurred to her to plant oak trees against the day when South Carolina might run out of hardwood. In a careful letter she compared the agriculture of England and South Carolina, somewhat to the advantage of the latter, and observed that "the poorer sort [here] are the most indolent people in the world or they could never be so wretched in so plentiful a country as this." Indolence was, in her view, pretty close to a deadly sin.

This precocious young woman who found men her own age a little boring was intrigued by the intelligent conversation of a man in his forties, Carolina's first native-born lawyer, Charles Pinckney. She had met Pinckney and his wife soon after her arrival, liked them both, and carried on a lively correspondence across the ten miles that separated the plantation from Charleston. He lent her books, encouraged her to report to him on her reading, and enjoyed the discipleship of so eager a pupil. Once, in 1741, she absentmindedly signed a letter to him "Eliza Pinckney."

Three years later in December 1744 Mrs. Pinckney died. On May 2, 1745, Eliza wrote her father thanking him for permission to marry Charles Pinckney and "for the fortune you are pleased to promise me." She also thanked him for the pains and money laid out for her education, which "I esteem a more valuable fortune than any you have now given me." She assured him that Mr. Pinckney was fully satisfied with her dowry.

To a cousin who had warned that she was so particular she was bound to "dye an old maid," she wrote: "But you are mistaken. I am married and the gentleman I have made choice of comes up to my plan in every tittle . . . I do him barely justice when I say his good Sence and Judgement, his extraordinary good nature and eveness of temper joynd to a most agreeable conversation and many valuable qualifications gives me the most agreeable prospect in the world."

She bore with equanimity the talk of the town about their somewhat precipitate marriage, but was righteously indignant when gossip told it that the late Mrs. Pinckney had been neglected in her last illness. Writing to that lady's sister, she said firmly that she would never have married a man who had been guilty of such a thing. As she had earlier striven to please her father, so now she made every effort to please her husband. "When I write to you," she told him, "I . . . desire . . . to equal even a Cicero or Demosthenes that I might gain your applause."

Her father seems to have worried lest the strong-minded independence in which he had reared her might not sit well with a husband, and she reassured him that "acting out of my proper province and invading his, would be inexcusable." She and Pinckney apparently agreed that her proper province was a spacious one, since she continued to supervise her father's plantations, assumed some responsibility for Pinckney's as well, and carried forward the experiments with indigo which were in midstream at the time of her marriage.

Her self-improving urge was as strong as ever. She wrote a long list of resolutions and planned to reread them daily. With God's help she hoped not to be "anxious or doubtful, not to be fearful of any accident or misfortune that may happen to me or mine, not to regard the frowns of the world." She planned to govern her passions, improve her virtues, avoid all the deadly sins, be a frugal manager while extending hospitality and charity generously, make a good wife, daughter, and mother, and a good mistress of servants. At the end of this long list of injunctions to herself for ideal behavior she made a typical note: "Before I leave my Chamber recolect in General the business to be done that day." Good advice for any administrator. Once she noted that "nobody eats the bread of idleness while I am here." It might well have been her lifetime motto.

Her married life was as busy as her single life had been. In ten months Charles Cotesworth Pinckney was born. Perhaps the childlessness of Pinckney's first marriage explains the extraordinary eagerness of both parents to cherish "as promising a child as ever parents were blessed with." Eliza could see "all his papa's virtues already dawning" in the infant. A friend in England was asked to find a set of educational toys described by John Locke, while his father set about designing toys to teach the infant his letters. "You perceive we begin bytimes," Eliza added, "for he is not yet four months old."

A second son was born and died. Then came Thomas and Harriott. Though Eliza Pinckney had slave nurses to suckle her infants, she was intensely preoccupied with the training, education, and shaping of her children.

In 1752 political maneuvering deprived Charles Pinckney of his seat as chief justice of the colony, and he left for England to serve as South Carolina's agent there. The family took a house in Surrey and lived much like their neighbors. Eliza Pinckney was appalled at the amount of time the English gentry wasted, especially in playing cards. On the other hand, she loved the theater and never missed a new performance if she could help it. She called on the widowed princess of Wales and found her informality and her interest in South Carolina and in "little domestick questions" very engaging. The boys were sent to school, and Harriott was taught at home. It was a good life, and she was in no hurry to return to South Carolina.

Increasingly concerned by developments in the Seven Years' War, fearful that France might take over a large part of North America, the Pinckneys decided to liquidate their Carolina estate and move to England. To this end they sailed the war-infested sea in 1758, taking Harriott and leaving their sons in school. Three weeks after they landed Charles Pinckney was dead. Eliza Pinckney at thirty-five was once again in charge of a large and complex plantation enterprise. It was just as well, she thought, to have so great a responsibility; otherwise the loss of this most perfect of husbands would have undone her.

> I find it requires great care, attention and activity to attend properly to a Carolina estate, tho but a moderate one, to do ones duty and make it turn to account, . . . I find I have as much business as I can go through of one sort or another. Perhaps 'tis better for me . . . . Had there not been a necessity for it, I might have sunk to the grave by the time in that Lethargy of stupidity which seized me after my mind had been violently agitated by the greatest shock it ever felt. But a variety of imployment gives my thoughts a relief from melloncholy subjects, . . . and gives me air and excercise.

In letter after letter she recited Pinckney's virtues, the same ones she had praised when she married him. His religious dedication, "free from sourness and superstition," his integrity,

charm, and good temper, "his fine address"— she thought she would never find his like again.

Fortunately she still loved books, agriculture, and her children. It was for the children she told herself (and them) that she worked so hard, overseeing the planting, buying, and selling, writing ceaselessly to England (in several copies since no ship was secure), nursing slaves through smallpox, supervising the education of Harriott. She expected reciprocal effort from her sons. She wrote Charles Cotesworth: "though you are very young, you must know the welfair of a whole family depends in a great measure on the progress you make in moral Virtue, Religion, and learning. . . . To be patient, humble, and resigned is to be happy. It is also to have a noble soul, a mind out of the reach of Envy, malice and every Calamity. And the earlier, my dear boy, you learn this lesson, the longer you will be wise and happy."

She was convinced that happiness for all her children depended in great measure on a "right Education," and she encouraged Harriott; she was "fond of learning and I indulge her in it. It shall not by my fault if she roams abroad for amusement, as I believe 'tis want of knowing how to imploy themselves agreeably that makes many women too fond of going abroad."

She thought highly of female talent. Once a letter from a friend in England came with the seal broken. Perhaps someone had read the letter? No matter; "it may teach them the art of writing prettily . . . and show how capable women are of both friendship and business."

She fell ill, lay four months in her chamber, but was too busy to die. A friend in England wanted seeds of all the trees in Carolina, and she was happy to oblige. The planting at Belmont, her plantation, was following an old-fashioned pattern; she decided to modernize, working harder, she said, than any slave. She revived silk-making experiments begun when Pinckney was alive and endeavored to teach the skill to other women. Harriott's education continued to be one of her chief joys: "For pleasure it certainly is to cultivate the tender mind, to teach the young Idea how to shoot, &c. especially to a mind so tractable and a temper so sweet as hers."

Though she still talked of going back to England, of taking her sons to Geneva for their final polishing, any observer could have foretold that it would never happen. She was busy and, therefore, happy, and the boys were doing well. Both, despite their long absence, were ardent in the American cause, and Thomas had astonished his schoolmates by his articulate opposition to the Stamp Act.

In 1768 Harriott at nineteen married a thirty-five-year-old planter, Daniel Horry, and set about replicating her mother's career. "I am glad your little Wife looks well to the ways of the household," Eliza wrote her new son-in-law; "the management of a Dairy is an amusement she has always been fond of, and 'tis a very useful one." Harriott was soon running much more than the dairy.

While Harriott was busy in the country, her mother set about planting a garden at the Horrys' town house. In her own well-organized household five slaves each had their appointed tasks; none was idle and none, she said, overworked. She herself was constantly industrious.

In such good order, then, were the family affairs in 1769 when Charles Cotesworth Pinckney at last came home from his sixteen-year sojourn in England, already an American patriot. He was at once admitted to the bar and in a month had been elected to the South Carolina Assembly. A year or so later Thomas arrived to join him. The children for whom she had seen herself as working so hard were all launched.

Perhaps, though it would have been out of character, other circumstances would have permitted Eliza Pinckney to slow down at forty-five. But public affairs were in turmoil, and in 1775 both her sons were commissioned

in the first regiment of South Carolina troops. Their business and financial affairs remained in the hands of their mother and sister, who were quite prepared to carry on while the men went to war.

It was 1778 before the full force of hostilities reached the Pinckneys. They had chosen Ashepoo, the family plantation belonging to Thomas Pinckney, as the safest place for all their valuables. It was a bad guess. Augustine Prevost's forces burned it to the ground on their way to Charleston, leaving Thomas—as he thought—wiped out and his mother's interest severely damaged. Charles Cotesworth wrote from his military post that of course whatever he had left when the war ended would be divided with them. Eliza wrote to Thomas: "Don't grieve for me my child as I assure you I do not for myself. While I have such children dare I think my lot hard? God forbid! I pray the Almighty disposer of events to preserve them and my grandchildren to me, and for all the rest I hope I shall be able to say not only contentedly, but cheerfully, God's Sacred Will be done!"

The loss of Ashepoo was only the beginning. British troops impressed horses, took provisions, commandeered houses. Eliza Pinckney had to take refuge in the country, leaving her town property to who could know what depredations. In the midst of all this stress Thomas was wounded, Charles Cotesworth, already suffering from malaria, was imprisoned, and two grandchildren were born. In 1780 the British captured Charleston, and by that time plenty had given way to pinched poverty. She owed sixty pounds to a creditor in England and could find no way at all to pay it. For a while it seemed that the fruit of thirty years' hard work was all lost.

Even before the war ended, however, it was clear that Eliza Pinckney's labors had accomplished much more than the building of a prosperous planting interest. She had created an enormously effective family. Planting and business, important as they were, had always taken second place to the upbringing and education of her children. Now, as adults, the three saw themselves, with her, as almost a single entity. The men, at war, often wrote their mother once, sometimes twice, a day. Harriott, who had been Tom's close friend and confidante before he was married, and whom he had always treated as an intellectual equal, continued after his marriage as his business agent and political adviser. For both brothers she managed plantations (as well as her own, after Daniel Horry died), handled money, and looked after their wives and children. They, in turn, took time from their pressing military duties to oversee the education of her son.

After the war, the pattern continued. Both Pinckney men moved into public service. Charles Cotesworth was a member of the Constitutional Convention; Thomas was elected governor of South Carolina by an overwhelming majority and was in office when the state ratified the Constitution. Both were part of the developing Federalist party. Each was to be a foreign envoy and to give his name to important treaties. These careers were made possible by the labors of their mother and sister.

In 1792 Eliza Pinckney developed cancer, and almost the entire family proposed to accompany her to Philadelphia, where a physician with considerable reputation in that field was to be found. She refused to go if they all came along: she could not risk the whole family on one ship. So, while Charles Cotesworth and his children reluctantly remained in Charleston, Harriott took her to Philadelphia. It was too late. She died and was buried there, George Washington at his own request serving as one of her pallbearers.

Reflections on the Microcosm

Different as these women were, each put family at the center of life. Eliza Pinckney and her three children viewed the world, not as

individuals, but *as a family*. A threat to one was a threat to all; fame and fortune were also shared. They took care of each other's interests, of each other's children, as a matter of course. Tom's rice crop failed and Charles Cotesworth's wife put 500 pounds at his disposal, "cheerfully," his brother noted. The family wanted Tom to stay in London. Earlier, when the British burned most of the family's movable assets, Charles Cotewsorth announced at once that all he had left was to be divided among the rest of them. When the brothers went abroad, Harriott had their power of attorney; she made sure their plantations were cared for, their debts paid. Together they took responsibility for the younger generation. Young Daniel Horry was a spendthrift and showed signs of becoming a monarchist. His grandmother and his uncles tried to set him right, and his debts were settled as a family responsibility. Meanwhile the young women in the family were trained by their aunt and grandmother so that they, too, could run plantations. By the time Eliza Pinckney died the family had a full-fledged "tradition" for many of its activities, and doubtless no one remembered that it had been created in two generations.

The Drinkers were equally knit together by kinship. The sons-in-law were brought into the family business and encouraged to help each other. When one had business reverses, the whole family helped out. The cousins were grouped around the grandparents and encouraged to see the family as their most basic commitment.

Jane Mecom's life was shaped by her relationship to Benjamin Franklin, but beyond the two of them lay a wide network of Franklin kin, in-laws, cousins in various degrees. Late in life Benjamin asked his sister to send him a detailed and complete list of all their kinfolk in Boston which he could use for reference. He was constantly being asked for help of one kind or another, and he wanted to be sure that he gave the proper priority to blood relations.

They clearly recognized some members of the clan as more "valuable" than others, but blood created a responsibility even for ne'er-do-wells.

Each of these women was pregnant within a month of marriage, and two continued to bear children into their late forties. Eliza Pinckney's family was unusually small for the time, but she was widowed at thirty-five.

Nor was it only their own children who kept women close to home. All three of these women were as much involved in raising a second generation as they had been with the first, and Jane Mecom, for a time, was responsible for four great-grandchildren. Grandmothering was an important part of their lifework.

All three believed in work as a moral value. They reserved their strongest criticisms for indolence in any form, and none of them saw old age as justification for idleness. For Jane Mecom and Elizabeth Drinker, "work" was largely domestic, though both dealt also in some mercantile ventures. Jane Mecom ran her own little shop for a while, and Elizabeth Drinker kept accounts for her husband's firm. Eliza Pinckney's work encompassed the larger world of plantation trade. Through most of her life she was busy with shipments, payments, factors, and the like, while she also planned and supervised the actual production of rice, indigo, silk, and the hundred other products of the relatively self-sufficient plantation. Though nominally working, first for her father, then for her husband, and finally for her children, she seems not to have felt any inhibition about acting in her own name, making her own decisions. The fact that legal ownership of land belonged to father or husband was of no great operational significance.

Woman's life in the eighteenth century was fundamentally influenced by marriage. In a day when conventional wisdom had it that for both men and women it was wise to marry close to home, all three did so. But the luck of the draw varied widely. There is little record of Edward Mecom's life, but circumstantial evidence suggests that Jane Mecom might have done better on her own. Elizabeth Drinker admired Henry, and his success in business provided her with a life of material comfort. Gradually, as she grew older, he was replaced at the center of her emotional ties by her son William, and her other children and grandchildren occupied her mind.

Eliza Pinckney was convinced that Charles Pinckney was incomparable, and despite various offers she never married again. During her marriage she had played the role of the properly subservient wife; her father had written to her husband the directions he had once sent to her; and her time had been much engaged in childbearing and child care. Widowed, she assumed the role of head of the family and continued to make vital decisions, even when her sons were grown and had families of their own. With their help she created the "Pinckney Family."

These were only three of millions of women who lived and worked and died in colonial America. In their experience we see much of the common life of eighteenth-century women, no matter what her social class. In another sense, of course, all three were uncommon women, whose achievements tell us something about the possibilities as well as the probabilities for women in their day and generation.

Questions for Study and Review

1. What regional variations in colonial life are suggested by these three self-portraits?

2. To what extent were the differences in these three women's lives attributable to residence (urban/rural), class, or region?

3. Compare the lives of Jane Franklin Mecom and Eliza Lucas Pinckney with that of Benjamin Franklin. What do the contrasting portraits tell us about the opportunities available to each sex?

4. Not until well into the twentieth century would most families be able to control the number and spacing of their children. How much of a difference would such control make in women's and in men's lives?

Suggested Readings

Mary Maples Dunn, "Saints and Sinners: Congregational and Quaker Women in the Early Colonial Period," *American Quarterly* (Winter 1978).

Mary Lynn Salmon, *Women and the Laws of Property in Early America* (1986).

Carol Berkin, *Within the Conjurer's Circle: Women in Colonial America* (1974).

Mary Beth Norton, "The Evolution of White Woman's Experience in Early America," *American Historical Review* (June 1984).

Gary B. Nash, "Poverty and Poor Relief in Pre-Revolutionary Philadelphia," *William and Mary Quarterly* (January 1976).

Nancy Shrom Dye and Daniel Blake Smith, "Mother Love and Infant Death, 1750–1920," *Journal of American History* (September 1986).

PART TWO

Birth of
a Nation

The process of revolution and nation building is most often understood in terms of military strategy and formal political development. In recent decades, increasing attention has been focused on the social and economic upheavals that preceded and followed the American War for Independence. The demonstrations and boycotts that fed revolutionary fervor in the 1760s and 1770s as well as the revolts against "hard money" and taxation that the Revolution fostered can be fully understood only by examining the experiences of common women and men in their local communities. Yet even these studies usually emphasize male-centered events—the Boston Tea Party, Paul Revere's ride, Shays's Rebellion, the Whisky Rebellion—or at least men's participation in such events.

The authors included in this section focus instead on women's experience of and involvement in the birth of the nation. Even in the mid-eighteenth century, women were in charge of buying most items for household consumption, including sugar, molasses, tea, and cloth. Thus, if boycotts against British goods were to succeed, women's support was essential. Such support required real devotion to the patriot cause since the loss of imported goods required housewives to replace British-made linen with homespun cloth and processed tea with home brews or coffee (the latter relatively unpopular in North America before the Revolution). These and other substitutions meant increased labor for women. A Massachusetts leader of the Daughters of Liberty, the organization that coordinated women's boycott efforts, assured her fellow colonists that added work or diminished comfort would not deter her patriot sisters: "I hope there are none of us but would sooner wrap ourselves in sheep and goatskin than buy English goods of a people who have insulted us in such a scandalous way."

Other women organized anti-tea leagues, sewing circles, and petition drives to support the patriot cause. In these ways, the economic necessity of women's work, which had been recognized for centuries, now took on

Women's real contributions to the birth of the new nation were often ignored or overlooked in favor of representations such as that in this engraving in which an idealized feminine figure offers the cup of liberty to the American eagle.

political significance as well. A few saw in the politicization of women's domestic labor the first step toward women's participation in formal politics. Abigail Adams was only the most famous of those who asked their patriot brothers (or, in her case, husband) to "remember the ladies" in the nation's new code of laws and to "be more generous and favorable to them than your ancestors!" More astonishingly, perhaps, a group of fifty-one women from Edenton, North Carolina, wrote a proclamation in 1774 that insisted on their right and duty to participate in the political activities of the day.

Some women took a more direct approach. Deborah Sampson (alias Robert Shurtleff) disguised her sex in order to join the Continental army. So did several hundred other women. The women of Groton, Massachusetts, though not interested in full-time soldiering, dressed in men's clothing and defended the local bridge from British troops retreating from Lexington and Concord. They captured a courier carrying valuable information, along with a number of comrades, and turned them over to military authorities. Many more women sought simply to protect hearth and home and frequently endured exploitation or abuse at the hands of enemy forces for their efforts.

As Linda Kerber demonstrates, during the Revolution women participated in every imaginable activity, from fund-raising to fighting, as individuals and in groups, on both sides and throughout all thirteen colonies.

Not all women and men, however, supported the patriot cause or sympathized with the British. Perhaps a third of all colonists were unmoved by revolutionary and parliamentary proclamations, unless or until troops appeared at their doorsteps. These women and men were caught up in other struggles—to make a good crop, to last out a bad winter, or to survive a difficult birth. Childbearing did not stop, of course, between the Declaration of Independence and the Surrender at Yorktown. In the midst of the Revolution, as well as before and after, women contributed to the nation's growth by bearing children. But even this most personal of events was reshaped by the battle for independence.

Women whose husbands fought in the war bore greater burdens in having to manage family farms and businesses as well as their households. Yet their husbands' absence probably relieved them of other burdens by increasing the interval between births. At the same time, the number of premarital pregnancies increased in the late eighteenth century, perhaps because of fears that sweethearts and fiancés might never return from battle.

So, too, according to Catherine Scholten, did the process of birth itself change. The desire for a national identity and for autonomy from Europe encouraged the establishment of local medical schools and sped the replacement of female midwives with male physicians, at least among affluent urban dwellers. As with revolutionary activities, the extent of women's participation in this new conduct varied by class, region, and race. Still, all women eventually found their lives and choices redefined by practices first adopted by the elite.

The development of homegrown schools and colleges did offer more direct benefits for women. Believing that only educated mothers could properly train sons for citizenship in the new nation, many writers argued for expanded educational opportunities for women. Yet the curriculum offered to the new generation of "Republican Mothers" tended to focus on domestic arts and traditional female skills. Moreover, in the new system of laws neither John Adams nor his fellow patriots did "remember the ladies." Instead, by codifying situations previously left to custom, they more often narrowed than expanded women's political and property rights in the years immediately following the British surrender at Yorktown. Thus, while women's indirect influence on politics expanded and women's early connections with evil were replaced by paeans to female moral and spiritual superiority, the ideal woman was now confined even more tightly within the bounds of domesticity.

More than educational or political innovation, economic change most thoroughly transformed the opportunities available to women in the New Republic. Here, too, a concern with national autonomy affected the policies advocated by political leaders, which in turn shaped everyday life. In his famous *Report on Manufactures*, for instance, Secretary of the Treasury Alexander Hamilton argued that the new nation could free itself from economic dependency on Europe only by establishing its own industries. The development of manufacturing, however, would require a new division of labor between women and men. The farmer, Hamilton insisted, would be provided "a new source of profit and support from the increased industry of his wife and daughters, invited and stimulated by the demands of neighboring manufactories." Thomas Jefferson, the United States' first Secretary of State and an opponent of Hamilton, placed greater faith in America's agrarian values and traditions. "I think our government will remain virtuous for many centuries," he wrote, "as long as they [the people] are chiefly agricultural." For Jefferson, wives and daughters were best employed as helpmates on the family farm.

When translated into everyday life, both Hamilton's and Jefferson's visions proved problematic. As Paul Johnson shows, too many children, too little land, and the "exhaustion" of what acres remained often left younger sons and daughters of all ages without an inheritance, at least one that allowed them to remain near their families and communities of origin. Such dispossessed individuals, male or female, had little opportunity to fulfill the Jeffersonian promise of agrarian peace and prosperity. Rather, these new citizens were both freed and forced from traditional entanglements of family and farm, released to fuel the industrial development planned by Hamilton. The families who supplied labor to industries, such as the family of Greenleaf and Abigail Patch, found themselves facing entirely new difficulties and dangers. In this new order, women and men often faced quite different obstacles and were offered different rewards. Thus did women and men, in families and communities up and down the Atlantic seaboard, begin to conceive of their choices in new ways as the nation itself struggled to life.

Suggested Readings

Alfred Young, ed., *The American Revolution: Explorations in the History of American Radicalism* (1976).

"Women and the Political Process in the United States," A Special Issue of *Signs: Journal of Women in Culture and Society* (Autumn 1977).

Michael Grossberg, *Governing the Hearth: Law and the Family in Nineteenth-Century America* (1985).

FOUR

Politicizing the Household: Sacrifice and Survival During the American Revolution

Linda K. Kerber

Betsy Ross, Molly Pitcher, Deborah Sampson, Abigail Adams—all heroines of the Revolution—are exceptional only in the attention they have attracted from scholars and novelists. The domestic and public activities of these heroines were quite common among colonial women, whose labors were critical to sustaining families and communities as tensions between the colonies and Great Britain erupted into war. Beginning in the mid-seventeenth century, as Koehler noted, housewives began translating domestic skills, such as sewing and brewing, into marketable commodities. It was the disruption of trade with Britain, however, from the 1760s through the 1780s, that encouraged women to adapt household resources to political ends.

Linda Kerber traces this politicization of the household in both rebel and Tory families and demonstrates how women's involvement in the Revolution—on either side—challenged traditional notions of virtue and citizenship. From the Sugar Act through the Boston Tea Party to the surrender at Yorktown, rebellious colonists, female and male, drew on every resource at their disposal to defeat the British forces. Through boycotts, spying, nursing, soldiering, fund-raising, and propagandizing, most mothers, wives, and daughters sup-

ported the efforts of their male relatives. A few, however, took issue with the loyalties proclaimed by their male kin and asserted their rights as independent agents to choose sides for themselves. They thereby raised important questions about the relationship between dependence and virtue, independence and citizenship.

By focusing on the activities of both the exceptional—such as Margaret Corbin—and the everyday—reflected in the efforts of thousands of women in manufacturing bullets—Kerber illustrates how uncommon even common women's lives became in the midst of revolutionary upheaval. She also suggests that the entrance of women into political agitation and military ventures blurred the boundaries between private and public spheres and promised to reshape women's and men's familial and community roles in the New Republic. It seemed for a moment that Anglo-American women might be gaining some of the authority in the local community and the larger political realm long accorded the Appamatuck and other Indian women described by Lebsock.

In the midst of revolution, it is also possible that "deviant" women found it easier to survive, even to thrive. Someone like Margaret Corbin might have found herself accused of witchcraft had she lived in Salem a century earlier; instead, she was a national heroine. Looking forward, Catherine Scholten's and Paul Johnson's articles suggest that women's contributions to the patriot effort were not fully rewarded in the New Republic. Perhaps fortunately for the success of the Revolution, the women described by Kerber could not see into that future.

"**P**atriotism in the Female Sex," wrote Abigail Adams as the American Revolution drew to a close, "is the most disinterested of all virtues. Excluded from honours and from offices, we cannot attach ourselves to the State of Government from having held a place of Eminence. Even in freest countrys our property is subject to the controul and disposal of our partners, to whom the Laws have given a sovereign Authority. Deprived of a voice in Legislation, obliged to submit to those Laws which are imposed upon us, is it not sufficient to make us indifferent to the publick Welfare? Yet all History and every age exhibit Instances of patriotic virtue in the female Sex; which considering our situation equals the most Heroick."

We cannot know how widely shared were these opinions, expressed in a private letter from wife to husband. They certainly challenged much of the accepted wisdom of the Revolutionary generation. It had been the common sense of eighteenth-century political theory that women had "less patriotism than men." Because women were excluded from honors and offices, the usual methods of attaching subjects' self-interest to the outcome of national policy, women's relationship to their nation seemed to be secondhand. They were thought to experience politics through husbands, fathers, sons.

This distrust of the female capacity to take politics seriously was present in the American colonies when the Revolution began and persisted long after the war's close. That many women shared this distrust is clear. "I can't

Abridged from *Women of the Republic: Intellect and Ideology in Revolutionary America*, by Linda K. Kerber. Copyright © 1980 The University of North Carolina Press. Reprinted by permission.

help exclaiming now and then, dreadful fruits of Liberty. I confess I have not such romantic notions of the Goddess," Margaret Livingston wrote shortly after the war began. "You know that our Sex are *doomed* to be obedient in every stage of life so that *we* shant be great gainers by this contest." The social correspondence of women from even the most political families—Jays, Livingstons, Pinckneys—often expressed the complaint that however the war turned out it would mean only inconvenience and trouble for them.

Could a woman be a patriot? If any experience could have provided unambivalent answers to that question, the Revolution ought to have done so. But the answers seemed little clearer at the end of the war—in part because memories of women who supported the Revolution were counterbalanced by memories of women who were loyalists. Evidence of unprecedented female political behavior in both camps was outweighed by the winners' scorn for the losers and by the belief that women's political choices had been controlled by male relatives. Women were expelled from patriot-held territory, for example, not because of their own political identities, but because of their husbands'; the burden rested heavily on the wife of the tory to prove that she indeed did not share her husband's political opinions. Few were prepared to agree that a wife and mother could also be an independent political being. Those who, like Abigail Adams, thought women could be both, faced a difficult task if they were to carry this idea past private conceptions. They would need to persuade a hostile public that expressive political behavior did not threaten the traditional domestic domain; by adopting the ideals of what may be called "Republican Motherhood," a patriotic woman could unite her seemingly contradictory loyalties to the home and to the state. Their task was made more difficult by the

This political cartoon comments on the American situation just before the Revolution. America is a naked, vulnerable woman. Lord North, British author of the Boston Port Bill, forcibly pours tea down America's unwilling throat, while leering politicians enjoy her distress. Britannia, powerless to help, covers her face and weeps.

liberal hesitancy to believe that propertyless people could make reasoned political decisions; yet even unmarried women who were independent property holders found resistance to their political claims. That women of the Revolutionary generation were not fully successful in their attempt ought not to blind us to their effort to articulate a political ideology that blended the domestic and public spheres. The creators and advocates of Republican Motherhood produced the terms and rhetoric in which much of the nineteenth- and twentieth-century debate on the proper dimensions of female patriotism would be expressed.

In 1769, mulling over what needed to be done to make the resistance to England effective, Christopher Gadsden formulated an explicit rationale for a direct ideological appeal to women that included domestic loyalties as well as a political consideration:

I come now to the last, and what many say and think is the *greatest difficulty* of all we have to encounter, that is, to persuade our wives to give us their assistance, without which 'tis impossible to succeed. I allow of the impossibility of succeeding without their concurrence. But, for my part, so far from doubting that we shall have it, I could wish, as our political salvation, at this crisis, depends altogether upon the strictest oeconomy, that the women could, with propriety, have the principal management thereof; for 'tis well known, that none in the world are better oeconomists, make better wives or more tender mothers, than ours. Only let their husbands point out the necessity of such a conduct; convince them, that it is the only thing that can save them and their children, from distresses, slavery, and disgrace; their affections will soon be awakened, and cooperate with their reason. When that is done, all that is necessary will be done; for I am persuaded, that they will be then as anxious and persevering in this matter, as any the most zealous of us can possibly wish.

Gadsden's formulation is traditional in its easy telescoping of "women" into wives. His appeal is not to women, but to the men who are their husbands; he does not seek to sway the independent single woman. But he did perceive that because women manage household economies, it would be easy for them to undermine political boycotts. Women would make political decisions whether they meant to or not. He also understood that they would make their decisions on the basis of their perceptions of their domestic duties and responsibilities. The men who sought to persuade them would have to do their persuading in women's terms: in terms of the ultimate security of children and homes. Republican rhetoric would have to be adapted to the protection of the women's domain if it were to be effective.

Perhaps men habitually overstated the need to appeal to women on the basis of their desire to protect domesticity. We have direct written expressions by women that justify boycotts squarely on the grounds of public political commitments. Indeed, they assert that women can be firmer than men in their patriotism. Milcah Martha Moore of Philadelphia copied a long verse into her commonplace book in 1768; it is based on the assumption that women can make up for men's political weaknesses.

Since the Men from a Party, on fear of a
    Frown,
Are kept by a Sugar-Plumb, quietly down,

Supinely asleep, and depriv'd of their Sight
Are strip'd of their Freedom, and rob'd of
    their Right.
If the Sons (so degenerate) the Blessing despise,
Let the Daughters of Liberty, nobly arise,
And tho' we've no Voice, but a negative
    here,
The use of the Taxables, let us forbear,
(Then Merchants import till yr. Stores are all
    full
May the Buyers be few and yr. Traffick be
    dull.)
Stand firmly resolved and bid Grenville to
    see
That rather than Freedom, we'll part with
    our Tea
And well as we love the dear Draught when
    adry,
As American Patriots,—our Taste we deny.

If purchasing was politicized, so was manufacture. In Newport, Rhode Island, Congregational minister Ezra Stiles played host to "ninety-two daughters of Liberty" who brought seventy spinning wheels at the break of day to his house and "spun and reeled, respiting and assisting one another" until 170 skeins were done. Because ordinary behaviors suddenly became charged with political significance, political decisions might be ascribed where none were intended, and even those who wished to remain neutral might find themselves accused of aligning themselves one way or another. If patriots wore homespun, could one wear an old silk dress? If "daughters of Liberty" brought their wheels to a communal spinning bee, could one stay at home?

The sharpest of these challenges to consumption behaviors came in the form of the tea boycott. Like the grape or lettuce boycotts of recent years, the tea boycott provided a relatively mild way of identifying oneself with the patriotic effort, for it was easy to refrain from drinking tea. If one wished, one could be

Colonial women demonstrated their support for the patriot cause by signing petitions and joining in boycotts against the importation and consumption of tea. This caricature suggests that many men found such activism on the part of women unusual and amusing.

emphatic, like the landlady with whom John Adams lodged briefly and who lectured him on the need to drink coffee, or like nine-year-old Susan Boudinot, daughter of a New Jersey patriot, who was taken to visit the tory governor William Franklin. When she was offered a cup of tea, she curtsied, raised it to her lips, and tossed the contents out the window. Doggerel verse on patriotic boycotts appeared in newspapers and in women's private papers, passed around from hand to hand. In Philadelphia, Hanna Griffitts referred to the tea act as North's "Ministerial blunder" and drafted a poem:

> . . . for the sake of Freedom's name,
>   (Since British Wisdom scorns repealing,)
> Come, sacrifice to Patriot fame,
>   And give up Tea, by way of healing,
> This done, within ourselves retreat,

> The Industrious arts of life to follow,
> Let the Proud Nabobs storm & fret,
>   They Cannot force our lips to swallow.

Occasionally political awareness became sharp enough to prompt a petition circulated and signed by women. In the 1830s women's petitions would be a familiar device, widely circulated by female antislavery societies. But they were virtually unknown before the 1770s. For many women, signing such a petition was surely their first political act. Fifty-one women of Edenton, North Carolina, endorsed the nonimportation Association resolves of 1774:

> As we cannot be indifferent on any occasion that appears nearly to affect the peace and happiness of our country, and as it has been thought necessary for the public good, to

enter into several particular resolves by a meeting of members deputed from the whole Province, it is a duty which we owe, not only to our near and dear relations and connections . . . but to ourselves, who are essentially interested in their welfare, to do everything as far as lies in our power, to testify our sincere adherence to the same; and we do therefore accordingly subscribe this paper, as a witness of our fixed intention and solemn determination to do so.

The dismay with which this sober and straightforward petition was received suggests its novelty. Arthur Iredell, who was living in England, wrote to his North Carolina relatives: "Is there a Female Congress at Edenton too? I hope not, for we Englishmen are afraid of the Male Congress, but if the Ladies, who have ever, since the Amazonian Era, been esteemd the most formidable Enemies, if they, I say, should attack us, the most fatal consequences is to be dreaded."

The prewar boycotts initiated the politicization of the household economy and marked the beginning of the use of a political language that explicitly included women. This politicization of the household economy intensified during the war. "Was not every fireside, indeed," John Adams would recall, "a theatre of politics?" Disruption of trade with Britain meant that consumption codes became self-enforcing. Nonconsumption depended on national policy rather than on individual choice, but other demands were addressed to women and to housekeepers. Sometimes the appeal made to women was patriotic, sometimes commercial, sometimes quasi-religious, sometimes all three. [The female] spinner was to feel strengthened by the sense that she was part of a long line of women stretching back to antiquity: "In this time of public distress, you have now, each of you, an opportunity not only to help to sustain your families, but likewise to cast your mite into the treasury of the public good."

Women saved rags for papermaking and for bandages; they turned in lead weights from windows to be melted down for bullets; they saved the family urine for saltpeter.

State statutes usually relied on the generic *he*, but those dealing with commodity production for the war made it very clear that women were specifically regarded as sources of the clothing and blankets the army needed. A New Jersey procurement act for November 1777, for example, made a point of prescribing penalties "if any person having any blankets to sell, or such sufficiency as to enable him or her to spare a part without distressing his or her family, and shall rate them at an exorbitant price." The amount expected from each county was large, and it is hard to imagine that the commissioners could have approached their quotas if women in large numbers had not taken to their looms. Male suppliers of clothing—tailors, weavers, shoemakers—were exempted from military service, but no sweeteners were offered for the services provided by women, only the threat that the items they made could be seized by the commissioners.

Old clothing collected for the army could rarely be used in the condition in which it was contributed. During the dreadful Valley Forge winter of 1777–1778, Mary Frazier of Chester County, Pennsylvania, rode

> day after day collecting from neighbors and friends far and near, whatever they could spare for the comfort of the destitute soldiers, the blankets, and yarn, and half worn clothing thus obtained she brought to her own house, where they would be patched, and darned, and made wearable and comfortable, the stockings newly footed, or new ones knit, adding what clothing she could give of her own.

Women undertook to police local merchants who hoarded scarce commodities. In May 1777, for example, a series of attacks were made on the Poughkeepsie, New York, home of Peter Mesier, a reputed loyalist who was rumored to be hoarding tea. Mesier's wife offered to sell the cache at four dollars a pound, but twenty-two women, accompanied by two Continental soldiers, demanded entry to her home, saying that they "would . . . have it at their own Price, and brought a Hammer and Scales, and proceeded to weigh as much as they chose to take, untill they had taken near One hundred weight . . . for which they left about Seventeen Pounds in Money." In July 1778 Abigail Adams reported that "a Number of Females, some say a hundred, some say more assembled with a cart and trucks, marched down to the Ware House" of an "eminent, wealthy, stingy Merchant" who was rumored to be hoarding coffee. When he refused to deliver the keys, "one of them seazd him by his Neck and tossed him into the cart. . . . he delivered the keys. . . . they . . . opened the Warehouse. Hoisted out the Coffee themselves, put it into trucks and drove off. . . . A large concourse of Men stood amazed silent Spectators." Throughout the war, open hostility to British fashion continued to be a way of mobilizing civilian enthusiasms and of offering a target for civilian anger. When the patriots recaptured Philadelphia in 1778, they celebrated the Fourth of July with understandable enthusiasm. Among their displays, Elizabeth Drinker reported, was "a very high Head dress . . . exhibited thro the Streets this afternoon on a very dirty Woman with a mob after her, with Drums &c by way of ridiculing that very foolish fashion." Of course women had been participants in crowds before the Revolution, but the war intruded into the family economy and gave more obvious and more frequent opportunity for the enforcement of consumption codes and for the display of aggressive political behavior by women.

The belief that consumption behaviors had political implications would persist long after the Revolution. With every international crisis in the years of the early Republic, women

would be asked to make contributions from the family economy to the public account. For example, at the beginning of a national drive to improve domestic manufactures in the fall of 1787, an anonymous author published an "Address to the ladies of America" in the *American Museum:* "Your country is independent of European power: and your modes of dress should be independent of a group of coquettes, milliners and manufacturers, who, from motives of vanity on one hand, and avarice on the other, endeavour to enslave the fancy of the whole world." Buying American wares became a patriotic gesture, intended to support "infant" manufacturers threatened by more fashionable products from abroad; it was up to American women to provide a protected market for domestic goods.

During the war women, like most men, were civilians. The role of the private citizen in a civil war can be vague and unclear; it is not surprising that whether whig or tory, women had something of a collective reputation for hesitant patriotism or outright neutrality. But woman soon discovered that in this civil war any theater of conflict could create violence that would change their lives. They might not be soldiers, but they were not immune from attack.

Documented cases of rape are relatively rare, but those we have are vicious in the extreme. Rape by the British was a crime for which there could be little redress. Those who reoccupied areas held by enemy troops gave low priority to documenting crimes for the sake of the record. We do have, however, the pathetic testimony, signed only with a mark, of thirteen-year-old Abigail Palmer, who was at home with her grandfather when the British troops came through Hunterdon County, New Jersey, in the winter of 1777. "A great number of soldiers Belonging to the British Army came there, when one of them said to the Deponent, I want to speak with you in the next Room & she told him she woud not go with him when he seizd hold of her & dragd her into a back Room and she screamd & begd of him to let her alone. . . . her Grandfather also & Aunt Intreated . . . telling them how Cruel & what a shame it was to Use a Girl of that Age after that manner, but . . . finally three of Said Soldiers Ravished her."

Mistreatment and indignity, the more frightening because the threat of rape was always present, were possible wherever armies roamed. Examples are easy to find, but difficult to quantify; they form a substantial segment of the memoir material compiled by both sides. The murder of Mrs. Caldwell in Connecticut Farms, New Jersey, by a British sharpshooter in 1780 took on the proportions of a patriotic myth; likewise, the loyalists made a legend of Flora McDonald's daughters, whose rebel captors in the fall of 1777 put "their swords into their bosoms, split down their silk dresses and, taking them out into the yard, stripped them of all their outer clothing." The loyalist Ann Hulton reported that "at Roxbury Mr. Ed. Brinleys wife whilst lying in, had a guard of Rebels always in her room, who treated her with rudeness & indecency, exposing her to the view of their banditti, as a sight 'See a tory woman' and stripd her & her Children of all their Linnen & cloths." The king's troops were even more cruel to Hannah Adams, the wife of Deacon Joseph Adams of Cambridge, Massachusetts; on their retreat from Concord, three soldiers broke into her room where she was lying in bed, "scarcely able to walk . . . to the fire, not having been to [her] chamber door . . . [since] being delivered in child-birth." They forced her outside with bayonets and set the house on fire while her five children were still inside.

Women were made refugees by the war. The war was so disruptive to family life that one begins to wonder whether the cult of domesticity—the ideological celebration of women's domestic roles—was not in large measure a response to the wartime disruption and threat of separation of families. Peace would bring renewed appreciation of what had once been taken for granted.

When the patriots evacuated New York City in 1776, Margaret Livingston moved from the city to Fairfield, Connecticut, only to find the British nearby. "I cant help thinking," she wrote, ". . . it would have been better for us to have staid in N.Y. the expence of moving has been very great & the loss of a good deal property in the City, makes me envy those who have had courage to stay." Many of the poor who had been cared for in the city almshouse had to leave also, and money was allocated to transport them to upstate counties. More than half of the approximately 550 who were sent out were women, and it is possible that more married women were subsumed under their husband's names, as they were in other lists. When Ezra Stiles counted the refugees who had come to New Haven in 1782, eighteen were male and twenty-eight female. Most unfortunate were the 170 Kentucky women and children taken captive by a force of British and Shawnee in June 1780; after a two-year internment in Canada, they were sent home in a condition that aroused public sympathy.

It was taken for granted that women would maintain the household economy while their menfolk were at war. Sarah Frazier described her grandmother's war effort: "All the cloth and linen that my Grandfather wore during the war were spun at home, most of it by her own hands. All the clothing of the family, (and it was not a small one) during this time was made at home except weaving. All the business of every kind, she attended to Farm, Iron Works, and domestic matters. In Summer as soon as it was light she had her horse saddled, rode over the farm and directed the men about their work, often rode down to the creek, where Sharpless' Iron Works are now, and was back at breakfast time to give her attention and toil to the children, servants, & household affairs." Abigail Adams maintained the family farm, hired and fired the hands, bought and sold lands. "Mrs. Adams Native Genius will Excel us all in Husbandry," James Warren reported. "She was much Engaged when I came along, and the Farm at Braintree Appeared to be Under Excellent Management."

Because the Revolution was a civil war, each adult had to assume a political identity and maintain it with sufficient clarity to satisfy the local authorities. Women had the advantage. Because they were not being recruited into the conflicting armies, their political choices were less carefully scrutinized than those of men; they could even shift back and forth between camps with some ease.

Patriots continually complained that women were moving into areas occupied by the British, bringing property and information behind enemy lines. "I have good reason to suspect," George Washington wrote, "that many persons (Women particularly) who obtain leave from the Executive Council of Pennsylvania to go and come to and from New York under pretence of visiting their Friends, have, in fact, no other Business but that of bringing out Goods to trade with." Henry Livingston complained that the British "were informed of every thing that passed among us and that Women were the most proper persons for that purpose."

Women who were intercepted in circulating British proclamations or passing information about American troops were numerically few, but dangerous enough to be taken seriously. In 1780, for example, some thirty-two women, along with over four hundred men, were brought to the attention of the Albany County Board of the New York State Commissioners for Detecting and Defeating Conspiracies, accused of being spies or sympathizers. Among the accused were women who had given sanctuary in their homes to loyalists and to British soldiers. Rachael Ferguson, confined in an Albany jail "for harbouring and entertaining a Number of Tories" en route from Canada,

was released on the very high bail of eight hundred pounds. Lidia Currey was similarly jailed for "assisting in concealing and harbouring Persons from the Enemy." A Mrs. Henderson of Dutchess County, New York, smuggled a message from a husband who was fighting with the British to his wife at home, and publicly "expressed herself much in favor of the Superiority and Success of the British Arms and observed that She had no doubt that finally they would subdue this Country and therefore that it would be best for all Persons to come in and submit."

Not only British sympathizers were suspected as conspirators. Pacifist Shakers were carefully watched. Founded by Mother Ann Lee, the Shaker sect had a strong appeal to women. The Albany committee interrogated Ann Standerren and two men with the carefully phrased question "whether they are principled against taking up Arms in defence of the American cause and whether they have not endeavored to influence other persons against taking up arms." When the three "answered in the affirmative," the committee resolved that they "be committed [to jail]." Not until December, when the board conceded that "many of the Persons of the said Persuasion [Shaking Quakers] have been reformed and that no further Evil is to be apprehended from her influence," was Standerren permitted to return home on the basis of a two hundred pound bond for good behavior.

Wives of tories, as a class, were regarded with partisan hostility, especially if their husbands had actually joined the British. In patriot areas, their homes might be robbed and plundered with relative impunity. After the fall of Ticonderoga, insecurity ran especially high on the New York frontier; it was suspected that tories were hiding out in the woods, secretly provided with supplies by their wives, and readying themselves to assist in the expected attack on Fort Schuyler. "The Women of those Enemies is still living among us," growled the chairman of the Tryon County Committee of Safety to Governor George Clinton. "Some behave very rudely at present, and have proved very active to support and spirit up the opposite Cause." The tory women saw their position rather differently. In a rare joint petition, signed with their marks and sent to the committee, they complained that "being left by . . . [their] Husbands and . . . [their] Effects sold," they were "reduced to the greatest distress imaginable." They "humbly" asked that they be provided for or that they be permitted to join their husbands, and eventually they got their request. In the summer of 1777, the Tryon County Committee of Safety rounded up eleven women and placed them under house arrest, and in October they were given seven days notice to leave.

Suspicion of tory wives was not confined to Tryon County. By the summer of 1780 New York State had passed "An Act for the Removal of the Families of Persons who may have joined the Enemy," justifying the removal on the basis of the "many and great Mischiefs" that arise "by permitting the Families of Persons who have joined the Enemy, to remain at their respective Habitations, inasmuch as such Persons frequently come out in a private Manner, to gain Intelligence and commit Robberies, Thefts and Murders . . . and are concealed and comforted by their respective Families." This measure empowered justices of the peace to give a twenty-day notice to the wives of persons who were with the enemy "that they depart this State . . . or repair to such Parts of it as are within the Power of the Enemy; and at their Discretion to take with them all or any of their Children, not above the Age of twelve Years."

There was little room in the patriot position for the admission that women might make political choices that were distinct from—and at odds with—those of their husbands. The Albany commission did permit one tory wife to remain after the passage of the expulsion law

on the grounds that "notwithstanding the Political Sentiments of her husband . . . Jane Moffit has always been esteemed a Friend to the American Cause." But in other cases a woman's harmlessness and her willingness to promise that she would not be a burden on the public treasury were the major considerations. Tories' wives who petitioned to be allowed to stay brought certificates signed by their patriot neighbors to the effect that they had "behaved themselves in an unexceptionable Manner" and that permitting them to remain would not be "detrimental to the Freedom and independence of this and the United States."

One of the most explicit of these pleas is a petition of twenty-one patriot women who had themselves been temporarily expelled from their homes in Wilmington, North Carolina, when the British occupied the town. When Wilmington was retaken in 1782, the Americans responded by issuing an order that summarily expelled the wives and children of absent loyalists. Women who signed the petition protesting this action included the wives of some of the most prominent patriots of the Cape Fear region. Anne Hooper, whose husband had signed the Declaration of Independence, signed first. Initially the petitioners bowed to tradition: "It is not the province of our sex to reason deeply upon the policy of the order." Yet they insisted that they had an obligation to respond, partly because the policy "must affect the helpless and innocent," partly because they suspected it had been drafted in retaliation for their own expulsion. The loyalists' wives had neither inspired the British expulsion order nor aided in its execution, said the patriot women. "On the contrary, they expressed the greatest indignation at it, and with all their power strove to mitigate our sufferings." Mrs. Hooper and her colleagues saw that there was a real difference between sending patriot wives to their friends on the outskirts of town, friends who had taken them in and made them feel comfortable, and expelling

"Town women" whose husbands were far away in Charleston and who lacked means of traveling there. The patriot women claimed a patriots' privilege. "If we may be allowed to claim any merit with the public for our steady adherence to the Whig principles of America . . . we shall hold it as a very signal mark of your respect for us if you will condescend to suffer to remain amongst us our old friends and acquaintances whose husbands, though estranged from us in political opinions, have left wives and children much endeared to us. . . . The safety of this State, we trust in God, is now secured beyond the most powerful exertions of our Enemies, and it would be a system of abject weakness to fear the feeble efforts of women and children." [In similar fashion,] Robert Morris's wife, Mary, watched the expulsion of women from Philadelphia with misgivings:

> My feelings [are] . . . wounded for the sufferings of a Number of my Sex in this State, who are compeld to leave it, by that Cruell Edict of our Counsel: a resolve which Obliges all the women whose Husbands are with the enemy, and Children whose parents are there, to repair to *them* Immediately; a determination like this which admits of no Exception, is unjust, and cruell, . . . there is many whose conduct has not Merited it, tho there is others that have, yet why not discriminate between the Innocent and guilty. . . . Mrs. Furgerson is determind not to go, she says they may take her life, but shall never banish her from Her Country.

Then she concluded wryly, "There are others [who are] . . . renderd happyer by the banishment of a worthless Husband and who by honest industry gains a Subsistence for themselves and Children."

The emergencies of war pulled women into political relationships and forced unfamiliar political choices. Women appear in substantial numbers among those who appealed for tax abatements because their property had been destroyed. Even menial jobs were politicized. Mary Pratt was turned out of her job as housekeeper for the South Carolina State House after the capture of Charleston "to make room for another person who was more attached to the British Government." Patriot forces, too, had employment to offer and new roles to suggest to sympathetic women who were willing to emerge, even if only to a modest extent, from their traditional domain. Women represent only a small proportion of those who came before committees of safety to testify against tories, but that these women would bring their traditionally private judgments of male political behavior into public tribunals is testimony to the intensity of wartime politics. Committees of safety had employment for "discreet Women, of known attachment to the American Cause" to search suspected women smugglers and tories for illegal papers. Abigail Adams seems to have been pulled into this effort. On April 21, 1776, she reported that "a number of Gentlemen who were together at Cambridge thought it highly proper that a Committee of Ladies should be chosen to examine the Torys Ladies, and proceeded to the choice of 3 Mrs. Winthrope, Mrs. Warren and your Humble Servant."

There were women who went to great risks for the patriot cause. Elizabeth Burgin came under suspicion for "helping the American prisiners to make their [es]cap" from New York in 1779. "The British offered," she reported, "a bounty of two Houndred pounds for taking me." Her friends smuggled her out to Long Island and then on to Philadelphia in a "wale boat," which was "chased by two Boats half way [across] the Sound." It was more than a month before she was able to get back to New York under a flag of truce to retrieve her children.

The American army offered political uses for traditional domestic skills. Conspicuous military heroines like Margaret Corbin were only a tiny proportion of the thousands of dependents who drifted after the troops. Wives and children who had no means of support when their husbands and fathers were pressed into service followed after and cared for their own men, earning their subsistence by cooking and washing for troops in an era when the offices of quartermaster and commissary were inadequately run.

The richest fictional portrait of such a woman was provided by James Fenimore Cooper in *The Spy: A Tale of the Neutral Ground,* published in 1821. Elizabeth Flanagan is "a female sutler, washerwoman, and . . . petticoat doctor to the troops. She was the widow of a soldier who had been killed in the service. . . . She constantly migrated with the troops. . . . sometimes the cart itself was her shop; at others the soldiers made her a rude shelter of such materials as offered." Her motive is not simply financial; she is as proud a patriot as any of Cooper's characters, with a clear sense of the value of her services to the political cause. "What would become of the States and liberty," she asks, "if the boys had never a clane shirt, or a drop to comfort them? Ask Captain Jack, there, if they'd fight . . . and they no clane linen to keep the victory in."

The real women who followed the troops were usually regarded as a nuisance, and they appear in orderly books in terms of what they might not do. Sometimes they are not to ride the wagons when the army moves; sometimes they are required to ride "as the weomin going on horses Back will deminish the Numbers of Drivers taken from the Army." When provisions were scarce in 1780, officers at West Point were instructed to "without Delay make the Strictest inpsection into the Carractor of the women who Draw [rations] in their Corps and Report on their honour the Names of Such as are Maryed to non Commsd officers, privates and Artificers." Married women were to be given certificates, unmarried women to be "sent off." Women who were permitted to stay might not draw provisions unless they washed clothes "at . . . a Reasonable Rate" fixed by "the Commanding officers of the Corps in which they Draw."

At Fishkill, New York, the wives of several artisans were employed as cooks; however, cooking was not regarded as a skilled trade, and the women were paid substantially less than their husbands. John Parsell, who was superintendent of the wheelwrights for two weeks, was paid fourteen shillings a day; Thomas Parsell, the foreman, was paid twelve shillings a day. Their relative Sarah Parsell was cook—at two shillings a day. The cook for the express riders was Mrs. Lloyd, wife of the hostler, and she was paid four dollars per month while her husband got ten dollars.

Even when given specific orders and employment, many women resisted military discipline. The pattern is clearly revealed in Washington's General Orders: from the beginning to the end of the war, his notes are dotted with the complaint that women slowed down the progress of the army. They are an "incumbrance," "a clog upon every movement." Women were sent with the slowest section of the moving troops, the baggage wagons, for two reasons. First, burdened as they were with children or pregnancies, the female dependents maintained the slowest pace. Second, it was an embarrassment to let them be seen with men. When the army retreated through Philadelphia after the battle of Germantown, Washington was explicit: baggage wagons were "to avoid the City entirely. . . . Not a woman belonging in the army is to be seen with the troops on their march." Much as he would have liked, Washington could not deny that in some sense the women did "belong" to the army. He was reduced to insisting that they be put to work or sent off to serve as nurses. Washington issued order after order forbidding women to ride in any wagon without leave in writing from the brigadier in command. "And," he added, "the Brigadiers are requested to be cautious in giving leave to those who are able to walk." By 1778 he was complaining that women were still in the wagons, [and] by the summer Washington was requiring permission in writing with the sole allowable basis of such permission being "inability to march." On the eve of Yorktown he was still fuming about the women encumbering the army.

The women not only had to be transported, they had to be fed. Washington was perplexed. "I cannot see," he wrote to Brig. Gen. John Stark at White Plains, "why the soldiers Wives in Albany should be supported at public expence. They may get most extravagant Wages of any kind of Work in the Country and to feed them, when that is the case, would be robbing the public and encouraging idleness." A year later, New York women whose husbands were away fighting in the west apparently demanded what we would now call dependents' allowances. Washington threw up his hands. "This is a thing which I have never known to be allowed, and which, if admitted in one instance, might be claimed by the whole army." He was helpless to change things, and conceded that "the New York troops will be at this post in a few days, when the Wives of as many Soldiers, as are generally allowed to follow the Army, may join and be subsisted as usual. If any remain, I cannot undertake to give an order for them to draw provisions." Washington's frustration affords an indirect glimpse of these hundreds of women who would not be separated from their husbands or from their ad hoc work in the camps, thus making it impossible to keep them off the wagons or from drawing their own subsistence rations. Like it or not, Washington was stuck with what even he had to refer to as the "Women of the Army."

The most common official position that the American forces offered women was that of nurse, an obvious employment of domestic skills. Occasionally military nurses could earn premium pay, but it is important to recognize

that, two generations before Florence Nightingale and Clara Barton upgraded the profession, the work of military nurses was largely custodial and therefore ill-paid. Women were recruited for this labor because, in Washington's words, if female nurses were not found, the army was "under the necessity of substituting in their place a number of men from the respective Regiments" who would then be "entirely lost in the proper line of their duty." Most of the skilled tasks of nursing were performed throughout the war by male surgeon's mates. The official duties left to the nurse were closer to those of the modern orderly, and only in the absence of the mates did nurses administer medicines. The formal job description below suggests the menial role of the army nurses and, in its direct warnings against drunkenness and theft, also reveals the nurses' low status in the hospital staff:

> The NURSES, in the absence of the Mates, administer the medicine and diet prescribed for the sick according to order; they obey all orders they receive from the Matron; not only to be attentive to the cleanliness of the wards and patients, but to keep themselves clean they are never to be disguised with liquor [a stricture which is not placed on the males]; they are to see that the close-stools or pots are emptied as soon as possible after they are used, into a necessary house. . . . they are to see that every patient, upon his admission into the Hospital is immediately washed with warm water, and that his face and hands are washed and head combed every morning . . . that their wards are swept over every morning or oftener if necessary and sprinkled with vinegar three or four times a day. All attempts to steal from, conceal the effects of, or otherwise defraud the patients . . . will be severely punished.

The pay scale that Congress established in 1777 for hospital staffs also confirms the limited status ascribed to women and the weakness of their bargaining position. Early in the war, Washington had begged for premium pay for nurses, and Dr. William Shippen, desperate for nurses for the hospital at Perth Amboy, New Jersey, reported that he had "been obliged to deviate from the regulations of the honorable Congress and allow them 10/per week instead of 3/9. The most ordinary woman here is able to earn much more, as there are so few women and so many men to work for. . . . the sick must suffer much unless well nursed and kept clean."

But as the hospital system was regularized, Washington's and Shippen's strictures were forgotten, and matrons and nurses were paid less well than stablehands. At a time when senior surgeons received four dollars per day and were entitled to six rations of food, matrons got only one-half dollar, and nurses' pay ranged from twenty-four cents to ninety cents per day, and one ration each. Wartime inflation drove up the salaries of physicians and surgeon's mates, but at the end of the war, when surgeon's mates got fifty dollars a month, matrons' salaries remained fifty cents a day.

One of the readiest ways for women to earn money had long been to run a boardinghouse. This employment had the advantage of making use of the form of capital that a widow or spinster was most likely to control and of requiring a relatively slight form of readjustment; one continued to live where one always had lived. Becoming a landlady might imply a lowering of status, but not perhaps so radical a fall as that suffered by a woman working for wages. The landlady remained self-employed while she did the work that was traditional for women to do. Self supporting women were frequently found as landladies.

And as landladies they were affected by the war. The influx of delegates to the Continental Congress meant a large number of respectable boarders for the boardinghouse keepers of Philadelphia. Sometimes landladies were paid for their services directly from the national treasury or by local committees of safety, which rented rooms to house officers and soldiers, employed women to cook meals for militia, and commandeered supplies from boardinghouse cellars. The double purposes of the medieval hotel—to care for the sick as well as to care for the traveler—had not yet fully disintegrated. Sick and wounded might be sent to private lodgings, and women were paid for their care.

Boardinghouses had political complexions. Members of Congress vied with each other to stay with Mary House. James Madison was a regular boarder and maintained a private correspondence with Mrs. House and her daughter after he had returned to Virginia. Eliza House married Nicholas Trist and became part of nationalist political circles in Virginia. When Rachel Farmer established a lodging house in Philadelphia in 1781, she argued that Congress owed her patronage because of what she had risked during the war: "Your Memorialist, did for many years keep a Respectable Tavern In New Brunswick, which Business she Resolved to Quit, at the Beginning of the War; but for the well Accommodateing the Gentlemen of our Army, & by the Solicittation of a Number of Gentlemen of Character, I Continued to keep a Publick House—the Consequence of which was, when the British took possession of that place, your Memorialist, had her House Burnt, & her Valluable Furniture Destroyed, & Rendered unable to prosecute Business."

In 1783 when the Continental Congress, threatened with civil uprising in Philadelphia, was searching for a convenient place to move, it was flooded with petitions of invitation. The people of Princeton, "desirous to testify their Respect for the supreme Legislature of America" and willing "to furnish the best in their power," sent an invitation signed by six women and thirty-six men. Mrs. Rock and Mrs. Know indicated that their accommodations were not good enough for members of Congress, but that they would take attendants; Mrs. [Richard]

Stockton offered "the whole House in which she lives, stables"; Mrs. Berrien offered "1 Room, 2 Beds, 2 Break & Dinners." A similar petition arrived from Trenton, though with fewer names and a caveat from five men who wished, reasonably enough, "to be excused from providing Dinners, as Congress do not dine at common Family hours."

Wartime also created another group of less cordial boardinghouse keepers—women who unwillingly housed soldiers during military occupation. Although the Americans paid for the services they commandeered of their own population, these payments were irregularly tendered, and the fees set by the Army. The British came in the role of conquerors, and so they had less compulsion to pay for services rendered; even people of loyalist sympathies hesitated before offering room to foreign soldiers. The British preferred to maintain as long as they could the fiction that they were welcomed voluntarily into women's homes.

The process of negotiation was carefully detailed by Elizabeth Drinker, a Philadelphia Quaker woman. Her politics were pacifist, but she was generally sympathetic to the British. When her husband, Henry, along with nineteen other Quaker men, was exiled by the patriots to Virginia, she was left alone in her home. She was there with four young children and several servants when the British entered the city at the end of September 1777. Not long after the battle of Germantown, she was repeatedly visited by a British officer who asked her to "take in a Sick or wounded Captain," but she was able to "put him off" by arguing that her husband was already a martyr and that she was all alone. But being alone also made her vulnerable; soldiers simply marched into her house to take what they needed. On the fifth of November a soldier came to ask for blankets. "Notwithstanding my refusal," she wrote, "he went up stairs and took one." On November 25, she was deeply frightened by "an enraged, drunken Man . . . with a sword in his hand, swearing about the House, after going 2 or 3 times up & down the Entry." Finally a male visitor, Chalkley James, disarmed the man and sent him on his way. When a courteous and respectable young officer called a few weeks later, looking for quarters and arguing "that it was a necessary protection at these times to have [an officer] . . . in the House," his words had some plausibility. She put him off by saying that she had to think about it, but he returned the next day and the next to ask again. "I told him that my sister was out [consulting their friends for advice] . . . that I expected that we who were at present 'lone women, would be excus'd he said he fear'd not, for tho I might put him off . . . yet a great number of Foreign Troops were to be quartered in this Neighbourhood, he believed they might be troublesome; we had a good deal of talk about the mal Behaveour of the British officers, which he by no means justify'd."

"I am straitend how to act, and yet determin'd," Elizabeth Drinker wrote. "I may be troubled with others much worse, for this man appears much of the Gentleman, but while I can keep clear of them, I intend to do so." But she really had no options, and Major Cramond moved in. With relief, she decided he was a "thoughtful sober young man." But she quickly discovered that the major did not come alone. "Cramond has 3 Horses 3 Cows 2 Sheep and 2 Turkeys with several Fowls in our Stable. He has 3 Servants 2 white Men and one Negro Boy call'd Damon, the Servants are here all day, but away at Night. He has 3 Hessians who take their turns to wate on him as messengers or order men." He entertained a great deal, inviting eleven or twelve officers to dine with him on January 5 and eight more on January 8. Despite Cramond's initial promise, his company stayed up late (on February 1 until midnight). Cramond expanded his possession of the house: "Our officer mov'd his lodgings from the bleu Chamber to the little front parlor, so that he has the two front parlors, a chamber up two pair of stairs for his bagage, and the Stable wholly to himself, besides the use of the kitchen." By the spring he had occupied even more territory. "Our Major took it into his Head to dine to day in the Summer House with another officer, he had 2 or 3 to visit him while they set there, so that when the House is kept open, I suppose we shall have them passing and repassing, which has not been the case hitherto; they behave well and appear pleas'd—but I don't feel so." She expressed no sorrow, therefore, when May 22 found the major packing to leave with the British (though other Quaker women of loyalist sympathies, like Sally Logan, were much distressed).

Jails were also scarce, and both British and Americans were likely to place prisoners, especially officers, under loose house arrest. Thus Catherine Heydshaw was paid £114 "for lodging, firing, candles and for dieting Hessian officers and soldiers" for a month in 1777, and Rachel Stille sent accounts for well over £300 to the Continental Congress for boarding British officers who were prisoners. American officers captured by the British were quartered with individuals on Long Island. When the war was over, those who had boarded the prisoners refused to return them until the cost of their lodging had been paid. The accounts of Abram Skinner, Commissary General of Prisoners, report some £800 paid to twelve women who had boarded American officers; women were perhaps 5 percent of the claimants.

Most of the civilian women who worked for the American cause, sometimes without pay, sometimes on a free-lance basis, did so unofficially. It is difficult to retrieve them, except anecdotally. Perhaps one of them, for whom the future chief justice John Marshall and other officers of the Virginia Continental Line organized a subscription, is as appropriate an epitome as we can find. The officers thanked

> Mrs Hay and her Daughter for their great attention and Tenderness to our Brother Officers, Prisoners in the City of Philadel-

phia. . . . they have come out at different times purely to serve the distressed at the risque of their Lives, and have actually assisted some officers in makeing their escape, besides nursing the sick & takeing particular care of the affects of the Deceased. Mrs Hay is a poor Widow, & any Little matter that Gentlemen chuse to contribute, can't fail of being acceptable and will be considered as a greatfull acknowledgement on their part for the Voluntary and Benevolent part she has acted.

The influence women exerted on the war effort of both whigs and tories is difficult to evaluate. Following Elizabeth Ellet's nineteenth-century anecdotal accounts, it has been traditional to assume that what women had to offer was moral support—emotional validation of the choices their men had independently made. But the shrill tone of public instructions to women—Washington ineffectively trying to keep them in line, economic planners anxiously seeking their cooperation—suggests both that women had significant services to render if they would and that their cooperation could not be taken for granted. The diaries that remain are decidedly not diaries of clinging vines. "I did not feel half so frighten'd as I expected to be," wrote fifteen-year-old Sally Wister. "'Tis amazing how we get reconciled to such things. Six months ago the bare idea of being within ten, aye, twenty miles, of a battle, wou'd almost have distracted me. And now, tho' two such large armies are within six miles of us, we can converse calmly of it." During the grim fall of 1776, Abigail Adams told her husband, "We are no ways dispiritted here, we possess a Spirit that will not be conquerd. If our Men are all drawn off and we should be attacked, you would find a Race of Amazons in America." Women discovered that they could be devious. The Quaker widow Margaret Hill Morris shielded a prominent loyalist refugee by tricking a patriot search party: "I put on a very simple look & cry[e]d out, bless me I hope you are not Hessians—say, good Men are you the Hessians? Do we look like Hessians? Ask[e]d one of them rudely. Indeed I dont know. Did you never see a Hessian? No never in my life but they *are Men,* & you are Men, & may be Hessians for anything I know."

Women gathered around each other for moral and emotional support. Elizabeth Drinker's prewar life had had a large share of calls and visits between friends, but during the dark days of her husband's exile and the British occupation, perhaps six women gathered around her virtually every day. The wives of the exiles formed what we would now call a mutual support group. They did the same in Wilmington, North Carolina, where, as we have seen, patriot wives were able to extrapolate from their own experience a sympathy for wives of their opponents. Those who were inclined to write wrote variants of the traditional phrase "Politics is not my affair" over and over again, but like it or not, politics had invaded their households. The "dreadful fruits of Liberty" were on every dinner table.

Questions for Study and Review

1. How did women's economic and political activities change from the prerevolutionary to the revolutionary period?

2. To what extent did women's, and men's, contributions to the Revolution differ according to wealth and status?

3. When wives disagreed with husbands over which side to support, how did this challenge conventional concepts of familial authority and political citizenship?

4. War is a recurrent theme in American history. Given the different causes, timing, and locations of military conflicts, what are some common effects on women's familial, community, and political roles?

Suggested Readings

Mary Beth Norton, *Liberty's Daughters: The Revolutionary Experience of American Women, 1750–1800* (1980).

Joan Hoff Wilson, "The Illusion of Change: Women and the American Revolution," in Alfred Young, ed., *The American Revolution: Explorations in the History of American Radicalism* (1976).

Jan Lewis, "The Republican Wife: Virtue and Seduction in the Early Republic," *William and Mary Quarterly* (October 1987).

Joy Day Buel and Richard Buel, Jr., *The Way of Duty: A Woman and Her Family in Revolutionary America* (1984).

Elizabeth Evans, *Weathering the Storm: Women of the American Revolution* (1975).

FIVE

"On the Importance of the Obstetrick Art": Changing Customs of Childbirth in America, 1760–1825

Catherine M. Scholten

The American Revolution dramatically affected the lives of women and men from Maine to Georgia; tales of daring and courage abound. Yet not all colonists were caught up in the revolutionary fervor, nor was war the only arena in which colonists waged life and death struggles. Among the one-fifth to one-third of colonists who failed to choose sides in the years of rebellion, and among women on all sides, the rhythms of reproduction could weigh as heavily as the horrors of war. The birth of a nation had a more literal if more mundane meaning than just military victory and political restructuring. Yet the two—the labors of childbirth and of nation building—were not unrelated.

Scholten carefully traces the transformation of childbearing in the years surrounding the Revolution from a communal event controlled by women to an isolated interaction between male physician and female patient. Though these changes initially affected only affluent, urban mothers, the patterns established among this group eventually affected the vast majority of American women. The century-long transformation of childbirth practices rendered labor less painful but also less communal; it assured that it would also be less female centered as it became more medically controlled.

Certainly similar changes would have occurred without a political revolution, and did in Great Britain and elsewhere. Nonetheless, heightened concern with establishing "American" institutions and expertise speeded the development of medical schools and professional associations in the New Republic. These, in turn, focused attention on "the obstetrick art," encouraging the replacement of female midwives with male physicians in the birthing rooms of the elite. Ironically, the success of this substitution would soon lead to demands for female physicians, both as an antidote to suspected improprieties resulting from male physicians' examinations of women and as an avenue for the Republic's talented daughters to contribute to the nation's future development.

The changes described by Scholten affected only a small proportion of women by 1825. For those who could not afford a physician, the communal, female-centered birth experience continued, though it was perhaps considered less desirable now that women had the alternative of male professionals, armed with anesthetics and forceps. Elizabeth Sandwich Drinker, whose life was sketched earlier by Scott, sought to preserve both the female intimacy of the old rituals alongside the greater safety of the new when her daughters began to experience the joys and dangers of childbirth. Scholten here traces the developments that allowed her such choices.

In October 1799, as Sally Downing of Philadelphia labored to give birth to her sixth child, her mother, Elizabeth Drinker, watched her suffer "in great distress." Finally, on the third day of fruitless labor, Sally's physician, William Shippen, Jr., announced that "the child must be brought forward." Elizabeth Drinker wrote in her diary that, happily, Sally delivered naturally, although Dr. Shippen had said that "he thought he should have had occasion for instruments," and clapped his hand on his side, so that the forceps rattled in his pocket.

Elizabeth Drinker's account of her daughter's delivery is one of the few descriptions by an eighteenth-century American woman of a commonplace aspect of women's lives—childbirth. It is of special interest to social historians because it records the participation of a man in the capacity of physician. Shippen was a prominent member of the first generation of American doctors trained in obstetrics and, commencing in 1763, the first to maintain a regular practice attending women in childbirth. Until that time midwives managed almost all deliveries, but with Shippen male physicians began to supplant the midwives.

The changing social customs and medical management of childbirth from 1760 to 1825 are the subjects of this article. By analyzing the rituals of childbirth it will describe the emergence of new patterns in private and professional life. It shows that, beginning among well-to-do women in Philadelphia, New York, and Boston, childbirth became less a communal experience and more a private event confined within the intimate family. In consequence of new perceptions of urban life and of women, as well as of the development of medical science, birth became increasingly regarded as a medical problem to be managed by physicians. For when Shippen, fresh from medical studies in London, announced his intention to practice midwifery in Philadelphia in 1763, he was proposing to enter a field considered the legitimate province of women. Childbearing had been viewed as the inevitable, even the divinely ordained, occasion of suffering for women; childbirth was an event shared by the female community; and delivery was supervised by a midwife.

During the colonial period childbearing occupied a central portion of the lives of women between their twentieth and fortieth years. Six to eight pregnancies were typical, and pregnant women were commonly described as "breeding" and "teeming." Such was women's natural lot; though theologians attributed dignity to carrying the "living soul" of a child and saluted mothers in their congregations with "Blessed are you among women," they also depicted the pains of childbirth as the appropriate special curse of "the Travailing Daughters of Eve." Two American tracts written specifically for lying-in women dwelt on the divinely ordained hazards of childbirth and advised a hearty course of meditation on death, "such as their pregnant condition must reasonably awaken them to."

Cotton Mather's pamphlet, *Elizabeth in Her Holy Retirement*, which he distributed to midwives to give to the women they cared for, described pregnancy as a virtually lethal condition. "For ought you know," it warned, "your Death has entered into you, you may have

Catherine M. Scholten, a doctoral candidate in history at the University of California, Berkeley when she read an earlier version of this article at the St. Louis meeting of the Organization of American Historians, April 1976, wished to thank Gunther Barth, J. William T. Youngs, Jr., Regina Morantz, and Linda Auwers for comments on that draft.

From "'On the Importance of the Obstetrick Art': Changing Customs of Childbirth in America, 1760 to 1825" by Catherine M. Scholten, *William and Mary Quarterly*, July 1977. Reprinted by permission of Pauline M. Scholten for the estate of Catherine M. Scholten.

conceived that which determines but about Nine Months more at the most, for you to live in the World." Pregnancy was thus intended to inspire piety. John Oliver, author of *A Present for Teeming American Women,* similarly reminded expectant mothers that prayer was necessary because their dangers were many. He noted that women preparing for lying-in "get linnen and other necessaries for the child, a nurse, a midwife, entertainment for the women that are called to the labour, a warm convenient chamber, and etc." However, "all these may be miserable comforters," argued Oliver, for "they may perchance need no other linnen shortly than a Winding Sheet, and have no other chamber but a grave, no neighbors but worms." Oliver counseled women to "arm themselves with patience" as well as prayer, and "abate somewhat those dreadful groans and cries which do so much to discourage their friends and relatives who hear them."

Surely women did not need to be reminded of the risks of childbirth. The fears of Mary Clap, wife of Thomas Clap, president of Yale College, surface even through the ritual phrases of the elegy written by her husband after her death in childbirth at the age of twenty-four. Thomas remembered that before each of her six lyings-in his wife asked him to pray with her that God would continue their lives together. Elizabeth Drinker probably echoed the sentiments of most women when she reflected, "I have often thought that women who live to get over the time of Child-bareing, if other things are favourable to them, experience more comfort and satisfaction than at any other period of their lives."

Facing the hazards of childbirth, women depended on the community of their sex for companionship and medical assistance. Women who had moved away at marriage frequently returned to their parents' home for the delivery either because they had no neighbors or because they preferred the care of their mothers to that of their in-laws. Other women summoned mothers, aunts, and sisters on both sides of the family, as well as female friends, when birth was imminent. Above all, they relied on the experience of midwives to guide them through labor.

Women monopolized the practice of midwifery in America, as in Europe, through the middle of the eighteenth century. As the recognized experts in the conduct of childbirth, they advised the mother-to-be if troubles arose during pregnancy, supervised the activities of lying-in, and used their skills to assure safe delivery. Until educated male physicians began to practice obstetrics, midwives enjoyed some status in the medical profession, enhanced by their legal responsibilities in the communities they served.

Some American midwives learned their art in Europe, where midwifery was almost exclusively the professional province of women. Though barber surgeons and physicians increasingly asserted their interest in midwifery during the seventeenth century, midwives and patients resisted the intruders. The midwives' levels of skill varied. Some acquired their medical education in the same way as many surgeons and physicians, by apprenticeship; some read manuals by more learned midwives and physicians; and after 1739, when the first British lying-in hospital was founded, a few were taught by the physicians who directed such hospitals. But more often than not, women undertook midwifery equipped only with folk knowledge and the experience of their own pregnancies.

Disparity of skills also existed among American midwives. Experienced midwives practiced alongside women who were, one physician observed, "as ignorant of their business as the women they deliver." By the end of the eighteenth century physicians thought that the "greater part" of the midwives in America took up the occupation by accident, "having first been *catched,* as they express it, with a woman in labour." The more diligent sought help from books, probably popular medical manuals such as *Aristotle's Master Piece.*

American midwives conducted their practice free, on the whole, from governmental supervision and control. Only two colonies appear to have enacted regulatory statutes, and it does not seem that these were rigorously enforced. In the seventeenth century Massachusetts and New York required midwives, together with surgeons and physicians, not to act contrary to the accepted rules of their art. More specifically, in 1716 the common council of New York City prescribed a licensing oath for midwives, which was similar to the oaths of England. The oath included an injunction— significant for the theme of this article—that midwives not "open any matter Appertaining to your Office in the presence of any Man unless Nessessity or Great Urgent Cause do Constrain you to do so." This oath, which was regularly re-enacted until 1763, suggests the common restriction of midwifery to women, excluding male physicians or barber surgeons, who, in any case, were few and usually ill trained. There are records of male midwives in New York, Philadelphia, Charleston, and Annapolis after 1740, but only onc, a Dr. Spencer of Philadelphia, had London training in midwifery, and it was said of another that "he attended very few natural labors."

Though their duties were not as well defined by law, American midwives served the community in ways similar to those of their British counterparts. In addition to assisting at childbed, they testified in court in cases of bastardy, verified birthdates, and examined female prisoners who pleaded pregnancy to escape punishment. Some colonials also observed the English custom of having the midwife attend the baptism and burial of infants. Samuel Sewall reported that Elizabeth Weeden brought his son John to church for christening in 1677, and at the funeral of little Henry in 1685 "Midwife Weeden and Nurse Hill carried the Corps by turns."

The inclusion of the midwife in these ceremonies of birth and death shows how women's relationships with their midwives went beyond mere respect for the latters' skill. Women with gynecologic problems would freely tell a midwife things "that they had rather die than discover to the Doctor." Grateful patients eulogized midwives. The acknowledgement of the services of one Boston midwife, recorded on her tombstone, has inspired comment since 1761. The stone informs the curious that Mrs. Phillips was "born in Westminster in Great Britain, and Commission'd by John Laud, Bishop of London in ye Year 1718 to ye Office of a Midwife," came to "this Country" in 1719, and "by ye Blessing of God has brought into this world above 3000 children."

We may picture Mrs. Phillips's professional milieu as a small room, lit and warmed by a large fire, and crowded by a gathering of family and friends. In daytime, during the early stages of labor, children might be present, and while labor proceeded female friends dropped in to offer encouragement and help; securing refreshments for such visitors was a part of the preparation for childbirth, especially among the well-to-do families with which we are concerned. Men did not usually remain at the bedside. They might be summoned in to pray, but as delivery approached they waited elsewhere with the children and with women who were "not able to endure" the tension in the room.

During the final stages of labor the midwife took full charge, assisted by other women. As much as possible, midwives managed deliveries by letting nature do the work; they caught the child, tied the umbilical cord, and if necessary fetched the afterbirth. In complicated cases they might turn the child and deliver it feet first, but if this failed, the fetus had to be destroyed. In all circumstances the midwife's chief duty was to comfort the woman in labor while they both waited on nature, and this task she could, as a woman, fulfill with social ease.

Until the mid-eighteenth century, attended childbirths in America were supervised by midwives, and midwifery was an almost exclusively female occupation. With the increasing sophistication of medical science and the development of obstetrics, men began to take over the practice. Gradually male physicians came to assume responsibility for presiding over deliveries. The gravestone in the photograph records the passing of Elizabeth Phillips, an officially licensed and particularly successful midwife, who, according to the stone, "has Brought into this world above 3000 Children."

Under the midwife's direction the woman in labor was liberally fortified with hard liquor or mulled wine. From time to time the midwife examined her cervix to gauge the progress of labor and encouraged her to walk about until the pains became too strong. There was no standard posture for giving birth, but apparently few women lay flat in bed. Some squatted on a midwive's stool, a low chair with an open seat. Others knelt on a pallet, sat on another woman's lap, or stood supported by two friends.

Friends were "welcome companions," according to one manual for midwives, because they enabled the woman in labor "to bear her pains to more advantage," and "their cheerful conversation supports her spirits and inspires her with confidence." Elizabeth Drinker endeavored to talk her daughter into better spirits by telling her that as she was thirty-nine "this might possibly be the last trial of this sort." Some women attempted to cheer the mother-to-be by assuring her that her labor was easy compared to others they had seen, or provoked laughter by making bawdy jokes.

For some attendants, a delivery could be a wrenching experience. Elizabeth Drinker relived her own difficult deliveries when her daughters suffered their labors, and on one such occasion she noted with irony, "This day is 38 years since I was in agonies bringing her into this world of troubles: she told me with tears that this was her birthday." For others the experience of assisting the labors of friends was a reminder of their sex. Sarah Eve, an unmarried twenty-two-year-old, attended the labor of a friend in 1772 and carried the tidings of birth to the waiting father. "None but those that were like anxious could be sensible of a joy like theirs," she wrote in her journal that night. "Oh! Eve! Adam's wife I mean—who could forget her today?"

After delivery, the mother was covered up snugly and confined to her bed, ideally for three to four weeks. For fear of catching cold she was not allowed to put her feet on the floor and was constantly supplied with hot drinks. Family members relieved her of household duties. Restless women, and those who could not afford weeks of idleness, got up in a week or less, but not without occasioning censure.

The social and medical hold of midwives on childbirth loosened during the half century after 1770, as male physicians assumed the practice of midwifery among urban women of social rank. Initially, physicians entered the field as trained practitioners who could help women in difficult labors through the use of instruments, but ultimately they presided over normal deliveries as well. The presence of male physicians in the lying-in chamber signaled a general change in attitudes toward childbirth, including a modification of the dictum that women had to suffer. At the same time, because medical training was restricted to men, women lost their position as assistants at childbirth, and an event traditionally managed by a community of women became an experience shared primarily by a woman and her doctor.

William Shippen, the first American physician to establish a steady practice of midwifery, quietly overcame resistance to the presence of a man in the lying-in room. Casper Wistar's *Eulogies on Dr. Shippen,* published in 1809, states that when Shippen began in 1763, male practitioners were resorted to only in a crisis. "This was altogether the effect of prejudice," Wistar remarked, adding that "by Shippen this prejudice was so done away, that in the course of ten years he became very fully employed." A few figures testify to the trend. The Philadelphia city directory in 1815 listed twenty-one women as midwives, and twenty-three men as practitioners of midwifery. In 1819 it listed only thirteen female midwives, while the number of men had risen to forty-two; and by 1824 only six female midwives remained in the directory. "Prejudice" similarly dissolved in Boston, where in 1781 the physicians advertised that they expected immediate payment for their services in midwifery; by 1820 midwifery in Boston was almost "entirely confined" to physicians. By 1826 Dr. William Dewees, professor of midwifery at the University of Pennsylvania and the outstanding American obstetrician of the early nineteenth century, could preface his textbook on midwifery with an injunction to every American medical student to study the subject because "everyone almost" must practice it. He wrote that "a change of manners within a few years" had "resulted in almost exclusive employment of the male practitioner."

Dewees's statement must be qualified because the "almost exclusive" use of men actually meant almost exclusive use among upper- and middle-class urban women. Female midwives continued throughout the nineteenth century to serve both the mass of women in cities and women in the country who were "without advantage of regular practitioners." During the initial years of their practice physicians shared obstetrical cases with midwives. On occasion Philadelphia women summoned Shippen together with their midwives, and Dewees reports that when he began to practice in the 1790s he depended on midwives to call him when instruments were needed. It is clear, however, that by the 1820s Dewees and his colleagues had established their own practice independent of midwives.

On one level the change was a direct consequence of the fact that after 1750 growing numbers of American men traveled to Europe for medical education. Young men with paternal means, like Shippen, spent three to four years studying medicine, including midwifery, with leading physicians in the hospitals of London and the classrooms of Edinburgh. When they returned to the colonies they brought back not only a superior set of skills but also British ideas about hospitals, medical schools, and professional standards.

In the latter part of the eighteenth century advanced medical training became available in North America. At the time of Shippen's return in 1762 there was only one hospital in the colonies, the Pennsylvania Hospital, built ten years earlier to care for the sick poor. Shippen and his London-educated colleagues saw that the hospital could be used for the clinical training of physicians, as in Europe. Within three years the Philadelphia doctors, led by John Morgan, established formal, systematic instruction at a school of medicine, supplemented by clinical work in the hospital. Morgan maintained that the growth of the colonies "called aloud" for a medical school "to increase the number of those who exercise the profession of medicine and surgery." Dr. Samuel Bard successfully addressed the same argument to the citizens of New York in 1768.

In addition to promoting medical schools, Morgan and Bard defined the proper practitioner of medicine as a man learned in science. To languages and liberal arts their ideal physician added anatomy, material medicine, botany, chemistry, and clinical experience. He was highly conscious not only of his duty to preserve "the life and health of mankind," but

also of his professional status, and this new emphasis on professionalism extended to midwifery.

The trustees of the first American medical schools recognized midwifery as a branch of medical science. From its founding in 1768, Kings College in New York devoted one professorship solely to midwifery, and the University of Pennsylvania elected Shippen professor of anatomy, surgery, and midwifery in 1791. By 1807 five reputable American medical schools provided courses in midwifery. In the early years of the nineteenth century some professors of midwifery began to call themselves obstetricians or professors of obstetrics, a scientific-sounding title free of the feminine connotations of the word midwife. Though not compulsory for all medical students, the new field was considered worthy of detailed study along the paths pioneered by English physicians.

Dr. William Smellie contributed more to the development of obstetrics than any other eighteenth-century physician. His influence was established by his teaching career in London from 1741 to 1758, and by his treatise on midwifery, first published in 1752. Through precise measurement and observation Smellie discovered the mechanics of parturition. He found that the child's head turned throughout delivery, adapting the widest part to the widest diameter of the pelvic canal. Accordingly, he defined maneuvers for manipulating an improperly presented child. He also recognized that obstetrical forceps, generally known for only twenty years when he wrote in 1754, should be used to rectify the position of an infant wedged in the mouth of the cervix, in preference to the "common method" of simply jerking the child out. He perfected the design of the forceps and taught its proper use, so that physicians could save both mother and child in difficult deliveries, instead of being forced to dismember the infant with hooks.

To Smellie and the men who learned from him, the time seemed ripe to apply science to a field hitherto built on ignorance and supported by prejudice. Smellie commented on the novelty of scientific interest in midwifery. "We ought to be ashamed of ourselves," he admonished the readers of his *Treatise,* "for the little improvement we have made in so many centuries." Only recently have "we established a better method of delivering in laborious and preternatural cases."

Some American physicians shared this sense of the new "Importance of the Obstetrick Art." Midwifery was not a "trifling" matter to be left to the uneducated, Thomas Jones of the College of Medicine of Maryland wrote in 1812. Broadly defined as the care of "all the indispositions incident to women from the commencement of pregnancy to the termination of lactation," it ranked among the most important branches of medicine. "With the cultivation of this branch of science," women could now "reasonably look to men for safety in the perilous conditions" of childbirth.

Jones maintained, as did other physicians, that the conditions of modern urban life produced special need for scientific aid in childbirth. Both rich and poor women in large cities presented troublesome cases to the physician. Pelvic deformities, abortions, and tedious labors Jones considered common among wealthy urban women because of their indolent habits and confining fashionable dress, and among the poor because of inadequate diet and long hours of work indoors. There was, he believed, a greater need for "well informed obstetrick practitioners in large cities than in country places."

Although it cannot be established that there was an increase in difficult parturitions among urban women, social as well as medical reasons account for the innovations in the practice of midwifery in such cities as Boston, Philadelphia, and New York. Physicians received their medical education in cities, and cities offered the best opportunities to acquire patients and live comfortably. Urban families of some means could afford the $12 to $15 minimum fee which Boston physicians demanded for midwife services in 1806. Obstetrics was found to be a good way to establish a successful general practice. The man who conducted himself well in the lying-in room won the gratitude and confidence of his patient and her family, and they naturally called him to serve in other medical emergencies. It was midwifery, concluded Dr. Walter Channing of Boston, that ensured doctors "the permanency and security of all their other business."

The possibility of summoning a physician, who could perhaps insure a safer and faster delivery, opened first to urban women. The dramatic rescue of one mother and child given up by a midwife could be enough to convince a neighborhood of women of a physician's value, and secure him their practice. Doctors asserted that women increasingly hired physicians because they became convinced "that the well instructed physician is best calculated to avert danger and surmount difficulties." Certainly by 1795 the women of the Drinker family believed that none but a physician should order medicine for a woman in childbed, and had no doubts that Dr. Shippen or his colleague Dr. Nicholas Way was the best help that they could summon.

Although she accepted a male physician as midwife, Elizabeth Drinker still had reservations about the use of instruments to facilitate childbirth and was relieved when Shippen did not have to use forceps on her daughter. Other women feared to call a physician because they assumed that any instruments he used would destroy the child. However, once the capabilities of obstetrical forceps became known, some women may have turned to them by choice in hope of faster deliveries. Such hope stimulated a medical fashion. By about 1820 Dewees and

Bard felt it necessary to condemn nervous young doctors from resorting unnecessarily to forceps.

The formal education of American physicians and the development of midwifery as a science, the desire of women for the best help in childbirth, the utility of midwifery as a means of building a physician's practice, and ultimately, the gigantic social changes labeled urbanization explain why physicians assumed the ordinary practice of midwifery among well-to-do urban women in the late eighteenth and early nineteenth centuries. This development provides insight into the changing condition of women in American society.

The development of obstetrics signified a partial rejection of the assumption that women had to suffer in childbirth and implied a new social appreciation of women, as admonitions to women for forbearance under the pain of labor turned to the desire to relieve their pain. Thus did Dr. Thomas Denman explain his life's work: "The law of a religion founded on principles of active benevolence, feelings of humanity, common interests of society, and special tenderness for women" demanded that men search for a method by which women might be conducted safely through childbirth. In his doctoral dissertation in 1812 one American medical student drew a distinction between childbirth in primitive societies and his own. In the former, "women are generally looked on by their rugged lords as unworthy of any particular attention," and death or injury in childbirth is "not deemed a matter of any importance." Well-instructed assistants to women in childbirth were one sign of the value placed on women in civilized societies.

The desire to relieve women in childbirth also signified a more liberal interpretation of scripture. At the University of Pennsylvania in 1804, Peter Miller, a medical student, modified the theological dictum that women must bear in sorrow. The anxieties of pregnancy and the anguish caused by the death of so many infants constituted sorrows enough for women, argued Miller. They did not need to be subjected to bodily pain as well. Reiterating this argument, Dewees bluntly asked, "Why should the female alone incur the penalty of God?" To relieve the pain of labor Dewees and his fellows analyzed the anatomy and physiology of childbirth and defined techniques for use of instruments.

If the development of obstetrics suggests the rise of a "special tenderness for women" on the part of men, it also meant that women's participation in medical practice was diminished and disparaged. A few American physicians instructed midwives or wrote manuals for them, but these efforts were private and sporadic, and had ceased by 1820. The increasing professionalization of medicine, in the minds of the physicians who formed medical associations that set the standards of the field, left little room for female midwives, who lacked the prescribed measure of scientific training and identity.

William Shippen initially invited midwives as well as medical students to attend his private courses in midwifery. His advertisement in the *Pennsylvania Gazette* in January 1765 related his experience assisting women in the country in difficult labors, "most of which was made so by the unskillful old women about them," and announced that he "thought it his duty to immediately begin" courses in midwifery "in order to instruct those women who have virtue enough to own their ignorance and apply for instructions, as well as those young gentlemen now engaged in the study of that useful and necessary branch of surgery." Shippen taught these private lessons until after the Revolution, when he lectured only to students at the University of Pennsylvania, who, of course, were male.

At the turn of the century Dr. Valentine Seaman conducted the only other known formal instruction of midwives. He was distressed by the ignorance of many midwives, yet convinced that midwives ought to manage childbirth because, unlike physicians, they had time to wait out lingering labors, and, as women, they could deal easily with female patients. In 1817 Dr. Thomas Ewell proposed that midwives be trained at a national school of midwifery in Washington, D.C., to be supported by a collection taken up by ministers. There is no evidence that Ewell's scheme, presented in his medical manual, *Letters to Ladies,* ever gained a hearing.

Seaman and Ewell, and other authors of midwives' manuals, presumed that if women mastered some of the fundamentals of obstetrics they would be desirable assistants in ordinary midwifery cases. In 1820 Dr. Channing of Boston went further in his pamphlet, *Remarks on the Employment of Females as Practitioners of Midwifery,* in which he maintained that no one could thoroughly understand the management of labor who did not understand "thoroughly the profession of medicine as a whole." Channing's principle would have totally excluded women from midwifery, because no one favored professional medical education for women. It was generally assumed that they could not easily master the necessary languages, mathematics, and chemistry, or withstand the trials of dissecting room and hospital. Channing added that women's moral character disqualified them for medical practice: "Their feelings of sympathy are too powerful for the cool exercise of judgement" in medical emergencies, he wrote; "they do not have the power of action, nor the active power of mind which is essential to the practice of the surgeon."

Denied formal medical training, midwives of the early nineteenth century could not claim any other professional or legal status. Unlike Great Britain, the United States had no extensive record of licensing laws or oaths defining the practice of midwifery. Nor were there any vocal groups of midwives who, conscious of their tradition of practice or associated with lying-in hospitals, were able to defend themselves against competition from physicians. American midwives ceased practice among women of social rank with few words uttered in their defense.

The victory of the physicians produced its own problems. The doctor's sex affected the relationships between women and their attendants in childbirth, and transformed the atmosphere of the lying-in room. In his advice to his male students Dewees acknowledged that summoning a man to assist at childbed "cost females a severe struggle." Other doctors knew that even the ordinary gynecologic services of a physician occasioned embarrassment and violated woman's "natural delicacy of feeling," and that every sensitive woman felt "deeply humiliated" at the least bodily exposure. Doctors recognized an almost universal repugnance on the part of women to male assistance in time of labor. Because of "whim or false delicacy" women often refused to call a man until their condition had become critical.

The uneasiness of women who were treated by men was sometimes shared by their husbands. In 1772 the *Virginia Gazette* printed a denunciation of male midwifery as immoral. The author, probably an Englishman, attributed many cases of adultery in England to the custom of employing men at deliveries. Even in labor a woman had intervals of ease, and these, he thought, were the moments when the doctor infringed on the privileges of the husband. It would be a matter of utmost indifference to him "whether my wife had spent the night in a bagnio, or an hour of the forenoon locked up with a man midwife in her dressing room." Such arguments were frequently and seriously raised in England during the eighteenth century. They may seem ludicrous, but at least one American man of Dr. Ewell's acquaintance suffered emotional conflict over hiring a male midwife. He sent for a physician to help his wife in labor, yet "very solemnly he declared to the doctor, he would demolish him if he touched or looked at his wife."

Physicians dealt with embarrassment of patients and the suspicion of husbands by observing the drawing-room behavior of "well-bred gentlemen." Dewees told his students to "endeavor, by well chosen conversation, to divert your patient's mind from the purpose of your visit." All questions of a delicate nature were to be communicated through a third party, perhaps the only other person in the room, either a nurse or an elderly friend or relative. The professional man was advised "never to seem to know anything about the parts of generation, further than that there is an orifice near the rectum leading to an os."

Physicians did not perform vaginal examinations unless it was absolutely important to do so, and they often had to cajole women into permitting an examination at all. Nothing could be more shocking to a woman, Shippen lectured his students, "than for a young man the moment he enters the Chamber to ask for Pomatum and proceed to examine the uterus." Doctors waited until a labor pain clutched their patients and then suggested an examination by calling it "taking a pain." During examination and delivery the patient lay completely covered in her bed, a posture more modest, if less comfortable, than squatting on a pallet or a birth stool. The light in the room was dimmed by closing the shutters during the day and covering the lamps at night. If a physician used forceps, he had to manipulate them under the covers, using his free hand as a guide. On this point doctors who read Thomas Denman's *Obstetrical Remembrancer* were reminded that "Degorges, one of the best obstetricians of his time, was blind."

The crowd of supportive friends and family disappeared with the arrival of the doctor. The physician guarded against "too many attendants; where there are women, they must talk." The presence of other women might increase the doctor's nervousness, and they certainly did not help the woman in labor. Medical men interpreted women's talk of other experiences with childbirth as mere gossip "of all the dangerous and difficult labours they ever heard any story about in their lives," which ought to be stopped lest it disturb the patient. Especially distracting were the bawdy stories visitors told, expecting the physician to laugh, too. Medical professors recommended "grave deportment," warning that levity would "hurt your patient or yourself in her esteem." Far from providing the consolation of a friend, the physician was often a stranger who needed to "get a little acquainted" with his patient. One medical text went so far as to coach him in a series of conversational ice breakers about children and the weather.

Etiquette and prudery in the lying-in chamber affected medical care. Physicians were frustrated by their inability to examine their patients thoroughly, for they knew full well that learning midwifery from a book was "like learning shipbuilding without touching timber." Examinations were inadequate, and the dangers of manipulating instruments without benefit of sight were tremendous. Dewees cautioned his students to take great care before pulling the forceps that "no part of the mother is included in the locking of the blades. This accident is frequent." Accidental mutilation of the infant was also reported, as the navel string had to be cut under the covers. Lecturers passed on the story of the incautious doctor who included the penis of an infant within the blades of his scissors.

In view of such dangers, the conflict between social values and medical practice is striking. The expansion of medical knowledge brought men and women face to face with social taboos in family life. They had to ask themselves the question, Who should watch a woman give birth? For centuries the answer had unhesitatingly been female relatives and friends, and the midwife. The science of obstetrics, developing in the eighteenth century, changed the answer. Though women might socially be the most acceptable assistants at a delivery, men were potentially more useful.

In consequence of the attendance of male physicians, by 1825, for some American women, childbirth was ceasing to be an open ceremony. Though birth still took place at home, and though friends and relatives still lent a helping hand, visiting women no longer dominated the activities in the lying-in room. Birth became increasingly a private affair conducted in a quiet, darkened room. The physician limited visitors because they hindered proper medical care, but the process of birth was also concealed because it embarrassed both patient and physician.

Between 1760 and 1825 childbirth was thus transformed from an open affair to a restricted one. As one consequence of the development of obstetrics as a legitimate branch of medicine, male physicians began replacing midwives. They began to reduce childbirth to a scientifically managed event and deprived it of its folk aspects. Strengthened by the professionalization of their field, these physicians also responded to the hopes of women in Philadelphia, New York and Boston for safe delivery. Although they helped some pregnant women, they hurt midwives, who were shut out of an area of medicine that had been traditionally their domain. All these innovations took place in the large urban centers in response to distinctly urban phenomena. They reflected the increasing privatization of family life, and they foreshadowed mid-nineteenth-century attitudes toward childbirth, mother, and woman.

Questions for Study and Review

1. Compare the domestic scenes described by Kerber with those described by Scholten. What might have happened when revolutionary activity and childbirth intersected in the same household?

2. In Europe and to some extent in the colonies, midwives were often accused of practicing witchcraft. What traits and practices of midwives might have led to such accusations?

3. What new insights does the replacement of midwives with physicians provide in terms of the effect of the Revolution on women, as midwives or mothers?

4. From the mid-nineteenth century through the early decades of the twentieth, numerous occupations—such as teacher, store clerk, librarian, and secretary—once filled almost exclusively by men would be redefined as "women's work." What does the redefinition of obstetrics as "men's work" tell us about the circumstances that lead to such changes in the sexual division of labor?

Suggested Readings

Judith Walzer Leavitt, *Brought to Bed: Child-bearing in America, 1750–1950* (1986).

Jane B. Donegan, *Women and Men Midwives: Medicine, Morality and Misogyny in Early America* (1978).

Sylvia Hoffert, *Private Matters: American Attitudes Toward Childbearing and Infant Nurture in the Urban North, 1800–1860* (1988).

SIX

The Modernization of Greenleaf and Abigail Patch: Land, Family, and Marginality in the New Republic

Paul E. Johnson

Individuals, families, and communities reacted differently to the economic and social changes of the postrevolutionary era. Battles over hard currency and increased taxes led some to active resistance, as in Shays's Rebellion and the Whisky Rebellion. Most citizens, however, like Greenleaf and Abigail Patch, sought to adapt to new conditions, hoping for the break that would send them on their way to financial security and a better life.

Uprooted from family and community by the death of parents, a failure to inherit land, and an inability to succeed at his trade of shoemaking, Greenleaf Patch almost did find through marriage the stability that had earlier eluded him. Alternating between agrarian, artisan, and industrial pursuits, however, he never achieved the success that seemed within his grasp. Abigail, whose upbringing prepared her to labor alongside but not in place of her husband, was perhaps fortunate to live in an era when a woman and her daughters could find in factories the means of supporting themselves. Yet she was no feminist foremother, seeking liberation from family claims. Rather, only a deep religious faith seems to have carried her through the economic trials and personal tragedies of a life filled with anxiety and disappointment.

Through a detailed portrait of a couple considered unremarkable in their own day, Paul Johnson demonstrates the halting first steps in what would one day culminate in a full-blown "industrial revolution." The social and economic transformations that began the process are here described as a series of disjointed and often disruptive modifications in the opportunities and expectations available to those living on the margins of society. Limited in their choices and often unaware of the consequences resulting from them, husbands and wives, parents and children, sons and daughters might suddenly find their places in the family and community significantly altered, even reversed.

When Alexander Hamilton called for women to enter factories or Thomas Jefferson for men to stay on farms, both seemed to envision stable and prosperous families in which men were breadwinners and women helpmates. Johnson shows that such a life was not obtainable by those Americans for whom economic upheaval coincided with other disruptions wrought by war and its aftermath—indebtedness, transiency, premarital pregnancy, alcoholism. Though in the midnineteenth century, as Thomas Dublin will show, farmers' daughters did finally live out Hamilton's dream, industrialization continued to subvert as often as it supported individual prosperity and familial stability.

This is the story of Mayo Greenleaf Patch and Abigail McIntire Patch, ordinary people who helped write a decisive chapter in American history: they were among the first New Englanders to abandon farming and take up factory labor. They did so because rural society had no room for them, and their history is a tale of progressive exclusion from an agrarian world governed by family, kinship, and inherited land. Mayo Greenleaf Patch was the youngest son of a man who owned a small farm. He inherited nothing, and in his early and middle years he improvised a living at the edges of the family economy. He grew up with an uncle and brother, combined farming and shoemaking with dependence on his wife's family in the 1790s, recruited a half-sister into schemes against his in-laws' property, then lived briefly off an inheritance from a distant relative. Finally, having used up his exploitable kin connections, he left the countryside and moved to a mill town in which his wife and children could support the family.

That is how Greenleaf and Abigail Patch made the journey from farm to factory. But they experienced their troubles most intimately as members of a family; their story can be comprehended only as family history. Greenleaf Patch was a failed patriarch. His marriage to Abigail McIntire began with an early pregnancy, was punctuated by indebtedness and frequent moves, and ended in alcoholism and a divorce. Along the way, a previously submissive Abigail began making decisions for the family, decisions that were shaped by an economic situation in which she but not her husband found work and by her midlife conversion into a Baptist church.

The outlines of the Patch family history are familiar, for recent scholarship on New England in the century following 1750 centers on its principal themes: the crisis of the rural social order in the eighteenth century, the beginnings of commercial and industrial society in the nineteenth, and transformations in personal and family life that occurred in transit between the two. The Patches shared even the particulars of their story—disinheritance, premarital pregnancy, alcoholism, transiency, indebtedness, divorce, female religious conversion—with many of their neighbors. In short, Abigail and Greenleaf Patch lived at the center of a decisive social transformation and experienced many of its defining events.

The story of the Patches throws light on the process whereby farmers in post-Revolutionary New England became "available" for work outside of agriculture. That light, however, is dim and oblique, and we must confront two qualifications at the outset. First, the Patches were obscure people who left incomplete traces of their lives. Neither Greenleaf nor Abigail kept a diary or wrote an autobiography, their names never appeared in newspapers, and no one bothered to save their mail. Apart from one rambling and inaccurate family reminiscence, their story must be reconstructed from distant, impersonal and fragmentary sources: wills and deeds, church records, tax lists, censuses, the minutes of town governments, court records, and histories of the towns in which they lived and the shoe and textile industries in which they worked. The results are not perfect. The broad outlines of the story can be drawn with confidence, and a few episodes emerge in fine-grained detail. But some crucial points must rest on controlled inference, others on inferences that are a little less controlled, still others on outright guesswork. Scholars who demand certainty should

From "The Modernization of Mayo Greenleaf Patch: Land, Family, and Marginality in New England, 1766–1818" by Paul E. Johnson, *The New England Quarterly*, vol. LV, no. 4, December 1982. Reprinted by permission of *The New England Quarterly* and the author.

stay away from people like Greenleaf and Abigail Patch. But historians of ordinary individuals must learn to work with the evidence that they left behind.

A second qualification concerns the problems of generalizing from a single case. It must be stated strongly that the Patches were not typical. No one really is. The Patches, moreover, can claim uniqueness, for they were the parents of Sam Patch, a millworker who earned national notoriety in the 1820s as a professional daredevil. The younger Patch's life was an elaborate exercise in self-destruction, and we might question the normality of the household in which he grew up. Indeed the history of the Patch family is shot through with brutality and eccentricity and with a consistent sadness that is all its own. The Patches were not typical but marginal, and that is the point: it was persons who were marginal to rural society who sought jobs outside of agriculture. The number of such persons grew rapidly in post-Revolutionary New England. This is the story of two of them.

✳

New England men of Greenleaf Patch's generation grew up confronting two uncomfortable facts. The first was the immense value that their culture placed on ownership of land. Freehold tenure conferred not only economic security but personal and moral independence, the ability to support and govern a family, political rights, and the respect of one's neighbors and oneself. New Englanders trusted the man who owned land; they feared and despised the man who did not. The second fact was that in the late eighteenth century increasing numbers of men owned no land. Greenleaf Patch was among them.

Like nearly everyone else in Revolutionary Massachusetts, Patch was descended from yeoman stock. His family had come to Salem in 1636, and they operated a farm in nearby Wenham for more than a century. The Patches were church members and farm owners, and their men served regularly in the militia and in town offices. Greenleaf's father, grandfather, and great-grandfather all served terms as selectmen of Wenham; his great-grandfather was that community's representative to the Massachusetts General Court; his older brother was a militiaman who fought on the first day of the American Revolution.

The Patches commanded respect among their neighbors, but in the eighteenth century their future was uncertain. Like thousands of New England families, they owned small farms and had many children; by mid-century it was clear that young Patch men would not inherit the material standards enjoyed by their fathers. The farm on which Greenleaf Patch was born was an artifact of that problem. His father, Timothy Patch, Jr., had inherited a house, an eighteen-acre farm, and eleven acres of outlying meadow and woodland upon his own father's death in 1751. Next door, Timothy's younger brother Samuel farmed the remaining nine acres of what had been their father's homestead. The father had known that neither Timothy nor Samuel could make a farm of what he had, and he required that they share resources. His will granted Timothy access to a shop and cider mill that lay on Samuel's land and drew the boundary between the two farms through the only barn on the property. It was the end of the line: further subdivision would make both farms unworkable.

Timothy Patch's situation was precarious, and he made it worse by overextending himself, both as a landholder and as a father. Timothy was forty-three years old when he inherited his farm, and he was busy buying pieces of woodland, upland, and meadow all over Wenham. Evidently he speculated in marginal land and/or shifted from farming to livestock raising. He financed his schemes on credit, and he bought on a fairly large scale. By the early 1760s Timothy Patch held title to 114 acres, nearly all of it in small plots of poor land.

Timothy Patch may have engaged in speculation in order to provide for an impossibly large number of heirs. Timothy was the father of ten children when he inherited his farm. In succeeding years he was widowed, remarried, and sired two more daughters and a son. In all, he fathered ten children who survived to adulthood. The youngest was a son born in 1766. Timothy named him Mayo Greenleaf.

Greenleaf Patch's life began badly: his father went bankrupt in the year of his birth. Timothy had transferred the house and farm to his two oldest sons in the early 1760s, possibly to keep the property out of the hands of creditors. Then, in 1766, the creditors began making trouble. In September Timothy relinquished twenty acres of his outlying land to satisfy a debt. By March 1767, having lost five court cases and sold all of his remaining land to pay debts and court costs, he was preparing to leave Wenham. Timothy's first two sons stayed on, but both left Wenham before their deaths, and none of the other children established households in the community. After a century as substantial farmers and local leaders, the Patch family abandoned their hometown.

Greenleaf Patch was taken from his home village as an infant, and his family's wanderings after that can be traced only through his father's appearances in court. By 1770 the family had moved a few miles north and west to Andover, where Timothy was sued by yet another creditor. Nine years later Timothy Patch was in Danvers, where he went to court seven times in three years. The court cases suggest that the family experienced drastic ups and downs. Some cases involved substantial amounts of money, but in the last, Timothy was accused of stealing firewood. He then left Danvers and moved to Nottingham West, New

Hampshire. There Timothy seems to have recouped his fortunes once again, for in 1782 he was a gambler-investor in an American Revolutionary privateer.

That is all we know about the Patch family during the childhood of Mayo Greenleaf Patch. About the childhood itself we know nothing. Doubtless Greenleaf shared his parents' frequent moves and their bouts of good and bad luck, and from his subsequent behavior we might conclude that he inherited his father's penchant for economic adventurism. He may also have spent parts of his childhood and youth in other households. Since he later named his own children after relatives in Wenham, he probably lived there in the families of his brother and uncle. We know also that during his youth he learned how to make shoes, and since his first independent appearance in the record came when he was twenty-one, we might guess that he served a formal, live-in apprenticeship. Even these points, however, rest on speculation. Only this is certain: Greenleaf Patch was the tenth and youngest child of a family that broke and scattered in the year of his birth, and he entered adulthood alone and without visible resources.

In 1787 Mayo Greenleaf Patch appeared in the Second (North) Parish of Reading, Massachusetts—fifteen miles due north of Boston. He was twenty-one years old and unmarried, and he owned almost nothing. He had no relatives in Reading; indeed no one named Patch had ever lived in that town. In a world where property was inherited and where kinfolk were essential social and economic assets, young Greenleaf Patch inherited nothing and lived alone.

Greenleaf's prospects in 1787 were not promising. But he soon took steps to improve them. In July 1788 he married Abigail McIntire in Reading. He was twenty-two years old; she was seventeen and pregnant. This early marriage is most easily explained as an unfortunate accident. But from the viewpoint of Greenleaf Patch it was not unfortunate at all, for it put him into a family that possessed resources that his own family had lost. For the next twelve years, Patch's livelihood and ambitions would center on the McIntires and their land.

The McIntires were Scots, descendants of highlanders who had been exiled to Maine after the Battle of Dunbar. Some had walked south, and Philip McIntire was among those who pioneered the North Parish in the 1650s. By the 1780s McIntire households were scattered throughout the parish. Archelaus McIntire, Abigail's father, headed the most prosperous of those households. Archelaus had been the eldest son of a man who died without a will, and he inherited the family farm intact. He added to the farm and by 1791 owned ninety-seven acres in Reading and patches of meadowland in two neighboring townships, a flock of seventeen sheep as well as cattle and oxen and other animals, and personal property that indicates comfort and material decency if not wealth. Of 122 taxable estates in the North Parish in 1792, Archelaus McIntire's ranked twenty-third.

In 1788 Archelaus McIntire learned that his youngest daughter was pregnant and would marry Mayo Greenleaf Patch. No doubt he was angry, but he had seen such things before. One in three Massachusetts women of Abigail's generation was pregnant on her wedding day, a statistic to which the McIntires had contributed amply. Archelaus himself had been born three months after his parents' marriage in 1729. One of his older daughters had conceived a child at the age of fourteen, and his only son would marry a pregnant lover in 1795.

Faced with yet another early pregnancy, Archelaus McIntire determined to make the best of a bad situation. In the winter of 1789/90, he built a shoemaker's shop and a small house for Greenleaf Patch and granted him use of the land on which they sat. At a stroke, Patch

was endowed with family connections and economic independence.

Greenleaf Patch took his place among the farmer-shoemakers of northeastern Massachusetts in 1790. The region had been exporting shoes since before the Revolution, for it possessed the prerequisites of cottage industry in abundance: it was poor and overcrowded and had access to markets through Boston and the port towns of Essex County. With the Revolution and the protection of footwear under the first national tariffs, with the expansion of the maritime economy of which the shoe trade was a part, and with the continuing growth of rural poverty, thousands of farm families turned to the making of shoes in the 1790s.

Their workshops were not entrepreneurial ventures. Neither, if we listen to the complaints of merchants and skilled artisans about "slop work" coming out of the countryside, were they likely sources of craft traditions or occupational pride. The trade was simply the means by which farmers on small plots of worn-out land maintained their independence.

The journal of Isaac Weston, a Reading shoemaker during the 1790s, suggests something of the cottage shoemaker's way of life. Weston was first and last a farmer. He spent his time worrying about the weather, working his farm, repairing his house and outbuildings, and trading farm labor with his neighbors and relatives. His tasks accomplished, he went hunting with his brothers-in-law, took frequent fishing trips to the coast at Lynn, and made an endless round of social calls in the neighborhood. The little shop at the back of Weston's house supplemented his earnings, and he spent extended periods of time in it only during the winter months. With his bags of finished shoes, he made regular trips to Boston, often in company with other Reading shoemakers. The larger merchants did not yet dominate the trade in country shoes, and Weston and his neighbors went from buyer to buyer bargaining as a group and came home with enough money to purchase leather, pay debts and taxes, and subsist for another year as farmers.

Isaac Weston's workshop enabled him to survive as an independent proprietor. At the same time, it fostered relations of neighborly cooperation with other men. He was the head of a self-supporting household and an equal participant in neighborhood affairs; in eighteenth-century Massachusetts, those criteria constituted the definition of manhood. Mayo Greenleaf Patch received that status as a wedding present.

Greenleaf and Abigail occupied the new house and shop early in 1790, and their tax listings over the next few years reveal a rise from poverty to self-sufficiency with perhaps a little extra. In 1790, for the first time, Greenleaf paid the tax on a small piece of land. Two years later he ranked fifty-sixth among the 122 taxpayers in the North Parish. Patch was not getting rich, but he enjoyed a secure place in the economy of his neighborhood. That alone was a remarkable achievement for a young stranger who had come to town with almost nothing.

With marriage and proprietorship came authority over a complex and growing household. Few rural shoemakers in the 1790s worked alone; they hired outside help and put their wives and children to work binding shoes. Isaac Weston brought in apprentices and journeymen, and Greenleaf Patch seems to have done the same. In 1790 the Patch family included Greenleaf and Abigail and their infant daughter, along with a boy under the age of sixteen and an unidentified adult male. In 1792 Patch paid the tax on two polls, suggesting that again the household included an adult male dependent. It seems clear that Greenleaf hired outsiders and (assuming Abigail helped) regularly headed a family work team that numbered at least four persons.

During the same years, Patch won the respect of the McIntires and their neighbors.

When Archelaus McIntire died in 1791, his will named Patch executor of the estate. Greenleaf spent considerable effort, including two successful appearances in court, ordering his father-in-law's affairs. In 1794 he witnessed a land transaction involving his brother-in-law, again indicating that he was a trusted member of the McIntire family. That trust was shared by the neighbors. In 1793 the town built a schoolhouse near the Patch home, and in 1794 and 1795 the parish paid Greenleaf Patch for boarding the schoolmistress and for escorting her home at the end of the term. Those were duties that could only have gone to a trusted neighbor who ran an orderly house.

✳

Greenleaf Patch's marriage to Abigail McIntire rescued him from the shiftless and uncertain life that had been dealt to him at birth. In 1787 he was a propertyless wanderer. By the early 1790s, he was the head of a growing family, a useful member of the McIntire clan, and a familiar and trusted neighbor. Greenleaf Patch had found a home. But his gains were precarious, for they rested on the use of land that belonged not to him but to his father-in-law. When Archelaus died, the title to the McIntire properties fell to his nineteen-year-old son, Archelaus, Jr. Young Archelaus was bound out to a guardian, and Patch, as executor of the estate, began to prey openly on the resources of Abigail's family. In succeeding years bad luck and moral failings would cost him everything that he had gained.

With Archelaus McIntire dead and his son living with a guardian, the household that the senior Archelaus had headed shrank to two women: his widow and his daughter Deborah. The widow described herself as an invalid, and there may have been something wrong with Deborah as well. In the will that he wrote in 1791, Archelaus ordered that his heir take care of Deborah. His son would repeat that order ten years later, when Deborah, still unmarried and still living at home, was thirty-five years old. Shortly after the death of Archelaus McIntire (and shortly before Patch was to inventory the estate), the widow complained to authorities that "considerable of my household goods & furniture have been given to my children" and begged that she be spared "whatever household furniture that may be left which is but a bare sufficiency to keep household." At that time two of her four daughters were dead, a third lived with her, and her only son was under the care of a guardian. The "children" could have been none other than Greenleaf and Abigail Patch, whose personal property taxes mysteriously doubled between 1791 and 1792. Greenleaf Patch had walked into a house occupied by helpless women and walked off with the furniture.

Patch followed this with a second and more treacherous assault on the McIntires and their resources. In November 1793 Archelaus McIntire, Jr. came of age and assumed control of the estate. Greenleaf's use of McIntire land no longer rested on his relationship with his father-in-law or his role as executor but on the whim of Archelaus, Jr. Patch took steps that would tie him closely to young Archelaus and his land. Those steps involved a woman named Nancy Barker, who moved into Reading sometime in 1795. Mrs. Barker had been widowed twice, the second time, apparently, by a Haverhill shoemaker who left her with his tools and scraps of leather, a few valueless sticks of furniture, and two small children. Nancy Barker, it turns out, was the half-sister of Mayo Greenleaf Patch.

In November 1795 Nancy Barker married Archelaus McIntire, Jr. She was thirty-one years old. He had turned twenty-three the previous day, and his marriage was not a matter of choice: Nancy was four months pregnant. Archelaus and Nancy were an unlikely couple, and we must ask how the match came about. Archelaus had grown up with three older

sisters and no brothers; his attraction and/or vulnerability to a woman nearly nine years his senior is not altogether mysterious. Nancy, of course, had sensible reasons for being attracted to Archelaus. She was a destitute widow with two children, and he was young, unmarried, and the owner of substantial property. Finally, Greenleaf Patch, who was the only known link between the two, had a vital interest in creating ties between his family and his in-law's land. It would be plausible—indeed it seems inescapable—to conclude that Nancy Barker, in collusion with her half-brother, had seduced young Archelaus McIntire and forced a marriage.

Of course, that may be nothing more than perverse speculation. Nancy and Archelaus may simply have fallen in love, started a baby, and married. Whatever role Greenleaf Patch played in the affair may have added to his esteem among the McIntires and in the community. That line of reasoning, however, must confront an unhappy fact: in 1795 the neighbors and the McIntires began to dislike Mayo Greenleaf Patch.

The first sign of trouble came in the fall of 1795, when town officials stepped into a boundary dispute between Patch and Deacon John Swain. Massachusetts towns encouraged neighbors to settle arguments among themselves. In all three parishes of Reading in the 1790s, only three disagreements over boundaries came before the town government, and one of those was settled informally. Thus Greenleaf Patch was party to half of Reading's mediated boundary disputes in the 1790s. The list of conflicts grew: after 1795 the schoolmistress was moved out of the Patch household; in 1797 Patch complained that he had been overtaxed (another rare occurrence), demanded a reassessment, and was reimbursed. Then he started going to court. In 1798 Greenleaf Patch sued Thomas Tuttle for nonpayment of a debt and was awarded nearly $100 when Tuttle failed to appear. A few months earlier, Patch had been hauled into court by William Herrick, a carpenter who claimed that Patch owed him $480. Patch denied the charge and hired a lawyer; the court found in his favor, but Herrick appealed the case, and a higher court awarded him $100.52. Six years later, Patch's lawyer was still trying to collect his fee.

There is also a question about land. In the dispute with John Swain, the description of Patch's farm matches none of the properties described in McIntire deeds. We know that Patch no longer occupied McIntire land in 1798, and town records identified him as the "tenant" of his disputed farm in 1795. Perhaps as early as 1795, Patch had been evicted from McIntire land.

Finally, there is clear evidence that the authorities had stopped trusting Mayo Greenleaf Patch. Nancy Barker McIntire died in 1798 at the age of thirty-four. Archelaus remarried a year later, then died suddenly in 1801. His estate—two houses and the ninety-seven-acre farm, sixty acres of upland and meadow in Reading, and fifteen acres in the neighboring town of Lynnfield—was willed to his two children by Nancy Barker. Archelaus's second wife sold her right of dower and left town, and the property fell to girls who were four and five years of age. Their guardian would have use of the land for many years. By this time Greenleaf and Abigail Patch had moved away, but surely authorities knew their whereabouts and that they were the orphans' closest living relatives. Yet the officials passed them over and appointed a farmer from Reading as legal guardian. The court, doubtless with the advice of the neighbors, had decided against placing Greenleaf Patch in a position of trust. For Patch it was a costly decision. It finally cut him off from property that he had occupied and plotted against for many years.

Each of these facts and inferences says little by itself, but together they form an unmistakable pattern: from the date of his marriage through the mid-1790s, Greenleaf Patch accu-

mulated resources and participated in the collective life of Abigail's family and neighborhood; from 1795 onward he entered the record only when he was fighting the neighbors or being shunned by the family. The promising family man of the 1790s was a contentious and morally bankrupt outcast by 1798.

Late in 1799 or early in 1800 Greenleaf and Abigail and their four children left Reading and resettled in Danvers, a community of farmer-shoemakers on the outskirts of Salem. We cannot know why they selected that town, but their best connection with the place came through Abigail. Danvers was her mother's birthplace, and she had an aunt and uncle, five first cousins, and innumerable distant relatives in the town. Indeed Abigail's father had owned land in Danvers. In 1785 Archelaus McIntire, Sr. had seized seven acres from John Felton, one of his in-laws, in payment of a debt. Archelaus, Jr. sold the land back to the Feltons in 1794 but did not record the transaction until 1799. Perhaps he made an arrangement whereby the Patches had use of the land. (Doubtless Archelaus was glad to be rid of Greenleaf Patch, but he may have felt some responsibility for his sister.)

Danvers was another shoemaking town, and the Patches probably rented a farm and made shoes. In 1800 the household included Greenleaf and Abigail, their children, and no one else, suggesting that they were no longer able to hire help. But this, like everything else about the family's career in Danvers, rests on inference. We know only that they were in Danvers and that they stayed three years.

Late in 1802 Greenleaf Patch received a final reprieve, again through family channels. His half-brother Job Davis (his mother's son by her first marriage) died in the fishing port of Marblehead and left Patch one-fifth of his estate. The full property included a butcher's shop at the edge of town, an unfinished new house, and what was described as a "mansion house" that needed repairs. The property,

In the postrevolutionary society that attached enormous value to land ownership, loss of land meant loss of status and respect. By the time the Patches reached the factory town of Pawtucket, they had been reduced to the circumstances depicted in this cartoon. Greenleaf abandoned his never-very-successful role as family breadwinner and turned to drink and theft. Abigail and her older children supported the family through work obtained from the town's textile mills. With her divorce from Greenleaf, Abigail exchanged a life characterized by male dominance and female subordination for one in which women became head of the household and family decision makers.

however, was mortgaged to the merchants William and Benjamin T. Reid. The survivors of Job Davis inherited the mortgage along with the estate.

The other heirs sold to the Reids without a struggle, but Greenleaf Patch, whether from demented ambition or lack of alternatives, moved his family to Marblehead early in 1803. He finished the new house and moved into it, reopened the butcher's shop, and ran up debts. Some of the debts were old. Patch owed Ebenezer Goodale of Danvers $54. He also owed Porter Sawyer of Reading $92 and paid a part of it by laboring at 75¢ a day. Then there were debts incurred in Marblehead: $70 to the widow Sarah Dolebar; a few dollars for building materials and furnishings bought from the

Reids; $50 to a farmer named Benjamin Burnham; $33 to Zachariah King of Danvers; $35 to Joseph Holt of Reading; another $35 to Caleb Totman of Hampshire County. Finally, there was the original mortgage held by the Reids.

Patch's renewed dreams of independence collapsed under the weight of his debts. In March 1803 a creditor repossessed the property up to a value of $150, and a few weeks before Christmas of the same year the sheriff seized the new house. In the following spring, Patch missed a mortgage payment, and Reids took him to court, seized the remaining property, and sold it at auction. Still, Patch retained the right to reclaim the property by paying his debts. The story ends early in 1805, when the Reids bought Greenleaf Patch's right of redemption for $60. Patch had struggled with the Marblehead property for two years, and all had come to nothing.

With this final failure, the Patches exhausted the family connections on which they had subsisted since their marriage. The long stay in Reading and the moves to Danvers and Marblehead were all determined by the availability of relatives and their resources. In 1807 the Patches resettled in Pawtucket, Rhode Island, the pioneer textile milling town in the United States. It was the climactic event in their history: it marked their passage out of the family economy and into the labor market.

When the family arrived in Pawtucket early in 1807, they found four textile mills surrounding the waterfall at the center of town. The mills were small and limited to the spinning of yarn, and much of the work was done by outworkers. Children picked and cleaned raw cotton in their homes, then sent it to the mills to be carded by other children. The cotton next went to the spinning rooms, where, with the help of water-driven machinery, a few skilled men, and still more children, it was turned into yarn. Millers put the yarn out to women, many of them widows with children, who wove it into cloth. There was thus plenty of work for Abigail and her older children, and it was they who supported the family in Pawtucket. Samuel, the second son, spent his childhood in the mills, and his sisters probably did the same. It is likely that Abigail worked as a weaver; certainly the wool produced on her father's farm suggests that she knew something about that trade.

That leaves only the father. Pawtucket was booming in 1807, and if Greenleaf Patch were willing and physically able, he could have found work. We know, however, that he did not work in that town. He drank, he stole the money earned by his wife and children, and he threatened them frequently with violence. Then, in 1812, he abandoned them. Abigail waited six years and divorced him in 1818. She re-

counted Greenleaf's drinking and his threats and his refusal to work, then revealed what for her was the determining blow: Greenleaf Patch had drifted back to Massachusetts and had been caught passing counterfeit money. In February 1817 he entered the Massachusetts State Prison at Charlestown. He was released the following August. Patch was fifty-two years old, and that is the last we hear of him.

❋

In a society that located virtue and respectability in the yeoman freeholder, Mayo Greenleaf Patch never owned land. We have seen some public consequences of that fact: his lifelong inability to attain material independence, the troubled relations with in-laws, neighbors, creditors, and legal authorities that resulted when he tried, and the personal and moral disintegration that accompanied unending economic distress.

Now we turn to private troubles, and here the story centers on Abigail McIntire Patch. Recent studies of late eighteenth- and early nineteenth-century family life have documented a decline of patriarchal authority, the creation of a separate and female-dominated domestic sphere, an increase in female religiosity, and, bound up with all three, the elevation of women's status and power within the home. Most of these studies center on middle- and upper-class women, and we are left to wonder whether the conclusions can be extended to women further down the social scale. In the case of Abigail Patch, they can: her story begins with patriarchy and ends with female control. In grotesque miniature, the history of the Patches is a story of the feminization of family life.

Abigail grew up in a family that, judged from available evidence, was ruled by her father. Archelaus McIntire owned a respected family name and a farm that he had inherited from his father and that he would pass on to his son; he was the steward of the family's past and future as well as its present provider. As a McIntire, he conferred status on every member of his household. As a voter he spoke for the family in town affairs; as a father and church member he led the family in daily prayers; and as a proprietor he made decisions about the allocation of family resources, handled relations with outsiders, and performed much of the heavy work.

Archelaus McIntire's wife and daughters were subordinate members of his household. He had married Abigail Felton of Danvers and had brought her to a town where she lived apart from her own family but surrounded by his; her status in Reading derived from her husband's family and not from her own. On the farm, she and her daughters spent long days cooking and cleaning, gardening, tending and milking cows, making cloth and clothing, and caring for the younger children—work that took place in and near the house and not on the farm. That work was essential, but New England men assumed that it would be done and attached no special importance to it. The notion of a separate and cherished domestic sphere was slow to catch on in the countryside, and if we may judge from the spending patterns of the McIntires, it played no role in their house. Archelaus McIntire spent his money on implements of work and male sociability— horses, wagons, well-made cider barrels, a rifle—and not on the china, tea sets, and feather beds that were appearing in towns and among the rural well-to-do. The McIntires owned a solid table and a Bible and a few other books, and there was a clock and a set of glassware as well. But the most valuable item of furniture in the house was Archelaus's desk. Insofar as the McIntires found time for quiet evenings at home, they probably spent them listening to the father read his Bible (the mother was illiterate) or keeping quiet while he figured his accounts.

As the fourth and youngest of Archelaus McIntire's daughters, Abigail had doubtless traded work and quiet subordination for security, for the status that went with being a female McIntire, perhaps even for peace and affection in the home. As she set up housekeeping with Mayo Greenleaf Patch, she doubtless did not expect things to change. Years later Abigail recalled that in taking a husband she wanted not a partner but "a friend and protector." For her part, Abigail spoke of her "duties" and claimed to have been an "attentive and affectionate wife." It was the arrangement that she had learned as a child: husbands protected their wives and supported them, wives worked and were attentive to their husbands' needs and wishes. All available evidence suggests that those rules governed the Patch household during the years in Reading.

Abigail and Greenleaf Patch maintained neither the way of life nor the standard of living necessary for the creation of a private sphere in which Abigail could have exercised independent authority. The house was small and there was little money, and the household regularly included persons from outside the immediate family. Greenleaf's apprentices and journeymen were in and out of the house constantly. For two summers the Patches boarded the schoolmistress, and Nancy Barker may have stayed with Greenleaf and Abigail before her marriage. With these persons present in hit-and-miss records, we may assume that outsiders were normal members of the Patch household.

At work, rural shoemakers maintained a rigid division of labor based on sex and age, and Greenleaf's authority was pervasive. Abigail's kitchen, if indeed it was a separate room, was a busy place. There she bound shoes as a semiskilled and subordinate member of her husband's work team, cared for the children (she gave birth five times between 1789 and 1799), did the cooking, cleaning, and laundry for a large household, and stared across the table at apprentices and journeymen who symbolized her own drudgery and her husband's authority at the same time. As Abigail Patch endured her hectic and exhausting days, she may have dreamed of wallpapered parlors and privacy and quiet nights by the fire with her husband. But she must have known that such things were for others and not for her. They had played little role in her father's house, and they were totally absent from her own.

Greenleaf Patch seems to have taken his authority as head of the household seriously. Available evidence suggests that he consistently made family decisions—not just the economic choices that were indisputably his to make but decisions that shaped the texture and meaning of life within the family.

Take the naming of the children. Greenleaf Patch was separated from his own family and dependent on McIntire resources, so when children came along we would expect him and Abigail to have honored McIntire relatives. That is not what happened. The first Patch child was a daughter born in 1789. The baby was named Molly, after a daughter of Greenleaf's brother Isaac. A son came two years later, and the Patches named him Greenleaf. Another daughter, born in 1794, was given the name Nabby, after another of Isaac Patch's daughters. A second son, born in 1798, was named for Greenleaf's uncle Samuel. That child died, and a son born the following year (the daredevil Sam Patch) received the same name. The last child was born in 1803 and was named for Greenleaf's brother Isaac. None of the six children was named for Abigail or a member of her family. Instead, all of the names came from the little world in Wenham—uncle Samuel's nine-acre farm, the shared barn and outbuildings, and the eighteen acres operated by brother Isaac—in which Greenleaf Patch presumably spent much of his childhood.

Religion is a second and more important sphere in which Patch seems to have made choices for the family. Abigail McIntire had grown up in a religious household. Her father had joined the North Parish Congregational Church a few days after the birth of his first child in 1762. Her mother had followed two months later, and the couple baptized each of their five children. The children in their turn became churchgoers. Abigail's sisters Mary and Mehitable joined churches, and her brother Archelaus, Jr. expressed a strong interest in religion as well. Among Abigail's parents and siblings, only the questionable Deborah left no religious traces.

Religious traditions in the Patch family were not as strong. Greenleaf's father and his first wife joined the Congregational church at Wenham during the sixth year of their marriage in 1736, but the family's ties to religion weakened after that. Timothy Patch, Jr. did not baptize any of his thirteen children, either the ten presented him by his first wife or the three born to Thomasine Greenleaf Davis, the nonchurchgoing widow whom he married in 1759. None of Greenleaf's brothers or sisters became full members of the church, and only his oldest brother Andrew owned the covenant, thus placing his family under the government of the church.

Among the Wenham Patches, however, there remained pockets of religiosity, and they centered, perhaps significantly, in the homes of Greenleaf's brother Isaac and his uncle Samuel. Uncle Samuel was a communicant of the church, and although Isaac had no formal religious ties, he married a woman who owned the covenant. The churchgoing tradition that Greenleaf Patch carried into marriage was thus ambiguous, but it almost certainly was weaker than that carried by his wife. And from his actions as an adult, we may assume that Greenleaf was not a man who would have been drawn to the religious life.

As Greenleaf and Abigail married and had children, the question of religion could not have been overlooked. The family lived near the church in which Abigail had been baptized and in which her family and her old friends spent Sunday mornings. As the wife of Greenleaf Patch, Abigail had three options: she could lead her husband into church; she could, as many women did, join the church without her husband and take the children with her; finally, she could break with the church and spend Sundays with an irreligious husband, The first two choices would assert Abigail's authority and independent rights within the family. The third would be a capitulation, and it would have painful results. It would cut her off from the religious community in which she had been born, and it would remove her young family from religious influence.

The Patches lived in Reading for twelve years and had five children there. Neither Greenleaf nor Abigail joined the church, and none of the babies was baptized. We cannot retrieve the actions and feelings that produced these facts, but this much is certain: in the crucial area of religious practice, the Patch family bore the stamp of Greenleaf Patch and not of Abigail McIntire. When Greenleaf and Abigail named a baby or chose whether to join a church or baptize a child, the decisions extended his family's history and not hers.

Abigail Patch accepted her husband's dominance in family affairs throughout the years in Reading, years in which he played, however ineptly and dishonestly, his role as "friend and protector." With his final separation from the rural economy and his humiliating failure in Marblehead, he abdicated that role. In Marblehead Abigail began to impose her will upon domestic decisions. The result, within a few years, would be a full-scale female takeover of the family.

In 1803 the sixth—and, perhaps significantly, the last—Patch child was baptized at Second Congregational Church in Marblehead. And in 1807, shortly after the move to Rhode Island, Abigail and her oldest daughter joined the First Baptist Church in Pawtucket. At that date Abigail was thirty-seven years old, had been married nineteen years, and had five living children. Her daughter Molly was eighteen years old and unmarried. Neither followed the customs of the McIntire or Patch families, where women who joined churches did so within a few years after marriage. Abigail and Molly Patch presented themselves for baptism in 1807 not because they had reached predictable points in their life cycles but because they had experienced religion and had decided to join a church.

At the same time (here was feminization with a vengeance) Abigail's daughters dropped their given names and evolved new ones drawn from their mother's and not their father's side of the family. The oldest daughter joined the church not as Molly but as Polly Patch. Two years later the same woman married under the name Mary Patch. Abigail's oldest sister, who had died in the year that Abigail married Greenleaf, had been named Mary. The second Patch daughter, Nabby, joined the Baptist church in 1811. At that time she was calling herself Abby Patch. By 1829 she was known as Abigail. The daughters of Abigail Patch, it seems, were affiliating with their mother and severing symbolic ties with their father. It should be noted that the father remained in the house while they did so.

In Pawtucket Abigail built a new family life that centered on her church and her female relatives. That life constituted a rejection not only of male dominance but of men. For five years Abigail worked and took the children to church while her husband drank, stole her money, and issued sullen threats. He ran off in 1812, and by 1820 Abigail, now officially head of the household, had rented a house and was taking in boarders. Over the next few years the Patch sons left home: Samuel for New Jersey, Isaac for the Northwest, Greenleaf for parts unknown. Abigail's younger daughter married and moved to Pittsburgh. Among the Patch children only Mary (Molly, Polly) stayed in Pawtucket. In 1825 Mary was caught committing adultery. Her husband left town, and Mary began calling herself a widow. Abigail closed the boardinghouse and moved into a little house on Main Street with Mary and her children sometime before 1830. She and her daughter and granddaughters would live in that house for the next quarter-century.

The neighbors remembered Abigail Patch as a quiet, steady little woman who attended the Baptist church. She did so with all of the Patch women. Mary had joined with her in 1807, and each of Mary's daughters followed in their turn: Mary and Sarah Anne in 1829, Emily in 1841. First Baptist was a grim and overwhelmingly female Calvinist church, subsidized and governed by the owners of Pawtucket's mills. The Articles of Faith insisted that most of humankind was hopelessly damned, that God chose only a few for eternal life and had in fact chosen them before the beginning of time, "and that in the flesh dwelleth no good thing." It was not a cheerful message. But it struck home among the Patch women.

Apart from the church, the women spent their time in the house on Main Street. Abigail bought the house in 1842—the first land that the Patches owned—and her granddaughters Mary and Emily taught school in the front room for many years. The household was self-supporting, and its membership was made up of women whose relations with men were either troubled or nonexistent. Abigail never remarried. We cannot know what preceded and surrounded the instance of adultery and the breakup of Mary's marriage, but she too remained single for the rest of her life. Sarah Anne Jones, one of the granddaughters, was thirty-six years old and unmarried when called before a church committee in 1853. Although she married a man named Kelley during the investigation, she was excommunicated "be-

cause she has given this church reason to believe she is licentious." Sarah Anne's sisters, the schoolteachers Mary and Emily, were spinsters all their lives. The lives of Abigail Patch and her daughter Mary Jones had been blighted by bad relations with men; the women whom they raised either avoided men or got into trouble when they did not. Abigail Patch lived on Main Street with the other women until 1854, when she died at the age of eighty-four.

We know little of what went on in that house. The women lived quietly, and former pupils remembered Abigail's granddaughters with affection. But beyond the schoolroom, in rooms inhabited only by the Patch women, there was a cloistered world. Within that world, Abigail and her daughter Mary reconstructed not only themselves but the history of their family.

Pawtucket celebrated its Cotton Centennial in 1890, and a Providence newspaperman decided to write about the millworker-hero Sam Patch. He asked Emily Jones, one of Abigail's aged granddaughters, about the Patch family history. Emily had been born after 1810, and her knowledge of the family's past was limited to what she had picked up from her mother and grandmother. Her response to the reporter demonstrated the selective amnesia with which any family remembers its history, but in this case the fabrications were sadly revealing.

Miss Jones told the newspaperman that her oldest uncle, Greenleaf Patch, Jr., had gone off to Salem and become a lawyer. That is demonstrably untrue. No one named Greenleaf Patch has ever been licensed to practice law in Massachusetts. About her uncle Sam Patch, Emily said: in the 1820s he operated a spinning mill of his own north of Pawtucket, but failed when his partner ran off with the funds; it was only then that he moved to New Jersey and became a daredevil. That too is a fabrication. What we know about Sam Patch is that he was an alcoholic with powerful suicidal drives, and that he succeeded in killing himself at the age of thirty. Miss Jones remembered that her youngest uncle, Isaac, moved to Illinois and became a farmer. That was true: in 1850 Isaac Patch was farming and raising a family near Peoria. It seems that Abigail Patch and Mary Patch Jones idealized the first two Patch sons by giving them successes and/or ambitions that they did not have. The third son was born in 1803 and grew up in a household dominated by Abigail and not by her dissipated husband; he became a family man. By inventing a similar ordinariness for the older sons, Abigail may have erased some of the history created by Mayo Greenleaf Patch.

Emily's memory of her grandfather provokes similar suspicions. We know that Greenleaf Patch lived in Pawtucket until 1812. But Miss Jones remembered that her grandfather had been a farmer in Massachusetts, and that he died before Abigail brought her family to Rhode Island. Greenleaf Patch, it seems, was absent from Abigail's house in more ways than one.

Questions for Study and Review

1. Analyze Hamilton's and Jefferson's plans for national development in light of the Patch family's history.

2. In what ways did Abigail Patch gain and demonstrate authority in the household as a result of the family's changing economic fortunes? Did she regard these as gains?

3. How did the options available to the Patch sons and daughters differ, and which were the most attractive alternatives for them?

4. In the late nineteenth and early twentieth centuries, mechanization would again transform women's labor, this time in both the factory and the household. Compare the advantages and disadvantages of this later period of technological change with those described by Johnson.

Suggested Readings

Nancy Cott, "Young Women and the Second Great Awakening in New England," *Feminist Studies* (Fall 1975).

Michael S. Hindus and Daniel Scott Smith, "Premarital Pregnancy in America, 1640–1971: An Overview and Interpretation," *Journal of Interdisciplinary History* (June 1975).

Cedric B. Cowing, "Sex and Preaching in the Great Awakening," *American Quarterly* (Fall 1968).

Daniel Lamar Jones, "The Strolling Poor: Transiency in Eighteenth Century Massachusetts," *Journal of Social History* (Spring 1975).

PART THREE

Remaking Society

By the 1820s, Alexander Hamilton's designs for industrial development were being realized. Fired by the entrepreneurial spirit of the Boston Associates, a group of economic innovators with a conservative social vision, textile towns sprang up in dozens of locations along the Merrimack and other New England rivers. The most famous of these, now a national park site, was Lowell, Massachusetts. This industrial village combined technological novelty with careful social planning. Whereas the Rhode Island employers who hired the Patch women assumed little responsibility for families outside the factory gates, Lowell mill owners offered to serve *in loco parentis* for young female operatives. Owners constructed boardinghouses within walking distance of their factories, assuring workers of lodging and landladies of full beds and steady rents.

Both boardinghouses and factories established strict rules of conduct and rigorous forms of discipline to reassure farm-bound parents of the safety of their factory-bound daughters. At first, the farmers' daughters who supplied the labor for industrialization found the Waltham-Lowell system exciting. New factories and refurbished houses, decent wages and working conditions, and the chance to gain some measure of independence and a taste of city life attracted large numbers of "country girls" to the mills. Amid the regulations and surveillance of overseers and landladies, young women who moved to mill villages carved out friendships, support networks, and a shared culture of labor and leisure. As Thomas Dublin demonstrates, the strength of these bonds allowed mill operatives to organize on their own behalf when wages and working conditions deteriorated.

Lowell's women workers described themselves as "daughters of freemen" who were proud of their "Patriotic Ancestors." By midcentury, however, the majority of these Yankee operatives had been replaced by workers with a different heritage, mostly immigrants from Ireland or French Canada. In tandem with commercial, industrial, and urban expansion throughout the

A new wave of religious fervor swept the nation during the Second Great Awakening. Revivalists such as the Reverend Charles Grandison Finney stressed good works as a means to personal salvation. This moral imperative gave reform-minded women opportunities to voice their concerns on social injustices of the time and to expand their influence outside the male-dominated political arena through evangelical societies, temperance organizations, and abolitionist groups.

Northeast, this shift in labor supply encouraged the development of new class distinctions in the opportunities open to and the images of women in society.

In the South, such divisions became clear earlier as a result of black women's relegation to manual labor under slavery. Though poor white women and even the wives of self-sufficient yeoman farmers might, out of necessity, labor in the fields, Southern ladies did not soil their hands. In the North, where slaves were less extensively employed, white women's domestic tasks from colonial days through the early years of the Republic included a good deal of hoeing, planting, and harvesting. Only with the rise of shops, factories, and urban markets did ladylike behavior demand that more affluent women withdraw from manual labor. Then the circumstances existed for starker distinctions between "ladies" and "mill girls."

The emergence and dissemination of a new ideal of womanhood depended greatly on improvements in printing that allowed newspapers, magazines, and that relatively new literary form, the novel, to reach mass audiences. A careful reading of these sources suggests that the "true woman" of the early nineteenth century was pious, pure, domestic, and submissive, enclosed within her separate sphere of family, home, and church. Such secular images were both reinforced and modified by the teachings of a new breed of evangelical ministers. The Reverend Charles Grandison Finney was the most famous of the revivalists who led the evangelical movement known as the Second Great Awakening. Tempering older messages about original sin and predestination, Finney and his followers stressed the individual's ability to participate in his or her own salvation and to pursue good works as a means of hastening the millennium. Often relying on women to carry the tidings to the unchurched, evangelical preachers reinforced that sense of female moral and spiritual superiority first instilled by the advocates of Republican Motherhood.

Women had long used the church as a vehicle for organizing voluntary efforts on behalf of the sick, orphaned, and destitute. In the 1830s, under the influence of evangelicalism, members of these organizations began to believe that such problems could be not only lessened but eliminated. The perfection of society would then open the door for Christ's Second Coming and a thousand years of joy, serenity, and justice. New associations emerged that were more fully infused with this millennial vision, encouraging women to step beyond home and church and into the public streets. These associations included temperance, peace, and moral reform societies, the last of which is examined by Carroll Smith-Rosenberg. She shows how "true women" employed perfectionist preachings to expand their sphere of activity into the public and political realm.

Seeking to eradicate prostitution, female moral reformers developed a critique of male vice and power just as female mill workers were developing critiques of capitalist greed and power. Women in both groups joined female friends and relatives in attempting to improve conditions in their own communities. Some of these women also explored links between the forms of oppression they experienced and those affecting women in other communities. Female abolitionists, for instance, most of whom had never set foot on a southern plantation, focused their efforts on alleviating the plight of slaves, especially ending the abuse of slave women.

Like their male counterparts, abolitionist women varied in their analysis of race relations and in their choice of political tactics and strategies. Such differences were rooted less in understandings of the slaves' condition than in the activists' own backgrounds. In the 1830s, evangelical women and men echoed William Lloyd Garrison's demand for the slaves' immediate emancipation without compensation to their former owners. By the 1840s, however, as revival leaders and many male abolitionists began criticizing women for venturing too far beyond their sphere, evangelical women retreated from this radical stance. In their place appeared a coterie of Quaker women and men who had long testified against slavery from within the Society of Friends and now did so within society at large.

Nancy Hewitt traces the appearance of and the expansion and division among female abolitionists in Rochester, New York. In that city, industrialization and rapid population growth, evangelical revivals and immigrant arrivals, bars and brothels inspired thousands of women to enter the public arena in the early nineteenth century. In pursuing social change, these women utilized new forms of activism or expanded the use of older ones, including petitions, boycotts, lectures, pamphlets, and prayer meetings. These female activists—rich and poor, Catholic and Protestant, black and white— followed various paths to social change, including those of moral reform, temperance, and peace as well as abolition.

Only one path, however, led to Seneca Falls, the site of the first women's rights convention in 1848. This route was carved out by Quaker abolitionists who used arguments for the slaves' emancipation as a model for demanding full equality for women. At Seneca Falls, and in Rochester two weeks later, a small circle of women met for the first time in formal convention to consider "the Rights of women, Politically, Socially, Religiously, and Industrially." Though those who organized the meeting received the support of husbands and fathers, they claimed that in general the "history of mankind is a history of repeated injuries and usurpations on the part of man toward woman, having in direct object the establishment of an absolute tyranny over her." Like the "daughters of freemen" at Lowell, women's rights advocates called on revolutionary precedents, using the Declaration of Independence as the model for enunciating women's grievances and asserting their "natural right" to equality.

By mid-century, the antebellum era's most radical female activists had joined men in founding utopian communities, advocating dress reform, vegetarianism, and spiritualism, and condemning slavery, racism, the use of alcohol and tobacco, and capital punishment. At the same time, women who were more committed to the tenets of true womanhood established single-sex associations and institutions to assist orphans and prostitutes as well as the intemperate, the insane, the blind, the deaf, and the delinquent. Along with labor leaders, free black activists, and male coworkers, these women began to transform the nation.

If as one historian claims, "the community [rather than the state or the nation] constituted the main arena of intellectual, social, and political life" throughout the nineteenth century, then common women and men trying to secure a better life for themselves, their families, their neighbors, and other people in need played a key role in remaking society.

Suggested Readings

Barbara Welter, "The Cult of True Womanhood, 1820–1860," *American Quarterly* (Summer 1966).

Gerda Lerner, "The Lady and the Mill Girl: Changes in the Status of Women in the Age of Jackson, 1800–1840," *Midcontinent American Studies Journal* (Spring 1969).

Nancy Cott, *The Bonds of Womanhood: "Woman's Sphere" in New England, 1780–1835* (1977).

Kathryn Kish Sklar, *Catharine Beecher: A Study in Domesticity* (1973).

Ronald G. Walters, *American Reformers, 1815–1860* (1978).

SEVEN

Building a Community of Labor: Women, Work, and Protest in Lowell

Thomas Dublin

In the second quarter of the nineteenth century, a full-blown industrial revolution reshaped New England's landscape, drawing farmers' daughters into new roles in the economy and the community. Generally unburdened by the transiency, premarital pregnancy, drinking, and indebtedness that plagued the Patch family, Lowell operatives helped sustain the family farm while themselves moving into a new urban order. Where the Patches had no home to return to and drifted from town to town, the mill workers Dublin describes here, knowing they could return to the farm whenever necessary, created a new community among the boardinghouses and factories of the mill village. Joining female kin and neighbors in the spinning rooms, training and covering for one another at work, sharing bed and board, these young Yankee women forged a peer culture new to American society.

Alexander Hamilton, one suspects, would have applauded both the Boston capitalists who built the mills and the farmers' daughters who labored there. Yet he would have been shocked when the latter began employing revolutionary rhetoric to protest economic exploitation. It was mill workers' sense of security—rooted in their heritage as "daughters of free men," in self-sufficient farms back home, and in the tight bonds of the mill community—that allowed them to protest long hours, speedups, wage cuts, and other attempts to channel the profits of industry only to owners.

Like Abigail Patch, mill women found within themselves the power to create a new autonomy. Unlike her, they forged collective responses to their exploitation that embraced not only women but men, not only family but friends. In their alliances with male workers, Lowell operatives maintained their new-found independence, adopted a variety of protest tactics, and even achieved some limited political successes.

By the late 1840s, however, just as their greatest victories were won, farmers' daughters began to leave the factories in large numbers. As working conditions deteriorated and immigrant women and men entered the mills in increasing numbers, the close-knit community unravelled, ending for a time the conditions that nurtured resistance. As Lowell operatives settled into new lives—perhaps as the wives of farmers or artisans, or as the schoolteachers, western migrants, or urban activists described in the following articles—Irish and French-Canadian workers quickly filled their places and began to create a new culture of work and protest.

In the years before 1850 the textile mills of Lowell, Massachusetts, were a celebrated economic and cultural attraction. Foreign visitors invariably included them on their American tours. Interest was prompted by the massive scale of the mills, the astonishing productivity of the power-driven machinery, and the fact that women comprised most of the workforce. Visitors were struck by the newness of both mills and city as well as by the culture of the female operatives. The scene stood in sharp contrast to the gloomy mill towns of the English industrial revolution.

Lowell, was, in fact, an impressive accomplishment. In 1820, there had been no city at all—only a dozen family farms along the Merrimack River in East Chelmsford. In 1821, however, a group of Boston capitalists purchased land and water rights along the river and a nearby canal, and began to build a major textile manufacturing center. Opening two years later, the first factory employed Yankee women recruited from the nearby countryside. Additional mills were constructed until, by 1840, ten textile corporations with thirty-two mills valued at more than ten million dollars lined the banks of the river and nearby canals. Adjacent to the mills were rows of company boarding houses and tenements which accommodated most of the eight thousand factory operatives.

As Lowell expanded, and became the nation's largest textile manufacturing center, the experiences of women operatives changed as well. The increasing number of firms in Lowell and in the other mill towns brought the pressure of competition. Overproduction became a

From "Women, Work, and Protest in the Early Lowell Mills: 'The Oppressing Hand of Avarice Would Enslave Us' " by Thomas Dublin, *Labor History*, Volume 27, Number 2. Copyright © 1986 by The Tamiment Institute. Reprinted by permission.

problem and the prices of finished cloth decreased. The high profits of the early years declined and so, too, did conditions for the mill operatives. Wages were reduced and the pace of work within the mills was stepped up. Women operatives did not accept these changes without protest. In 1834 and 1836 they went on strike to protest wage cuts, and between 1843 and 1848 they mounted petition campaigns aimed at reducing the hours of labor in the mills.

These labor protests in early Lowell contribute to our understanding of the response of workers to the growth of industrial capitalism in the first half of the nineteenth century. They indicate the importance of values and attitudes dating back to an earlier period and also the transformation of these values in a new setting.

The major factor in the rise of a new consciousness among operatives in Lowell was the development of a close-knit community among women working in the mills. The structure of work and the nature of housing contributed to the growth of this community. The existence of community among women, in turn, was an important element in the repeated labor protests of the period.

The pre-conditions for the labor unrest in Lowell before 1850 may be found in the study of the daily worklife of its operatives. In their everyday, relatively conflict-free lives, mill women created the mutual bonds which made possible united action in times of crisis. The existence of a tight-knit community among them was the most important element in determining the collective, as opposed to individual, nature of this response.

Before examining the basis of community among women operatives in early Lowell, it may be helpful to indicate in what sense "community" is being used. The women are considered a "community" because of the development of bonds of mutual dependence

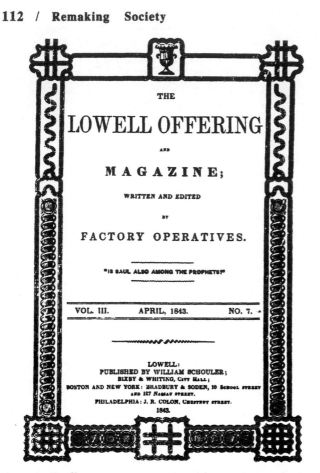

THE

LOWELL OFFERING

AND

MAGAZINE;

WRITTEN AND EDITED

BY

FACTORY OPERATIVES.

"IS SAUL ALSO AMONG THE PROPHETS?"

VOL. III.   APRIL, 1843.   NO. 7.

LOWELL:
PUBLISHED BY WILLIAM SCHOULER;
BIXBY & WHITING, CITY HALL;
BOSTON AND NEW YORK: BRADBURY & SODEN, 10 School street
AND 127 Nassau street.
PHILADELPHIA: J. R. COLON, Chestnut street.
1843.

The *Lowell Offering,* owner-sponsored but written and edited by the workers, featured fictional accounts of the mill workers' experiences. The publication in which Lowell operatives voiced their complaints about wage cuts and working conditions and advocated reform legislation was the *Voice of Industry.*

among them. In this period they came to depend upon one another and upon the larger group of operatives in very important ways. Their experiences were not simply similar or parallel to one another, but were inextricably intertwined. Furthermore, they were conscious of the existence of community, expressing it very clearly in their writings and in labor protests. "Community" for them had objective and subjective dimensions and both were important in their experience as women in the mills.

The mutual dependence among women in early Lowell was rooted in the structure of mill work itself. Newcomers to the mills were particularly dependent on their fellow operatives, but even experienced hands relied on one another for considerable support.

New operatives generally found their first experiences difficult, even harrowing, though they may have already done considerable hand-spinning and weaving in their own homes. The initiation of one of them is described in fiction in the *Lowell Offering:*

The next morning she went into the Mill; and at first the sight of so many bands, and wheels, and springs in constant motion, was very frightful. She felt afraid to touch the loom, and she was almost sure she could never learn to weave . . . the shuttle flew out, and made a new bump on her head; and the first time she tried to spring the lathe, she broke out a quarter of the treads.

While other accounts present a somewhat less difficult picture, most indicate that women only became proficient and felt satisfaction in their work after several months at the mills.

The textile corporations made provisions to ease the adjustment of new operatives. Newcomers were not immediately expected to fit into the mill's regular work routine. They were first assigned work as sparehands and were paid a daily wage independent of the quantity of work they turned out. As a sparehand, the newcomer worked with an experienced hand who instructed her in the intricacies of the job. The sparehand spelled her partner for short stretches of time, and occasionally took the place of an absentee. One woman described the learning process in a letter reprinted in the *Offering:*

> Well, I went into the mill, and was put to learn with a very patient girl. . . . You cannot think how odd everything seems. . . . They set me to threading shuttles, and tying weaver's knots, and such things, and now I have improved so that I can take care of one loom. I could take care of two if only I had eyes in the back part of my head. . . .

After the passage of some weeks or months, when she could handle the normal complement of machinery—two looms for weavers during the 1830s—and when a regular operative departed, leaving an opening, the sparehand moved into a regular job.

Through this system of job training, the textile corporations contributed to the development of community among female operatives. During the most difficult period in an operative's career, the first months in the mill, she relied

upon other women workers for training and support. And for every sparehand whose adjustment to mill work was aided in this process, there was an experienced operative whose work was also affected. Women were relating to one another during the work process and not simply tending their machinery. Given the high rate of turnover in the mill workforce, a large proportion of women operatives worked in pairs. At the Hamilton Company in July 1836, for example, more than a fifth of all females on the Company payroll were sparehands. Consequently, over forty percent of the females employed there in this month worked with one another. Nor was this interaction surreptitious, carried out only when the overseer looked elsewhere; rather it was formally organized and sanctioned by the textile corporations themselves.

In addition to the integration of sparehands, informal sharing of work often went on among regular operatives. A woman would occasionally take off a half or full day from work either to enjoy a brief vacation or to recover from illness, and fellow operatives would each take an extra loom or side of spindles so that she might continue to earn wages during her absence. Women were generally paid on a piece rate basis, their wages being determined by the total output of the machinery they tended during the payroll period. With friends helping out during her absence, making sure that her looms kept running, an operative could earn almost a full wage even though she was not physically present. Such informal work-sharing was another way in which mutual dependence developed among women operatives during their working hours.

Living conditions also contributed to the development of community among female operatives. Most women working in the Lowell mills of these years were housed in company boarding houses. In July 1836, for example, more than 73 percent of females employed by the Hamilton Company resided in company housing adjacent to the mills. Almost three-

Female workers at the Lowell mills formed a close-knit community that stressed moral support and cooperation among its members. One feature of the communal support system was informal job sharing. If a worker wished to have some time off, her co-workers willingly operated her loom so that she would be paid her usual piece work rate for that day.

fourths of them, therefore, lived and worked with each other. Furthermore, the work schedule was such that women had little opportunity to interact with those not living in company dwellings. They worked, in these years, an average of 73 hours a week. Their work day ended at 7:00 or 7:30 P.M., and in the hours between supper and the 10:00 curfew imposed by management on residents of company boarding houses there was little time to spend with friends living "off the corporation."

Women in the boarding houses lived in close quarters, a factor that also played a role in the growth of community. A typical boarding house accommodated twenty-five young women, generally crowded four to eight in a bedroom. There was little possibility of privacy within the dwelling, and pressure to conform to group standards was very strong. The community of operatives which developed in the mills it follows, carried over into life at home as well.

The boarding house became a central institution in the lives of Lowell's female operatives in these years, but it was particularly important in the initial integration of newcomers into urban industrial life. Upon first leaving her rural home for work in Lowell, a woman entered a setting very different from anything she had previously known. One operative, writing in the *Offering*, described the feelings of a fictional character: ". . . the first entrance into a factory boarding house seemed something dreadful. The room looked strange and comfortless, and the women cold and heartless; and when she sat down to the supper table, where among more than twenty girls, all but one were strangers, she could not eat a mouthful."

In the boarding house, the newcomer took the first steps in the process which transformed her from an "outsider" into an accepted member of the community of women operatives.

Recruitment of newcomers into the mills and their initial hiring was mediated through the boarding house system. Women generally did not travel to Lowell for the first time entirely on their own. They usually came because they knew someone—an older sister, cousin, or friend—who had already worked in Lowell. The scene described above was a lonely one—but the newcomer did know at least one boarder among the twenty seated around the supper table. The Hamilton Company Register Books indicate that numerous pairs of operatives, having the same surname and coming from the same town in northern New England, lived in the same boarding houses. If the newcomer was not accompanied by a friend or relative, she was usually directed to "Number 20, Hamilton Company," or to a similar address of one of the other corporations where her acquaintance lived. Her first contact with fellow operatives generally came in the boarding houses and not the mills. Given the personal nature of recruitment in this period, therefore, newcomers usually had the company and support of a friend or relative in their first adjustment to Lowell.

Like recruitment, the initial hiring was a personal process. Once settled in the boarding house a newcomer had to find a job. She would generally go to the mills with her friend or with the boarding house keeper who would introduce her to an overseer in one of the rooms. If he had an opening, she might start work immediately. More likely, the overseer would know of an opening elsewhere in the mill, or would suggest that something would probably develop within a few days. In one story in the *Offering,* a newcomer worked on some quilts for her house keeper, thereby earning her board while she waited for a job opening.

Upon entering the boarding house, the newcomer came under pressure to conform with the standards of the community of operatives. Stories in the *Offering* indicate that newcomers at first stood out from the group in terms of their speech and dress. Over time, they dropped the peculiar "twang" in their speech which so amused experienced hands. Similarly, they purchased clothing more in keeping with urban than rural styles. It was an unusual and

strongwilled individual who could work and live among her fellow operatives and not conform, at least outwardly, to the customs and values of this larger community.

The boarding houses were the centers of social life for women operatives after their long days in the mills. There they ate their meals, rested, talked, sewed, wrote letters, read books and magazines. From among fellow workers and boarders they found friends who accompanied them to shops, to Lyceum lectures, to church and church-sponsored events. On Sundays or holidays, they often took walks along the canals or out into the nearby countryside. The community of women operatives, in sum, developed in a setting where women worked and lived together, twenty-four hours a day.

Given the all-pervasiveness of this community, one would expect it to exert strong pressures on those who did not conform to group standards. Such appears to have been the case. The community influenced newcomers to adopt its patterns of speech and dress as described above. In addition, it enforced an unwritten code of moral conduct. Henry Miles, a minister in Lowell, described the way in which the community pressured those who deviated from accepted moral conduct:

A girl, suspected of immoralities, or serious improprieties, at once loses caste. Her fellow boarders will at once leave the house, if the keeper does not dismiss the offender. In self-protection, therefore, the patron is obliged to put the offender away. Nor will her former companions walk with her, or work with her; till at length, finding herself everywhere talked about, and pointed at, and shunned, she is obliged to relieve her fellow-operatives of a presence which they feel brings disgrace.

The power of the peer group described by Miles may seem extreme, but there is evidence in the writing of women operatives to corroborate his account. Such group pressure is illustrated by a story (in the *Offering*)—in which operatives in a company boarding house begin to harbor suspicions about a fellow boarder, Hannah, who received repeated evening visits from a man whom she does not introduce to the other residents. Two boarders declare that they will leave if she is allowed to remain in the household. The house keeper finally informed Hannah that she must either depart or not see the man again. She does not accept the ultimatum, but is promptly discharged after the overseer is informed, by one of the boarders, about her conduct. And, only one of Hannah's former friends continues to remain on cordial terms.

One should not conclude, however, that women always enforced a moral code agreeable to Lowell's clergy, or to the mill agents and overseers for that matter. After all, the kind of peer pressure imposed on Hannah could be brought to bear on women in 1834 and 1836 who on their own would not have protested wage cuts. It was much harder to go to work when one's roommates were marching about town, attending rallies, circulating strike petitions. Similarly, the ten-hour petitions of the 1840s were certainly aided by the fact of a tight-knit community of operatives living in a dense neighborhood of boarding houses. To the extent that women could not have completely private lives in the boarding houses, they probably had to conform to group norms, whether these involved speech, clothing, relations with men, or attitudes toward the ten-hour day. Group pressure to conform, so important to the community of women in early Lowell, played a significant role in the collective response of women to changing conditions in the mills.

In addition to the structure of work and housing in Lowell, a third factor, the homogeneity of the mill workforce, contributed to the development of community among female operatives. In this period the mill workforce was homogeneous in terms of sex, nativity, and age. Payroll and other records of the Hamilton Company reveal that more than 85 per cent of those employed in July, 1836, were women and that over 96 per cent were native-born. Furthermore, over 80 percent of the female workforce was between the ages of 15 and 30 years old; and only ten per cent was under 15 or over 40.

Workforce homogeneity takes on particular significance in the context of work structure and the nature of worker housing. These three factors combined mean that women operatives had little interaction with men during their daily lives. Men and women did not perform the same work in the mills, and generally did not even labor in the same rooms. Men worked in the picking and initial carding processes, in the repair shop and on the watchforce, and filled all supervisory positions in the mills. Women held all sparehand and regular operative jobs in drawing, speeding, spinning, weaving and dressing. A typical room in the mill employed eighty women tending machinery, with two men overseeing the work and two boys assisting them. Women had little contact with men other than their supervisors in the course of the working day. After work, women returned to their boarding houses, where once again there were few men. Women, then, worked and lived in a predominantly female setting.

Ethnically the workforce was also homogeneous. Immigrants formed only 3.4 percent of those employed at Hamilton in July, 1836. In addition, they comprised only 3 per cent of residents in Hamilton company housing. The community of women operatives was composed of women of New England stock drawn from the hill-country farms surrounding Lowell. Consequently, when experienced hands made fun of the speech and dress of newcomers, it was understood that they, too, had been "rusty" or "rustic" upon first coming to Lowell. This common background was another element shared by women workers in early Lowell.

The work structure, the workers' housing, and workforce homogeneity were the major elements which contributed to the growth of community among Lowell's women operatives. To best understand the larger implications of community it is necessary to examine the labor protests of this period. For in these struggles, the new values and attitudes which developed in the community of women operatives are most visible.

＊

In February, 1834, 800 of Lowell's women operatives "turned-out"—went on strike—to protest a proposed reduction in their wages. They marched to numerous mills in an effort to induce others to join them; and, at an outdoor rally, they petitioned others to "discontinue their labors until terms of reconciliation are made." Their petition concluded:

Resolved, That we will not go back into the mills to work unless our wages are continued . . . as they have been.
Resolved, That none of us will go back, unless they receive us all as one.
Resolved, That if any have not money enough to carry them home, they shall be supplied.

The strike proved to be brief and failed to reverse the proposed wage reductions. Turning-out on a Friday, the striking women were paid their back wages on Saturday, and by the middle of the next week had returned to work or left town. Within a week of the turn-out, the mills were running near capacity.

This first strike in Lowell is important not because it failed or succeeded, but simply because it took place. In an era in which women had to overcome opposition simply to work in the mills, it is remarkable that they would further overstep the accepted middle-class bounds of female propriety by participating in a public protest. The agents of the textile mills certainly considered the turn-out unfeminine. William Austin, agent of the Lawrence Company, described the operatives' procession as an "amizonian [sic] display." He wrote further, in a

letter to his company treasurer in Boston: "This afternoon we have paid off several of these Amazons & presume that they will leave town on Monday." The turn-out was particularly offensive to the agents because of the relationship they thought they had with their operatives. William Austin probably expressed the feelings of other agents when he wrote: ". . . notwithstanding the friendly and disinterested advice which has been on all proper occassions [sic] communicated to the girls ot the Lawrence mills a spirit of evil omen . . . has prevailed, and overcome the judgement and discretion of too many, and this morning a general turn-out from most of the rooms has been the consequence."

Mill agents assumed an attitude of benevolent paternalism toward their female operatives, and found it particularly disturbing that the women paid such little heed to their advice. The strikers were not merely unfeminine, they were ungrateful as well.

Such attitudes not withstanding, women chose to turn-out. They did so for two principal reasons. First, the wage cuts undermined the sense of dignity and social equality which was an important element in their Yankee heritage. Second, these wage cuts were seen as an attack on their economic independence.

Certainly a prime motive for the strike was outrage at the social implications of the wage cuts. In a statement of principles accompanying the petition which was circulated among operatives, women expressed well the sense of themselves which prompted the protest of these wage cuts:

UNION IS POWER

Our present object is to have union and exertion, and we remain in possession of our unquestionable rights. We circulate this paper wishing to obtain the names of all who imbibe the spirit of our Patriotic Ancestors, who preferred privation to bondage, and parted with all that renders life desirable—and even life itself—to procure independence for their children. The oppressing hand of avarice would enslave us, and to gain their object, they gravely tell us of the pressure of the time, this we are already sensible of, and deplore it. If any are in want of assistance, the Ladies will be compassionate and assist them; but we prefer to have the disposing of our charities in our own hands; and as we are free, we would remain in possession of what kind Providence has bestowed upon us; and remain daughters of freemen still.

At several points in the proclamation the women drew on their Yankee heritage. Connecting their turn-out with the efforts of their "Patriotic Ancestors" to secure independence from England, they interpreted the wage cuts as an effort to "enslave" them—to deprive them of their independent status as "daughters of freemen."

Though very general and rhetorical, the statement of these women does suggest their sense of self, of their own worth and dignity. Elsewhere, they expressed the conviction that they were the social equals of the overseers, indeed of the millowners themselves. The wage cuts, however, struck at this assertion of social equality. These reductions made it clear that the operatives were subordinate to their employers, rather than equal partners in a contract binding on both parties. By turning-out the women emphatically denied that they were subordinates; but by returning to work the next week, they demonstrated that in economic terms they were no match for their corporate superiors.

In point of fact, these Yankee operatives were subordinate in early Lowell's social and economic order, but they never consciously accepted this status. Their refusal to do so became evident whenever the mill owners attempted to exercise the power they possessed. This fundamental contradiction between the objective status of operatives and their consciousness of it was at the root of the 1834 turn-out

and of subsequent labor protests in Lowell before 1850. The corporations could build mills, create thousands of jobs, and recruit women to fill them. Nevertheless, they bought only the workers' labor power, and then only for as long as these workers chose to stay. Women could always return to their rural homes, and they had a sense of their own worth and dignity, factors limiting the actions of management.

Women operatives viewed the wage cuts as a threat to their economic independence. This independence had two related dimensions. First, the women were self-supporting while they worked in the mills and, consequently, were independent of their families back home. Second, they were able to save out of their monthly earnings and could then leave the mills for the old homestead whenever they so desired. In effect, they were not totally dependent upon mill work. Their independence was based largely on the high level of wages in the mills. They could support themselves and still save enough to return home periodically. The wage cuts threatened to deny them this outlet, substituting instead the prospect of total dependence on mill work. Small wonder, then, there was alarm that "the oppressing hand of avarice would enslave us." To be forced, out of necessity, to lifelong labor in the mills would indeed have seemed like slavery. The Yankee operatives spoke directly to the fear of a dependency based on impoverishment when offering to assist any women workers who "have not money enough to carry them home." Wage reductions, however, offered only the *prospect* of a future dependence on mill employment. By striking, the women asserted their actual economic independence of the mills and the determination to remain "daughters of freemen still."

While the women's traditional conception of themselves as independent daughters of freemen played a major role in the turn-out, this factor acting alone would not necessarily have triggered the 1834 strike. It would have led women as individuals to quit work and return to their rural homes. But the turn-out was a collective protest. When it was announced that wage reductions were being considered, women began to hold meetings in the mills during meal breaks in order to assess tactical possibilities. Their turn-out began at one mill when the agent discharged a woman who had presided at such a meeting. Their procession through the streets passed by other mills, expressing a conscious effort to enlist as much support as possible for their cause. At a mass meeting, the women drew up a resolution which insisted that none be discharged for their participation in the turn-out. This strike, then, was a collective response to the proposed wage cuts—made possible because women had come to form a "community" of operatives in the mill, rather than simply a group of individual workers. The existence of such a tight-knit community turned individual opposition of the wage cuts into a collective protest.

In October, 1836, women again went on strike. This second turn-out was similar to the first in several respects. Its immediate cause was also a wage reduction; marches and a large outdoor rally were organized; again, like the earlier protest, the basic goal was not achieved; the corporations refused to restore wages; and operatives either left Lowell or returned to work at the new rates.

Despite these surface similarities between the turn-outs, there were some real differences. One involved scale: over 1500 operatives turned out in 1836, compared to only 800 earlier. Moreover, the second strike lasted much longer than the first. In 1834 operatives stayed out for only a few days; in 1836, the mills ran far below capacity for several months. Two weeks after the second turn-out began, a mill agent reported that only a fifth of the strikers had returned to work: "The rest manifest *good 'spunk'* as they call it." Several days later he described the impact of the continuing strike on operations in his mills: "we must be feeble for months

to come as probably not less than 250 of our former scanty supply of help have left town." These lines read in sharp contrast to the optimistic reports of agents following the turn-out in February, 1834.

Differences between the two turn-outs were not limited to the increased scale and duration of the later one. Women displayed a much higher degree of organization in 1836 than earlier. To co-ordinate strike activities, they formed a Factory Girls' Association. According to one historian, membership in the short-lived association reached 2,500 at its height. The larger organization among women was reflected in the tactics employed. Strikers, according to one mill agent, were able to halt production to a greater extent than numbers alone could explain; and, he complained, although some operatives were willing to work, "it has been impossible to give employment to many who remained." He attributed this difficulty to the strikers' tactics: "This was in many instances no doubt the result of calculation and contrivance. After the original turn-out, they [the operatives] would assail a particular room—as for instance, all the warpers, or all the warp spinners, or all the speeder and stretcher girls, and this would close the mill as effectively as if all the girls in the mill had left."

Now giving more thought than they had in 1834 to the specific tactics of the turn-out, the women made a deliberate effort to shut down the mills in order to win their demands. They attempted to persuade less committed operatives, concentrating on those in crucial departments within the mill. Such tactics anticipated those of skilled mulespinners and loomfixers who went out on strike in the 1880s and 1890s.

In their organization of a Factory Girls' Association and in their efforts to shut down the mills, the female operatives revealed that they had been changed by their industrial experience. Increasingly, they acted not simply as "daughters of freemen" offended by the impositions of the textile corporations, but also as industrial workers intent on improving their position within the mills.

There was a decline in protest among women in the Lowell mills following these early strike defeats. During the 1837–1843 depression, textile corporations twice reduced wages without evoking a collective response from operatives. Because of the frequency of production cutbacks and lay-offs in these years, workers probably accepted the mill agents' contention that they had to reduce wages or close entirely. But with the return of prosperity and the expansion of production in the mid-1840s, there were renewed labor protests among women. Their actions paralleled those of working men and reflected fluctuations in the business cycle. Prosperity itself did not prompt turn-outs, but it evidently facilitated collective actions by women operatives.

In contrast to the protests of the previous decade, the struggles now were primarily political. Women did not turn-out in the 1840s; rather, they mounted annual petition campaigns calling on the State legislature to limit the hours of labor within the mills. These campaigns reached their height in 1845 and 1846, when 2,000 and 5,000 operatives respectively signed petitions. Unable to curb the wage cuts, or the speed-up and stretch-out imposed by mill owners, operatives sought to mitigate the consequences of these changes by reducing the length of the working day. Having been defeated earlier in economic struggles, they now sought to achieve their new goal through political action. The Ten Hour Movement, seen in these terms, was a logical outgrowth of the unsuccessful turn-outs of the previous decade. Like the earlier struggles, the Ten Hour Movement was an assertion of the dignity of operatives and an attempt to maintain that dignity under the changing conditions of industrial capitalism.

The growth of relatively permanent labor organizations and institutions among women was a distinguishing feature of the Ten Hour Movement of the 1840s. The Lowell Female Labor Reform Association was organized in 1845 by women operatives. It became Lowell's leading organization over the next three years, organizing the city's female operatives and helping to set up branches in other mill towns. The Association was affiliated with the New England Workingmen's Association and sent delegates to its meetings. It acted in concert with similar male groups, and yet maintained its own autonomy. Women elected their own officers, held their own meetings, testified before a state legislative committee, and published a series of "Factory Tracts" which exposed conditions within the mills and argued for the ten-hour day.

An important educational and organizing tool of the Lowell Female Labor Reform Association was the *Voice of Industry*, a labor weekly published in Lowell between 1845 and 1848 by the New England Workingmen's Association. Female operatives were involved in every aspect of its publication and used the *Voice* to further the Ten Hour Movement among women. Their Association owned the press on which the *Voice* was printed. Sarah Bagley, the Association president, was a member of the three-person publishing committee of the *Voice* and for a time served as editor. Other women were employed by the paper as travelling editors. They wrote articles about the Ten Hour Movement in other mill towns, in an effort to give ten-hour supporters a sense of the larger cause of which they were a part. Furthermore, they raised money for the *Voice* and increased its circulation by selling subscriptions to the paper in their travels about New England. Finally, women used the *Voice* to appeal directly to their fellow operatives. They edited a separate "Female Department," which published letters and articles by and about women in the mills.

Another aspect of the Ten Hour Movement which distinguished it from the earlier labor struggles in Lowell was that it involved both men and women. At the same time that women in Lowell formed the Female Labor Reform Association, a male mechanics' and laborers' association was also organized. Both groups worked to secure the passage of legislation setting ten hours as the length of the working day. Both groups circulated petitions to this end and when the legislative committee came to Lowell to hear testimony, both men and women testified in favor of the ten-hour day.

The two groups, then, worked together, and each made an important contribution to the movement in Lowell. Women had the numbers, comprising as they did over eighty per cent of the mill workforce. Men, on the other hand, had the votes, and since the Ten Hour Movement was a political struggle, they played a crucial part. After the State committee reported unfavorably on the ten-hour petitions, the Female Labor Reform Association denounced the committee chairman, a State representative from Lowell, as a corporation "tool." Working for his defeat at the polls, they did so successfully and then passed the following post-election resolution: "*Resolved,* That the members of this Association tender their grateful acknowledgements to the voters of Lowell, for consigning William Schouler to the obscurity he so justly deserves. . . ." Women took a more prominent part in the Ten Hour Movement in Lowell than did men, but they obviously remained dependent on male voters and legislators for the ultimate success of their movement.

Although co-ordinating their efforts with those of working men, women operatives organized independently within the Ten Hour Movement. For instance, in 1845 two important petitions were sent from Lowell to the State legislature. Almost ninety per cent of the signers of one petition were females, and more than two-thirds of the signers of the second were males. Clearly the separation of men and women in their daily lives was reflected in the Ten Hour petitions of these years.

The way in which the Ten Hour Movement was carried from Lowell to other mill towns also illustrated the independent organizing of women within the larger movement. For example, at a spirited meeting in Manchester, New Hampshire, in December, 1845—one presided over by Lowell operatives—more than a thousand workers, two-thirds of them women, passed resolutions calling for the ten-hour day. Later, those in attendance divided along male-female lines, each meeting separately to set up parallel organizations. Sixty women joined the Manchester Female Labor Reform Association that evening, and by the following summer it claimed over three hundred members. Female operatives met in company boarding houses to involve new women in the movement. In their first year of organizing, Manchester workers obtained more than 4,000 signatures on ten-hour petitions. While men and women were both active in the movement, they worked through separate institutional structures from the outset.

The division of men and women within the Ten Hour Movement also reflected their separate daily lives in Lowell and in other mill towns. To repeat, they held different jobs in the mills and had little contact apart from the formal, structured overseer-operative relation. Outside the mill, women tended to live in female boarding houses provided by the corporations and were isolated from men. Consequently, the experiences of women in these early mill towns were different from those of men, and in the course of their daily lives they came to form a close-knit community. It was logical that women's participation in the Ten Hour Movement mirrored this basic fact.

The women's Ten Hour Movement, like the earlier turn-outs, was based in part on the participants' sense of their own worth and dignity as daughters of freemen. At the same time, however, [it] also indicated the growth of a new consciousness. It reflected a mounting feeling of community among women operatives and a realization that their interests and those of their employers were not identical, that they had to rely on themselves and not on corporate benevolence to achieve a reduction in the hours of labor. One woman, in an open letter to a State legislator, expressed this rejection of middle-class paternalism: "Bad as is the condition of so many women, it would be much worse if they had nothing but your boasted protection to rely upon; but they have at least learnt the lesson which a bitter experience teaches, that not to those who style themselves their 'natural protectors' are they to look for the needful help, but to the strong and resolute of their own sex." Such an attitude, underlying the self-organization of women in the ten-hour petition campaigns, was clearly the product of the industrial experience in Lowell.

Both the early turn-outs and the Ten Hour Movement were in large measure dependent upon the existence of a close-knit community of women operatives. Such a community was based on the work structure, the nature of worker housing, and workforce homogeneity. Women were drawn together by the initial job training of newcomers; by the informal work sharing among experienced hands, by living in company boarding houses, by sharing religious, educational, and social activities in their leisure hours. Working and living in a new and alien setting, they came to rely upon one another for friendship and support. Understandably, a community feeling developed among them.

This evolving community as well as the common cultural traditions which Yankee women carried into Lowell were major elements that governed their response to changing mill conditions. The pre-industrial tradition of independence and self-respect made them particularly sensitive to management labor policies. The sense of community enabled them to transform their individual opposition to wage cuts and to the increasing pace of work into public protest. In these labor struggles women operatives expressed a new consciousness of their rights both as workers and as women. Such a consciousness, like the community of women itself, was one product of Lowell's industrial revolution.

The experiences of Lowell women before 1850 present a fascinating picture of the contradictory impact of industrial capitalism. Repeated labor protests reveal that female operatives felt the demands of mill employment to be oppressive. At the same time, however, the mills provided women with work outside of the home and family, thereby offering them an unprecedented point of entry into the public realm. That they came to challenge employer paternalism was a direct consequence of the increasing opportunities offered them in these years. The Lowell mills both exploited and liberated women in ways unknown to the pre-industrial political economy.

Questions for Study and Review

1. How and why were the experiences of Lowell mill operatives so different from those of Abigail Patch and her daughters?

2. Since young women were in the forefront of industrialization in New England, how might their ideas of family and community have differed from those of the farmers' sons they left behind?

3. How did opportunities for single women in early nineteenth-century New England compare with those of their counterparts in Salem? their foremothers in the Revolutionary era? their brothers in the same period?

4. How important to women's workplace protests and political activism of the twentieth century are the forms of community established in Lowell?

Suggested Readings

Thomas Dublin, *Women at Work: The Transformation of Work and Community in Lowell, Massachusetts, 1826–1860* (1979).

Mary Blewett, *Men, Women and Work: Class, Gender and Protest in the New England Shoe Industry, 1780–1910* (1988).

David Richard Kasserman, *Fall River Outrage: Life, Murder, and Justice in Early Industrial New England* (1986).

Philip Foner, ed., *The Factory Girls* (1977).

EIGHT

Beauty, the Beast, and the Militant Woman: Sex Roles and Sexual Standards in Jacksonian America

Carroll Smith-Rosenberg

Andrew Jackson was the symbol of an age. To many—both contemporaries and students of the Jacksonian era—he symbolized democracy, mobility, and individual achievement. To many middle-class matrons of the era, however, he symbolized all the evils that came with migration, family breakdown, and urbanization. A drinker and a duelist, an advocate of slavery, a man with few religious convictions who seemed to relish violence, the seventh president of the United States was even suspected of flaunting the seventh commandment—that forbidding adultery.

To women inspired by the religious revivals of the Second Great Awakening, it was Jackson's moral shortcomings that made him so representative of the common man. Faced by male vices and braced by the tenets of true womanhood and the perfectionist preachings of evangelicalism, female reformers shed the innately sinful image that had been associated with women since Biblical times and asserted their own moral and spiritual superiority. They resolved to institute a righteous order, including a single sexual standard defined by women's, not men's, morality.

Since the founding of the Republic, Americans had formed voluntary associations to assist the poor, house orphans, convert heathens, and care for the sick. When Alexis de Tocqueville visited the United States in the 1830s, he commented at length on this phenomenon. Yet he also claimed that once married, women were circumscribed "within the narrow circle of domestic interests and duties" beyond which they were forbidden to step by "the inexorable opinion of the public."

The Female Moral Reform Society (FMRS) examined by Smith-Rosenberg, with its millennial vision and militant action, demonstrates that voluntarism was also a powerful vehicle for married women's public concerns. Convinced that they were the proper arbiters of virtue in public as well as private, the organizers of the FMRS appealed for support from their country-bound sisters by detailing the horrors faced by city-bound sons and daughters. Separated from kin and community, young urban migrants were buffeted by economic, social, and sexual pitfalls. The perils faced by an Abigail Patch or an isolated Lowell mill operative were multiplied a hundredfold in New York City and other urban centers. Though originally concerned only with the dangers of unbridled sexual license and unprotected farmers' daughters, female moral reformers soon recognized the connections between low wages, inadequate housing, poor health, and moral vulnerability.

When they began to face heated criticism from civic leaders and ministers, these reformers also recognized that despite woman's widely proclaimed moral superiority, she was still very much restricted to home and hearth. Not yet prepared to launch a full-blown feminist attack, New York City's moral reformers nonetheless developed a pointed critique of men's power and mobilized a network of female activists in communities across the country to respond to the resulting depredations against women. Within a few years such critiques would embrace southern as well as northern men, would focus on the exploitation of black as well as white women, and would nurture the first formal campaign for women's rights in North America. The FMRS took the first steps along this path.

On a spring evening in May 1834, a small group of women met at the revivalistic Third Presbyterian Church in New York City to found the New York Female Moral Reform Society. The Society's goals were ambitious indeed; it hoped to convert New York's prostitutes to evangelical Protestantism and close forever the city's numerous brothels. This bold attack on prostitution was only one part of the Society's program. These self-assertive women hoped as well to confront that larger and more fundamental abuse, the double standard, and the male sexual license it condoned. Too many men, the Society defiantly asserted in its statement of goals, were aggressive destroyers of female innocence and happiness. No man was above suspicion. Women's only safety lay in a militant effort to reform American sexual mores—and, as we shall see, to reform sexual mores meant in practice to control man's sexual values and autonomy. The rhetoric of the Society's spokesmen consistently betrayed an unmistakable and deeply felt resentment toward a male-dominated society.

Few if any members of the Society were reformed prostitutes or the victims of rape or seduction. Most came from middle-class native American backgrounds and lived quietly respectable lives as pious wives and mothers. What needs explaining is the emotional logic which underlay the Society's militant and controversial program of sexual reform. I would like to suggest that both its reform program and the anti-male sentiments it served to express reflect a neglected area of stress in mid-19th

century America—that is, the nature of the role to be assumed by the middle-class American woman.

American society from the 1830s to the 1860s was marked by advances in political democracy, by a rapid increase in economic, social, and geographic mobility, and by uncompromising and morally relentless reform movements. Though many aspects of Jacksonianism have been subjected to historical investigation, the possibly stressful effects of such structural change upon family and sex roles have not. The following pages constitute an attempt to glean some understanding of women and women's role in antebellum America through an analysis of a self-consciously female voluntary association dedicated to the eradication of sexual immorality.

Women in Jacksonian America had few rights and little power. Their role in society was passive and sharply limited. Women were, in general, denied formal education above the minimum required by a literate early industrial society. The female brain and nervous system, male physicians and educators agreed, were inadequate to sustained intellectual effort. They were denied the vote in a society which placed a high value upon political participation; political activity might corrupt their pure feminine nature. All professional roles (with the exception of primary school education) were closed to women. Even so traditional a female role as midwife was undermined as male physicians began to establish professional control over obstetrics. Most economic alternatives to marriage (except such burdensome and menial tasks as those of seamstress or domestic) were closed to women. Their property rights were still restricted and females were generally considered to be the legal wards either of the state or of their nearest male relative. In the event of divorce, the mother lost custody of her children—even when the husband was conceded to be the

From "Beauty, the Beast and the Militant Woman: A Case Study in Sex Roles and Social Stress in Jacksonian America," by Carroll Smith-Rosenberg, *American Quarterly*, Vol. XXIII, No. 4, Fall (1971), pp. 562–84. Copyright © 1971 American Studies Association. Reprinted by permission of the publisher and the author.

erring party. Women's universe was bounded by their homes and the career of father or husband; within the home it was woman's duty to be submissive and patient.

Yet this was a period when change was considered a self-evident good, and when nothing was believed impossible to a determined free will, be it the conquest of a continent, the reform of society or the eternal salvation of all mankind. The contrast between these generally accepted ideals and expectations and the real possibilities available to American women could not have been more sharply drawn. It is not implausible to assume that at least a minority of American women would find ways to manifest a discontent with their comparatively passive and constricted social role.

Only a few women in antebellum America were able, however, to openly criticize their socially defined sexual identity. A handful, like Fanny Wright, devoted themselves to overtly subversive criticism of the social order. A scarcely more numerous group became pioneers in women's education. Others such as Elizabeth Cady Stanton, Lucretia Mott and Susan B. Anthony founded the women's rights movement. But most respectable women—even those with a sense of ill-defined grievance—were unable to explicitly defy traditional sex-role prescriptions.

I would like to suggest that many such women channeled frustration, anger and a compensatory sense of superior righteousness into the reform movements of the first half of the 19th century; and in the controversial moral reform crusade such motivations seem particularly apparent. While unassailable within the absolute categories of a pervasive evangelical world-view, the Female Moral Reform Society's crusade against illicit sexuality permitted an expression of anti-male sentiments. And the Society's "final solution"—the right to control the mores of men—provided a logical emotional redress for those feelings of passivity which we

have suggested. It should not be surprising that between 1830 and 1860 a significant number of militant women joined a crusade to establish their right to define—and limit—man's sexual behavior.

Yet adultery and prostitution were unaccustomed objects of reform even in the enthusiastic and millennial America of the 1830s. The mere discussion of these taboo subjects shocked most Americans; to undertake such a crusade implied no ordinary degree of commitment. The founders of the Female Moral Reform Society, however, were able to find both legitimization for the expression of grievances normally unspoken and an impulse to activism in the moral categories of evangelical piety. Both pious activism and sex-role anxieties shaped the early years of the Female Moral Reform Society. This conjunction of motives was hardly accidental.

The lady founders of the Moral Reform Society and their new organization represented an extreme wing of that movement within American Protestantism known as the Second Great Awakening. These women were intensely pious Christians, convinced that an era of millennial perfection awaited human effort. In this fervent generation, such deeply felt millennial possibilities made social action a moral imperative. Like many of the abolitionists, Jacksonian crusaders against sexual transgression were dedicated activists, compelled to attack sin wherever it existed and in whatever form it assumed—even the unmentionable sin of illicit sexuality.

New Yorkers' first awareness of the moral reform crusade came in the spring of 1832 when the New York Magdalen Society (an organization which sought to reform prostitutes) issued its first annual report. Written by John McDowall, their missionary and agent, the report stated unhesitatingly that 10,000 prostitutes lived and worked in New York City. Not only sailors and other transients, but men from the city's most respected families, were regular brothel patrons.

Lewdness and impurity tainted all sectors of New York society. True Christians, the report concluded, must wage a thoroughgoing crusade against violators of the Seventh Commandment.

The report shocked and irritated respectable New Yorkers—not only by its tone of righteous indignation and implied criticism of the city's old and established families. The report, it seemed clear to many New Yorkers, was obscene, its author a mere seeker after notoriety. Hostility quickly spread from McDowall to the Society itself; its members were verbally abused and threatened with ostracism. The society disbanded.

A few of the women, however, would not retreat. Working quietly, they began to found church-affiliated female moral reform societies. Within a year, they had created a number of such groups, connected for the most part with the city's more evangelical congregations. These pious women hoped to reform prostitutes, but more immediately to warn other God-fearing Christians of the pervasiveness of sexual sin and the need to oppose it. Prostitution was after all only one of the many offenses against the Seventh Commandment; adultery, lewd thoughts and language, and bawdy literature were equally sinful in the eyes of God. These women at the same time continued unofficially to support their former missionary, John McDowall, using his newly established moral reform newspaper to advance their cause not only in the city, but throughout New York State.

After more than a year of such discreet crusading, the women active in the moral reform cause felt sufficiently numerous and confident to organize a second city-wide moral reform society, and renew their efforts to reform the city's prostitutes. On the evening of May 12, 1834, they met at the Third Presbyterian Church to found the New York Female Moral Reform Society.

Nearly four years of opposition and controversy had hardened the women's ardor into a militant determination. They proposed through their organization to extirpate sexual license and the double standard from American society. A forthright list of resolves announced their organization:

> Resolved, That immediate and vigorous efforts should be made to create a public sentiment in respect to this sin; and also in respect to the duty of parents, church members and ministers on the subject, which shall be in stricter accordance with ... the word of God. ...
> Resolved, That the licentious man is no less guilty than his victim, and ought, therefore, to be excluded from all virtuous female society.
> Resolved, That it is the imperious duty of ladies everywhere, and of every religious denomination, to co-operate in the great work of moral reform.

A sense of urgency and spiritual absolutism marked this organizational meeting, and indeed all of the Society's official statements for years to come. "It is the duty of the virtuous to use every consistent moral means to save our country from utter destruction," the women warned. "The sin of licentiousness has made fearful havoc ... drowning souls in perdition and exposing us to the vengeance of a holy God." Americans hopeful of witnessing the promised millennium could delay no longer.

The motivating zeal which allowed the rejection of age-old proprieties and defied the criticism of pulpit and press was no casual and fashionable enthusiasm. Only an extraordinary set of legitimating values could have justified such commitment. And this was indeed the case. The women moral reformers acted in the conscious conviction that God imperiously commanded their work. As they explained soon after organizing their society: "As Christians we must view it in the light of God's word—we must enter into His feelings on the subject—engage in its overthrow just in the manner he would have us. . . . We must look away from all worldly opinions or influences, for they are perverted and wrong; and individually act only as in the presence of God." Though the Society's pious activism had deep roots in the evangelicalism of the Second Great Awakening, the immediate impetus for the founding of the Moral Reform Society came from the revivals Charles G. Finney conducted in New York City between the summer of 1829 and the spring of 1834.

Charles Finney, reformer, revivalist and perfectionist theologian from western New York State, remains a pivotal figure in the history of American Protestantism. The four years Finney spent in New York had a profound influence on the city's churches and reform movements, and upon the consciences generally of the thousands of New Yorkers who crowded his revival meetings and flocked to his churches. Finney insisted that his disciples end any compromise with sin or human injustice. Souls were lost and sin prevailed, Finney urged, because men chose to sin—because they chose not to work in God's vineyard converting souls and reforming sinners. Inspired by Finney's sermons, thousands of New Yorkers turned to missionary work; they distributed Bibles and tracts to the irreligious, established Sunday schools and sent ministers to the frontier. A smaller, more zealous number espoused abolition as well, determined, like Garrison, never to be silent and to be heard. An even smaller number of the most zealous and determined turned—as we have seen—to moral reform.

The program adopted by the Female Moral Reform Society in the spring of 1834 embraced two quite different, though to the Society's founders quite consistent, modes of attack. One was absolutist and millennial, an attempt to convert all of America to perfect moral purity. Concretely the New York women hoped to create a militant nationwide women's organization to fight the double standard and indeed any form of licentiousness—beginning of course in their own homes and neighborhoods. Only an organization of women, they contended, could be trusted with so sensitive and yet monumental a task. At the same time, the Society sponsored a parallel and somewhat more pragmatic attempt to convert and reform New York City's prostitutes. Though strikingly dissimilar in method and geographic scope, both efforts were unified by an uncompromising millennial zeal and by a strident hostility to the licentious and predatory male.

The Society began its renewed drive against prostitution in the fall of 1834 when the executive committee appointed John McDowall their missionary to New York's prostitutes and hired two young men to assist him. The Society's three missionaries visited the female wards of the almshouse, the city hospital and jails, leading prayer meetings, distributing Bibles and tracts. A greater proportion of their time, however, was spent in a more controversial manner, systematically visiting—or to be more accurate, descending upon—brothels, praying with and exhorting both the inmates and their patrons. The missionaries were especially fond of arriving early Sunday morning—catching women and customers as they awoke on the traditionally sacred day. The missionaries would announce their arrival by a vigorous reading of Bible passages, followed by prayer and hymns. At other times they would station themselves across the street from known brothels to observe and note the identity of customers. They soon found their simple presence had an important deterring effect, many men, with doggedly innocent expressions, pausing momentarily and then hastily walking past. Closed coaches, they also reported, were observed to circle suspiciously for upwards of an hour until, the missionary remaining, they drove away.

The Female Moral Reform Society did not depend completely on paid missionaries for the success of such pious harassment. The Society's executive committee, accompanied by like-thinking male volunteers, regularly visited the city's hapless brothels. The members went primarily to pray and to exert moral influence. They were not unaware, however, of the financially disruptive effect that frequent visits of large groups of praying Christians would have. The executive committee also aided the concerned parents (usually rural) of runaway daughters who, they feared, might have drifted to the city and been forced into prostitution. Members visited brothels asking for information about such girls; one pious volunteer even pretended to be delivering laundry in order to gain admittance to a brothel suspected of hiding such a runaway.

In conjunction with their visiting, the Moral Reform Society opened a House of Reception, a would-be refuge for prostitutes seeking to reform. The Society's managers and missionaries felt that if the prostitute could be convinced of her sin, and then offered both a place of retreat and an economic alternative to prostitution, reform would surely follow. Thus they envisioned their home as a "house of industry" where the errant ones would be taught new trades and prepared for useful jobs—while being instructed in morality and religion. When the managers felt their repentant charges prepared to return to society, they attempted to find them jobs with Christian families—and, so far as possible, away from the city's temptations.

Despite their efforts, however, few prostitutes reformed; fewer still appeared, to their benefactresses, to have experienced the saving grace of conversion. Indeed, the number of inmates at the Society's House of Reception was always small. In March 1835, for instance, the executive committee reported only fourteen women at the House. A year later, total admissions had reached but thirty—only four of whom were considered saved. The final debacle came that summer when the regular manager of the House left the city because of poor health. In his absence, the executive committee reported unhappily, the inmates seized control, and discipline and morality deteriorated precipitously. The managers reassembled in the fall to find their home in chaos. Bitterly discouraged, they dismissed the few remaining unruly inmates and closed the building.

The moral rehabilitation of New York's streetwalkers was but one aspect of the Society's attack upon immorality. The founders of the Female Moral Reform Society saw as their principle objective the creation of a woman's crusade to combat sexual license generally and the double standard particularly. American women would no longer willingly tolerate that traditional—and role-defining—masculine ethos which allotted respect to the hearty drinker and the sexual athlete. This age-old code of masculinity was as obviously related to man's social preeminence as it was contrary to society's explicitly avowed norms of purity and domesticity. The subterranean mores of the American male must be confronted, exposed and rooted out.

The principal weapon of the Society in this crusade was its weekly, *The Advocate of Moral Reform*. In the fall of 1834, when the Society hired John McDowall as its agent, it voted as well to purchase his journal and transform it into a national women's paper with an exclusively female staff. Within three years, the *Advocate* grew into one of the nation's most widely read evangelical papers, boasting 16,500 subscribers. By the late 1830s the Society's managers pointed to this publication as their most important activity.

Two themes dominated virtually every issue of the *Advocate* from its founding in January 1835, until the early 1850s. The first was an angry and emphatic insistence upon the lascivious and predatory nature of the American male. Men were the initiators in virtually every cause of adultery or fornication—and the source, therefore, of that widespread immorality which endangered America's spiritual life and delayed the promised millennium. A second major theme in the *Advocate's* editorials and letters was a

The Advocate of Moral Reform was the newspaper of the New York Female Moral Reform Society. Produced by an entirely female staff, the weekly became one of the nation's most widely read evangelical papers, with 16,500 subscribers. The *Advocate* gave women a voice to protest the evils of the double standard and to call for a national union of women. The editorial staff of the *Advocate* pursued moral reform to the point of publishing the names of men and organizations accused of exploiting women.

call for the creation of a national union of women. Through their collective action such a united group of women might ultimately control the behavior of adult males and of the members' own children, particularly their sons.

The founders and supporters of the Female Moral Reform Society entertained several primary assumptions concerning the nature of human sexuality. Perhaps the most central was the conviction that women felt little sexual desire; they were in almost every instance induced to violate the Seventh Commandment by lascivious men who craftily manipulated not their sensuality, but rather the female's trusting and affectionate nature. A woman acted out of romantic love, not carnal desire; she was innocent and defenseless, gentle and passive. "The worst crime alleged against [the fallen woman] in the outset," the *Advocate's* editors explained, "is . . . 'She is without discretion.' She is open-hearted, sincere, and affectionate. . . . She trusts the vows of the faithless. She commits her all into the hands of the deceiver."

The male lecher, on the other hand, was a creature controlled by base sexual drives which he neither could nor would control. He was, the *Advocate's* editors bitterly complained, powerful and decisive; unwilling (possibly unable) to curb his own willfulness, he callously used it to coerce the more passive and submissive female. This was an age of rhetorical expansiveness, and the *Advocate's* editors and correspondents felt little constraint in their delineation of the dominant and aggressive male. "Reckless," "bold," "mad," "drenched in sin" were terms used commonly to describe erring males; they "robbed," "ruined," and "rioted." But one term above all others seemed most fit to describe the lecher—"The Destroyer."

A deep sense of anger and frustration characterized the *Advocate's* discussion of such all-conquering males, a theme reiterated again and again in the letters sent to the paper by rural sympathizers. Women saw themselves with few defenses against the determined male; his will was far stronger than that of woman. Such letters often expressed a bitterness which seems directed not only against the specific seducer, but toward all American men. One representative rural subscriber complained, for example: "Honorable men; they would not plunder; . . . an imputation on their honour might cost a man his life's blood. And yet they are so passingly mean, so utterly contemptible, as basely and treacherously to contrive . . . the destruction of happiness, peace, morality, and all that is endearing in social life; they plunge into degradation, misery, and ruin, those whom they profess to love. O let them not be trusted. Their 'tender mercies are cruel.'"

The double standard seemed thus particularly unjust; it came to symbolize and embody for the Society and its rural sympathizers the callous indifference—indeed at times almost sadistic pleasure—a male-dominated society took in the misfortune of a passive and defenseless woman. The respectable harshly denied her their friendship; even parents might reject her. Often only the brothel offered food and shelter. But what of her seducer? Conventional wisdom found it easy to condone his greater sin: men will be men and right-thinking women must not inquire into such questionable matters.

But it was just such matters, the Society contended, to which women must address themselves. They must enforce God's commandments despite hostility and censure. "Public opinion must be operated upon," the executive committee decided in the winter of 1835, "by endeavoring to bring the virtuous to treat the guilty of both sexes alike, and exercise toward them the same feeling." "Why should a female be trodden under foot," the executive committee's minutes questioned plaintively, "and spurned from society and driven from a parent's roof, if she but fall into sin—while common consent allows the male to habituate himself to this vice, and treats him as not guilty. Has God made a distinction in regard to the two sexes in this respect?" The guilty woman too should be condemned, the Moral Reform Society's quarterly meeting resolved in 1838: "But let not the most guilty of the two—the deliberate destroyer of female innocence—be afforded even an 'apron of fig leaves' to conceal the blackness of his crimes."

Women must unite in a holy crusade against such sinners. The Society called upon pious women throughout the country to shun all social contact with men suspected of improper behavior—even if that behavior consisted only of reading improper books or singing indelicate songs. Church-going women of every village and town must organize local campaigns to outlaw such men from society and hold them up to public judgment. "Admit him not to your house," the executive committee urged, "hold no converse with him, warn others of him, permit not your friends to have fellowship with him, mark him as an evildoer, stamp him as a villain and exclaim, 'Behold the Seducer.'" The power of ostracism could become an effective weapon in the defense of morality.

A key tactic in this campaign of public exposure was the Society's willingness to publish the names of men suspected of sexual immorality. The *Advocate's* editors announced in their first issue that they intended to pursue this policy, first begun by John McDowall in his *Journal.* "We think it proper," they stated defiantly, "even to expose names, for the same reason that the names of thieves and robbers are published, that the public may know them and govern themselves accordingly. We mean to let the licentious know, that if they are not ashamed of their debasing vice, we will not be ashamed to expose them. . . . It is a justice which we owe each other." Their readers responded enthusiastically to this invitation. Letters from rural subscribers poured into the *Advocate,* recounting specific instances of seduction in their towns and warning readers to avoid the men described. The editors dutifully set them in type and printed them.

Within New York City itself the executive committee of the Society actively investigated charges of seduction and immorality. A particular target of their watchfulness was the city's employment agencies—or information offices as they were then called; these were frequently fronts for the white-slave trade. The *Advocate* printed the names and addresses of suspicious agencies, warning women seeking employment to avoid them at all costs. Prostitutes whom the Society's missionaries visited in brothels, in prison or in the city hospital were urged to report the names of men who had first seduced them and also of their later customers; they could then be published in the *Advocate.* The executive committee undertook as well a lobbying campaign in Albany to secure the passage of a statute making seduction a crime for the male participant. While awaiting the passage of the

measure, the executive committee encouraged and aided victims of seduction (or where appropriate their parents or employers) to sue their seducers on the grounds of loss of services.

Ostracism, exposure, and statutory enactment offered immediate, if unfortunately partial, solutions to the problem of male licentiousness. But for the seduced and ruined victim such vengeance came too late. The tactic of preference, women moral reformers agreed, was to educate children, especially young male children, to a literal adherence to the Seventh Commandment. This was a mother's task. American mothers, the *Advocate's* editors repeated endlessly, must educate their sons to reject the double standard. No child was too young, no efforts too diligent in this crucial aspect of socialization. The true foundations of such a successful effort lay in an early and highly pietistic religious education and in the inculcation of a related imperative—the son's absolute and unquestioned obedience to his mother's will. "Obedience, entire and unquestioned, must be secured, or all is lost." The mother must devote herself whole-heartedly to this task for self-will in a child was an ever-recurring evil. "Let us watch over them continually. . . . Let us . . . teach them when they go out and when they come in—when they lie down, and when they rise up. . . ." A son must learn to confide in his mother instinctively; no thought should be hidden from her.

Explicit education in the Seventh Commandment itself should begin quite early for bitter experience has shown that no child was too young for such sensual temptation. As her son grew older, his mother was urged to instill in him a love for the quiet of domesticity, a repugnance for the unnatural excitements of the theater and tavern. He should be taught to prefer home and the companionship of pious women to the temptations of bachelor life. The final step in a young man's moral education would come one evening shortly before he was to leave home for the first time. That night, the *Advocate* advised its readers, the mother must spend a long earnest time at his bedside (ordinarily in the dark to hide her natural blushes) discussing the importance of maintaining his sexual purity and the temptations he would inevitably face in attempting to remain true to his mother's religious principles.

Mothers, not fathers, were urged to supervise the sexual education of sons. Mothers, the Society argued, spent most time with their children; fathers were usually occupied with business concerns and found little time for their children. Sons were naturally close to their mothers and devoted maternal supervision would cement these natural ties. A mother devoted to the moral reform cause could be trusted to teach her son to reject the traditional ethos of masculinity and accept the higher—more feminine—code of Christianity. A son thus educated would be inevitably a recruit in the women's crusade against sexual license.

The Society's general program of exposure and ostracism, lobbying and education depended for effectiveness upon the creation of a national association of militant and pious women. In the fall of 1834, but a few months after they had organized their Society, its New York officers began to create such a woman's organization. At first they worked through the *Advocate* and the small network of sympathizers John McDowall's efforts had created. By the spring of 1835, however, they were able to hire a minister to travel through western New York State "in behalf of Moral Reform causes." The following year the committee sent two female missionaries, the editor of the Society's newspaper and a paid female agent, on a thousand-mile tour of the New England states. Visiting women's groups and churches in Brattleboro, Deerfield, Northampton, Pittsfield, the Stockbridges and many other towns, the ladies rallied their sisters to the moral reform cause and helped organize some forty-one new auxiliaries. Each succeeding summer saw similar trips by paid agents and managers of the Society

throughout New York State and New England. By 1839, the New York Female Moral Reform Society boasted some 445 female auxiliaries, principally in greater New England. So successful were these efforts that within a few years the bulk of the Society's membership and financial support came from its auxiliaries. In February 1838, the executive committee voted to invite representatives of these auxiliaries to attend the Society's annual meeting. The following year the New York Society voted at its annual convention to reorganize as a national society—The American Female Moral Reform Society; the New York group would be simply one of its many constituent societies.

This rural support was an indispensable part of the moral reform movement. The local auxiliaries held regular meetings in churches, persuaded hesitant ministers to preach on the Seventh Commandment, urged Sunday school teachers to confront this embarrassing but vital question. They raised money for the executive committee's ambitious projects, convinced at least some men to form male reform societies, and did their utmost to ostracize suspected lechers. When the American Female Moral Reform Society decided to mount a campaign to induce the New York State legislature to pass a law making seduction a criminal offense, the Society's hundreds of rural auxiliaries wrote regularly to their legislators, circulated petitions and joined their New York City sisters in Albany to lobby for the bill (which was finally passed in 1848).

In addition to such financial and practical aid, members of the moral reform society's rural branches contributed another crucial, if less tangible, element to the reform movement. This was their commitment to the creation of a feeling of sisterhood among all morally dedicated women. Letters from individuals to the *Advocate* and reports from auxiliaries make clear, sometimes even in the most explicit terms, that many American women experienced a depressing sense of isolation. The fact that social values and attitudes were established by men and oriented to male experiences only exacerbated women's feelings of inferiority and irrelevance. Again and again the Society's members were to express their desire for a feminine-sororial community which might help break down this isolation, lighten the monotony and harshness of life, and establish a counter-system of female values and priorities.

The New York Female Moral Reform Society quite consciously sought to inspire in its members a sense of solidarity in a cause peculiar to their sex, and demanding total commitment, to give them a sense of worthiness and autonomy outside woman's traditionally confining role. Its members, their officers forcefully declared, formed a united phalanx twenty thousand strong, "A UNION OF SENTIMENT AND EFFORT AMONG . . . VIRTUOUS FEMALES FROM MAINE TO ALABAMA." The officers of the New York Society were particularly conscious of the emotional importance of female solidarity within their movement—and the significant role that they as leaders played in the lives of their rural supporters. "Thousands are looking to us," the executive committee recorded in their minutes with mingled pride and responsibility, "with the expectation that the principles we have adopted, and the example we have set before the world will continue to be held up & they reasonably expect to witness our *united onward* movements till the conflict shall end in Victory."

For many of the Society's scattered members, the moral reform cause was their only contact with the world outside farm or village— the *Advocate* perhaps the only newspaper received by the family. A sense of solidarity and of emotional affiliation permeated the correspondence between rural members and the executive committee. Letters and even official reports inevitably began with the salutation, "Sisters," "Dear Sisters" or "Beloved Sisters." Almost every letter and report expressed the deep affection Society members felt for their like-thinking sisters in the cause of moral reform— even if their contact came only through letters and the *Advocate*. "I now pray and will not cease to pray," a woman in Syracuse, New York, wrote, "that your hearts may be encouraged and your hands strengthened." Letters to the Society's executive committee often promised unfailing loyalty and friendship; members and leaders pledged themselves ever ready to aid either local societies or an individual sister in need. Many letters from geographically isolated women reported that the Society made it possible for them for the first time to communicate with like-minded women. A few, in agitated terms, wrote about painful experiences with the double standard which only their correspondence with the *Advocate* allowed them to express and share.

Most significantly, the letters expressed a new consciousness of power. The moral reform society was based on the assertion of female moral superiority and the right and ability of women to reshape male behavior. No longer did women have to remain passive and isolated within the structuring presence of husband or father. The moral reform movement was, perhaps for the first time, a movement within which women could forge a sense of their own identity.

And its founders had no intention of relinquishing their new-found feeling of solidarity and autonomy. A few years after the Society was founded, for example, a group of male evangelicals established a Seventh Commandment Society. They promptly wrote to the Female Moral Reform Society suggesting helpfully that since men had organized, the ladies could now disband; moral reform was clearly an area of questionable propriety. The New York executive committee responded quickly, firmly—and negatively. Women throughout America, they wrote, had placed their trust in a female moral reform society, and in female officers. Women, they informed men, believed in both their own right and ability to combat the problem; it was decidedly a woman's, not a man's issue. "The paper is now in the right hands," one rural subscriber wrote: "This is the appropriate work for *women*. . . . Go on Ladies, go on, in the strength of the Lord."

In some ways, indeed, the New York Female Moral Reform Society could be considered a militant women's organization. Although it was not overtly part of the woman's rights movement, it did concern itself with a number of feminist issues, especially those relating to woman's economic role. Society, the *Advocate's* editors argued, had unjustly confined women to domestic tasks. There were many jobs in society that women could and should be trained to fill. They could perform any light indoor work as well as men. In such positions—as clerks and artisans—they would receive decent wages and consequent self-respect. And this economic emphasis was no arbitrary or inappropriate one, the Society contended. Thousands of women simply had to work; widows, orphaned young women, wives and mothers whose husbands could not work because of illness or intemperance had to support themselves and their children. Unfortunately, they had now to exercise these responsibilities on the pathetically inadequate salaries they received as domestics, washerwomen or seamstresses—crowded, underpaid and physically unpleasant occupations. By the end of the 1840s, the Society had adopted the cause of the working woman and made it one of their principal concerns—in the 1850s even urging women to join unions and, when mechanization came to the garment industry, helping underpaid seamstresses rent sewing machines at low rates.

The Society sought consciously, moreover, to demonstrate woman's ability to perform successfully in fields traditionally reserved for men. Quite early in their history they adopted the policy of hiring only women employees. From the first, of course, only women had been officers and managers of the Society. And after a few years, these officers began to hire women in preference to men as agents and to urge other charitable socie-ties and government agencies to do likewise. In February, 1835, for instance, the executive committee hired a woman agent to solicit subscriptions to the *Advocate*. That summer they hired another woman to travel through New England and New York State organizing auxiliaries and giving speeches to women on moral reform. In October of 1836, the executive officers appointed two women as editors of their journal—undoubtedly among the first of their sex in this country to hold such positions. In 1841, the executive committee decided to replace their male financial agent with a woman bookkeeper. By 1843 women even set type and did the folding for the Society's journal. All these jobs, the ladies proudly, indeed aggressively stressed, were appropriate tasks for women.

The broad feminist implications of such statements and actions must have been apparent to the officers of the New York Society. And indeed the Society's executive committee maintained discreet but active ties with the broader women's rights movement of the 1830s, 40s and 50s; at one point at least, they flirted with official endorsement of a bold woman's rights position. Evidence of this flirtation can be seen in the minutes of the executive committee and occasionally came to light in the articles and editorials appearing in the *Advocate*. As early as the mid-1830s, for instance, the executive committee began to correspond with a number of women who were then or were later to become active in the woman's rights movement. Lucretia Mott, abolitionist and pioneer feminist, was a founder and secretary of the Philadelphia Female Moral Reform Society; as such she was in frequent communication with the New York executive committee. Emma Willard, a militant advocate of women's education and founder of the Troy Female Seminary, was another of the executive committee's regular correspondents. Significantly, when Elizabeth Blackwell, the first woman doctor in either the United States or Great Britain, received her medical degree, Emma Willard wrote to the New York executive committee asking its members to use their influence to find her a job. The Society did more than that. The *Advocate* featured a story dramatizing Dr. Black-well's struggles. The door was now open for other women, the editors urged; medicine was a peculiarly appropriate profession for sensitive and sympathetic womankind. The Society offered to help interested women in securing admission to medical school.

One of the most controversial aspects of the early women's rights movement was its criticism of the subservient role of women within the American family, and of the American man's imperious and domineering behavior toward women. Much of the Society's rhetorical onslaught upon the male's lack of sexual accountability served as a screen for a more general—and less socially acceptable—resentment of masculine social preeminence. Occasionally, however, the *Advocate* expressed such resentment overtly. An editorial in 1838, for example, revealed a deeply felt antagonism toward the power exerted by husbands over their wives and children. "A portion of the inhabitants of this favored land," the Society admonished, "are groaning under a despotism, which seems to be modeled precisely after that of the Autocrat of Russia. . . . We allude to the tyranny exercised in the HOME department, where lordly man, 'clothed with a little brief authority,' rules his trembling subjects with a rod of iron, conscious of entire impunity, and exalting in his fancied superiority." The Society's editorialist continued, perhaps even more bitterly: "Instead of regarding his wife as a help-mate for him, and equal sharer in his joys and sorrows, he looks upon her as a useful article of furniture, which is valuable only for the benefit derived from it, but which may be thrown aside at pleasure." Such behavior, the editorial carefully emphasized, was not only commonplace, experienced by many of the Society's own members—even the wives of "Christians" and of ministers—but was accepted and even justified by society; was it not sanctioned by the Bible?

At about the same time, indeed, the editors of the *Advocate* went so far as to print an attack upon "masculine" translations and interpretations of the Bible, and especially of Paul's epistles. This appeared in a lengthy article written by Sarah Grimké, a "notorious" feminist and aboli-tionist. The executive committee clearly sought to associate their organization more closely with the nascent woman's rights movement. Calling upon American women to read and interpret the Bible for themselves, Sarah Grimké asserted that God had created woman the absolute equal of man. But throughout history, man, being stronger, had usurped woman's natural rights. He had subjected wives and daughters to his physical control and had evolved religious and scientific rationalizations to justify this domination. "Men have endeavored to entice, or to drive women from almost every sphere of moral action." Miss Grimké charged: "'Go home and spin' is the . . . advice of the domestic tyrant. . . . The first duty, I believe, which devolves on our sex now is to think for themselves. . . . Until we take our stand side by side with our brother; until we read all the precepts of the Bible as addressed to woman as well as to man, and lose . . . the consciousness of sex, we shall never fulfill the end of our existence." "Those who do undertake to labor," Miss Grimké wrote from her own and her sister's bitter experiences, "are the scorn and ridicule of their own and the other sex." "We are so little accustomed *to think for ourselves*," she continued,

> that we submit to the dictum of prejudice, and of usurped authority, almost without an effort to redeem ourselves from the unhallowed shackles which have so long bound us; almost without a desire to rise from that degradation and bondage to which we have been consigned by man, and by which the faculties of our minds, and the powers of our spiritual nature, have been prevented from expanding to their full growth, and are sometimes wholly crushed.

Each woman must re-evaluate her role in society; no longer could she depend on husband or father to assume her responsibilities as a free individual.

No longer, Sarah Grimké argued, could she be satisfied with simply caring for her family or setting a handsome table. The officers of the Society, in an editorial comment following this article, admitted that she had written a radical critique of woman's traditional role. But they urged their members, "It is of immense importance to our sex to possess clear and *correct* ideas of our rights and duties."

Sarah Grimké's overt criticism of woman's traditional role, containing as it did an attack upon the Protestant ministry and orthodox interpretations of the Bible, went far beyond the consensus of the *Advocate's* rural subscribers. The following issue contained several letters sharply critical of her and of the managers, for printing her editorial. And indeed the *Advocate* never again published the work of an overt feminist. Their membership, the officers concluded, would not tolerate explicit attacks upon traditional family structure and orthodox Christianity. Anti-male resentment and anger had to be expressed covertly. It was perhaps too threatening or—realistically—too dangerous for respectable matrons in relatively close-knit semi-rural communities in New York, New England, Ohio, or Wisconsin so openly to question the traditional relations of the sexes and demand a new and ominously forceful role for women.

The compromise the membership and the officers of the Society seemed to find most comfortable was one that kept the American woman within the home—but which greatly expanded her powers as pious wife and mother. In rejecting Sarah Grimké's feminist manifesto, the Society's members implicitly agreed to accept the role traditionally assigned a woman: the self-sacrificing, supportive, determinedly chaste wife and mother who limited her "sphere" to domesticity and religion. But in these areas her power should be paramount. The mother, not the father, should have final control of the home and family—especially of the religious and moral education of her children. If the world of economics and public affairs was his, the home must be hers.

And even outside the home, woman's peculiar moral endowment and responsibilities justified her in playing an increasingly expansive role, one which might well ultimately impair aspects of man's traditional autonomy. When man transgressed God's commandments, through licentiousness, religious apathy, the defense of slavery, or the sin of intemperance—woman had both the right and the duty of leaving the confines of the home and working to purify the male world.

The membership of the New York Female Moral Reform Society chose not to openly espouse the women's rights movement. Yet many interesting emotional parallels remain to link the moral reform crusade and the suffrage movement of Elizabeth Cady Stanton, the Grimké sisters and Susan B. Anthony. In its own way, indeed, the war for purification of sexual mores was far more fundamental in its implications for woman's traditional role than the demands for women's education—or even the vote.

Many of the needs and attitudes, moreover, expressed by suffragette leaders at the Seneca Falls Convention and in their efforts in the generation following are found decades earlier in the letters of rural women in the *Advocate of Moral Reform*. Both groups found women's traditionally passive role intolerable. Both wished to assert female worth and values in a heretofore entirely male world. Both welcomed the creation of a sense of feminine loyalty and sisterhood that could give emotional strength and comfort to women isolated within their homes—whether in a remote farmstead or a Gramercy Park mansion. And it can hardly be assumed that the demand for votes for women was appreciably more radical than a moral absolutism which encouraged women to invade bordellos, befriend harlots and publicly discuss rape, seduction and prostitution.

It is important as well to re-emphasize a more general historical perspective. When the pious women founders of the Moral Reform Society gathered at the Third Free Presbyterian Church, it was fourteen years before the Seneca Falls Convention—which has traditionally been accepted as the beginning of the woman's rights movement in the United States. There simply was no woman's movement in the 1830s. The future leaders were either still adolescents or just becoming dissatisfied with aspects of their role. Women advocates of moral reform were among the very first American women to challenge their completely passive, home-oriented image. They were among the first to travel throughout the country without male chaperones. They published, financed, even set type for their own paper and defied a bitter and long-standing male opposition to their cause. They began, in short, to create a broader, less constricted sense of female identity. Naturally enough, they were dependent upon the activist impulse and legitimating imperatives of evangelical religion. This was indeed a complex symbiosis, the energies of pietism and the grievances of role discontent creating the new and activist female consciousness which characterized the history of the American Female Moral Reform Society in antebellum America. Their experience, moreover, was probably shared, though less overtly, by the thousands of women who devoted time and money to the great number of reform causes which multiplied in Jacksonian America. Women in the abolition and the temperance movements (and to a lesser extent in more narrowly evangelical and religious causes) also developed a sense of their ability to judge for themselves and of their right to publicly criticize the values of the larger society. The lives and self-image of all these women had changed—if only so little—because of their new reforming interests.

Questions for Study and Review

1. In what ways were the activities of the FMRS extensions of the politicization of the household that began with the Revolution?

2. How did urbanization change the relations of women and men in the family and in the public sphere?

3. How did women's sense of moral and spiritual superiority both encourage and inhibit them from taking on new public roles?

4. In the 1910s and 1920s as in the 1960s, many women would come to favor a single sexual standard for women and men. Why did mid-nineteenth-century women view a more restrictive sexual standard as most beneficial to both sexes?

Suggested Readings

Carroll Smith-Rosenberg, *Religion and the Rise of the City: The New York City Mission Movement, 1812–1870* (1971).

Mary Ryan, "The Power of Women's Networks: A Case Study of Female Moral Reform in Antebellum America," *Feminist Studies* (Spring 1979).

Christine Stansell, *City of Women: Sex and Class in New York, 1789–1860* (1986).

Ronald G. Walters, ed., *Primers for Prudery: Sexual Advice to Victorian Americans* (1974).

Jed Dannenbaum, "The Origins of Temperance Activism and Militancy among American Women," *Journal of Social History* (Winter 1981).

Ellen Dubois and Linda Gordon, "Seeking Ecstasy on the Battlefield: Danger and Pleasure in the Nineteenth-Century Feminist Sexual Thought," *Feminist Studies* (Spring 1983).

NINE

Women's Antislavery Activism in Rochester, New York

Nancy A. Hewitt

When Sarah Grimké published her demand for recognition of women's complete equality with man in the *Advocate of Moral Reform* in 1838, she spoke from experiences in the campaign to end not only sexual but also racial slavery. For her, the two were deeply intertwined: Slave women were forced to submit to the sexual demands of planters and free women were trained to submit to the social authority of patriarchs. Daughters of a southern planter, Sarah and her sister Angelina infused abolitionism with a new vigor, but also with new tensions.

When they settled in Philadelphia in the 1820s and converted to Quakerism—the denomination with the longest history of antislavery protests— the Grimkés immediately gained celebrity status. As Southerners rejecting slavery; as eyewitnesses to the physical, psychological, and sexual brutality of the system; as women willing to speak out publicly before "promiscuous" audiences of men and women, the sisters initially captivated antislavery advocates even as they agitated opponents. Their success, however, soon intensified debates over women's proper role within antislavery societies. These debates resulted in the expansion of women's antislavery efforts but also

in greater conflict among female reformers and between female and male abolitionists.

Rochester, New York—home of Frederick Douglass and Susan B. Anthony, of Charles Grandison Finney's first major revival, and of hundreds of grass roots abolitionists—provides the setting for Hewitt's study of these developments at the local level. Here evangelically inspired white women, several of whom also belonged to the local Female Moral Reform Society, formed a women's antislavery circle in 1835 and joined in the massive petition campaign of 1837. This society dissolved amid controversies over women's place in the movement. A new association soon appeared comprised of both women and men, most of whom were Quakers. Many of these more radical abolitionists embraced women's rights by mid-century. In response, evangelical women reemerged, supporting their male kin in the recently created Liberty Party. Throughout these years, local black women also struggled to make their voices heard on the slave's behalf.

The various associations and alliances forged by Rochester's female abolitionists illuminate fundamental divisions in antebellum America's attitudes toward politics. Excluded from electoral politics, all women were forced to devise innovative means to induce social change. Their choice of moral suasion or constitutional law, of outraged demands or respectable appeals, of sexual and racial equality or "natural" hierarchies, reflected differences within society at large.

Few Rochester women had any direct contact with the lives of the female slaves they sought to free. We do not know what sense they would have made of Deborah White's claim, in a following article, that slave women carved out their own system of values and status within bondage. We do know that abolitionism led some women to challenge the dominant system of values, North and South. Such challenges ultimately affected the lives of all Americans by raising significant questions regarding the boundaries of women's lives, free or slave.

Northern women dedicated to the black slave's emancipation frequently organized themselves into associations for the promotion and management of antislavery fairs in the decades prior to the Civil War. These colorful markets, which were held periodically in communities throughout New England and Western New York, offered for sale goods both domestic and foreign produced by friends of the slave. The purpose was to raise money for the pursuit of slavery's abolition and to provide a means for females, themselves the victims of political disfranchisement and social discrimination, to participate in the struggle for reform. Indeed, the fairs organized by local women's antislavery sewing circles and ladies' antislavery societies were perhaps the only tactic that all abolitionists regarded as appropriate for female activists. Yet even the style and conduct of these fairs often reflected the profound division among female abolitionists over the tactics and strategies proper for women to pursue in the slave's cause. Always the clash was between those female reformers who advocated moral suasion, which allowed for the equal participation of men and women in the cause, and those who advocated an electoral solution that limited women to an auxiliary role in the cause.

The issue of woman's role in abolitionism was directly confronted at the May 1840 meeting of the American Anti-Slavery Society (AASS). Abby Kelley, a Quaker abolitionist, was elected to the Executive Committee that year. Her victory climaxed a series of clashes within the Society and led directly to its division. The division was rooted in three major issues: churches' support of slavery, political action, and the role of women. Those who remained within the AASS criticized churches' collaboration with slaveholders, advocated moral suasion as the primary means of social change, and supported the full and equal participation of women in the antislavery cause. Those who abandoned the AASS emphasized, instead, the continued potential for both churches and political parties to increase antislavery sentiment and the inappropriateness of women's direct efforts in either arena.

There were advocates of each position in Western New York. The first men's antislavery societies of Rochester and Monroe County, established in 1833 and 1834, respectively, supported William Lloyd Garrison's doctrine of immediate emancipation. A black and white women's antislavery society, founded in 1834 and 1835, respectively, declared themselves auxiliaries to the Garrison-led AASS. In 1837, some of Rochester's male antislavery leaders joined in the call for a state-wide society that would question political candidates on their antislavery stands. Three years later, several Rochesterians were involved in the founding of the Liberty Party and the advocacy of third party politics as the best antislavery strategy. Simultaneously, Garrisonian support among men and women was growing in Rochester, evidenced by the petition campaigns of 1837 and 1842, by participation in the AASS annual meetings, by coverage of local antislavery activities in *The Liberator,* and by the tours of AASS agents in Western New York.

One such agent, Abby Kelley, toured the region in 1840 and 1842 and helped organize the Western New York Anti-Slavery Society. The founding meeting brought together local advocates of both moral suasion and political

Abridged from "The Social Origins of Women's Antislavery Politics in Western New York" by Nancy Hewitt in *Crusaders and Compromisers: Essays on the Relationship of the Antislavery Struggle to the Antebellum Party System,* Alan M. Kraut, Ed. (Greenwood Press, Inc., Westport, CT, 1983), pp. 205–34. Copyright © 1983 by Alan M. Kraut. Used with permission. The author wishes to thank Alan M. Kraut, Jack McKivigan, and Judith Wellman for their generous assistance on this article.

One area in which women played an active public role was in the antislavery movement. Pictured here are members of the Philadelphia Anti-Slavery Society. Dissent over the best way to achieve the objective of ending slavery—whether through appeals to public sentiment or through political action—led to splits among groups of antislavery activists and abolitionists.

abolitionism. At the first annual meeting the following December, the advocates of the two positions resolved to work together. We "repudiate with indignation," they claimed,

> every sectarian, political, or other test, that may be attempted to be forced upon us as abolitionists; but though we may be of every form of religious and political opinions, Christian and Infidel, war men and peace men, voters and non-resistants, we unite for mutual co-operation to effect the one great object of converting the entire public to abolitionism.

Yet the breach between Rochester's moral suasion and political abolitionists ran far deeper than resolutions could heal. Abolitionism was an ideology that spoke as clearly to abolitionists' own social and economic concerns as to those of the slave. Rochester's antislavery men and women came from different social and economic situations and their abolitionism— both its ideological underpinnings and its expressions in action—continued to reflect these differences.

Moreover, women reformers faced a special obstacle in the 1830s and 1840s that did not affect their male counterparts. New definitions of womanhood, emerging during the first third of the nineteenth century, were constricting women's public role. The evangelical revivals of that era, led in Rochester by Charles Grandison Finney, had initially encouraged woman's antislavery activism as an extension of her piety. However, when abolitionists launched an attack on both churches that condoned slavery and those who remained silent on the issue, Finney and other evangelicals began to curb their support of some reform efforts. Specifically, many evangelicals charged that it was unseemly for women to play a public role in reform and that such behavior could only erode the Christian home, which was women's responsibility to preserve.

At the World Anti-Slavery Convention in London in 1840, one of Rochester's leading antislavery ministers, the Baptist Elon Galusha, assured his English counterparts that amongst his exceedingly numerous constituency in America the "ladies took no part in the business of societies" though he admitted that "a very small minority of the abolitionists . . . had allowed the innovation." Reverend Galusha was right in large part; most women chose to retreat into the domestic sphere or at least to shift their efforts into more socially acceptable church and charitable activities. Yet some pursued innovative roles in abolitionism with the support of male co-workers, and many of those who temporarily submitted to social pressure and retreated in the 1830s reemerged as active abolitionists in the 1850s.

The differences among abolitionist women—in their nativity, family background, religious affiliation, work experience, and economic status—were determining factors in the approach they adopted toward reform. Analysis of these differences among Rochester female reformers unearths the roots of female abolitionism in that hothouse of reform. By the 1830s, the village of Rochester was a burgeoning commercial center, the hub of an increasingly specialized agricultural hinterland, and one of the nation's fastest growing cities as well as a hotbed of religious and reform enthusiasms. With the opening of the Erie Canal in 1822, the city became a depot for goods, for people, and for social and political movements as they traveled between eastern urban centers and frontier communities. Rochester's demographic and institutional development was accordingly diversified and dynamic. During the 1830s and 1840s, Quakers, free blacks, and Irish and German immigrants joined New England Yankees and Maryland aristocrats on the community's radiating paths of settlement. Simultaneously, vil-

lage councils, schools, almshouses, and voluntary associations joined family and church at the loci of community governance. Improvements in transportation and communication and increases in population proceeded apace as did residential segregation and class and ethnic stratification.

These changes nurtured a large and vital community of social activists in Rochester and its hinterlands. From tract to temperance societies, benevolent institutions to woman's rights conventions, moral crusades to political campaigns, Rochesterians carved a profusion of pathways to social change in the first half of the nineteenth century. Women were prominent, often dominant, on these paths. Within the first decade of settlement, the wives of Rochester's religious, political, and business leaders had formed a missionary society, a charity school, and a Female Charitable Society. These activities were well supported by their male kin and by the ministers of Rochester's leading churches: First Presbyterian and St. Luke's Episcopal.

In the winter of 1834, a local antislavery paper, the *Rights of Man,* noted that "many benevolent ladies of Rochester, in years that are past, justly won the applause of the philanthropist and Christian, in their exertions on behalf of the oppressed and suffering *Greeks.*" Yet, noting that "the colored females in this village" had recently formed the first female antislavery society in Western New York, the editor wondered if there were "not motives quite as strong and patriotic to urge" benevolent ladies "onward in behalf of *their own* oppressed and suffering American sisters and brethren?" Regrettably, no further notice exists of the black women who introduced their sex into antislavery activity in Rochester. Their example, however, was followed by white women who formed the Rochester Female Anti-Slavery Society (RFASS) the next year.

Many of the women who led the RFASS in 1835 had been active previously in benevolent enterprises and a substantial majority had husbands or fathers who were active abolitionists. Yet these women were not, generally, members of the city's first families but rather of its most dynamic economic sector of shopkeepers and artisans. Indeed, the RFASS was refused the support of Mrs. Jonathan Child—the daughter of the city's founder, wife of its first mayor, sister-in-law of St. Luke's minister, and officer of the Charitable Society. She replied to their call for assistance by asserting that "combined public effort or co-operation" on the part of females could not be "exerted with propriety" on this subject. Unlike Mrs. Child, who was a Maryland-born Episcopalian aristocrat, Rochester's first female abolitionists were New Englanders or Eastern New Yorkers of middling economic circumstances and Presbyterian or Baptist faith. Several played prominent roles in the Finney-led revivals of 1830–31 and in 1835 turned their evangelical enthusiasm to "immediate emancipation" as the only proper response to slavery, which was "a gross violation of the law of God."

They obtained hundreds of their sisters' signatures on antislavery petitions circulated in Rochester and the surrounding county. The 600 female signatures collected in January 1837 and the 900 gathered the following September are the fullest testimony to the cause's appeal among Western New York women. Yet in the midst of national antislavery debates over women's role in abolitionism, the RFASS disappeared, and no new autonomous female antislavery society was formed for thirteen years. In the interim, men's political antislavery societies flourished as did a joint men's and women's society formed by a new group of local residents.

The signatures of Yankee, evangelical, middle-class women were augmented on the 1837 petitions by those of Hicksite Quaker women from rural New England and downstate New York. The number of these Quakers increased in Rochester from the late 1830s as did their visibility in antislavery circles. After 1840, the AASS concentrated its organizing efforts on this group, sending Quaker Abby Kelley into Western New York. Her labors were complemented by those of male AASS agents and of Lucretia Mott. Mott, a Philadelphia Quaker, provided a prominent voice for abolitionist and feminist concerns within Quaker meetings while Kelley translated that voice into worldly antislavery activity. These two women served as soul-stirring models for their religious sisters in Western New York.

In 1842 the activities of these antislavery and Quaker agents culminated in the founding of the Western New York Anti-Slavery Society (WNYASS). The founding meeting, held at the Washington Street Presbyterian Church, was presided over by Samuel D. Porter, a long-time abolitionist, a Liberty Party member, and the husband of an RFASS founder. A few Yankee, evangelical men joined Porter in the WNYASS, but the vast majority of his co-workers were Hicksite Quaker men and women. Women claimed an equal role in the Society from the beginning: Abby Kelley served on the 1842 resolutions committee while local women served as vice-presidents and members of the Executive Committee that first year. Between 1842 and 1850, women served as officers of the WNYASS, circulated petitions, formed sewing circles, and managed fund-raising fairs throughout Western New York.

In the 1840s, as RFASS members retreated from abolitionist to charitable circles, WNYASS women extended their critique of racial and sexual oppression. By 1848, many WNYASS members had become dissatisfied with Hicksite stands on slavery and women's rights and founded a new Quaker meeting. This association, the Yearly Meeting of Congregational Friends, adopted a "Basis of Religious Association" that established "an order of independent congregations" characterized by "perfect liberty of conscience" and "the equality of women." In the same year, these Quaker women joined Lucretia Mott and Elizabeth Cady Stanton at the Seneca Falls Women's Rights Convention and resolved,

> That being invested by their Creator with the same capabilities, and the same consciousness of responsibility for their exercise, it is demonstrably the right and duty of woman, equally with man, to promote every righteous cause by every righteous means . . . in private and in public, by writing and by speaking, by any instrumentalities to be used, and in any assemblies proper to be held.

A second woman's rights convention, publicized through the pages of Fredrick Douglass' *North Star,* was held in Rochester in August 1848.

While a small group of Rochester women were carrying on the work of moral suasion in increasingly feminist tones, male antislavery leaders were pursuing two distinct paths to abolitionism. Quaker artisans, shopkeepers, and farmers joined their female kin in the WNYASS and followed Garrisonian precepts of immediatism, moral suasion, and come-outerism. They were joined by a few Presbyterian and Unitarian merchants and professionals, but these men more often focused their attention on third party politics. Indeed, some of the latter group had triple affiliations, as WNYASS members, Liberty Party supporters, and antislavery Whigs. Multiple affiliations were not uncommon because many reformers viewed a vote for the Liberty Party more as an act of conscience than a choice of temporal leadership. Liberty Party leader, Samuel D. Porter, for instance, claimed that it was not electoral victory that Liberty Party men sought with their "appeal to the Ballot Box" but the "*moral effect of numbers.*"

Porter was one of several men who increased their third party political efforts during the 1840s, while their female kin retreated from the anti-slavery cause. In 1851, some of these women were wooed back to public action by Julia Griffiths, Fredrick Douglass' editorial assistant at the *North Star.* For the first time since 1837, Quaker and evangelical women joined forces in the public pronouncement of their antislavery sentiments: the occasion was the visit of Julia Griffith's countryman, the British abolitionist George Thompson.

By 1851, debates over third party politics and moral suasion had almost wholly rent national antislavery ranks. Yet within Rochester, Thompson's international stature, the opposition of the local press, and the passage of the Fugitive Slave Act caused abolitionists to close ranks. The massive and varied group of abolitionists that gathered to hear Thompson at Rochester's Corinthian Hall in January of 1851 encouraged local women to invite him back to the city for a grand Anti-Slavery Festival in April. The committee of ladies managing the festival included two former RFASS members, ten members of the WNYASS, Julia Griffiths, and eleven women who appeared in public antislavery ranks for the first time. In addition, the Committee included four members of the Union Anti-Slavery Sewing Society, a local association of black women who held fairs in support of Douglass' *North Star.*

The collective efforts in behalf of the Thompson Anti-Slavery Festival resulted in financial success, yet the Festival was the culmination, not the initiation, of women's unity in the antislavery cause. In the months that followed, white female abolitionists broke into two opposing camps. Their black co-workers, momentarily visible as their efforts converged with those of their white peers, once again faded from the public record. In June of 1851, Douglass helped to crystallize local divisions when he announced his conversion to political abolitionism and the merger of the *North Star* with the *Liberty Party Paper.*

While many local moral suasionists, male and female, withdrew their support from Douglass' new venture, political abolitionists applauded his decision. By 1851, the Liberty Party was all but defunct, most of its members having joined the Free Soilers in 1848. Still, several of Rochester's most important Liberty Party leaders, including Porter, were reluctant to accept the more limited antislavery stand of the new party. They were pleased to have such a prominent figure as Douglass advocate in print what they considered their more principled version of third party politics. Others, already having accepted Free Soil doctrines, believed that it would only be a matter of time before Douglass, too, moved from political abolitionism to political non-extension.

Applause did not always translate into subscriptions, however; and at least temporarily, the support of political abolitionists did not offset the loss of moral suasionists' subscriptions. Thus, Julia Griffiths wrote to Liberty Party leader Gerrit Smith that Douglass' "change on the Constitution has thinned our Subscription list considerably." In response, Griffiths continued, she was "forming an Anti-Slavery sewing circle," which, she trusted, would be "influential, permanent & efficient." She regretted that "bigotry precludes many of the *old* friends from joining" the new Rochester Ladies Anti-Slavery Sewing Society (RLASS).

During 1851, Rochester's white antislavery women followed male reformers' example and divided themselves into opposing camps. One, formed by WNYASS members, continued to criticize churches' collaboration with slaveholders, advocated moral suasion, and asserted women's right to full and equal participation in antislavery agitation. The other, the Rochester Ladies' Anti-Slavery Society (RLASS), consisted of former RFASS members and newcomers of similar backgrounds. They advocated continued faith in established religion and electoral politics and the establishment of a separate women's society to aid antislavery men seeking political leadership. Douglass exacerbated this division, and implicitly acknowledged the importance of women's support, when he suggested that those women who failed to follow his lead into political abolitionism had abandoned the cause entirely.

In a letter to Mrs. Samuel D. Porter, the first president of the RLASS, Douglass claimed that he looked to the new Society "for important services to the antislavery cause in Rochester. . . . At present, you have the field to yourselves," he continued, "and it is meet that you should occupy it." He was quickly reprimanded by Sarah Hallowell, a WNYASS member since 1842, who wrote, "For years (as we need not remind you,) we have labored earnestly and trustingly to get up Annual Fairs, as a means of aiding our cause." She acknowledged that the WNYASS women had recently changed their "modus operandi . . . devoting the principle part of our proceeds to the Boston Bazaar." Yet how could it be otherwise, for the Boston group, led by Garrison, Kelley, and other moral suasionists, continued to accept women as equal partners in antislavery agitation. Douglass was asking women who had worked as his equals to suddenly abandon that place and its attendant feminist implications for a separate and subordinate role. While refusing this change in their work, Hallowell assured Douglass that they never thought of "a final cessation of our associated efforts for the *slave*."

Both groups made their voices heard in support of the slave. Among moral suasionists, women were given a voice and vote in abolitionist strategies on principle. Even among political abolitionists, however, women's contributions to the cause, especially as fundraisers, allowed them to participate in the shaping of antislavery policies. Both groups of antislavery women were distinguished from their non-activist sisters in Rochester by their participation, in whatever capacity, in the public, and highly politicized, debates on slavery. Yet in the shaping of a new public and political role for women, their differences were more important than their similarities.

Political abolitionists emerged from New England villages already penetrated by commercial capitalism. In Rochester, such families' successes rested on the expansion of commerce and industry and the attendant separation of employer and employee, work and home, and men's and women's spheres. Thus, the process that increasingly relegated women to the domestic sphere, also moved their families toward the locus of economic power. Moral suasionist women from Quaker farming villages had long labored side-by-side with the men of their family and community. Differences between the particular tasks performed did not diminish the productive character of women's labor. The separation of work and home and the relegation of women to the latter increased as some men moved to shopkeeping and manufacturing in Rochester, but Quaker social and family circles continued to be dominated by agrarian lifeways, which necessitated the cooperation of household members on a seasonal and cyclical basis.

In community life as well as in labor, Quaker women shared public responsibilities with men that clearly differentiated them from their Yankee counterparts. Nineteenth-century Quaker farming communities, whether in western Massachusetts or on Long Island, maintained informal networks of social control and community welfare that had begun to break down in Yankee villages by the end of the eighteenth century. Quakers cared for the orphaned, old, destitute, and widowed in the midst of dense, kin-connected communities extended through generations of in-marrying neighbors. At the same time that such networks allowed for female economic dependence, the shared labors of agrarian life and women's autonomy in Quaker meeting fostered female independence. Moreover, as in early New England farming communities, the informal character of many social institutions and the importance of face-to-face interactions in community governance enhanced women's public roles and integrated them more fully into economic, social, and political relations.

By the early nineteenth century, the New England villages from which political abolitionists emerged were ordered communities whose hierarchies of status and authority were based on length of residence, wealth, and religious affiliation. New England villages were hardly heterogeneous in twentieth-century terms, but stratification within them was increasingly visible and increasingly a cause of concern. Religious and political leaders voiced even greater concern that geographic mobility, immigration, and economic change would burst the bonds of well-ordered communities and subvert the power of traditional authorities. The establishment of asylums to house deviant and disruptive individuals, the attempts to inculcate social control through religion and education, and the idealization of women as the agents of piety, purity, and order within the home were all employed to sustain the established order. Women were not yet seen as frail vessels. In fact, some memory of Revolutionary foremothers and the tenets of religious revivalism reinforced women's right to a public voice. However, their power was increasingly muted and manifested as feminine influence rather than direct action.

When Yankee women moved to Rochester, they encountered familiar forms whose elaboration and extension heightened their own subordination but also their families' power. Quaker women sought to reestablish the cooperative communities from which they came: they did so on the margins, figuratively and literally, of the city. A primary institutional expression of these divergent relations to local power and community life was the meeting-house. Both the Quaker meeting-house and the major evangelical churches were built at the center of the city in the early years of settlement. The frame building that housed the Hicksite Quakers was overwhelmed, however, by the stone edifices of nearby St. Luke's Episcopal Church and First Presbyterian Church and the more distant spires of the Bethel Free, Baptist, and Methodist churches. Moreover, while evangelical women worshiped in these central churches among fellow Rochesterians, Quakers held their most important sessions outside the city limits. Quarterly and Yearly meetings were held in central New York farming communities while the headquarters of the Congregational Friends was established at Waterloo, some fifty miles east of Rochester, to encourage friends to gather "from various parts of the moral vineyard."

While the revivalist tenets of the Second Great Awakening diffused the hierarchies of eighteenth-century New England church forms, evangelical churches retained the sex segregation of these earlier assemblies. Increased lay participation was accompanied by the elevation of the male minister's personal power while the elevation of woman to a pious and pure pedestal separated her further from the offices of religious authority. Even within evangelical societies that followed congregational forms, women's religious experience was mediated by male ministers, elders, and heads of households. Quakers considered the Inner Light, residing in the individual, as the source of religious truth. This emphasis on unmediated spiritual revelation along with women's right to an equal voice in religious affairs made the Quaker meeting one of the most democratic institutions in nineteenth-century America. Even though these Quaker principles did not always translate into full sexual equality, they provided the surest religious foundation for such equality. Congregational Friends increased the emphasis on the "progressive unfoldings of Divine Light" and on *equality of rights* irrespective of sex" while spiritualist doctrines accepted by some members of the group proclaimed the further diffusion of religious authority and the complete reliance on unmediated revelation through mediums of either sex. Thus, Quakers, emphasizing the Inner Light, gazed outward from Rochester for inspiration and fellowship; evangelicals, more dependent on external authority, established themselves as the city's moral center.

The distinctions in the social fabric of female moral suasionists' lives and that of their adversaries, the political abolitionists, can be detected by examining the Porters and the Posts, two prominent antislavery families in Rochester. At least eight Porter women and five Post women were involved in local antislavery activity, the former in the RFASS and the RLASS and the latter in the WNYASS. A comparison of their social and economic backgrounds and experiences with the forms of their antislavery activity will provide case studies of the general patterns described above.

Susan Porter, a member of the RFASS and the first president of the RLASS, was born Susan Farley in Waldoboro, Maine, in 1812. Her future husband, Samuel D. Porter, a native New Englander, had moved to Rochester in 1827 to clerk in his brother-in-law Everard Peck's bookstore. In 1831, Samuel accepted the tenets of Finneyite evangelicalism and joined the First Presbyterian Church while increasing his involvement in local reform activities. In 1835, Susan married Samuel, moved to Rochester, and joined him at First Presbyterian. The Porters' antislavery, temperance, and moral reform activities convinced them of the need for an evangelical congregation devoted to reform, and in 1836, they joined in the founding of the Bethel Free Presbyterian Church. They changed church membership again, in 1845 and 1855, each time staying within the Presbyterian fold but choosing to worship in a congregation filled with fellow reformers.

As the Porters increased their activities in evangelical and reform circles, Samuel was also improving his economic status. His success in land speculation combined with his kin connections to the commercially successful Peck family solidified the Porters' economic and social standing though the advocacy of antislavery kept Samuel from winning local political power. The expanding Porter family moved into the city's select Third Ward and, with the Pecks, gathered their kin around them, including Susan's sisters, Laura and Martha, and Samuel's father, stepmother, and three unmarried sisters. The extended family worked together in local commercial and professional enterprises and in various reform associations and worshipped together at the Washington Street Presbyterian Church or the First Unitarian Church.

Everard Peck was the most successful of the family members. Having moved to Rochester in its early years of settlement, he opened a bookstore, served as one of the village's first trustees, invested in milling and manufacturing enterprises, and played a leading role in tract, missionary, Bible, temperance, and early antislavery societies. By the 1840s, he was a comfortably established village patriarch with ties to First Presbyterian Church and Whig politics. Everard's first wife, a founder of the Charitable Society, died in 1831; his second wife, Martha Farley, joined her sister Susan in founding the local Orphan Asylum in 1837 and in the RLASS. Susan was married to the most upwardly mobile of the family members. The move from clerk to commercial capitalist and from the First to the Third Ward marked Samuel Porter as one of the new breed of boom town successes. Yet the Porters' continued commitment to evangelical perfectionism and antislavery distinguished them from those who combined upward mobility in the newly competitive commercial world with concern only for self-aggrandizement and social control.

Samuel's own kin may have influenced his perspective on these matters. His father was continually on the verge of economic collapse, being frequently saved from that fate by the labors of his wife and four daughters. Yet Samuel's father, stepmother, and sisters devoted as much time to the antislavery cause as did the more successful branches of the family. Their principled devotion to the cause despite their tenuous economic position likely reminded Samuel of his own good fortune, and the uses to which it should be put. At the same time, laboring for abolition in tandem with the more successful Porters and Pecks may have provided the less successful family members with a sense of stability and inclusion in the city's best circles that their own economic circumstances did not warrant.

The men and women of these families worked for the same causes in sex-segregated religious and reform associations. Susan Porter joined the Charitable Society and the RFASS in 1835, helped found the Orphan Asylum in 1837, labored in women's temperance and moral

reform societies during the 1840s, and joined the Home for Friendless Women at its founding in 1849, and the RLASS in 1851. Samuel Porter combined business with activity in Rochester's first men's antislavery society, in the Young Men's Moral Reform Society, the WNYASS, the Liberty Party, and the Industrial School. He also taught Sunday School, worked for temperance, and served on the all-male Boards of Trustees of the Orphan Asylum and the Home for Friendless Women.

When Fredrick Douglass announced his conversion to political abolitionism in 1851, Samuel Porter was one of his first and strongest supporters. When Julia Griffiths sought allies for her new Ladies' Anti-Slavery Society, she called immediately on Susan Porter and her kinswomen. Susan and her sisters were joined by Samuel's female relatives, by neighbors, and by fellow communicants from Presbyterian and Unitarian congregations. This close-knit network of kin, neighbors, and co-religionists from leading commercial and professional families aided fugitive slaves and free blacks and supported Douglass's paper and third party political efforts over the next fifteen years.

The Posts traveled a significantly different path to and through antislavery activism. Isaac and Amy Post were born into Long Island Quaker farming communities in 1800 and 1802, respectively. Isaac moved to a central New York Quaker community in the 1820s in search of better farmland, and Amy joined him there upon their marriage in 1828. Sarah Kirby soon journeyed from Long Island to aid her sister Amy in the care of her home and children; and the entire entourage moved on to Rochester in 1836. When Isaac gave up farming for butchering and then shopkeeping, Amy increased her activities in temperance and abolition campaigns. She was joined in this work by her sister Sarah, her daughter Mary, her aunt Phebe Willis, and her cousin Ann Willetts. Amy combined public activism with the rearing of five children in a household continually expanded by relatives, boarders, and free black and Irish servants. The Posts hosted local abolition, women's rights, and spiritualist circles as well as fugitive slaves and itinerant lecturers throughout the pre-Civil War period.

The Posts retained strong ties to the Quaker communities of Long Island and central New York. Many of their friends and fellow activists followed similar paths to Western New York and created a new Quaker community, knit together by associated religious and reform efforts and by intermarriage. Quaker families from Rochester and the surrounding farming communities met at the Yearly Meeting of Congregational Friends in Waterloo, New York, to discuss religion, slavery, temperance, education, Indian rights, capital punishment, communitarian settlements, labor reform, and women's rights. Back in Rochester, these same men and women joined in the establishment of spiritualist circles, manual labor schools, and anti-tobacco campaigns while the women worked separately to organize women's rights conventions, a working women's protective union, and antislavery fairs.

The Posts and their co-workers rarely found acceptance in the city's centers of economic and political power. Most established themselves as shopkeepers, artisans, or farmers in the early 1830s. Many, including the Posts, fell on hard times at least once in the next decade; several changed occupations several times without ever improving their economic status; and a few joined in the California Gold Rush or other westward movements in search of a better living. At best, moral suasionists entered the lower rungs of Rochester's middling classes, but they did not have the ties to local centers of business and politics of similarly situated political abolitionist families. While marginal to Rochester's dominant political and commercial sectors, moral suasionists sought to challenge and penetrate the social conscience and thereby shape the political and economic power of those sectors. Female supporters of political

abolitionists were indirectly linked to that sector through their male kin. Female moral suasionists had no such indirect ties; their influence would only be felt, they believed, if they announced their radical doctrines in bold and public voices. Yet because their ideas were likely to be rejected by local leaders, even had they been voiced by men, these women often turned to family, friends, and fellow reformers in Western New York and throughout the Northeast and Old Northwest to sustain their antislavery efforts.

The language and tactics of moral suasionist and political abolitionist women clearly reflect their contrasting social backgrounds, gender relations, and ideological perspectives on abolitionism. Moral suasionist women called on "all who have hearts to feel" to "come forward in the work of banishing slavery from the land" and to "be a 'light unto the world.'" Political abolitionist women stated in equally "plain terms, the course they design[ed] to pursue": our "object shall be to raise funds for Anti-Slavery purposes." Light to the world versus financier to the cause, direct action versus influence and support: these two opposing groups self-consciously and publicly articulated their positions on women's proper role in abolitionism. The antislavery fair mentioned in the beginning of this essay is an especially useful vane for detecting differences among antislavery women. Though fairs were universally popular in female abolitionist circles, the style and arrangement of fairs reflected the markedly different backgrounds and values of their organizers.

The Rochester Anti-Slavery Sewing Circle was a democratically organized association of WNYASS women devoted to the work of managing antislavery fairs. The term circle reflected the egalitarian structure of the association. Announcements of fairs appeared with the names of all Sewing Circle members unadorned by titles of office. A secretary and president were selected periodically for the fulfillment of particular duties relating to a fair or convention, but even these offices were defined by a task to be performed rather than a position to be filled. While most activities relating to WNYASS fairs took place in Rochester, fair committees included women from surrounding towns; and in several of these towns, women also formed independent sewing circles. One impetus for the formation of these circles was the desire of WNYASS women to reach the largest number of potential antislavery converts. In the winter of 1848, the WNYASS sponsored fairs in at least fourteen villages. The following November, the Fair Committee announced that the antislavery "friends in Western New York have opened a store for the benefit of the cause in eleven villages in the vicinity of Rochester."

Women advocates of political abolitionism in Rochester organized their fairs through the Rochester Ladies' Anti-Slavery Society, an association exclusively for women. Members generally belonged to no other antislavery society. This Society was hierarchically organized; the nineteen original members elected ten officers from among themselves to run the association. Published reports and announcements were accompanied by lists of the officers in rank order. All officers and members of the RLASS were Rochester residents, and all fairs managed by them were held in the city. This centralization was encouraged by the RLASS's concern with raising funds and by members' centrality to Rochester's social and economic institutions. A few women from surrounding towns did provide goods for the fairs, but the most substantial extra-local contributions came from England, Ireland, and Scotland. Aid from these areas could be accepted without impinging on the centralization of RLASS efforts.

The sale of articles from Britain aided the RLASS in attracting a new class of local citizens to the cause. The RLASS felt "amply repaid" for its labors at the March, 1852 Anti-Slavery Fair because a "class of Rochester citizens were reached" by Douglass' antislavery appeal "who had, in all probability, never heard it before."

The particular class attracted is suggested by the Society's prolonged praise of the Fair's "most saleable" items: "finely wrought baby linen, the exquisite seaweed baskets, the drawings, the collection of Irish shells, and the beautiful embroidery." In following years, they accompanied the sale of foreign goods "of surpassing beauty, richness, and elegance" with "eloquent and energetic" addresses by male abolitionists and "brilliant performances" on the "Piano Forte." The dramatic difference from WNYASS fairs is indicated by the latter's 1847 appeal for articles "both useful and ornamental," including "eggs, butter, cheese, cream, turkeys, hams, dried beef, pickles, and fruit" and other goods "of small as well as large value." The WNYASS women hoped that no one would "feel too poor, nor any too rich, to enlist in this holy cause" and asked for "the aid of men and women . . . the old and the young, the farmer, the mechanic, and the merchant."

The desire of the RLASS to raise funds and of the WNYASS to raise moral sentiments was also reflected in their different concerns with social etiquette. Both groups stepped beyond the bounds of the dominant definition of women's proper sphere, but they presented their transgression to the public in distinctly different manners. WNYASS women uniformly utilized their own first and last names in published reports and pronouncements without titles of marital status. They identified themselves repeatedly with "our sisters, crushed, abused, and bleeding under the lash" and believed that the "social mingling" of blacks and whites at antislavery fairs had "the effect to Kill prejudice." WNYASS extended this mingling to social affairs and traveling though it "caused great dissatisfaction in the Rochester community." As Mary Robbins Post wrote to her sister-in-law Amy, "we rejoice in the commotion for it gives signs of vitality."

Such commotion interfered, however, with the RLASS's plan to obtain funds "devoted to the diffusion of Anti-Slavery Sentiments by means of the Press and Lecturer; to the relief of the suffering Fugitive, and for such other Anti-Slavery objects as may present themselves." RLASS fairs raised five times as much money as those of the WNYASS. This pecuniary success was certainly tied in part to the RLASS's connections to leading families, connections nurtured by RLASS leaders' attention to social propriety whenever possible. Thus, RLASS women generally published reports and announcements under their married names. They did socialize with black abolitionists and Julia Griffiths boarded with the Douglass family despite rumors of improprieties. Yet these women never openly advocated the social mingling of the races nor do they appear to have encouraged it at their fairs or elsewhere. Nowhere in print did RLASS women refer to enslaved women as their sisters. Indeed, reports of the RLASS agent working among ex-slaves in Virginia indicate a paternalistic rather than a sisterly posture toward the "enslaved race": "The Freed people are not all thrifty, neither have they all the ability to improve their condition. Such we must assist and endeavor to elevate in the social scale. Instruction and encouragement will do much for them." RLASS women far surpassed most of their contemporaries in their attitudes toward race relations; yet to appeal to those contemporaries for funds, they had to walk a fine line between social commitment and social etiquette, aid to blacks and distance from them.

Differences between RLASS and WNYASS women in organization, appeals, and tactics were reflections of differences in their access to material resources as well as in the social bases of their activism. For instance, the "*Eating together* of 'Colored with White'" was a form of antislavery statement available to WNYASS women when fairs "came very short of realizing in a pecuniary point of view" the funds necessary for press and lecture campaigns. The RLASS was not only considerably more successful than the WNYASS in raising funds at fairs but also drew upon greater familial eco-

nomic resources. Thus, these women could mobilize the press and could bring key political and religious figures, such as Horace Greeley and Reverend Henry Ward Beecher, to Rochester to lecture. They were also able to fund fugitives' trips to Canada and to send food, clothing, and other goods to free blacks in Virginia. Moral suasionist women, in more limited economic circumstances, found it easier to offer a sustained antislavery commentary through their personal lifestyle than through the funding of antislavery projects. They ate sugar made from Massachusetts-grown rather than slave-produced beets, wore woolen rather than cotton clothing, sealed letters with antislavery wafers, and socialized in mixed racial company.

Differences in access to material resources and in social bases had more than local import: they were translated into distinct political ideologies that linked local female abolitionism into national antislavery movements. Moral suasionists believed "that when the ear of the American people can be gained, the downfall of slavery in this republic is certain." The goal of moral suasionists was to create a popular discourse on issues of national consequence and to articulate alternative social and political formations that would guarantee the broadest human freedoms. The concern with agitating the public mind allowed for the full participation of those—women, the poor, blacks—outside institutionalized forms of power. In turn, people structurally removed from such loci of power were likely to bring alternative visions of social order and social value to movements for social change. These activists did not so much seek to gain power as to make the powerful responsive to a popular voice that itself advocated the broadest and most thoroughly democratic principles of governance.

For political abolitionists, it was "the National Constitution . . . adopted by the people of the United States" that would "secure . . . the blessings of Liberty." To gain access to existing institutions, political abolitionists needed abundant material resources and popular support, but they could offer those structurally removed from political participation little in exchange for their efforts. Yet female members of Rochester's leading middle-class sector were willing to accept their own subordination in supporting the antislavery tactics of their male allies. For these women, the indirect benefits of male economic and political successes converged with the preachings of evangelical ministers and the teachings of popular literature: they were willing to sustain basic institutions that had rewarded their families well in the past if those institutions would guarantee fundamental human rights to blacks.

Moral suasionists sought to expose the contradictions posed by slavery in a democratic nation; political abolitionists sought to institutionalize a Constitutional resolution to those contradictions. Almost by definition, then, it was political abolitionists who claimed the final victory as the authors of a political emancipation. Yet moral suasionists had long asserted that "political action is only calculated to hold what moral suasion gains." Moreover, as advocates of an unpopular cause, both moral suasionists and political abolitionists began their campaigns by seeking to arouse the public in their own communities. As James Russell Lowell so eloquently wrote of antislavery agitators, "The public follows them step by step, occupying the positions they have successfully fortified and quitted, and it is necessary that they should keep in advance in order that people may not be shocked by waking up and finding themselves Abolitionists."

Male political abolitionists increasingly distanced themselves both from agitation and from their local base as they perceived the possibilities of a national electoral victory: they invested their labors in emancipation by law. In supporting their male kin, RLASS women accepted the continued domination of politics by white males though they hoped that the religious and moral principles advocated by antislavery males would make politics more responsive to all. Moral suasionists gradually lost their dominance

within the antislavery movement, rejecting participation in an electoral solution. Their continued strength lay in grass-roots organizing and the recruitment of the disfranchised and disaffected. Thus, moral suasionists and political abolitionists continued to challenge each other as they challenged the larger society. Advocates, respectively, of agitation and reform, their efforts often overlapped. They could coexist, but the distinctive social bases that underlay their efforts nullified their 1843 call for "mutual co-operation" in the cause of abolition.

Historian Gerda Lerner has claimed that women had a "peculiar relationship to political power" because of their history of disfranchisement. "Disfranchised groups in a democracy," she notes, "can hope to influence those holding political power by persuasion, by educational activities, and by exerting pressure in various forms." Both groups of women abolitionists in Rochester employed pressure, education, and persuasion; both developed and refined grass-roots organizing and fund raising techniques—most notably in the form of petition campaigns and antislavery fairs—that extended the power of the disfranchised. However, the differences in their social and economic bases led them to direct that new-found power to different ends.

Political abolitionist women sought to make common cause with male voters by providing local educational and economic support. Their goal was to influence the content rather than the structure of a political system in which their male kin and neighbors seemed to be gaining power. Moral suasionist women sought alliances with the disfranchised and with white males who rejected existing political structures. Abolitionism was only one crusade through which they hoped to redefine political, indeed all power, relations and to assure racial and sexual equality in the nation at large. Each group of female abolitionists expanded the human and financial resources of particular branches of the antislavery movement. Each also extended women's role in politics. RLASS women did so by demanding an auxiliary role in electoral campaigns focusing on antislavery issues; WNYASS women by working to reshape the structure of nineteenth-century politics by introducing methods of pressure and persuasion directly accessible to the disfranchised.

Questions for Study and Review

1. Given women's lack of direct access to the political arena, how did they hope to abolish a system as entrenched as slavery?

2. Did the differences among female and male abolitionists or between them and moral reformers limit or advance the cause of social change?

3. What was the relationship between women's antislavery activism and the conditions of southern slaves? between women's antislavery activism and the conditions of northern "free" women?

4. What were the similarities and differences between women's role in the antislavery movement of the nineteenth century and the civil rights movement of the twentieth?

Suggested Readings

Nancy A. Hewitt, *Women's Activism and Social Change: Rochester, New York, 1822–1872* (1984).

Gerda Lerner, "The Political Activities of Antislavery Women," in her *The Majority Finds Its Past: Placing Women in History* (1979).

Elizabeth Ann Bartlett, *Sarah Grimké: Letters on the Equality of the Sexes and Other Essays* (1988).

Blanche Glassmen Hersh, *The Slavery of Sex: Feminist-Abolitionism in America* (1978).

Paul Johnson, *The Shopkeeper's Millennium: Society and Revivals in Rochester, New York, 1815–1837* (1978).

PART FOUR

Expansion and Division

Expansion was the watchword of mid-nineteenth-century North Americans. With the purchase of the Louisiana Territory in 1803, the United States doubled in size. Over the next half-century, the population grew from fewer than seven million to almost thirty million, including an increase from less than one million to nearly four million slaves and an influx of several million new immigrants. Technological advances in agriculture, industry, transportation, and communication increased production of food, clothing, and hundreds of other goods and sped the movement of individuals and information across the nation. Americans traveled to both unexplored western territories and turbulent seaboard cities.

In 1810, New York became the first city to house 100,000 residents; after 1825, with the opening of the Erie Canal, it became the nation's unrivaled commercial as well as population center. Along the paths of canals, wagon trains, and railroads, boom towns sprang up, some to become thriving metropolises and others to fade away as the frontier passed. Chicago, a mere trading post in the early 1830s, had over 100,000 inhabitants by 1860.

Expansion fed the development of distinct regional economies in the North, South, and West and nurtured the accompanying social and political divisions. Expansion also reinforced divisions within each region—between long-settled native Americans and the newcomers who wanted their land, between African and African-American slaves and their ever more vigilant masters, between workers and employers both bent on gaining their fair share of new wealth, between women and men on southern plantations and western wagon trains and in Indian villages and northern urban neighborhoods.

Sometimes division meant confrontation, other times resistance, resignation, accommodation, or peaceful coexistence. Certain differences between the sexes, for instance, served positive ends, such as the distinct work and family roles of male and female slaves that helped them forge a more united front against owners

The opening of the American West is often depicted as a largely masculine achievement, as is obvious in this contemporary illustration. But women played a far more important role than merely supplying inspiration, as does the gauze-draped female figure here. Though women were indeed a minority in the westward migration, their unflagging labors during the journey and in the new settlements contributed substantially to the survival of their families and communities.

and overseers. Other differences, such as the tasks and responsibilities assigned midwestern husbands and wives, increased tension and dissension within families. The boundaries and meanings of all these divisions, between and within groups, constantly changed as numerical, geographical, and technological expansion transformed both society as a whole and individual members' relations with it and each other.

The expansion of European settlements had, from the beginning, forced changes in the lives of native Americans. By the early nineteenth century, those Indian nations on the eastern seaboard that had not been exterminated had adapted to new conditions. This involved changes in women's and men's roles. Iroquois and Cherokee women, for instance, like their predecessors among the Appamatuck, wielded significant economic, political, and religious power prior to colonization. Only the independent women of the Hispanic Southwest may have rivaled them in prestige and power. Such influential positions for females were at odds with European customs and expectations, encouraging Old World settlers to scorn Indians as uncivilized because they practiced a different sexual division of labor.

By the early nineteenth century, Americans of European descent were sufficiently dominant to force the reassignment of male and female tasks within Indian societies. Theda Perdue traces this process among southeastern Indians, such as the Creek and Cherokee. Christian missionaries and government agents encouraged these tribes to adopt "civilized" ways by introducing them to new technology—metal hoes for men and spinning wheels for women. Such interventions helped expand the influence of native American men in the family and the larger community, but did not provide them with the power to stop their tribes' removal to the West once white southerners' search for fertile cotton fields led to the Indians' land.

That search was fueled by the success of the cotton gin, invented in 1793 by Eli Whitney with the assistance of Mrs. Green, a planter's wife. This simple machine dramatically increased the speed with which slaves could separate seeds for short staple cotton. At a time when even some southerners were considering the advisability of freeing the slaves, the cotton gin's success assured that slavery and the slave trade would continue. An increase in the numbers of slaves and their concentration on larger plantations unintentionally encouraged the elaboration of family and community life among those in bondage. Since slave children were considered the property of the mother's owner, African-American females were central figures in the development of these more extensive kinship networks.

Deborah G. White reveals that slave women played critical roles in sustaining both communities and families. All-female work groups as well as extended kinship networks bound slaves together across plantations and generations. These networks were also crucial in the post-Civil war period, when newly freed blacks moved across the South to reunite with relatives or migrated west to find a better life.

White Americans and free blacks migrated westward for the same reasons throughout the nineteenth century. The construction of canals and then railroads increased both the speed and comfort of travel, as well as the profitability of shipping western agricultural goods eastward. Still, before the Civil War most migrants ventured beyond the Mississippi by wagon. The trip placed unusual demands on all those heading west—and in the 1840s and after a significant proportion of these travelers were women and children. Physical demands included crowded wagons, constant motion, fear of Indians (despite the relatively few hostile incidents), hot and dry or cool and wet weather, and the continuous need to haul water and collect fuel. In addition, the migrants had to deal with the psychological demands of the journey. Sorrow at leaving loved ones behind, anxiety about an unknown future, tensions increased by daily contact among fellow travelers, or isolation faced by a family traveling alone contributed significant stress.

Women, sometimes burdened with young children, seeking to maintain high domestic standards and Sabbath rest on the trail, and most often asked to jettison family heirlooms when the load had to be lightened, faced special hardships. Even as their numbers increased, women were nearly always outnumbered by men on wagon trains, and some found themselves isolated from female companionship. Yet many also found a new freedom and a personal pride by persevering in these struggles. The end of the journey offered much the same scenario—hardship and isolation combined with new opportunities and a heightened sense of self-worth.

John Mack Faragher examines the lives of these pioneers as they settled onto midwestern farms at mid-century. Emphasizing the importance of technology in increasing the productivity and profitability of agriculture, Faragher demonstrates the different effects that commercialization had on women and men. At a time when newly settled territories were becoming the battlegrounds for pro- and antislavery forces, less visible and less volatile struggles occurred on a daily basis over the power wielded by and the respect accorded wives and husbands. Less successful than their Cherokee and slave counterparts in gaining influence in the family, white women on the frontier suffered from trying to combine the realities of arduous labor with new ideals of domesticity and submissiveness. Still, they faced neither removal nor bondage; and over time, the critical importance of their labor to family survival and of their neighborly networks to community development opened greater opportunities for them in the areas of professional education and formal political participation.

In 1850, the frontier was still wide open, allowing Indians to be pushed further West, encouraging plantation owners to expand the slave system, and beckoning free white families and some newly arrived immigrants to seek a better life as pioneers. The mass migration that occurred in the early decades of the nineteenth century had different meanings for native Americans, African-Americans, and Euro-Americans and held different promises and possibilities for women and men in each of these groups. Expansion and division on the national level were two of the most important developments in the history of the United States in the mid-nineteenth century. So, too, were these same processes critical in the many local communities in which ordinary women and men collectively created expanded frontiers and chose sides in the divisions that followed.

Suggested Readings

Suzanne Lebsock, *The Free Women of Petersburg: Status and Culture in a Southern Town, 1784–1860* (1984).

Jean Fagin Yellin, ed., *Incidents in the Life of a Slave Girl Written by Herself, by Harriet A. Jacobs* (1987).

Steven M. Stowe, *Intimacy and Power in the Old South: Ritual in the Lives of the Planters* (1987).

John Mack Faragher, *Sugar Creek: Life on the Illinois Prairie* (1986).

Pamela Herr, *Jessie Benton Fremont: American Woman of the 19th Century* (1987).

TEN

Domesticating the Natives: Southern Indians and the Cult of True Womanhood

Theda Perdue

The "queen of the Appamatuck" and her tribeswomen from seventeenth-century Virginia would not have felt out of place among the eighteenth-century Cherokee. In this and other southeastern tribes, women played prominent economic, political, and religious roles, supported by strong bonds among extended networks of female relatives. Yet by the 1830s, when the Cherokee were forcibly removed from Georgia, Alabama, North Carolina, and Tennessee to new lands in Oklahoma, the economic, political, and familial authority of the tribe's women had been severely undercut. Andrew Jackson, Martin Van Buren, and a long series of southern judges, politicians, and planters were responsible for the removal of the Cherokee; government agents and Christian missionaries, including women, were responsible for the reorganization of sex roles among the Cherokee.

The ideals of true womanhood and the evangelical preachings that inspired Anglo-American women to initiate charitable and reform efforts proved problematic when applied to Cherokee society. Among the aboriginal Cherokee, women farmed and men hunted. Women thus remained closer to home and labored on the land, which was inherited through the female line. Indeed,

when he married, a husband went to live with his wife's family so that she could continue to work on the female-centered family farm. Women also held important positions in religion and politics and practiced a sexual openness considered at best immodest by European standards.

The arrival of missionaries and government agents brought dramatic transformation to the Cherokee community. Men were encouraged to farm and women to spin. Male authority and control over trade, war, and property were reinforced. Eventually large numbers of Cherokees adopted Christianity, constitutional law, and the English alphabet, even slavery. This embrace of Anglo-American lifeways weakened not only women's power but the power of the Cherokee as a whole.

Southern planters began coveting Indian lands, and once they had the support of leading politicians, no amount of civilization, not even a favorable ruling by the U.S. Supreme Court, could save the Indian nation. The resistance of some tribal members to further Anglo-American intrusions was considered an additional rationale for the tribe's removal.

In either case—the adoption of Anglo-American culture or its rejection—Cherokees and especially Cherokee women lost economic and political independence and power as King Cotton moved west. As Deborah G. White shows in the next article, slave women and men also had to contend with challenges from planters and politicians to their preferred gender roles and relations. Yet as African and African-American presence in the South rapidly increased, that of native Americans declined. They left behind lessons about the benefits of "civilization" and a trail of tears.

Southern Indians stand apart culturally and historically from other native Americans. Building of temple mounds, an elaborate ceremonial life, a complex belief system, riverine agriculture, and matrilineal descent characterized their aboriginal culture. Southern Indians embraced European culture with such enthusiasm and success that they came to be known as the "five civilized tribes." They acquired this sobriquet in the half-century after the ratification of the United States Constitution, a time when many southern Indians came to believe that their physical survival depended on adopting an Anglo-American lifestyle and value system. These Indians gradually abandoned hunting and subsistence agriculture, the practice of blood vengeance, their traditional religious beliefs and practices, and other aspects of their aboriginal way of life. Some individual Indians succeeded so well that they became culturally indistinguishable from their white neighbors. They owned large plantations, operated successful businesses, attended Christian churches, promoted formal legal and judicial systems, and wrote and conversed in the English language.

An integral part of this cultural transformation was a redefinition of gender roles. Just as men could no longer follow their aboriginal pursuits of hunting and warfare, women could no longer behave in what was perceived to be a "savage" or "degraded" way. Instead, they had to attempt to conform to an Anglo-American ideal characterized by purity, piety, domesticity, and submissiveness. A true woman was essentially spiritual rather than physical. She occupied a separate sphere apart from the

From "Southern Indians and the Cult of True Womanhood" by Theda Perdue, *The Web of Southern Social Relations: Women, Family and Education* edited by Walter J. Fraser, Jr., et al. Copyright © 1985 by the University of Georgia Press. Reprinted by permission.

ambition, selfishness, and materialism that permeated the man's world of business and politics. Her proper place was the home, and because of her spiritual nature, she imbued her home with piety, morality, and love. The home was a haven from the outside world, and in its operation a true woman should excel. Openly submissive to men, a true woman influenced them subtly through her purity and piety.

Traditionally southern Indians had a very different view of womanhood. Indian women occupied a separate sphere from that of men, but they had considerable economic, political, and social importance. While men hunted and went to war, women collected firewood, made pottery and baskets, sewed clothes, cared for children, and cooked the family's food. These tasks certainly fell within the nineteenth-century definition of domesticity, but the sphere of Indian women extended beyond home and hearth to encompass economic activities that seemed far less appropriate to their sex. In particular, women farmed in a society that depended primarily on agriculture for subsistence, and women performed most of the manual labor with men assisting only in clearing fields and planting corn. This inequitable division of labor elicited comments from most Euro-American observers. On his 1797 tour of the Cherokee country, Louis-Philippe, who later would become king of France, observed: "The Indians have all the work done by women. They are assigned not only household tasks; even the corn, peas, beans, and potatoes are planted, tended, and preserved by the women." In the economy of southern Indians, therefore, women did what Euro-Americans considered to be work—they farmed—while men did what was considered sport—they hunted.

This arrangement was amazing in that women did not seem to object to doing most of the work. In the early nineteenth century, a missionary commented on the willingness with

Native women performed the greater share of the labor required to keep their communities prosperous and were thus valued highly in their society. They routinely handled economic transactions and took part in important religious events, such as the Green Corn Ceremony pictured here. As overseers of the community's agricultural efforts, the women had the privilege of presenting the new corn as a sacrifice. *Green Corn Dance* painting by Joseph Henry Sharp, from the Thomas Gilcrease Institute of American History and Art, Tulsa, Oklahoma.

which the women toiled: "Though custom attached the heaviest part of the labor of the women, yet they were cheerful and voluntary in performing it. What others have discovered about the Indians I cannot tell, but though I have been about nineteen years among the Cherokees, I have perceived nothing of that slavish, servile fear, on the part of women, so often spoke of." One reason women may have worked so gladly was that they received formal recognition for their economic contribution and they controlled the fruit of their labor. In the Green Corn Ceremony, the southern Indians' most important religious event, women ritually presented the new crop, which was sacrificed to the fire, and when Europeans occasionally purchased corn from Indians in the eighteenth century, they bought it from women. Women may also have labored without complaint

because farming was one of the determinants of gender. Southern Indians distinguished between the sexes on other than merely biological grounds. Women were women not only because they could bear children but also because they farmed, and men who farmed came to be regarded sexually as women. Men hunted, therefore, because hunting was intrinsically linked to male sexuality; women farmed because farming was one of the characteristics that made them women.

The matrilocal residence pattern of southern Indians probably contributed to the association of women and agriculture. A man lived in the household of his wife's lineage, and buildings, garden plots, and sections of the village's common field belonged to her lineage. A man had no proprietary interest in the homestead where he lived with his wife or in the land his wife farmed. Nor was a husband necessarily a permanent resident in the household of his wife's lineage. Polygamy was common, and he might divide his time between the lineages of his wives. Furthermore, southeastern Indians frequently terminated their marriages, and in the event of divorce, a man simply left his wife's household and returned to his mother's house and his own lineage. Because southeastern Indians were also matrilineal, that is, they traced kinship only through the female line, children belonged to the mother's lineage and clan rather than to the father's, and when divorce occurred, they invariably remained with their mothers. Men, therefore, had no claim on the houses they lived in or the children they fathered.

John Lawson tried to explain matrilineal lineage, which he considered an odd way of reckoning kin, by attributing it to "fear of Imposters; the Savages knowing well, how much Frailty possesses *Indian* women, betwixt the Garters and the Girdle." Women in southern Indian tribes did enjoy considerable sexual freedom. Except for restraints regarding incest and menstrual taboos, Indian women were relatively free in choosing sexual partners, engaging in intercourse, and dissolving relationships. All southern Indians condoned premarital sex and divorce, which were equally female or male prerogatives, but attitudes toward adultery varied from one tribe to another.

Indian women usually displayed a sense of humor and a lack of modesty regarding sexual matters. One member of Lawson's expedition took an Indian "wife" for a night. The couple consummated their marriage in a room occupied by other members of the company and guests at the wedding feast. In the morning the groom discovered that both his bride and his shoes were gone. So brazen and skilled were most Cherokee women that Louis-Philippe concluded that "no Frenchwoman could teach them a thing." When his guide made sexual ad-

vances to several Cherokee women in a house they visited, he recorded in his journal that "they were so little embarrassed that one of them who was lying on a bed put her hand on his trousers before my very eyes and said scornfully, *Ah, sick.*"

Compared to the other southern Indians, Louis-Philippe decided, the Cherokees were "exceedingly casual" about sex. Although all southern Indians had certain common characteristics—they were matrilineal and matrilocal, women farmed, and both sexes enjoyed some sexual freedom—Cherokee women had the highest degree of power and personal autonomy. The trader James Adair maintained that the Cherokees "have been a considerable while under a petticoat-government." In Cherokee society, women spoke in council and determined the fate of war captives. Some even went on the warpath and earned a special title, "War Woman." In fact, Cherokee women were probably as far from the "true women" of the early nineteenth-century ideal as any women Anglo-Americans encountered on the continent. When the United States government and Protestant missionaries undertook the "civilization" of native Americans in the late eighteenth century, however, the Cherokees proved to be the most adept at transforming their society.

Until the late eighteenth century, Europeans had few relations with Cherokee women other than sexual ones. Europeans were primarily interested in Indian men as warriors and hunters and considered women to be of little economic or political significance. After the American Revolution, native alliances and the deerskin trade diminished in importance. All the Indians still had that Europeans valued was land. George Washington and his advisers devised a plan which they believed would help the Indians recover economically from the depletion of their hunting grounds and the destruction experienced during the Revolution while making large tracts of Indian land available for white settlement. They hoped to convert the Indians into farmers living on isolated homesteads much like white frontiersmen. With hunting no longer part of Indian economy, the excess land could be ceded to the United States and opened to whites.

The Cherokees traditionally had lived in large towns located along rivers. These towns were composed of many matrilineal households containing several generations. A woman was rarely alone: her mother, sisters, and daughters, with their husbands, lived under the same roof, and other households were nearby. Beyond the houses lay large fields which the women worked communally. Originally, these towns had served a defensive purpose, but in the warfare of the eighteenth century, they became targets of attack. In the French and Indian War and the American Revolution, soldiers invaded the Cherokee country and destroyed towns and fields. As a result, Cherokees began abandoning their towns even before the United States government inaugurated the civilization program. When a government agent toured the Cherokee Nation in 1796, he passed a number of deserted towns; at one site he found a "hut, some peach trees and the posts of a town house," and at another there was only a "small field of corn, some peach, plumb and locust trees."

Agents appointed to implement the civilization program encouraged this trend. They advised the Cherokee to "scatter from their towns and make individual improvements also of cultivating more land for grain, cotton &c. than they could while crowded up in towns." The Cherokees complied: "They dispersed from their large towns,—built convenient houses,—cleared and fenced farms, and soon possessed numerous flocks and herds." By 1818 missionaries complained that "there is no place near us where a large audience can be collected as the people do not live in villages, but scattered over the country from 2 to 10 miles apart." The breaking up of Cherokee towns resulted in a

very isolated existence for women because new households often consisted of only one nuclear family. This isolation occurred just at the time when the work load of women was increasing.

In a letter of 1796, George Washington advised the Cherokees to raise cattle, hogs, and sheep. He pointed out that they could increase the amount of corn they produced by using plows and that they could also cultivate wheat and other grains. Apparently addressing the letter to the men, Washington continued: "To these you will easily add flax and cotton which you may dispose of to the White people, or have it made up by your own women into clothing for yourselves. Your wives and daughters can soon learn to spin and weave." Washington apparently knew nothing about traditional gender roles, and the agents he sent usually had little sympathy for the Indian division of labor. They provided plows to the men and instructed them in clearing fields, tilling soil, and building fences. Women received cotton cards, spinning wheels, and looms.

The women, politically ignored in the eighteenth century and bypassed in the earlier hunting economy, welcomed the opportunity to profit from contact with whites. In 1796, agent Benjamin Hawkins met with a group of Cherokee women and explained the government's plan. He reported to Washington that "they rejoiced much at what they had heard and hoped it would prove true, that they had made some cotton, and would make more and follow the instruction of the agent and the advice of the President." According to a Cherokee account, the women proved far more receptive to the civilization program than the men: "When Mr. Dinsmore, the Agent of the United States, spoke to us on the subject of raising livestock and cotton, about fifteen years ago, many of us thought it was only some refined scheme calculated to gain an influence over us, rather than to ameliorate our situation and slighted his advice and proposals; he then addressed our women, and presented them with cotton seeds for planting; and afterwards with cards, wheels and looms to work it. They acquired the use of them with great facility, and now most of the clothes we wear are of their manufacture." Two censuses conducted in the early nineteenth century reveal the extent to which women accepted their new tasks. In 1810 there were 1,600 spinning wheels and 467 looms in the Cherokee Nation; by 1826 there were 2,488 wheels and 762 looms.

In 1810, one Cherokee man observed that the women had made more progress toward civilization than the men: "The females have however made much greater advances in industry than the males; they now manufacture a great quantity of cloth; but the latter have not made proportionate progress in agriculture; however, they raise great herds of cattle, which can be done with little exertion." At the same time, women continued to do most of the farming, and many even raised livestock for market. This extension of woman's work concerned government agents because many men were not acquiring the work habits considered essential to "civilized" existence. They had not been able to accomplish a shift in gender roles merely by introducing the tools and techniques of Western culture. Gender roles as well as many other aspects of Cherokee culture proved extremely difficult to change.

Cultural change came more easily, however, among Cherokees who already had adopted the acquisitive, materialistic value system of white Americans. Turning from an economy based on hunting, they took advantage of the government's program and invested in privately owned agricultural improvements and commercial enterprises. They quickly became an economic elite separated from the majority of Cherokees by their wealth and by their desire to emulate whites. In the early nineteenth century, members of this economic elite rose to positions of leadership in the Cherokee Nation because of the ease and effectiveness with which they dealt with United States officials. Gradually they transformed Cherokee political institutions into replicas of those of the United States. This elite expected Cherokee women to conform to the ideals of the cult of true womanhood, that is, to be sexually pure, submissive to fathers and husbands, concerned primarily with spiritual and domestic matters, and excluded from politics and economic activities outside the home. In 1818, Charles Hicks, who later would become principal chief, described the most prominent men in the nation as "those who have kept their women & children at home & in comfortable circumstances." Submissive, domestic wives were a mark of prominence.

Cherokees learned to be true women primarily through the work of Protestant missionaries whom tribal leaders welcomed to the nation. In 1800 the Moravians arrived to open a school, and in the second decade of the nineteenth century Congregationalists supported by the interdenominational American Board of Commissioners for Foreign Missions, Baptists and Methodists joined them. Except for the Methodists, missionaries preferred to teach children in boarding schools, where they had "the influence of example as well as precept." In 1819 President James Monroe visited the American Board's Brainerd mission and approved "of the plan of instruction; particularly as the children were taken into the family, taught to work, &c." This was, the president believed, "the best & perhaps the only way to civilize and Christianize the Indians." For female students, civilization meant becoming true women.

Mission schools provided an elementary education for girls as well as boys. Either single women or the wives of male missionaries usually taught the girls, but all students studied the same academic subjects, which included reading, writing, spelling, arithmetic, geography, and history. Examinations took place annually and were attended by parents. The teachers questioned students in their academic subjects as well as Bible history, catechism, and hymns, and "the girls showed specimens of knitting, spinning, mending, and fine needlework."

Mastery of the domestic arts was an essential part of the girls' education because, according to one missionary, "all the females need is a proper education to be qualified to fill any of the relations or stations of domestic life." The children at the mission schools performed a variety of tasks, and the division of labor approximated that in a typical Anglo-American farming family. The boys chopped wood and plowed fields, and the girls milked, set tables, cooked meals, washed dishes, sewed clothing, knitted, quilted, did laundry, and cleaned the houses. Because their fathers were wealthy, many students were not accustomed to such menial labor. Missionaries endeavored to convince them that "the charge of the kitchen and the mission table" was not degrading but was instead a "most important station," which taught them "industry and economy."

The great advantage of teaching Cherokee girls "industry and economy" was the influence they might exert in their own homes. One girl wrote: "We have the opportunity of learning to work and make garments which will be useful to us in life." Another girl expressed gratitude that missionaries had taught the students "how to take care of families that when we go home we can take care of our mother's house." A missionary assessed the impact of their work: "We cannot expect that the influence of these girls will have any great immediate effect on their acquaintance—but I believe in each case it is calculated to elevate the families in some degree, with which they are connected." Although missionaries and students expected the domestic arts learned in the mission schools to improve their parental home, they believed that the primary benefit would be to the homes the girls themselves established. Missionary

Sophia Sawyer specifically hoped to "raise the female character in the Nation" so that "Cherokee gentlemen" could find young women "sufficiently educated for companions." In 1832 missionaries could report with satisfaction that the girls who had married "make good housewives and useful members of society."

The marriages missionaries had in mind were not the Cherokees' traditional polygamous or serial marriages. Louis-Philippe had believed that such a marriage "renders women contemptible in men's eyes and deprives them of all influence." A monogamous marriage was supposedly liberating to women because these "serve exclusively to heighten the affections of a man." Although the Cherokee elite accepted most tenets of Western civilization, some balked at abandoning the practice of polygamy. The chief justice was one who had more than one wife, but these marriages differed from traditional ones in which a man lived with his wives in their houses. Polygamous members of the elite headed more than one patriarchal household. They recognized the desirability of monogamous unions, however, encouraged others to enter into them, and sent their children to mission schools where they were taught polygamy was immoral.

In practice, religious denominations confronted the problem of polygamy in different ways. Moravians apparently allowed converts to keep more than one wife. The American Board required a man "to separate himself from all but the first." Perhaps because some of their chief supporters were polygamists, the governing body in Boston advised missionaries in the field to be "prudent and kind" when dealing with the "tender subject" and to instruct polygamous converts "in the nature and design of marriage, the original institution, and the law of Christ, that they may act with an enlightened conviction of duty." American Board ministers sometimes remarried in a Christian service couples who had lived for years in "a family capacity." Missionaries also rejoiced when they united in matrimony young couples of "industrious habits & reputable behavior" who were "very decent and respectable in their moral deportment."

Achieving "moral deportment" at the mission schools was no simple matter, but missionaries considered the teaching of New England sexual mores to be one of their chief responsibilities. According to some reports, they enjoyed success. In 1822, American Board missionaries reported: "Mr. Hall thinks the moral influence of the school has been considerable.... The intercourse between the young of both sexes was shamefully loose. Boys & girls in their teens would strip & go into bathe, or play ball together naked. They would also use the most disgustingly indecent language, without the least sense of shame. But, when better instructed, they became reserved and modest." To maintain decorum, the missionaries tried to make certain that girls and boys were never alone together: "When the girls walk out any distance from the house they will be accompanied by instructors." Male and female students normally attended separate classes. When Sophia Sawyer became ill in 1827 she reluctantly sent the small girls to the boys' school but taught the larger girls in her sickroom. Miss Sawyer so feared for the virtue of the older girls that she asked the governing board "could not the boys at Brainerd be at some other school." The Moravians did resort to separate schools. The American Board, however, simply put locks on the bedroom doors.

Even with these precautions, difficulties arose. In 1813 the Moravians recorded in their journal: "After prayer we directed our talk toward Nancy, indirectly admonishing her to abstain from the lust which had gripped her. She seemed not to have taken it to heart, for instead of mending her ways she continues to heap sin upon sin." Nancy Watie later moved to an American Board mission along with her cousin Sally Ridge. Their fathers were prominent in the Cherokee Nation, and they had left strict instructions that their daughters be supervised constantly and their purity preserved. A problem occurred when teenage boys in the neighborhood began calling on the girls at the mission. At first, the young people decorously sat in front of the fire under the watchful eyes of the missionaries, but soon the conversation shifted from English to Cherokee, which none of the chaperones understood. Suspecting the worst, the missionaries ordered the suitors to "spend their evenings in some other place." A year later, however, the missionaries reported that despite their care, the girls "had given themselves up to the common vices."

The missionaries did not, of course, intend to cloister the young women to the extent that they did not meet suitable young men. Sophia Sawyer observed: "Like all females they desire the admiration of men. They can easily be shown that the attention, or good opinion of men without education, taste, or judgement is not worth seeking, & to gain the affection or good opinion of the opposite character, their minds must be improved, their manner polished, their persons attended to, in a word they must be qualified for usefulness." Attracting the right young men was permissible and even desirable.

The girls' appearance was another concern of the missionaries. Ann Paine related an attempt to correct the daughter of a particularly prominent Cherokee: "Altho' her parents supplied her with good clothes, she was careless and indifferent about her appearance.—I often urged her attention to these things and offered as a motive her obligation to set a good example to her nation as the daughter of their chief. Told her how the young ladies of the North were taught to govern their manners and tempers and of their attention to personal appearance. She never appeared more mortified than in hearing of her superiority of birth, and of the attention she ought to pay to her personal appearance." Paine soon had "the

satisfaction of witnessing her rapid improvement." Four years later, Sophia Sawyer complained about the female students in general:
"I have had to punish several times to break
bad habits respecting cleanliness in their clothes,
books, & person—I found them in a deplorable
situation in this respect. The largest girls I had
in school were not capable of dressing themselves properly or of folding their clothes when
taken off." Sometimes concern for the students'
appearance went beyond clothing. One girl
wrote a correspondent: "Mr. Ellsworth told me
I had better alter my voice. He said I spoke like
a man."

In addition to a neat, feminine appearance,
respectable men presumably also admired piety
in young women and probably expected them
to be more pious than they themselves were.
The missionaries clearly believed that the female
students in mission schools were more serious
about religion than the male students, and they
encouraged this emotion. Nancy Reece wrote
her northern correspondent that "after work at
night the girls joined for singing a special hymn
Mr. Walker wrote for them & then go to worship services." Many of the girls wrote about
their spiritual lives. A ten-year-old confided in
a letter that "some of the girls have been serious about there wicked hearts and have retired
to their Chambers to pray to God. . . . I feel as
though I am a great sinner and very wicked
sinner."

The piety of the girls at the mission station
was manifest in other ways. They organized a
society to raise money to send missionaries
into heathen lands. The American Board agreed
to pay them for clothing they made, and they
in turn donated the money to mission work.
They also sold their handiwork to local Cherokee women. The piety of the girls extended
beyond the school and into the community.
Once a month, neighboring women would
gather at the mission for a prayer meeting "that
missionary labors may be blessed." One missionary reported with satisfaction that "the

females have a praying society which is well
attended, and they begin to do something by
way of benevolence."

Of the several hundred Cherokee girls who
attended mission schools, the best example of
"true womanhood" was Catharine Brown. She
was sixteen or seventeen years old when she
arrived at the Brainerd mission. She had some
European ancestry, and although she had grown
up in a fairly traditional Cherokee household,
she spoke and read a little English. The missionaries reported that, despite the absence of
a Christian influence in her childhood, "her
moral character was ever good." Her biogra-
pher added: "This is remarkable, considering
the looseness of manner then prevalent among
the females of her nation, and the temptations
to which she was exposed, when during the
war with the Creek Indians, the army of the
United States was stationed near her father's
residence. . . . Once she even fled from her
home into the wild forest to preserve her
character unsullied." When she applied for
admission to Brainerd, the missionaries hesitated because they feared that she would object to the domestic duties required of female
students. They later recalled that she was "vain,
and excessively fond of dress, wearing a profusion of ornaments in her ears." Catharine
"had no objection" to work, however, and shortly
after her admission, her jewelry disappeared
"till only a single drop remains in each ear."
After she became a part of the mission family,
Catharine became extremely pious: "She spent
much time in reading the Scriptures, singing,
and prayer." She attended weekly prayer
meetings and helped instruct the younger girls
in the Lord's Prayer, hymns, and catechism. In
1819, Catharine received baptism. Her intellectual achievements were also remarkable, and
soon the missionaries sent her to open a female
school at the Creek Path Mission station. There
she fulfilled not only her spiritual and educational responsibilities, but also her domestic
ones. Visitors reported: "We arrived after the

family had dined, and she received us, and spread a table for our refreshment with the unaffected kindness of a sister." When her father proposed to take the family to Indian territory, Catharine was appropriately submissive. Although she did not want to go, she acquiesced to his wishes and prepared to leave for the West. Catharine's health, however, was fragile. She became ill, and "as she approached nearer to eternity her faith evidently grew stronger." In July 1823, "this lovely convert from heathenism died."

Few women in the Cherokee Nation could equal Catharine Brown, and perhaps the majority of Cherokee women had little desire to be "true women." The historical record contains little information about the Cherokee masses, but from the evidence that does exist, we can infer that many Cherokees maintained a relatively traditional way of life. Continuing to exist at the subsistence level, they rejected Christianity and mission schools and relied on local councils rather than the central government dominated by the elite. Borrowing selectively from the dominant white society, a large number of women also maintained a semblance of their aboriginal role. As late as 1817, a council of women petitioned the Cherokee National Council to refrain from further land cessions, and in 1835 at least one-third of the heads of households listed on the removal roll were women. Some probably were like Oo-dah-less who, according to her obituary, accumulated a sizable estate through agriculture and commerce. She was "the support of a large family" and bequeathed her property "to an only daughter and three grand children." Other women no doubt lived far more traditionally, farming, supervising an extended household, caring for children and kinsmen, and perhaps even exercising some power in local councils.

Although the feminine ideal of purity, piety, submissiveness, and domesticity did not immediately filter down to the mass of Cherokees, the nation's leaders came to expect these qualities

in women. Therefore, the influence of the cult of true womanhood probably far exceeded the modest number of women trained in mission schools. The Cherokee leaders helped create a new sphere for women by passing legislation that undermined matrilineal kinship and excluded women from the political process. In the first recorded Cherokee law of 1808, the national council, which apparently included no women, established a police force "to give their protection to children as heirs to their father's property, and to the widow's share." Subsequent legislation gave further recognition to patrilineal descent and to the patriarchal family structure common among men of wealth. In 1825 the council extended citizenship to the children of white women who had married Cherokee men, another act that formally reorganized descent. Legislation further isolated women by prohibiting polygamy and denied women the right to limit the size of families by outlawing the traditional practice of infanticide. In 1826 the council decided to call a constitutional convention to draw up a governing document for the tribe. According to legislation that provided for the election of delegates to the convention, "No person but a free male citizen who is full grown shall be entitled to vote." Not surprisingly, when the convention met and drafted a constitution patterned after that of the United States, women could neither vote nor hold office. The only provisions in the Cherokee legal code reminiscent of the power and prestige enjoyed by aboriginal women were laws that protected the property rights of married women and prohibited their husbands from disposing of their property without consent.

The elite who governed the Cherokee Nation under the Constitution of 1827 regarded traditionalists with considerable disdain. Having profited from the government's civilization program, most truly believed in the superiority of Anglo-American culture. Some leaders and, to an even greater extent, United States officials tended to question the ability of traditionalists to make well-informed, rational decisions. This lack of faith provided a justification for those highly acculturated Cherokees who in 1835, without tribal authorization, ceded Cherokee land in the Southeast contrary to the wishes of the vast majority of Indians. The failure of many Indian women to conform to the ideals of womanhood may well have contributed to the treaty party's self-vindication. Perhaps they believed that the land could have little meaning for the Cherokees if women controlled it, that the Indians must still depend primarily on hunting if women farmed, and that the Indians had no notion of ownership if men had no proprietary interest in their wives.

Of all the southern tribes, the Cherokees provide the sharpest contrast between the traditional role of women and the role they were expected to assume in the early nineteenth century. In this period, the Cherokees excluded women, who originally had participated in tribal governance, from the political arena. Women in other tribes had been less active politically; consequently, their status did not change as dramatically. All southern nations, however, did move toward legally replacing matrilineal with patrilineal descent and restricting the autonomy of women. In 1824, for example, the Creeks passed one law prohibiting infanticide and another specifying that upon a man's death, his children "shall have the property and his other relations shall not take the property to the injury of His children."

Men of wealth and power among the Creeks, Choctaws, and Chickasaws as well as the Cherokees readily accepted the technical assistance offered through the government's civilization program and gradually adopted the ideology it encompassed. Although these changes occurred at different rates among southern Indians, women began to fade from economic and political life in the early nineteenth century. Just as the traditional female occupation, farming, became commercially viable, men took over and women became only secondarily involved in subsistence. Women, of course, still had their homes and families, but their families soon became their husband's families, and domesticity brought influence, not power. Similarly, purity and piety seemed almost anachronistic in a culture and age that tended to value the material above the spiritual. Perhaps all that remained for women was what historian Nancy Cott has called "bonds of womanhood," but Indian women did not even develop closer ties to other women. Living a far more isolated existence than ever before, they no longer shared labor and leisure with mothers, daughters, and sisters. Instead they spent most of their time on remote homesteads with only their husbands and children.

This separate sphere in which Indian women increasingly lived in the nineteenth century could hardly give rise to a woman's rights movement, as some historians have suggested it did among white women, because true womanhood came to be associated with civilization and progress. Any challenge to the precepts of the cult of true womanhood could be interpreted as a reversion to savagery. Ironically, by the end of the century, some white Americans had come to view the traditional status of Indian women in a far more favorable light. In 1892 the author of an article in the *Albany Law Review* applauded the revision of property laws in the United States to protect the rights of married women and noted that such a progressive practice had long existed among the Choctaw and other southern Indians. This practice, however, was only a remnant of a female role that had been economically productive, politically powerful, and socially significant but had been sacrificed to the cult of true womanhood.

Questions for Study and Review

1. What were the perceived benefits of the Anglo-American lifestyle that encouraged many Indians to adopt the programs put forth by missionaries and agents?

2. How might southern planters' experience with the Cherokee have shaped their attitudes toward civilizing and Christianizing the slaves?

3. How would you compare the empowering and the restrictive effects of the cult of true womanhood on Anglo-American and native American women?

4. Other groups—African-Americans, Hispanics, Asians and a variety of European immigrants—also had to decide how much to adapt to and adopt Anglo-American lifestyles and values. What factors would affect the degree to which ethnic or black communities retained distinctive customs and cultures?

Suggested Readings

Mary E. Young, "Women, Civilization, and the Indian Question," in Mabel E. Deutrich, ed., *Clio Was a Woman: Studies in the History of American Women* (1980).

Glenda Riley, *Women & Indians on the Frontier, 1825–1915* (1984).

Barbara Welter, "She Hath Done What She Could: Protestant Women's Missionary Concerns in Nineteenth-Century America," *American Quarterly* (Winter 1978).

Anthony F. C. Wallace, *The Death and Rebirth of the Seneca* (1969).

Janet Lecompte, "The Independent Women of Hispanic New Mexico, 1821–1846," *Western Historical Quarterly* (January 1981).

ELEVEN

Female Slaves: Sex Roles and Social Status in the Antebellum Plantation South

Deborah G. White

Like native Americans, Africans had developed complex economic, political, and social systems long before contact with Europeans. The critical importance of women to agricultural production in Africa paralleled that of their counterparts in Cherokee society. The significance of women's labor and the centrality of the mother–child bond in many West African societies were carried to the New World along with cargoes of slaves. Forced to labor on tobacco, rice, and cotton plantations, black women and men sustained much of this African heritage, yet much was also lost under the oppressive conditions of labor and life.

Though scholars have long recognized the importance of African legacies in such areas as religion, music, cooking, dress, and folktales, they have paid less attention to how these legacies differentially affected women's and men's roles in the family and community. White notes the new meanings given to the very idea of family and community under bondage, where legal marriage, property rights, and parental and public authority were severely restricted. She also illuminates the ways that present-day controversies over black female-headed households and gender roles within black urban communities have shaped studies of slavery. White rejects both modern studies that overemphasize black women's power (the matriarch thesis of Daniel Moynihan and others) and those that overemphasize black men's power (the patriarchal portrait of historians Eugene Genovese and Herbert Gutman among others).

In their place, White shows how women and men shared the burdens of slavery, though they often did so in single-sex groups. Focusing on female slaves who were engaged in a startling array of tasks, she finds that they developed their own criteria of skill and status within the slave community. Yet this did not create separate so much as complementary female and male spheres of activity in the black family and community.

It took the resources of both women and men to survive slavery. Slavery necessitated and the slave community rewarded female strength, expertise, and authority. The survival of African and African-American families and cultures cannot be understood without recognizing women's central role in their preservation, a role that sheds new light as well on women's and men's relations among Anglo-Americans and native Americans. Claiming that in the past historians of slavery have "placed too much emphasis on what men could not do rather than on what women could do and did," White shows how female slaves not only survived their bondage but also helped to shape the African-American family and community that would emerge in freedom.

In his 1939 study of the black family in America, sociologist E. Franklin Frazier theorized that in slave family and marriage relations, women played the dominant role. Specifically, Frazier wrote that "the Negro woman as wife or mother was the mistress of her cabin, and, save for the interference of master and overseer, her wishes in regard to mating and family matters were paramount." He also insisted that slavery had schooled the black woman in self-reliance and self-sufficiency and that "neither economic necessity nor tradition had instilled in her the spirit of subordination to masculine authority." The Frazier thesis received support from other social scientists, including historians Kenneth Stampp and Stanley Elkins, both of whom held that slave men had been emasculated and stripped of their paternity rights by slave masters who left control of slave households to slave women. In his infamous 1965 national report, Daniel Patrick Moynihan lent further confirmation to the Frazier thesis when he alleged that the fundamental problem with the modern black family was the "often reversed roles of husband and wife," and then traced the origin of the "problem" back to slavery.

Partly in response to the criticism spawned by the Moynihan Report, historians reanalyzed antebellum source material, and the matriarchy thesis was debunked. For better or worse, said historians Robert Fogel and Stanley Engerman, the "dominant" role in slave society was played by men. Men were dominant, they said, because men occupied all managerial and artisan slots, and because masters recognized the male head of the family group. From historian John

From *Journal of Family History,* Volume 12, Numbers 1–3, 1987. Copyright © JAI Press Inc. 1987. Reprinted by permission of JAI Press Inc.

Blassingame we learned that by building furnishings and providing extra food for their families, men found indirect ways of gaining status. If a garden plot was to be cultivated, the husband "led" his wife in the family undertaking. After a very thoughtful appraisal of male slave activities, historian Eugene Genovese concluded that "slaves from their own experience had come to value a two-parent, male-centered household, no matter how much difficulty they had in realizing the ideal." Further tipping the scales toward patriarchal slave households, historian Herbert Gutman argued that the belief that matrifocal households prevailed among slaves was a misconception. He demonstrated that children were more likely to be named after their fathers than mothers, and that during the Civil War slave men acted like fathers and husbands by fighting for their freedom and by protecting their wives and children when they were threatened by Union troops or angry slaveholders.

With the reinterpretation of male roles came a revision of female roles. Once considered dominant, slave women were now characterized as subordinated and sometimes submissive. Fogel and Engerman found proof of their subordinated status in the fact that they were excluded from working in plow gangs and did all of the household chores. Genovese maintained that slave women's "attitude toward housework, especially cooking, and toward their own femininity," belied the conventional wisdom "according to which women unwittingly helped ruin their men by asserting themselves in the home, protecting their children, and assuming other normally masculine responsibilities." Gutman found one Sea Island slave community where the black church imposed a submissive role upon married slave women.

In current interpretations of the contemporary black family the woman's role has not been "feminized" as much as it has been "deemphasized." The stress in studies like those done by Carol Stack and Theodore Kennedy is not on roles per se but on the black family's ability to survive in flexible kinship networks that are viable bulwarks against discrimination and racism. These interpretations also make the point that black kinship patterns are not based exclusively on consanguineous relationships but are also determined by social contacts that sometimes have their basis in economic support.

Clearly then, the pendulum has swung away from the idea that women ruled slave households, and that their dominance during the slave era formed the foundation of the modern day matriarchal black family. But how far should that pendulum swing? This paper suggests that we should tread the road that leads to the patriarchal slave household and the contemporary amorphous black family with great caution. It suggests that, at least in relation to the slave family, too much emphasis has been placed on what men could not do rather than on what women could do and did. What follows is not a comprehensive study of female slavery, but an attempt to reassess Frazier's claim that slave women were self-reliant and self-sufficient through an examination of some of their activities, specifically their work, their control of particular resources, their contribution to their households, and their ability to cooperate with each other on a daily basis. Further, this paper will examine some of the implications of these activities, and their probable impact on the slave woman's status in slave society, and the black family.

At the outset a few points must be made about the subject matter and the source material used to research it. Obviously, a study that concentrates solely on females runs the risk of overstating woman's roles and their importance in society. One must therefore keep in mind that this is only one aspect, although a very critical one, of slave family and community life. In addition, what follows is a synthesis of the probable sex role of the average slave woman on plantations with at least twenty slaves. Information about female slaves cannot be garnered from sources left by slave women because they left few narratives, diaries or letters. The dearth of source material makes it impossible to draw conclusions about the slave woman's feelings. Second, even given the ex-slave interviews, a rich source material for this subject, it is almost impossible to draw conclusions about female slave status from an analysis of their individual personalities. Comments such as that made by the slave woman, Fannie, to her husband Bob, "I don't want no sorry nigger around me," perhaps say something about Fannie, but not about all slave women. Similarly, for every mother who grieved over the sale of her children there was probably a father whose heart was also broken. Here, only the activities of the slave woman will be examined in an effort to discern her status in black society.

Turning first to the work done by slave women, it appears that they did a variety of heavy and dirty labor, work which was also done by men. In 1853, Frederick Olmsted saw South Carolina slaves of both sexes carting manure on their head to the cotton fields where they spread it with their hands between the ridges in which cotton was planted. In Fayetteville, North Carolina, he noticed that women not only hoed and shovelled but they also cut down trees and drew wood. The use of women as lumberjacks occurred quite frequently, especially in the lower South and Southwest, areas which retained a frontier quality during the antebellum era. Solomon Northup, a kidnapped slave, knew women who wielded the ax so perfectly that the largest oak or sycamore fell before their well-directed blows. An Arkansas ex-slave remembered that her mother used to carry logs. On Southwestern plantations women did all kinds of work. In the region of the Bayou Boeuf women were expected to "plough, drag, drive team, clear wild lands, work on the highway," and

GATHERING THE CANE.

Although female slaves might perform the same tasks as male slaves, including heavy field labor, some occupations were considered "female work." Such tasks included cooking, sewing, spinning, weaving, washing, doctoring, and midwifery.

do any other type of work required of them. In short, full female hands frequently did the same kind of work as male hands.

It is difficult, however, to say how often they did the same kind of field work, and it would be a mistake to say that there was no differentiation of field labor on Southern farms and plantations. The most common form of differentiation was that women hoed while men plowed. Yet, the exceptions to the rule were so numerous as to make a mockery of it. Many men hoed on a regular basis. Similarly, if a field had to be plowed and there were not enough male hands to do it, then it was not unusual for an overseer to command a strong woman to plow. This could happen on a plantation of twenty slaves or a farm of five.

It is likely, however, that women were more often called to do the heavy labor usually assigned to men after their childbearing years.

Pregnant women, and sometimes women breastfeeding infants, were usually given less physically demanding work. If slave women began childbearing when about twenty years of age and had children at approximately two and a half year intervals, at least until age thirty-five, slave women probably spent a considerable amount of time doing tasks which men did not do. Pregnant and nursing women were classified as half-hands or three-quarter hands and such workers did only some of the work that was also done by full hands. For instance, it was not unusual for them to pick cotton or even hoe, work done on a regular basis by both sexes. But frequently, they were assigned to "light work" like raking stubble or pulling weeds, which was often given to children and the elderly.

Slave women might have preferred to be exempt from such labor, but they might also have gained some intangibles from doing the same work as men. Anthropologists have demonstrated that in societies where men and women are engaged in the production of the same kinds of goods and where widespread private property is not a factor, participation in production gives women freedom and independence. Since neither slave men nor women had access to, or control over, the products of their labor, parity in the field may have encouraged equalitarianism in the slave quarters.

But bondswomen did do a lot of traditional "female work" and one has to wonder whether this work, as well as the work done as a "half-hand" tallied on the side of female subordination. In the case of the female slave, domestic work was not always confined to the home, and often "women's work" required skills that were highly valued and even coveted because of the place it could purchase in the higher social echelons of the slave world. For example, cooking was definitely "female work" but it was also a skilled occupation. Good cooks were highly respected by both blacks and whites, and their occupation was raised in status because the masses of slave women did not cook on a regular basis. Since field work occupied the time of most women, meals were often served communally. Female slaves, therefore, were, for the most part, relieved of this traditional chore, and the occupation of "cook" became specialized.

Sewing too was often raised above the level of inferior "woman's work." All females at one time or another had to spin and weave. Occasionally each woman was given cloth and told to make her family's clothes, but this was unusual and more likely to happen on small farms than on plantations. During slack seasons women probably did more sewing than during planting and harvesting seasons, and pregnant women were often put to work spinning, weaving and sewing. Nevertheless, sewing could be raised to the level of a skilled art, especially if a woman sewed well enough to make the white family's clothes. Such women were sometimes hired out and allowed to keep a portion of the profit they brought their master and mistress.

Other occupations which were solidly anchored in the female domain, and which increased a woman's prestige, were midwifery and doctoring. The length of time and extent of training it took to became a midwife is indicated by the testimony of Clara Walker, a former slave interviewed in Arkansas, who remembered that she trained for five years under a doctor who became so lazy after she had mastered the job that he would sit down and let her do all the work. After her "apprenticeship" ended she delivered babies for both slave and free, black and white. Other midwives learned the trade from a female relative, often their mother, and they in turn passed the skill on to another female relative.

A midwife's duty often extended beyond delivering babies, and they sometimes became known as "doctor women." In this capacity they cared for men, women and children. Old women, some with a history of midwifery and some without, also gained respect as "doctor women." They "knowed a heap about yarbs [herbs]," recalled a Georgia ex-slave. Old women had innumerable cures, especially for children's diseases, and since plantation "nurseries" were usually under their supervision, they had ample opportunity to practice their art. In sum, a good portion of the slave's medical care, particularly that of women and children, was supervised by slave women.

Of course, not all women were hired-out seamstresses, cooks, or midwives; a good deal of "female work" was laborious and mundane. An important aspect of this work, as well as of the field work done by women, was that it was frequently done in female groups. As previously noted, women often hoed while men plowed. In addition, when women sewed they usually did so with other women. Quilts were made by women at gatherings called, naturally enough, "quiltins." Such gatherings were attended only by women and many former slaves had vivid recollections of them. The "quiltin's and spinnin' frolics dat de women folks had" were the most outstanding remembrances of Hattie Anne Nettles, an Alabama ex-slave. Women also gathered, independent of male slaves, on Saturday afternoons to do washing. Said one ex-slave, "they all had a regular picnic of it as they would work and spread the clothes on the bushes and low branches of the tree to dry. They would get to spend the day together."

In addition, when pregnant women did field work they sometimes did it together. On large plantations the group they worked in was sometimes known as the "trash gang." This gang, made up of pregnant women, women with nursing infants, children and old slaves, was primarily a female work gang. Since it was the group that young girls worked with when just being initiated into the work world of the plantation, one must assume that it served some kind of socialization function. Most likely, many lessons about life were learned by twelve-year-old girls from this group of women who were either pregnant or breastfeeding, or who were grandmothers many times over.

It has been noted that women frequently depended on slave midwives to bring children into the world; their dependence on other slave women did not end with childbirth but continued through the early life of their children. Sometimes women with infants took their children to the fields with them. Some worked with their children wrapped to their backs, others laid them under a tree. Frequently, however, an elderly woman watched slave children during the day while their mothers worked in the field. Sometimes the cook supervised young children at the master's house. Mothers who were absent from their children most of the day, indeed most of the week, depended on these surrogate mothers to assist them in child socialization. Many ex-slaves remember these women affectionately. Said one South Carolin-

ian: "De old lady, she looked after every blessed thing for us all day long en cooked for us right along wid de mindin'."

Looking at the work done by female slaves in the antebellum South, therefore, we find that sex role differentiation in field labor was not absolute but that there was differentiation in other kinds of work. Domestic chores were usually done exclusively by women, and certain "professional" occupations were reserved for females. It would be a mistake to infer from this differentiation that it was the basis of male dominance. A less culturally biased conclusion would be that women's roles were different or complementary. For example, in her overview of African societies, Denise Paulme notes that in almost all African societies, women do most of the domestic chores, yet they lead lives that are quite independent of men. Indeed, according to Paulme, in Africa, "a wife's contribution to the needs of the household is direct and indispensable, and her husband is just as much in need of her as she of him." Other anthropologists have suggested that we should not evaluate women's roles in terms of men's roles because in a given society, women may not perceive the world in the same way that men do. In other words, men and women may share a common culture but on different terms, and when this is the case, questions of dominance and subservience are irrelevant. The degree to which male and female ideologies are different is often suggested by the degree to which men and women are independently able to rank and order themselves and cooperate with members of their sex in the performance of their duties. In societies where women are not isolated from one another and placed under a man's authority, where women cooperate in the performance of household tasks, where women form groups or associations, women's roles are usually complementary to those of men, and the female world exists independently of the male world. Because women control what goes on in their world, they rank and order themselves vis à vis other women, not men, and they are able to influence decisions made by their society because they exert pressure as a group.

Elements of female slave society—the chores done in and by groups, the intrasex cooperation and dependency in the areas of child care and medical care, the existence of high echelon female slave occupations—may be an indication, not that slave women were inferior to slave men, but that the roles were complementary and that the female slave world allowed women the opportunity to rank and order themselves and obtain a sense of self which was quite apart from the men of their race and even the men of the master class.

That bondswomen were able to rank and order themselves is further suggested by evidence indicating that in the community of the slave quarters certain women were looked to for leadership. Leadership was based on either one or a combination of factors, including occupation, association with the master class, age, or number of children. It was manifested in all aspects of female slave life. For instance, Louis Hughes, an escaped slave, noted that each plantation had a "forewoman who . . . had charge of female slaves and also the boys and girls from twelve to sixteen years of age, and all the old people that were feeble." Bennett H. Barrow repeatedly lamented the fact that Big Lucy, one of his oldest slaves, had more control over his female slaves than he did: "Anica, Center, Cook Jane, the better you treat them the worse they are. Big Lucy, the Leader, corrupts every young negro in her power." When Elizabeth Botume went to the Sea Islands after the Civil War, she had [as] a house servant a young woman named Amy who performed her tasks slowly and sullenly until Aunt Mary arrived from Beaufort. In Aunt Mary's presence the obstreperous Amy was "quiet, orderly, helpful and painstaking."

Another important feature of female life, bearing on the ability of women to rank and order themselves independently of men, was the control women exercised over each other by quarreling. In all kinds of sources there are indications that women were given to fighting and irritating each other. From Jesse Belflowers, the overseer of the Allston rice plantation in South Carolina, Adele Petigru Allston learned that "mostly mongst the Women," there was "goodeal of quarling and disputing and telling lies." Harriet Ware, a northern missionary, writing from the Sea Islands in 1863 blamed the turmoil she found in black community life on the "tongues of the women." The evidence of excessive quarreling among women hints at the existence of a gossip network among female slaves. Anthropologists have found gossip to be a principal strategy used by women to control other women as well as men. Significantly, the female gossip network, the means by which community members are praised, shamed, and coerced, is usually found in societies where women are highly dependent on each other and where women work in groups or form female associations.

In summary, when the activities of female slaves are compared to those of women in other societies a clearer picture of the female slave sex role emerges. It seems that slave women were schooled in self-reliance and self-sufficiency but the "self" was more likely the female slave collective than the individual slave woman. On the other hand, if the female world was highly stratified and if women cooperated with each other to a great extent, odds are that the same can be said of men, in which case neither sex can be said to have been dominant or subordinate.

There are other aspects of the female slave's life that suggest that her world was independent of the male slave's and that slave women were rather self-reliant. It has long been recognized that slave women did not derive traditional benefits from the marriage relationship, that there was no property to share and essential needs like food, clothing, and shelter were not provided by slave men. Since in almost all societies where men consistently control women, that control is based on male ownership and distribution of property and/or control of certain culturally valued subsistence goods, these realities of slave life had to contribute to female slave self-sufficiency and independence from slave men. The practice of "marrying abroad," having a spouse on a different plantation, could only have reinforced this tendency. We have yet to learn what kind of obligations brothers, uncles, and male cousins fulfilled for their female kin, but it is improbable that wives were controlled by husbands whom they saw only once or twice a week. Indeed, "abroad marriages" may have intensified female intradependency.

That fact that marriage did not yield traditional benefits for women, and that "abroad marriages" existed, does not mean that women did not depend on slave men for foodstuffs beyond the weekly rations, but since additional food was not guaranteed, it probably meant that women along with men had to take initiatives in supplementing slave diets. Female house slaves, in particular, were especially able to supplement their family's diet. Mary Chestnut's maid Molly, made no secret of the fact that she fed her offspring and other slave children in the Confederate politician's house. "Dey gets a little of all dat's going," she once told Chestnut. Frederick Douglass remembered that his grandmother was not only a good nurse but a "capital hand at catching fish and making the nets she caught them in." Eliza Overton, an ex-slave, remembered how her mother stole, slaughtered, and cooked one of her master's hogs. Another ex-slave was not too bashful to admit that her mother "could hunt good ez any man." Women, as well as men, were sometimes given the opportunity to earn money. Women often sold baskets they had woven, but they also earned money by burning charcoal for blacksmiths,

and cutting cordwood. Thus, procuring extra provisions for the family was sometimes a male and sometimes a female responsibility, one that probably fostered a self-reliant and independent spirit.

The high degree of female cooperation, the ability of slave women to rank and order themselves, the independence women derived from the absence of property considerations in the conjugal relationship, "abroad marriages," and the female slave's ability to provide supplementary foodstuffs are factors which should not be ignored in considerations of the character of the slave family. In fact, they conform to the criteria most anthropologists list for that most misunderstood concept—matrifocality. Matrifocality is a term used to convey the fact that women *in their role as mothers* are the focus of familial relationships. It does not mean that fathers are absent; indeed two-parent households can be matrifocal. Nor does it stress a power relationship where women rule men. When *mothers* become the focal point of family activity, they are just more central than are fathers to a family's continuity and survival as a unit. While there is no set model for matrifocality, . . . certain elements are constant. Among these elements are female solidarity, particularly in regard to their cooperation within the domestic sphere. Another factor is the economic activity of women which enables them to support their children independent of fathers *if they desire to do so or are forced to do so.* The most important factor is the supremacy of the mother-child bond over all other relationships.

Female solidarity and the "economic" contribution of bondswomen in the form of medical care, foodstuffs, and money has already been discussed; what can be said of the mother-child bond? We know from previous works on slavery that certain slaveholder practices encouraged the primacy of the mother-child relationship. These included the tendency to sell mothers and small children as family units, and to accord special treatment to pregnant and nursing women and women who were exceptionally prolific. We also know that a husband and wife secured themselves somewhat from sale and separation when they had children. Perhaps what has not been emphasized enough is the fact that it was the wife's childbearing and her ability to keep a child alive that were crucial factors in the security achieved this way. As such, the insurance against sale which husbands and wives received once women had borne and nurtured children heads the list of female contributions to slave households.

In addition to slaveowner encouragement of close mother-child bonds there are indications that slave women themselves considered this their most important relationship. Much has been made of the fact that slave women were not ostracized by slave society when they had children out of "wedlock." Historians have usually explained this aspect of slave life in the context of slave sexual norms which allowed a good deal of freedom to young unmarried slave women. However, the slave attitude concerning "illegitimacy" might also reveal the importance that women, and slave society as a whole, placed on the mother role and the mother-child dyad. For instance, in the Alabama community studied by Charles S. Johnson in the 1930s, most black women felt no guilt and suffered no loss of status when they bore children out of wedlock. This was also a community in which, according to Johnson, the role of the mother was "of much greater importance than in the more familiar American family group." If slave women were not ostracized for having children without husbands, it could mean that the mother-child relationship took precedence over the husband-wife relationship.

The mystique which shrouded conception and childbirth is perhaps another indication of the high value slave women placed on motherhood and childbirth. Many female slaves claimed that they were kept ignorant of the details of conception and childbirth. For instance, a female slave interviewed in Nashville,

noted that at age twelve or thirteen, she and an older girl went around to parsley beds and hollow logs looking for newborn babies. "They didn't tell you a thing," she said. Another ex-slave testified that her mother told her that doctors brought babies, and another Virginia ex-slave remembered that "people was very particular in them days. They wouldn't let children know anything." This alleged naiveté can perhaps be understood if examined in the context of motherhood as a *rite de passage*. That conception and childbirth were cloaked in mystery in antebellum slave society is perhaps an indication of the sacredness of motherhood. When considered in tandem with the slave attitude toward "illegitimacy," the mother-child relationship emerges as the most important familial relationship in the slave family.

Finally, any consideration of the slave's attitude about motherhood and the expectations which the slave community had of childbearing women must consider the slave's African heritage. In many West African tribes the mother-child relationship is and has always been the most important of all human relationships. To cite one of many possible examples, while studying the role of women in Ibo society, Sylvia Leith-Ross asked an Ibo woman how many of ten husbands would love their wives and how many of ten sons would love their mothers. The answer she received demonstrated the precedence which the mother-child tie took: "Three husbands would love their wives but seven sons would love their mothers."

When E. Franklin Frazier wrote that slave women were self-reliant and that they were strangers to male slave authority he evoked an image of an overbearing, even brawny woman. In all probability visions of Sapphire danced in our heads as we learned from Frazier that the female slave played the dominant role in courtship, marriage and family relationships, and later from Elkins that male slaves were reduced to childlike dependency on the slave master. Both the Frazier and Elkins theses have been overturned by historians who have found that male slaves were more than just visitors to their wives' cabins, and women something other than unwitting allies in the degradation of their men. Sambo and Sapphire may continue to find refuge in American folklore but they will never again be legitimized by social scientists.

However, beyond the image evoked by Frazier is the stark reality that slave women did not play the traditional female role as it was defined in nineteenth-century America, and regardless of how hard we try to cast her in a subordinate or submissive role in relation to slave men, we will have difficulty reconciling that role with plantation realities. When we consider the work done by women in groups, the existence of upper echelon female slave jobs, the intradependence of women in childcare and medical care; if we presume that the quarreling or "fighting and disputing" among slave women is evidence of a gossip network and that certain women were elevated by their peers to positions of respect, then what we are confronted with are slave women who are able, within the limits set by slaveowners, to rank and order their female world, women who identified and cooperated more with other slave women than with slave men. There is nothing abnormal about this. It is a feature of many societies around the world, especially where strict sex role differentiation is the rule.

Added to these elements of female interdependence and cooperation were the realities of chattel slavery that decreased the bondsman's leverage over the bondswoman, made female self-reliance a necessity, and encouraged the retention of the African tradition which made the mother-child bond more sacred than the husband-wife bond. To say that this amounted to a matrifocal family is not to say a bad word. It is not to say that it precluded male-female cooperation, or mutual respect, or traditional romance and courtship. It does, however, help to explain how African-American men and women survived chattel slavery.

Questions for Study and Review

1. What new definitions of family and community were created for slaves? by slaves?

2. If both native Americans and Africans were considered outcasts, why was the fate of one removal and the other enslavement?

3. How did women's roles and status within the slave community compare with black women's roles and status in the larger plantation society and with white women's roles and status in that society?

4. If slavery did not automatically lead to Daniel Moynihan's vision of twentieth-century black matriarchy, how did the slave experience continue to shape African-American families and communities into modern America?

Suggested Readings

Deborah Gray White, *Ar'n't I A Woman?: Female Slaves in the Plantation South* (1985).

Ira Berlin, "Time, Space and the Evolution of Afro-American Society in British Mainland North America," *American Historical Review* (February 1980).

Charles Joyner, *Down by the Riverside: A South Carolina Slave Community* (1984).

Elizabeth Fox-Genovese, *Within the Plantation Household: Black and White Women of the Old South* (1988).

James Horton, "Freedom's Yoke: Gender Conventions among Antebellum Free Blacks," *Feminist Studies* (Spring 1986).

TWELVE

The Midwestern Farm Family at Midcentury

John Mack Faragher

James K. Polk won the presidency of the United States in 1844 with the promise to annex Texas and expand the nation's boundaries. Editor John L. O'Sullivan assured his fellow Americans that annexation was "the fulfillment of our manifest destiny to overspread the continent allotted by providence for the free development of our yearly multiplying millions." In the 1830s, 1840s, and 1850s, thousands of young men—mostly northern, native-born, and white—committed themselves to forwarding that destiny. After the defeat of Black Hawk's forces in 1832 removed the fear of hostile Indians, the Midwest became the haven for those seeking to escape overused agricultural areas and overcrowded cities of the east.

This migration was dominated by men, particularly during the Gold Rush of 1849, but women played a critical part in establishing family farms and stable communities on the new frontier. In areas that were battlegrounds for pro- and anti-slavery forces—such as Missouri and Nebraska—and in neighboring territories, less volatile struggles occurred between women and men over the distribution of work, resources, and power. Cherokee and slave women were accorded recognition by male kin for their labors despite the oppressive settings in which they worked. As

Faragher demonstrates, white women on the frontier fought a losing battle for similar acknowledgment of their contributions.

Pioneer wives were often less enthusiastic than their husbands at the prospect of moving west. The trip itself expanded women's work as they continued to clean, cook, and care for children while taking on new tasks—such as collecting buffalo chips for fuel or substituting for men as drivers and scouts when emergencies demanded they do so. Once settled, however, women's contributions to the move and to the new settlement were rarely rewarded with increased status or authority.

As Faragher shows, technological improvements, commercialization, and the tenets of true womanhood converged to obscure the significance of farm wives' productivity. Here the complementary nature of women's and men's labor did not lead to greater equality between the sexes. Nor did the introduction of agricultural machines provide the opportunities for western farm wives that industrial technology once offered farmers' daughters back east. Nonetheless, western expansion and the economic developments and political crises it generated could not have occurred without women's participation. "One cannot avoid being struck by the enormousness of women's work load," Faragher concludes, yet "men gave women minimal recognition for their work." Nonetheless, women continued to labor on the family farm as they had done for centuries.

Farming in the antebellum Midwest was part of a way of life that stretched back through the centuries, a way of life on the verge of a fundamental reordering. Families were at the center of this rural political economy; working lives were regulated principally through families. Work was organized by a domestic division of labor, roles and routines were set by family patterns, production decisions determined by a calculus of family needs.

American farmers were not peasants. They enjoyed a freedom of movement which set them off radically from their European peasant contemporaries.

Westward emigrations of men and families reduced demographic pressures in many parts of the East (indeed some sections lost too many people) and opened the way for structural changes in farming. As the eastern seaboard became more a part of the Atlantic market, a new regional division of labor occurred, and the commercial centers provided lucrative markets for farm products. Seventeenth-century opinion had stressed and valued self-sufficient farming and the closed circle of family labor. Farmers clung to these old attitudes tenaciously, but commercial values stressing economic rationality in market terms were more salient under the changed circumstances. Farming moved increasingly toward commercialization and specialization to meet the market demands of nascent urban communities. The view of farming as a business rather than a way of life was ascendant, if not dominant, in the Northeast by the first years of the nineteenth century.

Those who emigrated to the geographic and social periphery of the nation, on the other hand, met a different set of conditions. The move itself usually required some years of rather primitive living, but even after the early hunting-farming stage of pioneering had passed, the dominant fact of life in the Midwest was the isolation of farmers from the commerce of the East. Full entry of midwestern agriculture into the growing urban-industrial economy required effective transportation links with urban markets.

The notion of farm self-sufficiency should not conjure up images of isolated, impoverished farmers, out of economic and cultural touch with their peers. There was a good deal of social intercourse in the Midwest. In all but the rawest frontier regions there was an important social division of labor. In the first place, farm families could not produce all their necessities at home; husbandry and domestic arts had to be supplemented by the trades and crafts of the small villages and towns. In this way it was "possible for the skilled and enterprising settler to achieve a standard of living high in proportion to his wealth as measured in cash values." Moreover, the need of the Midwest for effective local administration, particularly in land and law, and the development of a local cultural apparatus (education, the press, the arts) further precluded pure subsistence and demanded the exchange of products and services.

Midwestern life had as its cultural context a capitalist economic system in which the principal regulator of economic affairs was the market, but it existed in relative isolation from that market. These facts had important consequences. In the first place, nearly every farmer's son hoped to make his entry into the commercial system and better his lot, and to this end he tried to turn a profit on whatever surpluses he could squeeze out of his farm. Largely laboring under commercial hopes, settlement was under way in the four principal home states of the overland emigrants—Indiana, Illinois, Iowa, and Missouri—by 1825, and the opening of these areas was completed after the Black Hawk War of 1832.

But entrepreneurial aspirations alone were not sufficient to make a capitalist revolution in midwestern agriculture. There were structural problems to be solved. The takeoff into commercial growth was stymied by midwestern isolation and poor transportation; even enterprising farmers were frustrated by prohibitive farm-to-market distances. Occasionally a farmer with easy access to a river would load up a raft or flatboat and float his produce down to the Mississippi and thence to St. Louis or even New Orleans. Such interregional trade along the Ohio and Mississippi river system fostered the growth of river towns; a similarly hopeful trade on the Great Lakes contributed to the prominence, exuberance, and growth of Chicago before 1850. More commonly, however, farmers bartered their dressed hogs, bacon, or wheat for goods at the general store or for the services of local craftsmen, and shopkeepers, in turn, shipped the produce to agents down the river.

During the second quarter of the century the hopes and expectations of midwestern farmers paved the way for the changes introduced by the railroads; these finally solved the transportation problem and brought the Midwest fully into the market. The decisive moment of change came in the mid-1850s. As far as future developments were concerned, the nascent commercial trends and structures were unquestionably the most important aspects of the years before 1850, and historians emphasize them most. But we are concerned here with the actual way of life of the majority of farm families in the Midwest. Until the Civil War (and the period of overland emigration to the Pacific Coast was mostly antebellum), most midwesterners lived by the traditional means of family self-sufficiency, whatever their aspirations.

The general shift to commercialism that began in the Midwest during the 1850s was accompanied by a revolution in farm technology. The steel plow, drill, reaper, mower, and thresher, although inventions of the 1830s, became commonly available during the fifties and were only fully utilized in response to the huge market demands, labor shortages, and high prices of the Civil War. Until the Civil War the self-sufficiency of midwestern farmers was in large measure a feature of the means of production: hand power did not provide the average midwestern farm family with enough productivity to turn to strict commercialism.

The technology of most midwestern farms, then, was a traditional force, tying men and women to the hand-power heritage. The essential tools of the farm—the ones the overland emigrants carried in their wagons—were the chopping ax, broadax, frow, auger, and plane. Farmers used these tools to manufacture their own farm implements—hoes, rakes, sickles, scythes, cradles, flails, and plows—resorting to the blacksmith for ironwork.

Hand technology set upper limits on the number of acres that a family could cultivate in a season; the only way productivity could be increased beyond that limit was by adding field hands. Working at maximum output, a farm family with two economically active males could utilize perhaps fifty acres of growing land with the traditional technology. Of these, perhaps one acre was devoted to the home garden, a score to small grain crops, the remainder to corn. In order simply to survive, a family required at least half an acre for the garden, the same for grain, and some ten acres in corn. Corn was the most essential; according to one observer, "it affords the means of subsistence to every living thing about his place." Before the 1850s the majority of midwestern families fell between these limits: most families lived on farms with forty to fifty improved acres.

As to livestock, an ox, or preferably a yoke of oxen, was essential, although when first starting out some families made do working a cow. Cows were necessary for milk and its products, however, and working them as draught animals negatively affected dairy production. A few sheep of mongrel breeds were necessary for wool, but mutton was almost never eaten. Geese and ducks were sometimes butchered, but they were valued most for their down. A family's meat supply was provided by the ever-present brood of chickens and the herd of swine, a dozen or more being necessary for a medium-sized family. These animals were frequently unsheltered, although on the better farms cattle might have a lean-to shelter for winter.

A farm family could gradually increase its level of consumption by clearing, draining, and preparing more land, and by increasing the size and improving the breed of its livestock. Then there came a limit, when the level of technology was a fetter on further expansion without resort to hired labor. The limit came, however, after the level of consumption had been raised to the level of contemporary comfort. "A backwoods farm," wrote an English observer, "produces everything wanted for the table, except coffee and rice and salt and spices." To the list of supplementals could be added occasional dry goods, shoes, and metal for farm implements. A self-sufficient family could produce enough for its annual table, along with a small trading surplus, but the task required the close attention of men and women to the needs of the land and the demands of the seasons.

The dominant paradigm of farm life was the cycle: the recurrence of the days and seasons, the process of growth and reproduction. Hand-power technology did not deceive men into thinking they could overcome nature; their goal was to harmonize man's needs with natural forces as best they could. The length of the working day, for example, was largely determined by the hours of sunlight. Candles and grease lamps were common but expensive, and the hearth's flickering light was too dim for more than a little work after dark. So most work was largely confined to daylight: up and at work by dawn, nights for sleeping. And in keeping with this daily round, midwesterners told time by the movements of the sun, not the clock. There was a variety of time phrases so rich they nearly matched the clock for refinement; the hours before sunrise, for example, were distinguished thus: long before day, just before day, just comin' day, just about daylight, good light, before sunup, about sunup, and, finally, sunup. Each period of the day was similarly divided.

The seasons imposed the same kind of rule as the sun. The farm's work demands were primarily shaped by the seasons, each quarter calling upon husbandmen and housewife to perform appointed tasks. The farming year opened in mid-March when thaws called the tenants outside. Land had to be cleared, drained, manured, and plowed, fields sown, gardens planted. Sheep, grown woolly, needed washing and shearing, geese plucking. In the hardwood stands farmers might spend a few days collecting and rendering maple sap, or searching out and hiving bees.

As the sun approached summer solstice, the work load increased with the day's length. The corn needed cultivation and hilling until it was strong enough to compete successfully with the weeds and "laid by" till harvest. There was hay to make, garden crops to nurture, gather, and replant, and often a winter wheat crop to harvest and thresh. In August, with the corn laid by and harvest coming, men took the opportunity for a respite; these were the dog days when "onery" farmers took long naps and "progressive" farmers mended fences. But August was soon overwhelmed by the frantic pace of September's harvest. Summer grain had to be cut, bound, and shocked within a critically short period, the corn picked, the last round of garden vegetables safely packed away in cold storage while still fresh.

Days continued to shorten, but after harvest the pace of work slowed as well. Still the grain needed threshing, the corn husking and cribbing, there was perhaps fruit to pick, dry, or preserve in a variety of ways, possibly pickles and kraut to make. These and other activities prepared the way for winter: sowing the winter wheat, making firewood, daubing the cracks in old cabins, barns, and outbuildings, banking dirt around foundations to keep out some of the cold, and butchering enough hogs for salted and smoked meat until the spring again provided a larder of milk, eggs, and poultry.

Summer's activity was counterbalanced by winter's leisure. The daily chores of the farm—tending livestock, hauling wood and water, the domestic routine—continued. But there was comparatively little opportunity for productive activity in the winter, aside from work in the woodlot. So winter months were occupied with general farm repair and improvement, visiting neighbors, trading the surpluses that summer's labor had produced. In late winter farmers would begin to plan the plantings of the next season, setting out planting dates in traditional fashion by carefully determining with the farm almanac the timing of the phases of the moon and the rising and falling of astrological signs.

Encouraged by their subordination to the natural world, the people of the Midwest held to a traditional animistic conception of the universe: the inanimate world was infused with will, feeling, and spirit. As William Oliver, an English visitor and resident of Illinois in the 1840s, wrote, "There is a good deal of superstition or belief in witchdraft, omens, lucky times, etc." The world could be best understood by analogy (if an animal disturbed the afterbirth, that baby would take on some trait of the beast) or contrast (cold hands, warm heart) or the rule of "firsts" (if a women cries on her wedding day she will cry throughout her married life).

Many of the beliefs were employed in a half-embarrassed way, perhaps pulled out only in times of emergencies like sickness, death, disaster; others were the stock-in-trade of midwestern life.

The cycle of the seasons encouraged a traditional view of work as well. Work was the expenditure of human energy to meet given tasks. When wheat was ready for harvesting, for example, men would readily work fifteen-hour days to bring it in before the precious grain was shed on the ground. On the other hand, when seasonal demands slackened, as in winter, a man might quit early without qualms, and few worried when a winter storm closed in the family for a few days. The persistent pace of modern labor, measured not by natural cycles but by the clock, was almost unknown to midwesterners. By the same token, work was understood not as the opposite of leisure but as life's requirement for all creatures regardless of sex or age. Men, women, and children would share life's burdens.

The common work of the farm was, then, divided among family members, but the principal division of work was by sex. Men and women worked in different areas, skilled at different tasks, prepared and trained for their work in different ways. In an economy based on the family unit, women and men in midwestern society achieved common goals by doing different jobs.

Sex and gender is a foundation of individual and social identity in all human societies. For historians (as well as other social scientists), the proper place to begin an understanding of gender roles is by reconstructing and examining the customary ways in which men and women divided the work of society among themselves. Such an approach employs an active, concrete concept of gender roles: gender roles are social regularities observed in what men and women do and the ways they think and feel about what they do, as well as how and why they do what they do.

The life of a midwestern farm woman entailed constant and often backbreaking labor. While the men of the family worked to produce cash crops, the women assumed responsibility for the never-ending domestic chores of cooking, cultivating, butchering, spinning, weaving, and sewing. Gathering fuel was also women's work. Here a farm woman pushes a barrow of buffalo chips, the only fuel available on the nearly treeless Great Plains.

The functional principles of the general divisions of work by sex on the midwestern farm were quite clear and quite strict in application. In only a few areas did the work of men and women overlap. Most clearly, men were occupied with the heaviest work. First, they had responsibility for work with the broadax. If the family was taking up new wooded ground—as many Oregon emigrants would be doing, for example—the land had to be cleared. Frequently a farmer would gird the trees with his ax the first season to kill foliage, felling trees and removing stumps in the following winters. Logrolling, when the men of the neighborhood joined together to clear a field belonging to one of them, was a common late-winter social event for men. Construction, including making fences, was also a male job, as was the ongoing work in the family woodlot. Wood was chopped, hauled and stacked, or dumped near the house.

Men also controlled work with the plow. For new land a breaking plow, drawn by several yoke of oxen, was often needed, especially in prairie sod. Working improved acres was easier, but still hard, heavy work. And within the limitations of available labor and marketability, men were usually itching to put new land to the plow, so the plow was associated with work of the heaviest sort and understood to be male. Work in the cleared and plowed fields, where grain or corn grew, also fell to male control and supervision. Men plowed in the spring or winter, sowed their wheat broadcast (until the 1850s), and planted their corn in hills. Men and boys harrowed and weeded until harvest, when they picked the corn together and cooperated in bringing in the wheat, men cradling and boys binding. Fieldwork kept men extremely busy. Two mature men on fifty acres of corn and wheat land spent three-quarters of the whole growing season plowing, planting, and harvesting, exclusive of any other work.

There was plenty of other work to do. Men were responsible for upkeep and repair of tools, implements, and wagons and care of the draft animals, the oxen, mules, or horses. Hogs and sheep, both pretty much allowed to roam, were herded, fed, and tended by men and boys. Finally, men were responsible for cleanup and maintenance of the barn, barnyard, fields, and woodlot. This meant ditching and trenching, innumerable repairs on all the things that could—and did—break, laying down straw and hay, and hauling manure.

Less important in fact, but work which nonetheless played an important role in male thinking, was hunting. For the early pioneers game provided most of the protein in the family diet. By mid-century those pioneer days had passed in the Midwest. But the rifle remained in its central place over the door or mantle long after the emergencies that might call it out had gone the way of the forests. Hunting remained, if only as an autumn sport or shooting match, a central aspect of male identity. The hunting legacy had one practical consequence for male work loads: men had primary responsibility for slaughtering and butchering large farm animals. Indeed, when hogs ran wild, they were sometimes picked off by rifle shot. Hunting was the male activity that most embodied men's self-conceived role—keystone of the hearth, defender of the household, the main provider.

In fact, women were more centrally involved in providing subsistence for the farm family than men. Nearly all the kinds of food consumed by farm families were direct products of women's work in growing, collecting, and butchering. An acre or so of improved land near the house was set aside for the domestic garden. After husbands had plowed the plot, farm women planted their gardens. Housewives began by setting out onions and potatoes in early April, following up later that month by

planting lettuce, beets, parsnips, turnips, and carrots in the garden, tomatoes and cabbages in window boxes indoors. When danger of late frosts had passed, the seedlings were moved outside and set out along with May plantings of cucumbers, melons, pumpkins, and beans. Women also frequently laid down a patch of buckwheat and a garden of kitchen and medicinal herbs—sage, peppers, thyme, mint, mustard, horseradish, tansy, and others.

The garden required daily attention. At first the seedlings needed hand watering. Then crops required cultivation, and the everlasting battle against weeds began. Garden harvesting could commence in late April and was a daily chore throughout the summer, supplying fresh vegetables for the family table.

Wives and daughters were also traditionally responsible for the care of henhouse and dairy. After a dormant winter poultry came alive in the spring. The farm-wise woman carefully kept enough chickens to produce both eggs for the kitchen and to set hens for a new flock of spring roasters. From late spring to late fall the family feasted regularly on fresh-killed rooster, selected and usually butchered by the housewife. Daughters and young boys gathered the eggs that were another mainstay of the summer diet. Women's responsibility for the henhouse extended even to cleaning out the manure by the bucket load.

Cows were sheltered in whatever served as a barn, and men's general supervision there relieved women of having to shovel the stalls. But women milked, tended, and fed the animals. The milking and the manufacture of butter and cheese was one of their central tasks. Cows were milked first thing in the morning and the last thing at night; housewives supervised the milking but parceled the job out to children as soon as they were able. Boys, however, with their father's sanction would rebel from milking; "the western people of the early days entertained a supreme contempt for a man who attended the milking." Making good butter was a matter of pride among farm women. The churn had to be operated with patience and persistence if the butter was to come.

> Come butter, come;
> Come butter, come;
> Little Johnny's at the gate,
> Waiting for his buttered cake.
> Come butter, come.

The meter marked the up and down of the churn. When it had come, the butter was packed into homemade, hand decorated molds, and pounds of it [were] consumed each week. Cheesemaking was less general; ripened cheeses were the product of a minority. Nearly all women, however, were trained in the manufacture of cottage cheese and farmer's cheese. Dairy production was especially important to the household and central to the definition of women's work. In 1839 a Springfield, Illinois, newspaper reprinted with horror a report that New England women were pressuring their husbands to take over the milking.

There were some areas of food production where women's and men's operations overlapped, but these were the exceptions. When hogs were butchered in fall, men from several farms might work together; it was mainly when it became necessary to supplement the meat supply that women helped men to slaughter and dress the animal. In any event, women were always a part of the butchering, there to chop the scraps and odd pieces into sausage, prepare the hams for curing, and cook the ribs immediately. At other social and almost ritual occasions of food preparation—making cider or apple butter, rendering maple sugar—men and women regularly worked side by side. All of the work of the orchard was often a joint project.

The sexes also sometimes combined their energies during planting. If not preoccupied with field planting, men might help to set out garden seed. More likely, however, field planting would fall behind the schedule set by zodiac or moon, and men called their womenfolk out to help. Women most often assisted in the cornfield. "Tarpley made a furrow with a single-shovel plow drawn by one horse," Iowa farmer woman Elmira Taylor remembered of the 1860s. "I followed with a bag of seed corn and dropped two grains of seed each step forward." A farmer with no sons worked his daughters in the fields at planting time without a second thought.

Food preparation was, of course, women's work, and by all reports midwestern men kept women busy by consuming great quantities at mealtime. Wives were responsible for preparing three heavy meals a day; most farm wives spent their entire mornings cooking and tried to save afternoons for other work. Included in the daily midwestern diet were two kinds of meat, eggs, cheese, butter, cream (especially in gravies), corn in one or more forms, two kinds of bread, three or four different vegetables from the garden or from storage, several kinds of jellies, preserves, and relishes, cake or pie, and milk, coffee, and tea. Making butter and cheese were only two of the innumerable feminine skills needed to set the farm table.

Corn, for example, was served fresh, softened with lye and fried (hominy), parched, preserved as a relish, ground green and cooked in a pudding, or ground into meal from which mush, flapjacks, johnnycake, pone, or corn bread were prepared. Bread baking, whether with corn or wheat, was a daily task. Pork was salted and packed, brined and smoked, or pickled. Chickens were roasted, fried, or stewed. Vegetables were boiled fresh or pickled for storage, cabbage was salted down and cut fine or made into kraut, peppers and spices were dried, fruit was dried or preserved.

Women cooked on the open hearth, directly over the coals; it was low, back-breaking work that went on forever; a pot of corn mush took from two to six hours with nearly constant stirring. Cast-iron, wood-burning cook stoves were available in Illinois in the mid-1840s, and by 1860 most midwestern women had been given the opportunity to stand and cook. The next great improvement in domestic technology was the general introduction of running water in close proximity to the kitchen. But throughout the antebellum Midwest, water had to be carried to the house, sometimes from quite a distance, and that invariably was women's work. Domestic work—housecleaning, care of the bedding, all the kitchen work, in addition to responsibility for decorating and adding a "woman's touch"—was a demanding task under the best of circumstances, and farms offered far from the best. The yard between the kitchen and barn was always covered with enough dung to attract hordes of summer houseflies. In those days before screen doors kitchens were infested; men and women alike ignored the pests. In wet months the yard was a mess of mud, dung, and cast-off water, constantly tracked into the house. A cleanly wife had to be a constant worker.

A farmer was said to be a jack-of-all-trades. But women's work outdistanced men's in the sheer variety of tasks performed. In addition to their production of food, women had complete responsibility for all manufacture, care, and repair of family clothing. During the first half of the nineteenth century, domestic manufacture gave way to industrial production of thread and cloth, but in the Midwest, from 1840 to 1860, while home manufactures declined, they remained an important activity for women. On the Taylor homestead in southeastern Iowa, for example, the assessed valuation of household manufactures declined from $73 in 1850 to $50 in 1860, but this marked a decline, not an end to the use of the wheel and loom: in 1861 Elmira Taylor spun her own wool, took it to a mill to be carded, and wove it into cloth throughout the winter on her mother-in-law's loom.

Midwestern homespun was mostly of flax and wool, supplemented by a little homegrown cotton or purchased cotton thread. A few sheep and a quarter-acre of flax were enough to supply the largest family. Farm wives sowed flax in March, harvested it in June (replanting immediately with a sterile-soil crop like potatoes), and prepared it that summer by soaking and sun-drying it to rot the outer coating. Men lent a hand by crushing the flax on the flax break to remove the inner fibers and washing and shearing the sheep, but from that point it was a woman's operation. Spinning wheels were in universal use; each household required separate wheels for wool and flax. Wool had first to be carded into lean bunches, then spun on the great wheel; the spinner paced back and forth, whirling the wheel with her right hand, manipulating the wool and guiding the yarn on the spindle with her left. Two miles of yarn, enough for two to four yards of woven wool, required pacing over four miles, a full day's work. An excellent spinner, sitting at the smaller flax wheel, could spin a mile of linen thread in a day.

The yarn was woven into wool and linen cloth or more commonly combined into durable linsey-woolsey on homemade looms. If cotton was available it was woven with wool warp to make jean. The giant loom dominated cramped living quarters when in use; it was knocked down and put away when weaving was completed. The cloth still had to be shrunk and sized (fulled)—a job usually put out to the fulling mill if one were nearby—and dyed, sometimes from home dyes, but increasingly with commercial dyes bought at local stores. Nearly all farm clothing was cut from this cloth. Coarser tow cloth, made from the short-fiber, darker parts of the flax, was used for toweling, bandage, menstrual cloth, rags, or rough field clothing. Pillows and mattresses were made of tow and stuffed with the down women collected from the geese and ducks in their charge. The finest homespun, the pure linen bleached scores of times till it reached its characteristic color, was reserved for coverlets, tablecloths, appliqué, and stitchery. For their annual clothing a family of four would require a minimum of forty yards of cloth, or at least two full weeks at the wheel and loom for an experienced housewife. This work was, of course, spread throughout the available time, and one could expect to find women spinning or weaving at almost any time of the day, at every season of the year.

Every wife was a tailor, fitting and cutting cloth for her own slip-on dresses and those of her daughters, her son's and husband's blouses and pantaloons, and the tow shirts of the younger ones. If there was "boughten" cloth available—cotton or woolen broadcloth, gingham or calico—it was used for dress-up clothing, home-tailored of course. Socks, mittens, and caps were knit for winter wear, but every adult went sockless and children barefoot in summer. Underclothes were not manufactured or worn, for they were considered an unnecessary extravagance.

Worn pants and shirts were continually mended, garments too worn to be saved used for patches, and every scrap of every kind of cloth that passed through the house was saved for the special purpose it would one day find. As an old Kentucky woman remembered,

> You see you start out with just so much caliker; you don't go to the store and pick it out and buy it, but the neighbors will give you a piece here and a piece there, and you will have a piece left every time you cut out a dress, and you take what happens to come and that's predestination. But when it comes to cuttin' out why you're free to choose your patterns. The Lord sends in the pieces, but we can cut 'em out and put 'em together pretty much to suit ourselves.

Sewing was the consummate feminine skill, a domestic necessity but one practiced and refined until in the hands of many it achieved the status of an art form. Girls were taught to sew before they were taught to read, and started on a four- or nine-patch quilt cover as soon as they could hold a needle. Coverlets, counterpanes,

crocheted samplers, and most especially the elaborate patchwork or appliqué front pieces for quilts were the highest expression of the material culture of women. With patchwork, appliqué, and quilt stitchery, utility was a secondary consideration; these were primarily modes of creative artistry for women. One farm woman testified to the importance of this avenue for her: "I would have lost my mind if I had not had my quilts to do."

On a more mundane level, clothes had to be washed, and women made their own soap for both the clothes and the family who wore them. Women loaded hardwood ashes into the ash hopper, poured water over, and collected the lye in the trough below. They boiled kitchen fats and grease, added the lye, and if everything was going well the soap would "come" after long, hot hours of stirring. They poured the hot soap into molds or tubs and stored it. Soapmaking was a big, all-day job, done only two or three times a year. Monday, by all accounts, was the universal washday. Rainwater was used for washing, or alternately a little lye was added to soften well water. The water was heated in the washtub over hearth or stove, soap added, and clothes were pounded against a washboard, then rinsed, wrung out by hand, and hung. The lye, harsh soap, and hot water chapped and cracked the skin; women's hands would often break open and bleed into the tub. In the winter, the clothes were hung outside where sore, wet hands would freeze painfully, or inside, draped over chairs or lines, steaming up the windows and turning the whole place clammy. Ironing and mending were also allocated one day each week.

To women fell a final task. Women bore the children and nursed them for at least the first few months, and in this they worked completely alone. Even after weaning, farm women remained solely responsible for the supervision of young children; both boys and girls were under their mother's supervision until the boys were old enough to help with the fieldwork, at about ten years, at which time they came under their father's guidance. Girls, of course, remained apprenticed to the housewife's craft. Farm mothers put their charges to work "almost as soon as they could walk," and although they could not contribute materially until they were five or six, the correct work attitude had by then been instilled. There was plenty that children could do around the garden, dairy, and henhouse; they watered, fed the animals, collected eggs, milked, hauled water, weeded, and performed innumerable other chores that housewives could never have finished but for the work of their children.

Midwestern farm mothers had relatively large families. The mean family size in the Midwest in 1850 was 5.7. The mean size of emigrating families in their full childbearing phase was 7.6. In her lifetime, then, a farm woman could expect to raise five or six children of her own. These children helped significantly with the burden of farm work, but not without the expenditure of a great deal of physical and emotional energy by their mothers.

To determine the full occupations of women, their total work load, we must consider the social effects of childbearing as well as child-rearing. Miscarriages, stillbirths, birth accidents, and infant mortality took a terrible toll on the energies and spirit of women. Counting infant deaths alone, one in five children died before its fifth birthday, and prenatal losses were at least as high. Childbirth certainly was a central experience for farm women. It was no occasional or unique event but occurred with demanding regularity.

Over half the emigrant women gave birth to their first child within their first year of marriage, another quarter the second year, and fully 98 percent by the end of the third. Thereafter a mean of 29.0 months intervened between births throughout a woman's twenties and thirties. For their most vital years farm women lived under the dictatorial rule of yet another cycle, a two-and-a-half year cycle of childbirth, of which nineteen or twenty months were spent in advanced pregnancy, infant care, and nursing. Until her late thirties, a woman could expect little respite from the physical and emotional wear and tear of nearly constant pregnancy or suckling.

Given the already burdensome tasks of women's work, the additional responsibilities of the children were next to intolerable. Women must have searched for some way of limiting the burden. It is possible that mothers introduced their babies to supplemental feeding quite early and encouraged children's independence in order to free themselves from the restrictions of nursing, which had to seriously limit their capacity to work. There is almost no mention of child-feeding practices in the literature, but there are some indirect indications that babies were soon consuming "bread, corn, biscuits and pot-likker" right along with their parents. On the other hand, there was a prevalent old wives' notion that prolonged nursing was protection against conception. To achieve a twenty-nine-month cycle without practicing some form of self-conscious family limitation, women would have had to nurse for at least a year.

Short of family planning, there was no easy choice for women in the attempt to reduce the burden of child care. Other groups had practiced family limitation before this time, but the need for labor may have been a mitigating factor here. It comes as no surprise, then, that as soon as it was possible, children were pretty much allowed and encouraged to shift for themselves, to grow as they might, with relatively little parental or maternal involvement in the process.

By no means were men the "breadwinners" of this economy. Both women and men actively participated in the production of family subsistence. Indeed, women were engaged in from one-third to one-half of all the food production of the farm, the proportions varying with regional and individual differences. Of

This engraving displays only a few of the many tasks farm women routinely performed: spinning, childcare, candle-making, and gardening. Women toiled from sunrise to long past sunset to do these chores so essential to the survival of their families.

the farm staples—meat, milk, corn, pumpkins, beans, and potatoes—women produced the greater number as a product of their portion of the division of labor. Women were also likely to be found helping men with their portion at peak planting time. To this must be added the extremely important work of clothing manufacture, all the household work, and the care of the children. To be sure, men and women alike worked hard to make their farms produce. But one cannot avoid being struck by the enormousness of women's work load.

In 1862, in its first annual report, the Department of Agriculture published a study by Dr. W. W. Hall on the condition of farm women. "In plain language," Hall proclaimed, "in the civilization of the latter half of the nineteenth century, a farmer's wife, as a general rule, is a laboring drudge. . . . It is safe to say, that on three farms out of four the wife works harder, endures more, than any other on the place; more than the husband, more than the 'farm hand,' more than the 'hired help' of the kitchen." In his recommendations for improvements in women's condition, Hall's report supplements our view of farm work. The practice of many farmers of letting their wives cut the firewood and haul the water, especially in the cold of winter, needed correction. Men should be responsible for providing a root cellar for potatoes and other vegetables, otherwise wives were compelled to go out in the cold "once or twice every day, to leave a heated kitchen, and most likely with thin shoes; go to the garden with a tin pan and hoe, to dig them out of the wet ground and bring them home in slosh or rain." Equally perilous for women were the extremes of heat and cold encountered in washing and hanging the winter laundry; men were stronger and should take that job. "The truth is, it perils the life of the hardiest persons, while working over the fire in cooking or washing, to step outside the door of the kitchen for an instant, a damp, raw wind may be blowing, which coming upon an inner garment throws a chill or the clamminess of the grave over the whole body in an instant of time." Men should make sure that women had ample time to produce the clothing needed for the coming season, or at least not hold their wives responsible when because of overwork they fell behind. By the same token, women should be allowed to purchase cloth for an adequate winter dress; too many women were underdressed, principally owing to their husband's niggardly attitudes.

Hall lamented the lack of attention to women's needs and recommended to men that they adopt a more sympathetic attitude. "There are 'seasons' in life of women which, as to some of them, so affect the general system, and the mind also, as to commend them to our warmest sympathies. . . . Some women, at such times, are literally insane. . . ." Husbands had to be patient and affectionate or risk driving their wives to a "lunatic's cell." In addition, a man should realize that his wife loved finery and beauty and should supply her "according to his ability, with the means of making her family and home neat, tasteful and tidy." Hall reminded the farmer that "his wife is a social being; that she is not a machine, and therefore needs rest, and recreation, and change." If hands were to be hired perhaps help in the kitchen was worth considering. Women should be allowed to get out of the house once in a while to do a little visiting with other people; in fact, it was a good idea for both husband and wife to dress up and step out for the day now and then.

More comprehensively, Hall insisted that women be given full authority within their domestic sphere. As the husband was master of the fields, so the wife must be mistress of the household. Husbands should not contradict a wife's domestic authority but must "make the wife's authority in her domain as imperative as their own." Most important "let the farmer never forget that his wife is his best friend, the most steadfast on earth; would do more for him in calamity, in misfortune, and sickness than any other human being, and on this account, to say nothing of the marriage vow, made before high Heaven and before men, he owes to the wife of his bosom a consideration, a tenderness, a support, and a sympathy, which should put out of sight every feeling of profit and loss the very instant they come in collision with his wife's welfare as to her body, her mind, and her affections. No man will ever lose in the long run by so doing."

Hall's report was a mixture of constructive suggestions and temporizing platitudes; it is unlikely that many farmers or farm women ever saw, let alone heeded, its advice. In the end it is more important for what it suggests concerning the working relations of husbands and wives than for its proposed reforms. Hall implicitly leveled a harsh indictment against farmers: that they were insensitive to the work load of their wives and drove women past reasonable limits; that they did not comprehend the natural or psychological needs of their wives; that they refused to give women the respect and authority that was their due. Hall attributed the problem to calculations of profit and loss which ignored social and emotional needs (although he made his appeal to men on the very same basis: "no man will ever lose in the long run").

The report adds depth to what we have thus far seen and suggests that the division of labor was structured in favor of men, that it exploited women, and that it was perpetuated, in part, by a masculine attitude of superiority. Daniel Drake, who visited the Midwest in the late 1830s, concluded that the farmer's wife was one who "surrounded by difficulties or vexed with hardships at home, provided with no compensation for what she has left behind, pines away, and wonders that her husband can be so happy when she is so miserable." The true inequality in the division of labor was clearly expressed in the aphorism, "A man may work from sun to sun, but a woman's work is never done." The phrase has a hollow ring to us today, but it was no joke to farm women, who by all accounts worked two or three hours more each day than men, often spinning, weaving, or knitting late into the dark evening hours.

There are some areas of women's participation in farm life that suggest a higher status. Cross-cultural studies indicate that the responsibility for exchanging goods and services with persons outside the family tends to confer family power and prestige. "The relative power of women is increased if women both contribute to subsistence *and also* have opportunities for extra domestic distribution and exchange of valued goods and services." In the Midwest, the products of dairy, henhouse, garden and loom were often the only commodities successfully exchanged for other family necessities. Powder, glass, dyes, crockery, coffee, tea, store cloth, metal utensils, and sugar were bought on credit from the local merchant; butter, cheese, eggs, vegetables, homespun, and whiskey were the main items offered in trade to pay the tab.

However, while it was true that women traded, the proceeds were not credited to them individually, but to the family in general. Commodity exchange in corn and grain surpluses, on the other hand, was most frequently used for male economic pursuits: paying off the farm mortgage, speculating in new lands, and as innovations in technology became available, experimenting with new farm equipment. Men's product was for male use; women's product was for the family. It has been claimed that "there was no doubt of her equality in those days because she showed herself capable in all the tasks of their life together, and she was proud to know that this was true. Her position and dignity and age-old strength was that of the real help-mate in everything that touched the welfare of the family and the home." From

a modern perspective equal work may seem a first step toward sexual equality, but the question of power is not only a question of what people do but also of the recognition they are granted for what they do and the authority that recognition confers. There is little evidence to suggest that men, for their part, gave women's work a second thought. That it was a woman's lot to work that hard was simply taken for granted.

Indeed, one theme of midwestern folksongs was the lament of the husband wronged by the wife who refused to perform her appointed tasks.

Come all you wary bachelors,
Come listen unto me
Come all you wary bachelors,
Who married once would be.

Before my wife was married
She was a dainty dame.
She could do all kinds of cunjer work,
Like butter, cheese an' cream.

She'd weed her father's oats an' flax,
And milk the cows I know;
And when she would return at night
She could spin a pound of tow.

But since my wife got married,
Quite worthless she's become.
An' all that I can say of her
She will not stay at home.

She will wash herself, an' dress herself,
An' a-visiting she will go;
An' that's the thing she'd rather do
In place of spinning tow.

One looks in vain for evidence of songs that sang the praises of women's diligence. Even the woman accomplished at all of her duties was likely to fall short in male estimation.

She could wash and she could brew,
She could cut and she could sew,
But alas and alas! she was dumb, dumb,
  dumb.

She could sweep with the broom,
She could work at the loom,
But alas and alas! she was dumb, dumb, dumb.

She could card and she could spin,
She could do most anything,
But alas and alas! she was dumb, dumb, dumb.

She was pretty, she was smart,
An' she stole away my heart,
But alas, in the door she was dumb, dumb, dumb.

Men and women were locked into productive harmony. The farm could not exist without the cooperative labor of both sexes. Yet men gave women minimal recognition for their work. Women, fully equal in production, were not granted the status of equality.

Despite its interdependence, the character of men's and women's work was essentially different. Women's work was dominated by the omnipresent awareness of the immediate usefulness of her product, be it milk, cabbage, eggs, or flax. Whatever processing was required she herself performed. Her view was inward, to her household and family. For them she was not simply to provide food and clothing and keep up the house, but to do these things with imagination and care: by gardening industriously, by preserving, drying, and storing to overcome the limitations of nature, by preparing the season's fare with distinction, by dyeing, bleaching, and cutting clothes in ways to please, and by keeping not only a clean but a well-appointed house. The joys of women's work lay in the satisfactions of accomplishment—of bread well made, butter nicely molded, quilts intended for heirlooms—and in the variety of skills each woman had to master. Women who worked up to this standard were good wives; those who failed on these counts were cast in male folklore as improvident slatterns.

Men, for their part, worked long, monotonous, solitary hours at a single pursuit in the fields, plowing row after row, hoeing hill after hill. Hamilton remembered work in the cornfield: "Usually you cultivated the corn with a hired man or two. But you each had your own 'land,' maybe two dozen rows each was working on, a row at a time. So you did not pass close as the two or three crossed and recrossed the fields, stopping, uncovering corn, pulling cockleburrs." Such work would produce, it was hoped, quantities of staple grain great enough to sustain the family and provide a surplus, but there was little satisfaction in the immediate labor. The flavor of male work was quantitative: acres, fields, bushels—all measured a man's work. Neither the corn nor the grain was immediately consumable but required processing; the connections between production and consumption—the full cycle of work—was not embodied in a man's own activity. The cyclical nature of farm women's work might allow her to see in a flowering field of blue flax the linen for next summer's chemise. For men the fields would yield not usable, tangible articles—bread or hominy—but bushels; quantities, not things.

On the self-sufficient farm, or farms approaching self-sufficiency, the character of men's work was a powerful link between the field and the house. The housewife converted the corn to hominy, the grain to bread, while the farmer looked on: only woman could realize the product of man. But the somewhat abstract nature of men's work enabled them to envision another mode within which they were not dependent upon their wives to fulfill their labor. The market could connect men's work to a larger social process and remunerate them in the tokens of commerce. In order to qualify as social labor, work had to have this characteristic: to be able to reach out and connect the family to the larger social world. Woman's work, always cyclical, always looking inward, did not qualify; it was hidden by domestic draperies. Men's work, even in the pre-commercial Midwest, encouraged a kind of economic vision women could not ordinarily achieve.

Questions for Study and Review

1. Considering the contributions of Lowell mill operatives, of native American and African-American women, and of pioneer wives, how was antebellum economic development shaped overall by women's work?

2. Under what circumstances did technology enhance women's—and men's—opportunities and status, or limit them?

3. In what ways would the conflicts over western territories between pro- and antislavery forces have affected women's and men's relations and power?

4. In the 1920s and 1950s, advances in household technology promised women less work and more leisure. What does women's experience with technological change in the first half of the nineteenth century suggest about the limits of these benefits?

Suggested Readings

John Mack Faragher and Christine Stansell, "Women and Men on the Overland Trail to California and Oregon, 1842–1867," *Feminist Studies* (#2/3, 1975).

Joan M. Jensen, *Loosening the Bonds: Mid-Atlantic Farm Women, 1750–1850* (1986).

Julie Roy Jeffrey, *Frontier Women: The Trans-Mississippi West, 1840–1880* (1979).

Glenda Riley, "'Not Gainfully Employed': Women on the Iowa Frontier," *Pacific Historical Review* (May 1980).

Jeanne Boydston, "'To Earn Her Daily Bread': Housework and Antebellum Working-Class Subsistence," *Radical History Review* (#35, June 1986).

PART FIVE

Civil War and Reconstruction

Civil War and Reconstruction—two events upon which both much blood and much ink have been spilled. As the nation was ripped in two and then partially repaired, families and communities North and South were transformed. High death and injury rates, inadequate transportation and communication, demands for more soldiers and more workers assured that mothers and sons, wives and husbands, sisters and brothers—whatever their race, region, or class—would be changed by the war.

In some cases, the war expanded opportunities for women—as nurses, as civil servants, and even as soldiers; as volunteer or paid workers in the thousands of local aid societies North and South; or as female slaves momentarily freed from constant surveillance by the absence of owners and overseers. Individual women engaged in an amazing array of activities. Rose O'Neal Greenhow, a Washington, DC, hostess, served as a Confederate informant and was honored by Jefferson Davis as the "hero" of Bull Run. Harriet Tubman was an even more valuable spy for the Union cause. An ex-slave who had made numerous journeys into the South to rescue runaways, she provided detailed reports on the southern terrain, worked as a nurse and courier, and guided several Union forays into Confederate territory.

Women performed medical as well as military miracles. Kate Cummings of Alabama and Hannah Ropes of Massachusetts were two of the tens of thousands of Civil War nurses, only 3,200 of whom were formally paid for services on either side. Dr. Maggie Walker, honored for her medical services to Union soldiers (some of which were performed after she was placed in a prisoner of war camp by Confederate troops) was the first woman to receive the Congressional Medal of Honor. Phebe Yates Pember, a South Carolina widow who served as superintendent in Richmond's largest hospital, gained a reputation as a brilliant administrator. Loretta Janeta Velasquez outfitted an entire cavalry unit after her planter husband's death in rebel ranks. Black women, North and South, were more likely to join the war effort as camp

197

As so often in American history, an idealized female figure is used to rally support to a cause perceived as moral and just. The fierce-eyed female warrior depicted here as the Spirit of '61 is also an apt symbol for the legions of women who worked during the war—for both sides—in local aid societies, as nurses, as intelligence gatherers, and even as soldiers.

followers or to be pressed into service as cooks, laundresses, and nurses. Susie King Taylor, for example, served with an African-American regiment in the South and recorded her experiences in *Reminiscences of My Life in Camp with the 33rd United States Colored Troops*. Ex-slave Harriet Brent Jacobs and Quaker school teacher Julia Wilbur labored as agents of northern women's antislavery societies, assisting black women and men who found their way into "contraband" camps behind Union lines.

Lori D. Ginzberg details the activities of thousands of women who served in the United States Sanitary Commission or in its local branches. She analyzes the importance of these labors for both local women seeking to aid male relatives and neighbors and for women leaders trying to shape new means by which to influence the nation's social and political development. The activities Ginzberg describes were reflective of hardship as well as hope, frustration as well as innovation. War brought loneliness and poverty, widowhood and grief to many. It also brought separation from family and friends; it increased the number of poorly paid jobs for women suddenly forced to support themselves and their children; it lengthened the hours spent in fields for women left behind to manage farms; and it introduced the disruptions of migration for camp followers or those caught in the path of battle.

Black and white, North and South, rich and poor, women labored on behalf of Union and Confederate causes. Few gained fortune, some gained fame, most simply got along as best they could. Many recorded their thoughts in letters and diaries, perhaps fearing they would not survive the cataclysm or hoping to pass on a memento of these convulsive times to children and grandchildren. One such chronicler recorded the ambivalence of women toward war as deaths and prices mounted. Commenting on a series of inflation-induced bread riots in Richmond, Virginia, in 1863, she wrote:

> I am for a tidal wave of peace—and I am not alone. . . . Here, in Richmond, if we can afford to give $11 for a pound of bacon, $10 for a small dish of green corn, and $10 for a watermelon, we can have a dinner of three courses for four persons. . . . Somebody, somewhere, is mightily to blame for all this business, but it isn't you nor I nor yet the women who . . . were only hungry.

Irish women involved in the New York City draft riots of the same year, native American women whose husbands and sons fought for a nation that spurned them, frontier women struggling to keep the farm and family intact, textile operatives turning out both uniforms and burial shrouds, wives of the South's small farmers who battled to save a slave system from which they did not profit or at least the state's right doctrines that sustained it, and widows and orphans on all sides must have shared these thoughts, at least now and then.

When the "tidal wave of peace" came, it did not wash away the hardships and doubts nor did it crush the spirit and pride of those who survived the war. Once again, the experiences of women and men differed by race, region, and class as well as by sex. Southern blacks had freedom but not the resources to enjoy it. Northern whites and blacks had victory, but the price in dead, wounded, maimed, imprisoned, and missing was high. Most southern whites had neither resources nor victory and harbored wounds that neither medicine nor time healed.

Americans shared the enormous consequences of the war—the loss of a generation of young men, more rapid industrialization and the intensified commercialization of agriculture, an increasingly powerful and centralized national government, the encouragement of further western migration, and the tensions of incorporating blacks, at least black men, into the country's ranks of voters. These changes and the national policies that spawned them comprised the formal history of Reconstruction, but it was their impact on and implementation in local communities that shaped the lives of most women and men.

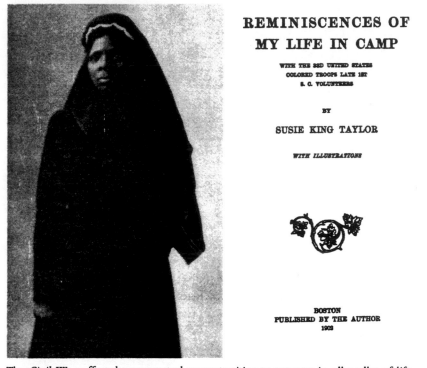

REMINISCENCES OF
MY LIFE IN CAMP

WITH THE 33D UNITED STATES
COLORED TROOPS LATE 1ST
S. C. VOLUNTEERS

BY

SUSIE KING TAYLOR

WITH ILLUSTRATIONS

BOSTON
PUBLISHED BY THE AUTHOR
1902

The Civil War offered unexpected opportunities to women in all walks of life.
Susie King Taylor, shown here in a military uniform, served with the 33rd United
States Colored Troops and later recorded her experiences in a book.

Of the million men who served in the Confederate Army, more than one-fourth died. Another 360,000 perished in Union ranks. The South lost $2 billion in property, raising immense economic and social barriers for defeated whites and freed black women and men trying to build new lives. Though Northern missionaries and teachers, many of them women, traveled south to educate freed blacks, and though the Freedmen's Bureau sent agents to assist needy families of both races, most Americans reconstructed their lives without outside help. Nonetheless, they were not untouched by state and federal programs. Jacqueline Jones traces survival efforts among southern blacks, offering a moving portrait of the limits and opportunities of freedom and the ways they were shaped by both black initiative and federal and especially state obstructiveness.

One of the most fundamental transformations resulting from Reconstruction was the incorporation of African-Americans into the political system. Former slaves were emancipated by the Thirteenth Amendment and granted citizenship by the Fourteenth. Black men were given voting rights by the Fifteenth, or, more precisely, could not be denied the vote "on account of race, color, or previous condition of servitude." For southern blacks of both sexes, attempts to claim these "rights" often led to retribution, including physical violence.

For northern women who had fought for abolition and woman's rights, the ratification of the Reconstruction amendments spelled the end of their hopes for admission to full citizenship. The inclusion of the words "male inhabitants" to define voters in the Fourteenth Amendment dealt women of all races and regions a setback on the road to equality. As a result, many white women formerly sympathetic to the slave's plight became less enamored of racial equality as they pursued more ardently the advancement of women's interests.

In the late nineteenth century, the western territories provided fruitful terrain for both blacks seeking economic independence and women seeking political influence. By then, Jim Crow laws in the South had deprived African-Americans of much they had been promised or had hoped for in the first glow of Union victory. In the North, industrial development and increasing immigration shaped most women's and men's lives more forcefully than did the right to vote. On the frontier, which was rapidly closing, native Americans found their societies again restructured as the federal government settled the remaining members of once-powerful tribes on small reservations scattered across the Far West. Native-born Americans in the same region saw their economic hopes revived as the Homestead Act (1862), the Morrill Land Grant Act (1862), the completion of the transcontinental railroad (1869), and passage of ever more generous land allotments in the 1870s testified to Congress's commitment to continued expansion.

In each region, reconstructing families and communities in the postwar period required the labor of ordinary women and men, some of whom gained distinct advantages in the midst of upheaval. At the same time, others suffered serious setbacks or found themselves caught in a new version of older constraints and conflicts.

Suggested Readings

Gerda Lerner, ed., *Black Women in White America: A Documentary History* (1973).

C. Vann Woodward, ed., *Mary Chestnut's Civil War* (1981).

Dorothy Sterling, ed., *We Are Your Sisters: Black Women in the Nineteenth Century* (1984).

Jacqueline Jones, *Soldiers of Light and Love: Northern Teachers and Georgia Blacks, 1865–1973* (1980).

Ellen Carol DuBois, *Feminism and Suffrage: The Emergence of an Independent Women's Movement in America, 1848–1869* (1978).

THIRTEEN

A Passion for Efficiency: The Work of the United States Sanitary Commission

Lori D. Ginzberg

When Confederate guns opened fire on Fort Sumter on the morning of April 12, 1861, the lives of all Americans were transformed. Amid the agony and brutality of civil war, women and men offered their services and their lives to one side or the other. In the North, the Sanitary Commission and its local soldiers' aid societies drew professional and business men, reform-minded women, and thousands of mothers, daughters, and wives from hundreds of towns and cities into a systematic plan for providing food, clothing, and medical care to Union forces.

The Commission itself was founded by leading male philanthropists and entrepreneurs, but the day-to-day work was carried out by women, some of whom—such as Josephine Shaw and Louisa Lee Schuyler—held positions equivalent to those of corporate or political leaders. Younger, single women were especially attracted to this new work and were enthusiastic about its businesslike organization. Keeping in step with the greater systematization and coordination demanded by war, female voluntarists shed much of the emotional and moral rhetoric of earlier public efforts, adopting instead an ethos of order and efficiency.

Though individual heroines such as Clara Barton and Mother Bickerdyke have received more scholarly attention, the most significant contributions of women—North and South, white and black—were made collectively through the preparation of bandages, clothing, and food packages; the raising of funds; and the care provided at battlesites, in hospitals, and in prisoner-of-war and contraband camps. In the North, the local soldier's aid societies and the Sanitary Commission to which they were attached provided the vehicle for most women's activism.

At the end of the war, women leaders in New York City claimed that "from this hour the Womanhood of our country is knit in a common bond, which the softening influences of Peace must not, and shall not weaken and dissolve." They did not; and women's voluntary organizations expanded and became increasingly efficient in the postwar years. Even in the midst of battlefield chaos, local aid societies had hoped that their care packages would find their way to "hometown boys." In the aftermath of war, as Ginzberg aptly demonstrates, the centralization and professionalization of benevolent and reform efforts threatened to diminish women's role in politics and society at the very moment when women felt most qualified to extend their efforts in new directions.

Throughout the rest of the century, activist women eager to maintain their significance in local communities and to expand into state and national arenas were forced to wrestle with the new forms of association forged in wartime. In addition, they struggled with the question of woman's enfranchisement and access to the formal political arena, a question raised with the return of peace and the enfranchisement of black men.

This war "is exactly like a revival," cried eighteen-year old Josephine Shaw, "—a direct work of God, so wonderful are some of the conversions." For Shaw as for many of her contemporaries, the war promised all the passion and purpose that had been lacking in the previous decade. Indeed, many, especially among the children of abolitionists, referred blissfully to the struggle for the "redemption of the nation," and to the "jubilee" which would follow the North's victory. Yet these and other young women's actions would undermine the enthusiasm of their words; wartime relief work celebrated explicitly business, not evangelical, principles, and the "conversions" which Shaw suggested signalled not a millennial vision of society but a glorification of the new virtues of efficiency and order. The themes which pervaded efforts at sustaining the soldiers contrasted sharply with those of an earlier age: nationalism, discipline, centralization and, above all, efficiency, became the watchwords for a new benevolence. In spite of Shaw's initial enthusiasm, the war deadened, rather than awakened, the flickering utopian impulse of her parents' generation.

Civil war benevolent workers established the first centralized, quasi-public organization for the relief of United States soldiers: the Sanitary Commission, along with its women's branches, furnished food, clothing, and nurses for the nation's first "modern" war. The "Sanitary Elite," men and women such as Henry Bellows, Louisa Lee Schuyler, Frederick Law Olmsted, and Josephine Shaw Lowell, reacted against the utopian hopefulness of their parents' generation by appealing to national loyalty, not individual moral perfection; urging manly exertion rather than feminine feeling; scorning humanitarianism and exulting in the reality of war.

The women who built the Woman's Central Association of Relief [W.C.A.R.] in New York, the Sanitary Commission's main branch, reached new heights of organizational fervor in the work of supplying the army, training and sending nurses and agents to the front, and establishing local and regional centers for the systematization of their work. In contrast to previous benevolent organizations, they displayed an elaborate concern for the details of organizational structure itself. Similarly, unlike antebellum benevolence, Civil War relief extolled a language of wartime discipline which for the leaders of the Sanitary Commission defined the essential nature of the war experience.

The women who would become the officers of the W.C.A.R. were born between 1828 (Abby Woolsey, Ellen Collins) and 1843 (Josephine Shaw Lowell). Louisa Lee Schuyler, the undisputed leader in the work, was twenty-four when the war began; Josephine Shaw joined the Executive Committee in 1863 when she was only twenty. Caroline Lane was twenty-two in 1863, Georgeanna Woolsey was twenty-nine, and Angelina Post was probably in her twenties. Of the eight women on the Executive Committee that year (there were also six men), only two were married. The builders of the machinery of war relief had barely begun their adult lives when they ventured to systematize on a national scale the feeding, clothing, and healing of the soldiers.

None of these young women signed the "Appeal to the Women of New York" which launched the Woman's Central Association of Relief in April 1861. Those whose names appear were older, established figures in benevolence; of the ninety-one women who signed, only two were unmarried. The women who actually ran the day-to-day operations of the

The United States Sanitary Commission, organized to provision the Union Army and to provide relief for the wounded, gave many women opportunities to work in organizations from the local level to the highest administrative levels.

W.C.A.R. had neither the status nor the influence to be considered essential to a public appeal. Nevertheless, it was these younger women, rather than the thousands of middle-aged women who organized local aid societies, who best characterized the changing style of that work. They approached their careers with a vision nurtured in the decade of the 1850s and a fervor inspired by war.

The war experience confirmed to many younger women that "calls of humanity" were less pertinent to the war effort than were calls to order. Over four years of war, unaffiliated women such as Clara Barton and Mary Bickerdyke found themselves with a shrinking role in the work at the front, as the Sanitary Commission solidified its hold on all aspects of the collection and distribution of supplies, the assignment of nurses in the field, and the development of a new rhetoric of order. Al-though there were still women who trespassed boldly over official restrictions in the name of "humanity," a new spirit pervaded the war. The Sanitary Commission, far from glorifying "pure benevolence," sought to control it, to discipline the ardor of women who, notwithstanding regulations, sought to bring "womanly influence" to the army.

In his introductory essay to Brockett and Vaughan's *Woman's Work in the Civil War,* Sanitary Commission president Henry Bellows sought to ensure that people's postwar memories would be free of any sentimental bias about nurses' importance to the war effort. Bellows praised at length the women at home who provided food and clothing for the army; only then did he reluctantly move "to a consideration of what naturally occupies a larger space in this work—however much smaller it was in reality, i.e., to the labors of the women who actually went to war...." Bellows honored those who worked in camps and hospitals as "persons of exceptional energy ... which ... hardly submitted itself to any rules except the impulse of devoted love for the work...." They were, he readily admitted, "as rare as heroines always are...." Yet nursing was not, he insisted, women's important contribution to the war effort; the ongoing, steady, businesslike work—the submission to rules, in fact—was what maintained the nation through its long struggle.

Indeed, the business of benevolence on the home front, not the activism of ultraists or the self-sacrifice of female nurses, most precisely characterized the changes which the Civil War experience catalyzed. Three days after the war began, a group of women in Bridgeport, Connecticut, organized the first Soldiers Aid Society in the North. Within the week societies had been established in dozens of cities and towns. Anxious for work to do in the first flush of wartime enthusiasm, church congregations and established benevolent organizations began sewing for the soldiers, packing boxes of food, and picking lint for bandages. By war's end thousands of societies had been organized to supply the Army with badly needed food and clothing. Women's Civil War work—in sewing societies as well as under government contracts—introduced a new scale to women's benevolent efforts.

On April 25, 1861, fifty or sixty women met at the New York Infirmary for Women and Children, founded by Doctors Elizabeth and Emily Blackwell, to plan an organization which would coordinate the disparate efforts by women in New York. "The importance of systematizing and concentrating the spontaneous and earnest efforts now making [sic] by the women of New York ... must be obvious to all reflecting persons," the "Appeal" began. "Numerous societies, working without concert, organization, or head ... are liable to waste their enthusiasm in disproportionate efforts...." The society would coordinate the collection and distribution of supplies, and would screen and train women nurses for the military hospitals. Even in this earliest document, the proposed organization was clear about its relationship to antebellum ideals: it sought to bring order from the supposed chaos of benevolent enthusiasm. "It will at once appear that without a central organization, with proper authority, there can be no efficiency, system, or discipline in this important matter of nurses—" stated the "Appeal." Signed by ninety-one "Most Respected Gentlewomen," the "Appeal" asked women, doctors, and ministers to meet at the Cooper Institute the following Monday.

Some two to three thousand women and many of New York's most prominent benevolent men attended the founding of the W.C.A.R. Demonstrating the federal government's approbation of the women's work, Vice-President Hannibal Hamlin addressed the audience. A committee of twelve men and twelve women was appointed to govern the organization. The W.C.A.R. (and the other organizations which would eventually become regional branches of the Sanitary Commission) differed dramatically from older benevolent societies in the vastness of its scale, the scope of its distribution of war resources, and its leaders' almost obsessive concern with organizational matters. In other respects as well, the organization of the W.C.A.R. signalled a new departure for benevolent organization. In September 1861 the W.C.A.R. became an auxiliary to the Sanitary Commission "at its own generous instance, ... retaining full powers to conduct its own affairs in all respects independently of the Commission...." The ambiguity of the W.C.A.R.'s position was indicated by the *New York Times* description which informed the public that the W.C.A.R. "was ... incorporated with (or rather was auxiliary of) the U.S. Sanitary Commission...." Although they displayed a certain contempt for the "female values" supposedly exemplified by the mass of women, both female and male leaders of the Sanitary Commission worked closely together, showing, according to Bellows, "no disposition to discourage, underrate, or dissociate from each other." The relations between the women and men who led the Civil War relief organizations indicated a new assumption about the "professionalism" of benevolence.

By 1862, according to William Maxwell, "most women of the North had been brought into direct relation with the commission." The network of civilian aid was, in theory, rigidly structured. Hundreds of local aid societies performed the mundane work of gathering supplies for the soldiers; thousands of women knit and sewed, canned and dried foods, and packed cartons which they sent to a regional office. These offices in turn sent supplies to one of twelve railroad centers; some sent materials directly to the national office. The central offices mailed the boxes to hospitals and agents at the front. In addition, women organized "Refreshment Saloons" for passing soldiers along key railroad routes. The local societies and branches, by distributing supplies solely through the Sanitary Commission and its agents, acknowledged the principles of nationalism and efficiency propounded by the organization. In 1864 the Buffalo depot announced with no little pride that "thus far we have never lost a package."

The central offices in New York, Boston, and Chicago, besides shipping out huge accumulations of boxes, administered an enormous relief organization. Managers maintained a copious correspondence with hundreds of local societies, sent out a steady stream of lecturers, and ran an occasional "Woman's Council" in Washington to reignite the fervor of those who had enlisted, in the common phrase, "for the war." The *New York Times* reported that the W.C.A.R.'s "rooms present[ed] the aspect of a busy warehouse. . . ." Louisa Lee Schuyler, Mary Livermore, Angelina Post, Ellen Collins, and Abby May spent long days and weeks in the offices, each fulfilling specific although broadly-defined responsibilities. Schuyler, for example, supervised publications, appointed regional managers, and scheduled lec-

turers. In addition, she sternly delegated duties to her coworkers: "I know how you dislike all this responsibility . . . which is so very little in itself," she wrote her friend Angelina Post, "but I don't think it will do you any harm. . . ." Both she and Ellen Collins, who chaired the committee on supplies, worked beyond the generally accepted office hours of nine to six; Collins frequently took work home in order to complete the meticulous charts of the W.C.A.R.'s supplies and distribution.

In 1863 the W.C.A.R. announced its adoption of the "Boston Plan for Sectional Divisions," a system developed by Abby May for appointing Associate Managers to bring the work of systematizing relief to local communities. The Associate Managers, women chosen for their administrative skill and local influence, supervised communication between sewing circles and the central organization. They distributed Sanitary Commission literature and reports from the front, and kept the central office in touch with the needs and activities of women throughout their region. Often they organized new societies as they toured an area. They bridged—and were torn by—the local concerns and nationalizing tendencies of wartime benevolence.

The qualifications for an Associate Manager reflected the difficulties of the job. "It is very desirable that they should be ladies against whom no local prejudices exist," instructed Schuyler, "& who are able to *work along* with the country people of the little villages, which I know is no easy task, requiring both tact & sympathy. Of course, earnestness, zealousness & energy are indispensable." "You will see from the enclosed circular that the duties may be summed up in the word *influence*," Schuyler wrote Lydia Wallace, the new Associate Manager for Syracuse:

We want someone who will help us to investigate floating reports about the Commission . . . —who will keep the interests of the commission before the people of her section & help to give them that confidence in it which we feel so deeply ourselves—& finally who will keep us informed of the spirit of the people about her. . . .

The New England Woman's Auxiliary Association, in correspondence with 750 societies early in the war, relied on each Associate Manager to report on "the state of affairs in her neighborhood. . . ." In return, the Association sent information from Washington about which supplies were most needed. Thus sewing circles in cities as well as isolated rural areas could work on the appropriate projects in order that "not one unneeded stitch may be set."

The women who accepted the appointment of Associate Manager identified with and worked ardently to achieve the central office's standard of efficiency. They filled with some pride their recognized role in a national organization. M. M. Miller noted that "except for being *under orders* & working beyond my present sphere, I shall not have much more to do, than I am now doing *without* the name [of Associate Manager]." Nevertheless she accepted the position, proud that it would be thought helpful. Eliza B. Culver felt "very much flattered" by the appointment; her "only hesitation at accepting the position at once is on account of incompetency." Yet she too agreed to take the job, and was soon writing bitterly to Schuyler that "patriotism is about *dead* in [this] County. . . ."

The offices in New York and Boston were flooded with descriptions of local populations from their Associate Managers. Women described problems ranging from their household cares to the ambiguous loyalties of local aid societies. "I am the mother of a family of six children," wrote Harriet Wing in response to an invitation to become an Associate Manager, "— *two sons* absent in the Army! . . . with my present domestic arrangements I have nearly the whole of my time to devote to the Soldiers— and *I do it*. . . . It is a necessity of my being while my Country is bleeding to do all that my puny arm can do." Many women actively engaged in war-

time benevolence wrote with some bitterness of the ambivalent sympathies with the war or with the Sanitary Commission manifested by the local populace, and of the weak commitment to steady work exhibited by the other women. From Sharon, Connecticut, Helen Smith reported an "aversion to systematized action on the part of working members . . .": her tone indicated both exasperation with the local society and her own identification with the rhetoric and organizational style of the national organization.

The phrases used to describe the work of the war—efficiency, machinery, harnessing enthusiasm, order—captured both the tone and the actual experience which a new generation brought to benevolence. Asking "How can we best help our camps and hospitals?" the W.C.A.R. estimated that "fully one-half of the People's voluntary contributions in the aid of the Army, . . . has been wasted, because not systematically distributed by central organization." Amateurs, continued the argument, injured the army's morale: "It must be remembered that private charity, patriotism, and humanity . . . do far less for our soldiers than Government is doing every day." Private charity, was, in fact, dangerous to the war. "The Commission recognized the depth of the National impulses that were at work," asserted another Sanitary Commission document, "the immense mischief they do if allowed to run wild, and the good they might do if organized and regulated. . . . Its endeavor has been and is to direct this stream into measured channels. . . ." "The women—God bless them!— think that it requires nothing but a good and loving heart to aid the poor soldier," observed Bellows. "But I can assure you, that however ardent and warm the heart, its pulsations . . . must be regulated by order and method."

In spite of the notorious inefficiency of the Northern army during the Civil War, Sanitary Commissioners evoked a military model to describe their own concerns: the Commission, Bellows boasted, "has followed the regulations of army life. . . ." "Only the most persistent and strenuous resistance to an impulsive benevolence," warned the Commission in its first *Bulletin*, "the most earnest and obstinate defense of a guarded and methodized system of relief, can save the public from imposition, and the Army from demoralization." This refrain, consciously opposed to the prewar rhetoric, was continuously heard by women throughout the war.

Those women and men who administered war relief were unabashed in their commitment to "business relations" which, the W.C.A.R. insisted, "have been found indispensable. . . ." Women's work in the war, recalled Mary Livermore, like that of "the best business houses," was characterized by "money-making enterprises, whose vastness of conception, and good business management, yielded millions of dollars. . . ." This rhetoric was contagious, affecting many local societies. "At first, simply a Charity, [the Ladies' Industrial Aid Association] became also an Industrial School," stated its *Report* proudly, "and we hope to make it a *self-supporting business*, in which Ladies step in between Government and the Seamstress. . . ." The Civil War, according to a proud Henry Bellows, "brought [women's] business habits and methods to an almost perfect finish. . . . They showed . . . a perfect aptitude for business, and proved . . . that men can devise nothing too precise, too systematic or too complicated for women. . . ." The Commission's insistence on business principles seemed to erase any lingering attachment to "sentimental" benevolence. The "ultimate end" of the Sanitary Commission, admitted its leaders, "is neither humanity nor charity. It is to economise for the National service the life and strength of the National soldier."

Ideas of female propriety and descriptions of home—both traditionally arenas for paeans to benevolent femininity—adapted to the new language of efficiency and professionalism. Louisa Lee Schuyler advised women who planned to form soldiers' aid societies to invite a man to preside at their founding meeting. "This formality, which may appear unnecessary to some," she insisted, "is, in reality, important to any efficient action on the part of the Society." Similarly, Mary Livermore described her return home after a long day at the Sanitary Commission rooms in terms that were assumed to be relevant only for men:

> Wearied in body, exhausted mentally, I . . . hail the streetcar, which takes me to my home. Its pleasant order and quiet, its welcome rest, its cheerful companionship, its gayety . . . all seem strange and unnatural after the experiences of the day. It is as if I had left the world for a time, to refresh myself in a suburb of heaven. . . ."

It was no coincidence that these women turned to this imagery in describing their wartime experiences; the Sanitary Commission waged a continuing struggle to convince women in local communities that their benevolent work must parallel the ongoing contribution of men. In its first *Bulletin*—whose very existence indicated that the work was to continue indefinitely—the Commission reiterated that "We have warned [the women] from the first that they were enlisted for the war. . . . There is no longer novelty or artificial excitement to sustain their activity. Only a steady principle of patriotic humanity can be depended on for continued labors in this holy cause." The article went on to urge women to make war work their daily business. ". . . *I* must, *we all must* buckle on the armor & work with all our might" agreed one Associate Manager.

An earlier generation had thought that a benevolent impulse would ensure the world's salvation; the women and men of the Commission sought to channel this "moral" force, to control erratic bursts of wartime enthusiasm through persevering labor. Louisa Lee Schuyler's correspondence emphasized this point again and again; she herself worked long hard hours administering war relief, and expected no less from her coworkers. "There seems to be a growing feeling . . . ," she wrote, "that the work of the Commission is really at an end. They

In order to raise money for their work, the Sanitary Commission organized fairs where wealthy patrons bought and sold a wide variety of goods, with profits going to the Commission.

should be *entirely dispossessed of any such idea.* Our work is to last as long as the war does & probably longer. . . . At the Convention of women held in Washington last January, nothing impressed the minds of those present so much as the manifest *stability* of this work."

From small towns and rural areas around the North, women active in their local auxiliaries wrote about their efforts to conform to the central office's standards of efficiency and hard work. "We meet every Tuesday," wrote L. R. James from Ogdensburg, New York, a town on the Canadian border, "and give ourselves credit for perseverance . . . as we have never adjourned our meetings in summer or winter since we were first organized for more than one or two weeks." L. M. Brown promised on behalf of her society "to work with more system and regularity than heretofore." *The Soldier's Aid,* a publi-

cation of the Rochester society, reminded women "that the service required . . . is something more than the result of occasional spasms of patriotism; that it is *work,* undisguised, continuous work, that we must render."

The qualities aspired to by local aid societies were admired as well in individual women. The women who organized the New York Metropolitan fair, which raised enormous sums of money from fashionable society for the Sanitary Commission, were the "creme de la creme" of New York society; the Commission, true to form, praised them primarily for their "administrative ability." A report on the Northwestern Sanitary fair was effusive in this respect: "Enough is said of the marvelous energy and wise business talent displayed by the ladies who had the Fair in hand, when it is stated that from beginning to end, . . . there was perfect system, and no break, no jars in the machinery." The new generation of elite women received the most ardent commendations for these virtues. "Kate [Wormeley] is a most thoroughly satisfactory woman," wrote Georgeanna Woolsey in her journal, in part because she had "not a single grain of mock-sentiment about her." Wormeley, according to Brockett and Vaughan, was indeed "endowed with extraordinary executive ability. . . ." Admiration for the nurses on the Hospital Transports was expressed in telling terms: "As for the ladies, they are just what they should be, efficient, wise, active as cats, merry, light-hearted, thoroughbred, and without the fearful tone of self-devotedness about them that sad experience makes one expect in benevolent women." Wormeley described the requisite characteristics of a Hospital Transport nurse unequivocally: "No one must come here who cannot put away all feeling," she wrote her mother. "Do all you can, and be a machine. . . ."

Above all, the young leaders of corporate benevolence admired business aptitude. Louisa Lee Schuyler granted Ellen Collins the highest compliment she knew: she was "systematic and methodical, and enjoy[ed] the business side of the work. . . ." Similarly, Julia Curtis praised Collins' meticulous charts ("a marvel of method and clearness"), which described in efficient detail the W.C.A.R.'s supplies. Schuyler attributed Abby May's purported "superior ability" to her admirable "system and efficiency." The Commission's final thanks to women after the war's end praised them, significantly, for two predominantly "male" activities: wage-earning and warring. "Your volunteer work has had all the regularity of paid labor," noted this document admiringly. "In a sense of responsibility, in system . . . you have rivalled the discipline, the patience, the courage, of soldiers in the field. . . ."

Henry Bellows overflowed with such praise. "The distinctive features in woman's work in this war," he wrote in his "Introduction" to Brockett and Vaughan's postwar tribute, "were

magnitude, system, thorough co-operativeness with the other sex, distinctness of purpose, business-like thoroughness in details, sturdy persistency to the close." The women who ran the branch offices in particular, agreed Brockett and Vaughan, "exhibited business abilities, order, foresight, judgement and tact, such as are possessed by very few of the most eminent men of business in the country."

Louisa Lee Schuyler, a close coworker of Bellows', embodied and celebrated traits which refuted previous ideals of female benevolence. Hers was a veritable passion for efficiency, business-like discipline, and unsentimental hard work, epitomizing in her own career the transformations in benevolence which the Civil War period strengthened. Schuyler was only twenty-four years old when she and her mother, Eliza Hamilton Schuyler, attended the founding meeting of the W.C.A.R. Yet from the start she assumed her mother's place on the Executive Committee and soon chaired the Committee of Correspondence, on whose behalf she wrote and received thousands of letters over the next four years. In fact, Schuyler operated the W.C.A.R., made contact with its numerous branches, and prepared its reports and publications. Schuyler prided herself on her ability to *systematize* the work of the W.C.A.R. and its auxiliaries. Taking on the obstacles of "religious feeling, localism, and sentimentalism" to rationalize "the 'production of supplies,'" she adopted the language of war—and disdained that of "femininity"—to express a wholly new conception of benevolence. She frequently referred to her coworkers as having military status; Angelina Post was her "chief of staff" who knew well "the likes and dislikes of her commanding officer" and Joseph Parrish was the "Colonel" to his "L*t* Co*l*." It was Schuyler who continually impressed on the women with whom she corresponded that they had all "enlisted for the war."

Schuyler's counterparts in Chicago, who operated the Northwestern Sanitary Commission, displayed more by their actions than their words a commitment to efficiency. Mary Ashton Rice Livermore and Jane Currie Blaikie Hoge were older than the New York leaders; they had developed in the benevolent institutions of the 1850s the skills necessary for their war work. In 1848 Jane and Abraham Hoge had moved to Chicago from Pittsburgh. Jane, who had been secretary of the Pittsburgh Orphan Asylum, plunged immediately into benevolent endeavors. In 1858 she helped found the Chicago Home for the Friendless; it was there that she met Mary Livermore, recently moved from Boston to Chicago, who was also interested in the institution. Like many of their generation and class, the two women became coworkers in a variety of institutionally-based benevolent works: besides the Home for the Friendless, they were prominent in work for the Home for Aged Women and the Hospital for Women and Children. When the war began, they moved easily into relief work, unaware of the dramatic shift toward a national base that their work would take.

Within one month of the war's beginning, Chicago boasted twelve or more aid societies. Soon, Dorothea Dix appointed Hoge and Livermore as general agents to recruit female nurses. Eventually the two women would have four thousand aid societies and a number of Soldiers' Homes under their direction. In addition to their administrative duties, both Hoge and Livermore travelled to army camps, attended Woman's Councils in Washington, and originated and executed the massive citywide fundraising fair, which became a model for other large fairs.

Henry Bellows insisted that "Everywhere, well educated women were found fully able to understand and explain . . . the public questions involved in the war:"

> . . . Everywhere started up women acquainted with the order of public business; able to call, and preside over public meetings of their own

sex; act as secretaries and committees, draft constitutions and bye-laws [sic], open books, and keep accounts with adequate precision, appreciate system, and postpone private inclinations or preferences to general principles; enter into extensive correspondence with their own sex; cooperate in the largest and most rational plans proposed by men. . . .

The war encouraged the virtues which best accorded with that work: efficiency and the subordination of enthusiasm to routine. In addition, the war, in part because of the great demand for the products of benevolent labor, placed benevolence in the center of the public eye. For the first time, debates took place over organizational issues which antebellum benevolence had previously hidden from public scrutiny.

Throughout the war, Northerners battled one another over the values which the Sanitary Commission and the W.C.A.R. represented. Women and men, nurses and doctors, "amateurs" and "professionals," religious and scientific benevolence—all sought to define the relationship between older notions of benevolence and the evolving demand for public service. In particular, tensions over paying wages, centralizing corporate functions, relating benevolence to government, and using funds solely for administrative purposes all came into the open. These disputes flooded the pages of Sanitary Commission and W.C.A.R. reports, forced lecturers into the field to defend a particular organizing style, and instigated vociferous local disputes over where funds and energy would be best spent.

These differences emerged publicly in a conflict between the Sanitary Commission and a rival organization, founded in November, 1861, the Christian Commission. The Christian Commission, which sent ministers and tract distributors to relieve the "temporal and spiritual" wants of the soldiers, was organized by the leaders of the prewar Benevolent Empire. Its strength derived from evangelical ministers, the

American Tract Society, and "disaffected areas," where grassroots support emerged from loosely affiliated church congregations.

The debate between the two commissions involved a conflict between an evangelical and a new "scientific," or liberal, style of benevolence; in practice, it centered around the benefits of paying or not paying benevolent workers, or agents. The Christian Commission claimed that unpaid workers were the more pure of heart, the Sanitary Commission that they were inefficient. Volunteers, explained a W.C.A.R. pamphlet, were "unreliable for permanent, systematic, and subordinate labor." In response to charges that its agents were unbusinesslike, the Christian Commission retorted that the Sanitary Commission was not a "Christian" organization, that it represented *"partisan, political views. . . ."* "It is attacked for its *sectarianism,*" cried Louisa Lee Schuyler indignantly. ". . . It is accused of squandering the people's money regardless of the oft-repeated statement . . . that *experience* has taught the true economy to be the employment of salaried workers."

Conflict also arose over the centralized, government-oriented structure and rhetoric which the Sanitary Commission and its branches so forcefully advocated. Commission publications constantly reiterated that the war was being fought for a *national,* not a local idea; that supplies had therefore to be sent where they were needed, regardless of people's loyalties to their own state's troops; and that women had to abandon localist notions of benevolence (or "statishness") to unite in support of centralized relief. The Commission, with a characteristic sense of its own importance, likened itself to none other than the federal government. "Because it is an 'arm of Government,'" declared a report of the New England Women's Auxiliary Association, the Sanitary Commission functioned better than could any local or state agency.

Sanitary leaders stressed the importance of its "practical lesson on the blessings of National Unity" so frequently as to make clear that people resisted their rejection of localism. Indeed, in spite of this constant barrage of rhetoric, the women's branches "had steadily to contend with the natural desire of the Aid Societies for local independence, and to reconcile neighborhoods to the idea of being merged and lost in large generalizations." Julia N. Crosby of Poughkeepsie explained to the aid society of which she was a member the "great necessity" of aiding the Sanitary Commission. "But I found the old American spirit of independence too strong for my argument," she wrote, caught between annoyance and pride, "and the plan was decidedly opposed. This was . . . from a natural unwillingness to become, after three & a half years of independent existence, in any sense a branch Society." "Do not denounce us as a very unmanageable, obstinate set of [women]," Crosby pleaded to Schuyler, "but give us still your sympath[ies]. . . ." The *Third Annual Report* of the Hartford Soldier's Aid Association defended its

position as an independent organization, ready to distribute of our supplies wherever the need is most urgent, [because] we are permitted to know of wants supplied and benefits conferred which it is impossible to communicate through the general channels of relief.

Such reports were anathema to the officers and loyal workers of the Sanitary Commission.

Some communities reacted to the Sanitary Commission's appeals to nationalism by questioning the integrity of the Commission itself. Loyal representatives of the Sanitary Commission wrote frantically of the negative rumors which circulated throughout their towns. People were suspicious of an organization which seemed to absorb enormous amounts of money and still cried out for more, which urged local effort but refused to allow aid societies to provide for local soldiers, and which so self-consciously aspired to a status akin to that of the federal government. Ophelia Wait assured Schuyler anxiously that *she* for one did not believe that well-known philanthropists were "engaged in the nefarious business of plundering the public. . . ." "Unsupported slanders"—that the Sanitary Commission's officers were pocketing its funds and that its agents were selling food to the soldiers—plagued local societies' fundraising efforts. Especially after the large urban fairs, many thought the Commission rich, and resisted sending it money or supplies.

Indeed, the Sanitary Commission itself viewed the "popular benevolence" which exerted itself for the large fundraising fairs as an obstacle in its campaign to encourage system and regularity among contributors. First, the fairs celebrated local pride and wealth; the official account of the Brooklyn and Long Island fair called the event "the first great act of self-assertion ever made by the City of Brooklyn." Second, the fairs netted unwieldy sums of money, which the women donated to the Commission. The first large fair, in Chicago, organized by Mary Livermore and Jane Hoge, netted between $86,000 and $100,000. The Boston fair, held in December, 1863, earned a profit of nearly $146,000, and that of Brooklyn and Long Island earned $400,000. But no fair compared to New York's, which imitated Chicago's innovations on a New York scale. The very wealthy bought and sold elegant goods from Paris and Rome; antiques, silver, handmade quilts, and tapestries were exhibited and purchased—the city, complained Harriet Woolsey, was in a "disgusting state of fashionable excitement." Held in a large building in Union Square, the extravaganza netted two million dollars for the Sanitary Commission's coffers.

The Sanitary Commission did praise the efficiencies and abilities of the women, many of whom represented an older generation of benevolent women, who had organized the

fairs. Yet tension arose over such huge sums of money raised in so short a time. "The Fairs held in our large cities," explained the New Haven General Soldier's Aid Society, "had netted such large amounts that many persons . . . regarded the sums inexhaustible, and seemed to consider their duty ended in that channel." As people throughout the North learned of the fairs' profits, they ceased to send as steady a supply of aid. The Sanitary Commission and the W.C.A.R. spent a great deal of energy convincing people of their unending duty—not only to the war effort, but, as importantly, it seemed, to the Sanitary Commission itself.

When the need for war work did end in April 1865, the leaders of the Civil War relief organizations expressed a profound ambivalence, perhaps more dismayed than relieved at the cessation of war. An article in the Commission's *Bulletin* about the Northern victory was entitled, amazingly, "The Crisis." "What will the Commission do now?" it asked. "Will it wind up its affairs, make a final report of its proceedings and disband, or continue its work?" In its own *Final Report* the W.C.A.R. admitted to its "mingled feelings of joy and sorrow" at the onset of peace.

Schuyler, Post, Collins, and the other W.C.A.R. administrators postponed the inevitable closing of the rooms where they had spent four long years. "We had a little informal chat to-day among the boxes. . . ," one W.C.A.R. worker wrote to Angelina Post. "Our Ch*m* [sic] bless her, agrees with me, that it would be in very bad taste for *us* to be the first to show signs of wishing to relax our efforts: that the gentlemen of the Commission will not be slow to inform us, so soon as it is necessary to narrow our sphere of operation. . . ." Louisa Lee Schuyler had trouble believing that the July 1865 board meeting was the W.C.A.R.'s last: "I haven't got used to the passive tense yet," she confessed to Post. Before adjourning the meeting Schuyler proposed a social gathering at her home in

Dobbs Ferry in October. "I couldn't bear to have the dear, old people, disperse & go away, without fixing some time for meeting again somewhere . . . ," she acknowledged, in a rare admission of sentiment.

To compound their own ambivalences about the end of the work, the managers of the W.C.A.R. were overwhelmed by letters from women around the North, expressing dismay at the completion of their shared labors. "Sometimes we wonder what we shall do, and how we shall feel when the sad necessity for such work no longer exists . . . ," wrote L. R. James. Minnie Brooks expressed great happiness upon receiving a photograph of the New York managers. "I think much of [the W.C.A.R.] and shall continue to more and more," she informed Schuyler, "as time hallows those days, and we are permitted to realize more and understand better, the times in which we were permitted to live and work." ". . . [T]hose last letters!" Schuyler scrawled to Post:

> Hundreds & hundreds of them—so full of feeling, so sad at the breaking up of their intercourse with us. . . . They send their love, they want our photographs, they want us to advise them what to do next. . . . It is almost impossible to read over these letters without crying, or choking rather for me. We are all feeling the break-up very deeply. . . .

"It is worth a dozen years of hard work—this ending," Schuyler concluded. "Henceforth the women of America are banded in town and country, as the men are from city and field," resolved the W.C.A.R.'s *Final Report*. "We have wrought, and thought, and prayed together . . . and from this hour the Womanhood of our country is knit in a common bond, which the softening influences of Peace must not, and shall not weaken or dissolve."

True to form, the Sanitary Commission indulged in no idle rhetoric. Almost before the war had ended, its leaders were making plans for their continued work. "The machinery of the Commission is still in good working order, and only needs to be contracted in some directions and extended in others," promised the Sanitary Commission *Bulletin*. The Commission proposed that women's aid societies help the returning soldiers adjust to civilian life and, in some cases, build institutions to assist the disabled. Only the women who were linked to the Sanitary Commission, the article claimed, could help the returning soldier "collect his claims upon the Government he has sustained. . . ." "We recommend you to impress on every aid society on your books, the importance of making itself the local centre of all that concerns the welfare of returning soldiers, in its own neighborhood," instructed a member of the Sanitary Commission's Supply Department. He advocated centrally located asylums for invalid veterans, maintaining to the end the lessons of the war, that "State and sectional feeling should be steadily withstood in favor of a larger and more patriotic sentiment. . . ." The Commission had no intention of slackening its wartime campaign on behalf of systematic benevolence. "That we should profit by the instructive experience of the past four years is plainly a duty now," claimed its leaders.

At the final board meeting of the W.C.A.R., Henry Bellows proposed having the organization's history written. Several members suggested, logically, that Louisa Lee Schuyler write it. Unwilling to undertake such a project ("I am not capable of doing anything of the kind—& don't mean to") and in any case nearing a breakdown from overwork, she sat "upon pins & needles" throughout the discussion. The work was never written in any official sense.

But Louisa Lee Schuyler, Henry Bellows, and the other leaders of the "Sanitary Elite" were not without a sense of their own importance and of the significant changes in benevolence which they had helped bring about. With characteristic self-consciousness they sought to determine the historical image they would leave behind. In spite of her exhaustion, Schuyler made sure to have photographs of W.C.A.R. members made and sent to representatives in local communities. In addition, she sought carefully to preserve the image of the W.C.A.R. which best represented her ideal. Schuyler left her own "private S.C. Diary" with Angelina Post when she went to Europe after the war ("Don't show this to anyone," she warned), and also instructed Post about how to preserve W.C.A.R. documents:

> I don't think there is anything in the gentlemen's letters which requires erasing, but those letters from Aunt Mary! . . . Take a pen, & scribble all over the personal parts you think *may give offense*. I remember parts which the New Haven people might not like. And where you think best, tear out whole pages or the entire letter—& destroy them. . . . I think Mrs. Olmsted's letters may need to have the pen & scissors freely used.

With whatever editing Post did do, there are nevertheless mountains of documentation about the Commission and its auxiliaries, much of it the elaborate trivia of a corporation's accounts. "There are twenty-five large, thick books, still standing upon our shelves," read the W.C.A.R.'s *Final Report,* "in which every one of your invoiced letters . . . have been carefully preserved . . . Let those who want to understand our work in the truest sense, read over these hundreds, or rather thousands of letters. . . ." The leaders had no intention of limiting the lessons of wartime benevolence to the war itself.

The legacy of the Sanitary Commission was an elitist and conservative repudiation of "female benevolence." Commission leaders such as Henry Bellows and Louisa Lee Schuyler "regarded the spontaneous benevolence of the American people . . . as a great danger to the discipline of the army which it was their business to limit and control." Sanitary Commission publications as well as individuals' correspondence over and over linked a concern for effi-

ciency and professionalism with a growing denigration of the rhetoric of "female benevolence." "Spontaneous" benevolence, particularly on the part of women, had to be efficiently disciplined into appropriate channels.

The language of "femininity" and "masculinity" pervaded this rhetoric as it had earlier commitment to an evangelical vision of social change. Patriotism, insisted the Sanitary Commission, the clergy, and numerous other writers, was a "manly" virtue, the counterbalance, perhaps, to humanitarianism which had long been recognized as "feminine." Ministers, suspicious of "charity and compassion," fervently celebrated the "manly" emotions requisite for battle. The Sanitary Commission, proclaimed one of its leaders in a remarkable statement, was the child of two parents:

> . . . on the one side, the motherly love which kept swelling up night and day . . . in such a stream as threatened to overrun all bounds. On the other side, the manly demand for law and system to guide and control this great moving tide. . . . Except for that union—the masculine with this feminine element—that tremendous tide of love, and impulse, and anxious tenderness, would ere long have been met by pointed bayonets and turned back, and forbidden entrance to the camp and hospital.

The metaphor could not have been clearer—or more violent to antebellum sensibilities. Without the controlling influence of "paternal" discipline, "female benevolence" and its representatives would be thwarted by the sword.

Many women in local aid societies resisted this transformation, recognizing that the denigration of "benevolent femininity" signalled the adoption of masculine professionalism as the new symbol of social service. There was no universal rush to embrace the new emphasis on efficiency and nationalism, the forthright glorification of the "Sanitary Elite," and the attendant plaudits accorded organizational skills over humanitarian impulse. Many women were still reluctant to replace the rhetoric of gender identity with one of professional interest, or to accept the "masculinization" of the ideology of benevolence. Nonetheless, a critical divide had been crossed during the hours, weeks, months, and years devoted to war work.

If benevolent women (and a few men) sought in the 1830s and early 1840s to "control" male passions by infusing the "male realm" with "female virtues," the Civil War gave a new generation an opportunity to reverse completely that rhetoric. Increasingly, "male values" were viewed as necessary to control and limit a "female" effusion of emotion, sensibility, or passion; either those sensibilities would submit to "law and system" or they would become entirely ineffective. The wartime "masculinizing" of the ideology of benevolence consolidated trends which had been apparent in the 1850s. It pushed women—many of whom continued to accept an ideology of inherent gender characteristics and "female values"—further from the symbolic and real centers of social and political power.

Questions for Study and Review

1. How did women's experiences of and contributions to the Civil War differ from those during the American Revolution?

2. In what ways might southern women's wartime efforts have paralleled or diverged from those of northern women?

3. How did the Civil War reshape the public activities of women in local communities and their relation to national policies and programs?

4. War generally expands women's public labors and familial authority and government often draws on female voluntary efforts to support official military actions. Yet in the aftermath of the Civil War, World War I, and World War II, women faced political rejection and division and economic restriction. What are the common elements that contributed to these situations?

Suggested Readings

Elizabeth Brown Pryor, *Clara Barton: Professional Angel* (1987).

Michael B. Chesson, "Harlots or Heroines? A New Look at the Richmond Bread Riot," *Virginia Magazine of History and Biography* (April 1984).

Jonathan Weiner, "Female Planters and Planters' Wives in Civil War and Reconstruction, 1850-1870," *Alabama Review* (April 1977).

John R. Brumgardt, ed., *Civil War Nurse: The Diary and Letters of Hannah Ropes* (1980).

FOURTEEN

Freed Women? The Civil War and Reconstruction

Jacqueline Jones

"Devastated, demoralized, and destitute" is how one historian described the post-Civil War South. As the primary battlefield during both the war and the peace that followed, this region experienced more dramatic and traumatic changes than any other section of the country. In the decade and a half of upheaval, plantation mistresses sought to maintain their families' estates, often as sole managers in the absence of male kin, while slave women and men struggled to expand their freedom and to sustain or re-create black family and community life. While northern women joined local soldier's aid societies, the products of which were channeled into the massive United States Sanitary Commission, southern women labored individually or through informal associations, and without the assistance of the Confederate government in dispensing their relief.

Black women found the war years especially difficult. Black men were hauled off to war alongside planters and their sons or forced into munitions factories, or became convinced that flight across Union lines was the best hope for freedom. Black women were often left behind on plantations to fend for themselves and their children. The end of the war and the guarantee of freedom relieved blacks of both sexes of the burdens of slavery, yet caused new problems of unemployment, homelessness, and racial violence. As the federal government struggled to erect a legal framework for reconstructing the nation, black families struggled simply to survive.

African-Americans traveled across the South to reconnect with long-lost kin, to find a better piece of land or a higher wage, and to track down those government agents who they heard would supply them with forty acres and a mule. As they attempted to throw off the psychological and physical legacies of bondage, black women and men also redefined their relations with each other and with white society.

Jones examines the contradictory meanings of emancipation, tracing the struggle of black women and men to give substance to their new-found freedom. Not unexpectedly, "southern planters could not reconcile themselves" to the new order. Yet even northern whites "feared that black people's desire for family autonomy" and "the preference among wives and mothers to eschew wage work in favor of attending to their own households" represented the failure of ex-slaves to adopt proper attitudes and behaviors. Documenting the variety of ways black women adapted to freedom and its limits, Jones demonstrates how they gained respect and authority in their communities even as they continued to be viewed as "a despised caste" by the larger white society.

In the Reconstruction South, white farm wives often were accorded less respect and authority within their family and community than were their black counterparts, though later in the century many poor whites moved toward a similar concern with elevating women's status. Yet white farm families rarely had to contend with the kinds of physical violence and emotional tension under which newly freed men and women suffered in the post-war South. Nor could blacks, even with the joint efforts of women and men, overcome the political repression, economic exploitation, and social ostracism heaped upon them when Reconstruction ended without significantly redistributing power or resources between the races.

Soon after he assumed the position of assistant commissioner of the Louisiana Freedmen's Bureau in 1865, Thomas W. Conway had an opportunity to state his policy regarding families of southern black Union soldiers. The northern federal agent found distressing the reports that former slaveowners near Port Hudson had, "at their pleasure," turned freedwomen and children off plantations "and [kept] their pigs chickens and cooking utensils and [left] them on the levee a week in a starving condition. . . ." Still, he remained firmly convinced that the government should not extend aid to soldiers' dependents; Conway wanted the "colored Soldiers and their families . . . to be treated like and expected to take care of themselves as white Soldiers and their families in the north." Moreover, the commissioner observed, the bureau "could not compel the planters to retain those women if their husbands were not on the place, unless contracts had been made with them." He appreciated the sacrifices that black men had made for the "Noble Republic," but with their wages from military service (no matter how meager or unpredictable) "and the amount which can be earned by an industrious woman," he saw no reason why their families could not "be maintained in at least a comfortable manner." The freed people needed only to demonstrate "a little economy and industry" and they would become self-supporting.

The postbellum debate over the fate of the emancipated slaves cast the major white participants into new roles which they embraced with varying degrees of enthusiasm. Neoabolitionists now sought to implement their notions about the moral significance of honest toil, and standard bearers of the northern Republican "free labor" ideology—Union military officials, carpetbagging planters, and Freedmen's Bureau agents—intended to provide the former slaves with the opportunity to exchange their labor in a new competitive marketplace that would replace the slavemarkets of old. These whites feared that black people's desire for family autonomy, as exemplified by the "evil of female loaferism"—the preference among wives and mothers to eschew wage work in favor of attending to their own households—threatened to subvert the free labor experiment. Like the Irish and French-Canadian immigrant women who labored in New England textile mills to help support their families, freedwomen were considered exempt from the middle-class ideal of full-time domesticity. Still, the irony did not escape the notice of one Yankee journalist: Of a newly arrived northern planter in the South, he wrote in 1866, "An abolitionist making women work in the fields, like beasts of burden—or men!"

For their part, southern planters could not reconcile themselves to the fact of emancipation; they believed that "free black labor" was a contradiction in terms, that blacks would never work of their own free will. An unpredictable labor situation therefore required any and all measures that would bind the freed people body and soul to the southern soil. Black women—who had reportedly all "retired from the fields" in the mid-1860s—represented a significant part of the region's potential work force in a period when cotton planters' fears about low agricultural productivity reached almost hysterical proportions. Ultimately, southern whites embarked on a "Prussian road" of authoritarian labor arrangements, but not without stopping along the way to alternately accommodate, cajole, and brutalize the people

In African-American families after emancipation, domestic chores were perceived to be the major responsibility of women, but when necessary women joined men in the field. Children, too, had tasks to perform—washing, cutting and carrying wood, and supervising younger children.

whom they had once claimed to care for and know so well. Thus by the end of the Civil War, it was clear that the victorious Yankees and the vanquished Confederates agreed on very little when it came to rebuilding the war-torn South; but one assumption they did share was that black wives and mothers should continue to engage in productive labor outside their homes.

Throughout this era of bloodshed and turmoil, freed blacks resisted both the northern work ethic and the southern system of neoslavery: "Those appear most thriving and happy who are at work for themselves," noted one perceptive observer. The full import of their preference for family sharecropping over gang labor becomes apparent when viewed in a national context. The industrial North was increasingly coming to rely on workers who had yielded to employers all authority over their working conditions. In contrast, sharecropping husbands and wives retained a minimal amount of control over their own productive energies and those of their children on both a daily and seasonal basis. Furthermore, the sharecropping system enabled mothers to divide their time between field and housework in a way that reflected a family's needs. The system also removed wives and daughters from the menacing reach of white supervisors. Here were tangible benefits of freedom that could not be reckoned in financial terms.

Emancipation was not a gift bestowed upon passive slaves by Union soldiers or presidential proclamation; rather, it was a process by which black people ceased to labor for their masters and sought instead to provide directly for one another. Control over one's labor and one's family life represented a dual gauge by which true freedom could be measured. Blacks struggled to weld kin and work relations into a single unit of economic and social welfare so that women could be wives and mothers first and laundresses and cotton pickers second. The experiences of black women during these years revealed both the strength of old imperatives and the significance of new ones; in this regard their story mirrors on a personal level the larger drama of the Civil War and Reconstruction.

✻

The institution of slavery disintegrated gradually. It cracked under the weight of Confederate preparations for war soon after cannons fired on Fort Sumter in April 1861 and finally crumbled (in some parts of the South many years after the Confederate surrender) when the last slaves were free to decide whether to leave or remain on their master's plantation. The specific ways in which southern defense strategy affected blacks varied according to time and place; before the war's end a combination of factors based on circumstance and personal initiative opened the way to freedom for many, but often slowly, and only by degrees. For women, the welfare of their children was often the primary consideration in determining an appropriate course of action once they confronted—or created—a moment ripe with possibilities.

Three individual cases suggest the varying states of awareness and choice that could shape the decisions of slave women during this period of upheaval. In 1862 a seventy-year old Georgia bondswoman engineered a dramatic escape for herself and twenty-two children and grandchildren. The group floated forty miles down the Savannah River on a flatboat and finally found refuge on a federal vessel. In contrast, Hannah Davidson recalled many years later that she and the other slaves on a Kentucky plantation lived in such rural isolation—and under such tyranny—that they remained in servitude until the mid-1880s: "We didn't even know we were free," she said. Yet Rosaline Rogers, thirty-eight years old at the war's end and mother of fourteen children, kept her family together on her master's Tennessee plantation, even after she was free to leave: "I was given my choice of staying on the same plantation, working on shares, or taking my family away, letting them out [to work in return] for their food and clothes. I decided to stay on that way; I could have my children with me." But, she added, the arrangement was far from satisfactory, for her children "were not allowed to go to school, they were taught only to work."

The logic of resistance proceeded apace on plantations all over the South as slaveholders became increasingly preoccupied with the Confederacy's declining military fortunes. On a Mississippi plantation, Dora Franks overheard her master and mistress discuss the horror of an impending Yankee victory. The very thought of it made the white woman "feel lak jumpin' in de well," but, Dora Franks declared, "from dat minute I started prayin' for freedom. All de res' of de women done de same." Slaves did not have to keep apprised of rebel maneuvers on the battleground to take advantage of novel situations produced by an absent master, a greenhorn overseer, or a nervous mistress uncertain how to maintain the upper hand. Under these conditions black women, men, and children slowed their workpace to a crawl. "Awkward," "inefficient," "lazy," "erratic," "ungovernable," and "slack" (according to exasperated whites), they left weeds in the cotton fields, burned the evening's supper to a crisp, and let the cows trample the corn.

Their chains loosened by the distractions of war, many slaves challenged the physical and emotional resolve of whites in authority. For the vast majority, however, the war itself only intensified their hardships. As the Confederacy directed more of its resources and manpower toward the defense effort, food supplies became scarce throughout the region. Planters and local government officials, anxious in the midst of black (and even white) rebels on their own soil and uncertain about the future of their new nation, reacted violently to isolated cases of real and imagined insubordination. The owner of a Georgia coastal plantation was so infuriated by the number of his slaves who had fled to Union lines that he took special precautions to hold onto his prized cook; he bound her feet in iron stocks so that "she had to drag herself around her kitchen all day, and at night she was locked into the corn-house."

During wartime the responsibility for the care of the children, the ill, and the elderly devolved upon slave women to an even greater extent than had been the case during the antebellum period. Military mobilizations wreaked havoc on the already fragile ties that held slave families together. Efforts to restrict slave mobility prevented husbands from visiting their "broad" wives on a regular basis and discouraged cross-plantation marriages in general. Confederate slave impressment policies primarily affected men, who were put to work on military construction projects and in armies, factories, and hospitals. The practice of "refugeeing" highly valued slaves to the interior or to another state also meant that the strongest, healthiest men were taken away from plantation wives and children.

During the conflict, at different times in different parts of the South, the approaching Union army provided slaves with both an opportunity and an incentive to flee from their masters. Soon after the Union forces took control of the South Carolina Sea Islands, Elizabeth Botume, a newly arrived northern teacher, observed a refugee mother and her three children hurrying toward a government steamer:

A huge negress was seen striding along with her hominy pot, in which was a live chicken, poised on her head. One child was on her back with its arms tightly clasped around her neck, and its feet about her waist, and under each arm was a smaller child. Her apron was tucked up in front, evidently filled with articles of clothing. Her feet were bare, and in her mouth was a short clay pipe. A poor little yellow dog ran by her side, and a half-grown pig trotted on before.

To women like the Louisiana mother who brought her dead child ("shot by her pursuing master") into a Yankee army camp, "to be buried, as she said, *free,*" Union territory symbolized the end of an old life and the beginning of a new one. But it was an inauspicious beginning. Crowded together, often lacking food, shelter, and medicine, these human "contraband of war" lived a wretched existence. Moreover, in 1863 the refugee settlements—and virtually any areas under federal control—became targets for military officials seeking black male conscripts. Black men wanted to defend their families and fight for freedom, and almost a quarter of a million served the Union war effort in some formal capacity—half as soldiers, the rest as laborers, teamsters, craftsmen, and servants. However, the violent wrenching of draftees from their wives and children caused great resentment among the refugees. The women of one camp, wrote Elizabeth Botume, "were proud of volunteers, but a draft was like an ignominious seizure."

Whether southern black men volunteered for or were pressed into Union military service, the well-being of their families remained a constant source of anxiety for them. Wives and children who remained behind in Confederate territory on their master's plantation, and even some of those who belonged to owners sympathetic to the northern cause, bore the brunt of white men's anger as a way of life quickly began to slip away. Frances Johnson, a Kentucky slave woman whose husband was a Union soldier, reported that in 1864 her master had told her, "all the 'niggers' did mighty wrong in joining the Army." One day the following spring, she recalled, "my masters son . . . whipped me severely on my refusing to do some work for him which I was not in a condition to perform. He beat me in the presence of his father who told him [the son] to 'buck me and give me a thousand' meaning thereby a thousand lashes."

In an effort to stay together and escape the vengeance of southern whites, some families followed their menfolk to the front lines. But soldiers' wives, denounced as prostitutes and "idle, lazy vagrants" by military officials, found that the army camps offered little in the way of refuge from callousness and abuse. The payment of soldiers' wages was a notoriously slow and unpredictable process, leaving mothers with responsibility for the full support of their children. The elaborate application procedures discouraged even qualified women from seeking aid from the Army Quartermaster Department. A few wives found jobs as laundresses and cooks in and around the camps, but gainful employment was not easy to come by during such chaotic times. Meanwhile, not only did many families lack basic creature comforts in the form of adequate clothing and shelter, they were at times deprived of what little they did have by Union officers who felt that the presence of black wives impaired the military efficiency of their husbands. At Camp Nelson, Kentucky, in late 1864, white soldiers leveled the makeshift shantytown erected by black women to house their children and left four hundred persons homeless in bitterly cold weather.

Although many women had no choice but to seek food and safety from northern troops, often with bitterly disappointing results, others managed to attain relative freedom from white interference and remain on or near their old homesites. In areas where whites had fled and large numbers of black men had marched—or been marched off—with the Union army, wives, mothers, daughters, and sisters often grew crops and cared for each other. For example, several hundred women from the Combahee River region of South Carolina made up a small colony unto themselves in a Sea Island settlement. They prided themselves on their special handicrafts sent to their men "wid Mon'gomery's boys in de regiment": gloves and stockings made from "coarse yarn spun in a tin basin and knitted on reed, cut in the swamps." Together with men and women from other areas, the "Combees" cultivated cotton and potato patches, gathered ground nuts, minded the children, and nursed the ill.

The end of the war signaled the first chance for large numbers of blacks to leave their slave quarters as a demonstration of liberty. Asked why she wanted to move off her master's South Carolina plantation, the former slave Patience responded in a manner that belied her name: "I must go, if I stay here I'll never know I'm free."

During the first fearful months of freedom, many black women and men traveled to nearby towns to escape the masters who had extracted so much pain and suffering from them. But before long a reverse migration occurred among those people who had to return to the countryside in order to search for work. The degree to which the antebellum elite persisted (in both a social and economic sense) varied throughout the South. Nevertheless, the failure of the federal government to institute a comprehensive land confiscation and redistribution program, combined with southern whites' systematic refusal to sell property or extend credit to the former slaves, meant that the majority of blacks would remain economically dependent upon the group of people (if not the individuals) whom they had served as slaves. The extent of black migration out of the South during this period was negligible—and understandable, considering the lack of viable job opportunities for blacks elsewhere in the country. Most freed people remained concentrated in the Cotton Belt, in the vicinity of their enslavement; the proximity of kin groupings helped to determine precisely where they would settle.

Indeed, whites felt that blacks as a race would

gradually die out as a result of their inability to care for themselves and work independent of the slaveholder's whip. The eagerness with which blacks initially fled the plantations convinced these white men that only "Black Laws" limiting their freedom of movement would insure a stable labor force. The Yankees' vision of a free labor market, in which individual blacks used their wits to strike a favorable bargain with a prospective employer, struck the former Confederates as a ludicrous idea and an impossible objective.

When it came to reconstructing southern society, northerners were not all of the same stripe. But those in positions of political authority tended to equate freedom with the opportunity to toil on one's own behalf. Yankees conceived of the contract labor system as an innovation that would ensure the production of cotton (necessary for the New England textile industry) and protect blacks against unbridled exploitation at the hands of their former masters. If a person did not like the terms or treatment accorded by an employer, he or she should look for work elsewhere, thereby encouraging diehard rebels to conform to enlightened labor practices. In time, after a thrifty household had accumulated a little cash, it could buy its own land and become part of the independent yeomanry. To this end northern Republicans established the Freedmen's Bureau, which oversaw contract negotiations between the former slaves and their new masters.

The contract system was premised on the assumption that freed people would embrace gainful employment out of both economic necessity and natural inclination. Still, the baneful effects of slavery on the moral character of blacks caused whites like Bureau Commissioner Oliver O. Howard to express the pious hope that, initially, "wholesome compulsion" would lead to "larger independence" for the masses. "Compulsion" came in a variety of shapes and sizes. For the Yankee general stationed in Richmond and determined to get the families

of black soldiers off federal rations, it amounted to "hiring out" unemployed women or creating jobs for them in the form of "a grand *general* washing establishment for the city, where clothing of any one will be washed gratis." Indeed, even many northern teachers commissioned to minister to the freed blacks believed that hard manual labor would refresh the souls of individual black women and men even as it restored the postwar southern economy.

If few slave women ever had the luxury of choosing between different kinds of work, freedwomen with children found that economic necessity bred its own kind of slavery. Their only choice was to take whatever work was available—and that was not much. Field hands and domestic servants who decided to stay on or return to their master's plantation and work for wages needed the children's help to make ends meet; at times it seemed as if only seasoned cotton pickers would be able to eat.

All women had to contend with the problem of finding and keeping a job and then depending upon white employers for payment. The largest single category of grievances initiated by black women under the Freedmen's Bureau "complaint" procedures concerned nonpayment of wages, indicating that many workers were routinely—and ruthlessly—defrauded of the small amounts they had earned and then "run off the place." Few southern planters had reserves of cash on hand after the war, and so they "fulfilled" commitments to their employees by charging prices for supplies so exorbitant that workers were lucky if they ended the year even, rather than indebted to their employer.

The bureau recommended that blacks receive a monthly wage ($10–12 per month for adult men, $8 for women) and that employers refrain from using physical force as a means of discipline. However, thousands of freed blacks contracted for rations, clothing, and shelter only, especially during the period 1865–1867. Employers retained unlimited authority in using various forms of punishment and felt free to disregard the agreements at the first sign of recalcitrance on the part of their laborers. Prohibitions against movement on and off the plantation were routine; blacks had to promise to "have no stragling about their houses and not to be strowling about at night," and they needed written permission to go into town or visit relatives nearby. The bureau tolerated and even, in most cases, approved these harsh terms. As the teacher Laura Towne noted, "enforcement" of the contracts usually meant ensuring that "the blacks don't break contract and [then] compelling them to submit cheerfully if the whites do."

Most northerners in positions of formal authority during the Reconstruction period detested southern planters as Confederate rebels but empathized with them as fledgling capitalists attempting to chain their workers to a "free labor" contract system. Moreover, few Union officials were inclined to believe that freedwomen as a group should contribute anything less than their full muscle power to the rebuilding of the region's economic system.

High rates of geographical mobility (as blacks moved about the southern countryside, in and out of towns, and to a lesser extent, to new homes in the southwestern part of the region) make it difficult to pinpoint with any precision the number of black women in specific kinds of jobs immediately after the war. Charlie Moses's mother moved the family from one Louisiana farm to another in search of work; "We jus' travelled all over from one place to another," he recalled. Freedwomen accepted any work they could find; in Columbia, South Carolina, they took the places of mules and turned screws to press cotton. The seasonal nature of agricultural labor meant that families often had to locate new sources of employment. When the cotton-picking season ended, for instance, Mingo White and his mother cut and hauled wood on an Alabama plantation. However, the overwhelming majority of women continued to work as field hands cultivating cotton for white landowners.

Other freedwomen relied on their cooking, gardening, dairying, and poultry-raising experience in an effort to make money as petty tradeswomen. In Aiken, South Carolina, a roving Yankee newspaper correspondent noted with approval that a black woman given 50 cents one day had appeared the next selling cakes and fresh fruit purchased with the money. Some women peddled berries, chickens, eggs, and vegetables along the road and in towns.

Other women tried to turn special talents and skills into a secure means of making a living. Nevertheless, former slaves were too poor to pay much for the services of midwives and seamstresses, and whites proved unreliable customers, to say the least. Even the small number of literate women who aspired to teaching had to rely on the fortunes of local black communities, most of which were unable to support a school on a regular basis. Susie King Taylor taught pupils in Savannah soon after the war; she and other independent instructors could hardly compete with a free school operated by a northern freedmen's aid society, the American Missionary Association (AMA). As a result, she was eventually forced from teaching into domestic service. A tiny number of teachers did qualify for aid from the Freedmen's Bureau or a private group like the AMA. In Georgia between 1865 and 1870, for example, perhaps seventy-five freedwomen received a modest salary for at least a few months from a northern source. However, New Englanders eager to help the cause of freedmen's education preferred to commission white teachers from the northern and midwestern states.

Although the freed people remained largely dependent upon whites for employment and supplies, strikes and other forms of group labor resistance began to surface soon after the Yankee invasion of the south. During the busy harvest season in the fall of 1862, for instance, female field hands on a Louisiana sugar plantation in Union-occupied territory engaged in a slowdown and then refused to work at all until the white landowner met their demand for wages. Then men on the plantation also struck within a week. The planter, fearful that his entire crop would be lost if it were not cut and processed immediately, finally agreed to pay them. And in 1866, the "colored washerwomen" of Jackson, Mississippi, organized themselves and established a price code for their services. Though the strike in June of that year was unsuccessful, according to Philip Foner it marked the "first known collective action of free black working-women in American history, as well as the first labor organization of black workers in Mississippi."

Slowly and grudgingly some whites began to learn a basic lesson of Reconstruction: Blacks' attitudes toward work depended on the extent of their freedom from white supervision. Edward S. Philbrick, a shrewd Yankee planter masquerading as a missionary on the South Carolina Sea Islands, marveled in March 1862 over the ability of former slaves to organize themselves and prepare hundreds of acres for planting cotton "without a white man near them." Frances B. Leigh, daughter of the renowned actress and abolitionist Fanny Kemble but more similar in temperament to her slaveholding father, returned to the family's Georgia estate in 1866 and soon discovered that the elderly freed people were "far too old and infirm to work for me, but once let them get a bit of ground of their own given to them, and they became quite young and strong again." One day she discovered that the aged Charity—"who represented herself as unable to move"—walked six miles almost every day to sell eggs (from her own chickens) on a neighboring plantation.

In their desire for household determination and economic self-sufficiency, blacks challenged the intentions of bureau agents and northern and southern planters alike. Northerners underestimated the extent to which black people would be prevented from accumulating cash and acquiring property. On the other hand,

southerners had not counted on the leverage wielded by workers determined to pry concessions out of them in the form of days off and garden privileges, and to press their own advantage during times of labor shortages. Some of this leverage assumed the form of meaningful political power at the local and state levels; for example, South Carolina rice workers (as members of the Republican party) played a vital role in that state's political process until Reconstruction ended in 1877. Ultimately, in making certain decisions about how family labor was to be organized, black people not only broke with the past in defiance of the white South, they also rejected a future of materialistic individualism in opposition to the white, middle-class North.

✳

The northerner's hope that black workers would be able to pursue their interests as individuals did not take into account the strong family ties that bound black households tightly together. More specifically, although black women constituted a sizable proportion of the region's labor force, their obligations to their husbands and children and kin took priority over any form of personal self-seeking. For most black women, then, freedom had very little to do with individual opportunity or independence in the modern sense. Rather, freedom had meaning primarily in a family context. Freedwomen derived emotional fulfillment and a newfound sense of pride from their roles as wives and mothers. Only at home could they exercise considerable control over their own lives and those of their husbands and children and impose a semblance of order on the physical world.

The withdrawal of black females from wage-labor—a main theme in both contemporary and secondary accounts of Reconstruction—occurred primarily among the wives and daughters of able-bodied men. (Women who served as the sole support for their children or other family members had to take work wherever they could find it.) According to a South Carolina newspaper writer in 1871, this development necessitated a "radical change in the management of [white] households as well as plantations" and proved to be a source of "absolute torment" for former masters and mistresses. The female field hand who plowed, hoed, and picked cotton under the ever-watchful eye of an overseer came to symbolize the old order.

Employers made little effort to hide their contempt for freedwomen who "played the lady" and refused to join workers in the fields. To apply the term ladylike to a black woman was apparently the height of sarcasm; by socially prescribed definition, black women could never become "ladies," though they might display pretensions in that direction. The term itself had predictable racial and class connotations. White ladies remained cloistered at home, fulfilling their marriage vows of motherhood and genteel domesticity. But black housewives appeared "most lazy"; they stayed "out of the fields, doing nothing," demanding that their husbands "support them in idleness."

In their haste to declare "free labor" a success, even northerners and foreign visitors to the South ridiculed "lazy" freedwomen working within the confines of their own homes. Hypocritically—almost perversely—these whites questioned the "manhood" of husbands whom they charged were cowed by domineering female relatives. South Carolina Freedmen's Bureau agent John De Forest, for example, wrote that "myriads of women who once earned their own living now have aspirations to be like white ladies and, instead of using the hoe, pass the days in dawdling over their trivial housework, or gossiping among their neighbors." He disdained the "hopeless" look given him by men told "they must make their wives and daughters work."

Most southern and northern whites assumed that the freed people were engaged in a misguided attempt to imitate middle-class white norms as they applied to women's roles. In fact, however, the situation was a good deal more complicated. First, the reorganization of female labor resulted from choices made by *both* men and women. Second, it is inaccurate to speak of the "removal" of women from the agricultural work force. Many were no longer working for a white overseer, but they continued to pick cotton, laboring according to the needs and priorities established by their own families.

An Alabama planter suggested in 1868 that it was "a matter of pride with the men, to allow all exemption from labor to their wives." He told only part of the story. There is good reason to suspect that wives willingly devoted more time to childcare and other domestic matters, rather than merely acquiescing in their husbands' demands. A married freedwoman, the mother of eleven children, reminded a northern journalist that she had had "to nus' my chil'n four times a day and pick two hundred pounds cotton besides" under slavery. She expressed at least relative satisfaction with her current situation: "I've a heap better time now'n I had when I was in bondage."

The humiliations of slavery remained fresh in the minds of black women who continued to suffer physical abuse at the hands of white employers and in the minds of freedmen who witnessed or heard about such acts. At this point it is important to note only that freedmen attempted to protect their womenfolk from rape and other forms of assault; as individuals, some intervened directly, while others went to local Freedmen's Bureau agents with accounts of beatings inflicted on their wives, sisters, and daughters. Bureau records include the case of a Tennessee planter who "made several base attempts" upon the daughter of the freedman Sam Neal (his entire family had been hired by the white man for the 1865 season). When Neal protested the situation, he was deprived of his wages, threatened with death, and then beaten badly by the white man and an accomplice. As a group, men sought to minimize chances for white male–black female contact by removing their female kin from work environments supervised closely by whites.

In the late 1860s this tug of economic and psychological warfare between planters determined to grow more cotton and blacks determined to resist the old slave ways culminated in what historians have called a "compromise"— the sharecropping system. It met the minimal standards of each party—a relatively reliable source of labor for white landowners, and, for freed people (more specifically, for families), a measure of independence in terms of agricultural decision making. Sharecroppers moved out of the old cabins and into small houses scattered about the plantation. Contracts were renegotiated around the end of each calendar year; families not in debt to their employers for equipment and fertilizer often seized the opportunity to move in search of a better situation. By 1870 the "fifty-fifty" share arrangement under which planters parceled out to tenants small plots of land and provided rations and supplies in return for one-half the crop predominated throughout the Cotton South.

Although 1870 data present only a static profile of black rural households in the Cotton South, it is possible to make some generalizations (based on additional forms of evidence) about the status of freedwomen five years after the war. The vast majority (91 percent) lived in rural areas. Illiterate and very poor (even compared to their poor white neighbors), they nonetheless were not alone, and shared the mixed joys of work and family life with their husbands, children, and nearby kin. Fertility rates declined very slowly from 1830 to 1880; the average mother in 1870 had about six or seven children. The lives of these women were severely circumscribed, as were those of other family members. Most of the children never had an opportunity to attend school—or at least not with any regularity—and began to work in the fields or in the home of a white employer around the age of ten or twelve. Young women found it possible to leave their parents' home earlier than did the men they married. As a group, black women were distinguished from their white neighbors primarily by their lower socioeconomic status and by the greater reliance of their families on the work they did outside the realm of traditional domestic responsibilities.

Within the limited public arena open to blacks, the husband represented the entire family, a cultural preference reinforced by demographic and economic factors. In 1870, 80 percent of black households in the Cotton Belt included a male head and his wife (a proportion identical to that in the neighboring white population).

Landowners, merchants, and Freedmen's Bureau agents acknowledged the role of the black husband as the head of his family at the same time they encouraged his wife to work outside the home. He took "more or less land according to the number of his family" and placed "his X mark" on a labor agreement with a landowner. Kin relationships were often recognized in the text of the contract itself. Indeed, just as slaveholders had opportunistically dealt with the slave family—encouraging or ignoring it according to their own perceived interests—so postbellum planters seemed to have had little difficulty adjusting to the fact that freedmen's families were structured "traditionally" with the husband serving as the major source of authority. Patrick Broggan, an employer in Greenville, Alabama, agreed to supply food and other provisions for wives and children—"those who do not work on the farm"—"at the expense of their husbands and Fathers," men who promised "to work from

Monday morning until Saturday night, faithfully and lose no time. . . ."

The Freedmen's Bureau's wage guidelines mandated that black women and men receive unequal compensation based on their sex rather than their productive abilities or efficiency. Agents also at times doled out less land to families with female (as opposed to male) household heads. Moreover, the bureau tried to hold men responsible for their wives' unwillingness to labor according to a contractual agreement. For example, the Cuthbert, Georgia, bureau official made one black man promise "to work faithfully and keep his wife in subjection" after the woman refused to work and "damned the Bureau" saying that "all the Bureaus out cant make her work."

A black husband usually purchased the bulk of the family's supplies (either in town or from a rural local merchant) and arranged to borrow or lease any stock animals that might be needed in plowing. He received direct payment in return for the labor of a son or daughter who had been "hired out." Finally, complaints and criminal charges lodged by black men against whites often expressed the grievances of an entire household.

Thus the sexual division of labor that had existed within the black family under slavery became more sharply focused after emancipation. Wives and mothers and husbands and fathers perceived domestic duties to be a woman's major obligation, in contrast to the slave master's view that a female was first and foremost a field or house worker and only incidentally the member of a family. Women also worked in the fields when their labor was needed. At planting and especially harvest time they joined their husbands and children outside. During the late summer and early fall some would hire out to white planters in the vicinity to pick cotton for a daily wage. In areas where black men could find additional work during the year—on rice plantations or in phosphate mines or sugar mills, for example—they left their "women and children to hoe and look after the crops. . . ." Thus women's agricultural labor partook of a more seasonal character than that of their husbands.

The rural *paterfamilias* tradition exemplified by the structure of black family relationships after the Civil War did not challenge the value and competence of freedwomen as fieldworkers. Rather, a distinct set of priorities determined how wives and mothers used their time in terms of housework, field labor, and tasks that produced supplements to the family income. Thus it is difficult to separate a freedwoman's "work" from her family-based obligations; productive labor had no meaning outside the family context. These aspects of a woman's life blended together in the seamless fabric of rural life.

Since husbands and wives had different sets of duties, they needed each other to form a complete economic unit. As one Georgia black man explained to George Campbell in the late 1870s, "The able-bodied men cultivate, the women raise chickens and take in washing; and one way and another they manage to get along." When both partners were engaged in the same kind of work, it was usually the wife who had stepped over into her husband's "sphere." For instance, Fanny Hodges and her husband wed the year after they were freed. She remembered, "We had to work mighty hard. Sometimes I plowed in de fiel' all day; sometimes I washed an' den I cooked. . . ." A family's ability to obtain financial credit from one year to the next depended upon the size of past harvests and the promise of future ones. Consequently the crop sometimes took precedence over other chores in terms of the allocation of a woman's energies.

The status of black women after the war cannot be separated from their roles as wives and mothers within a wider setting of kinship obligations. More than one-third of all black households in the Cotton Belt lived in the immediate vicinity of people with the identical (paternal) surname, providing a rather crude—and conservative—index of local kinship clusters. As the persons responsible for child nurture and social welfare, freedwomen cared not only for members of their nuclear families, but also for dependent relatives and others in need. This postemancipation cooperative impulse constituted but one example of a historical "ethos of mutuality" developed under slavery.

The former slaves' attempts to provide for each other's needs appear to be a logical and humane response to widespread hardship during the 1860s and 1870s. But whites spared from physical suffering, including southern elites and representatives of the northern professional class, often expressed misgivings about this form of benevolence. They believed that any able-bodied black person deserved a "living" only to the extent that he or she contributed to the southern commercial economy. Blacks should reap according to the cottonseed they sowed.

Too many blacks, according to bureau agent John De Forest, felt obliged to look after "a horde of lazy relatives" and neighbors, thus losing a precious opportunity to get ahead on their own. This tendency posed a serious threat to the South's new economic order, founded as it was, in De Forest's view, on individual effort and ambition. He pointed to the case of Aunt Judy, a black laundress who barely eked out a living for herself and her small children. Yet she had "benevolently taken in, and was nursing, a sick woman of her own race. . . . The thoughtless charity of this penniless Negress in receiving another poverty-stricken creature under her roof was characteristic of the freedmen. However selfish, and even dishonest, they might be, they were extravagant in giving." By calling the willingness to share a "thoughtless" act, De Forest implied that a "rational" economic being would labor only to enhance her own material welfare.

The racial self-consciousness demonstrated by black women and men within their own kin networks found formal, explicit expression in the political arena during Reconstruction. As Vincent Harding and others have shown, freedmen actively participated in postwar Republican politics, and leaders of their own race came to constitute a new and influential class within black communities. Class relationships that had prevailed before the war shifted, opening up possibilities of cooperation between the former slaves and nonelite whites. The two groups met at a historical point characterized by landlessness and economic dependence, but they were on two different trajectories—the freed people on their way up (no matter how slightly) from slavery, the poor whites on their way down from self-sufficiency. Nevertheless, the vitality of the political process, tainted though it was by virulent racial prejudice and violence, provided black men with a public forum distinct from the private sphere inhabited by their womenfolk.

Black men predominated in this arena because, like other groups in nineteenth-century America, they believed that males alone were responsible for—and capable of—the serious business of politicking. This notion was reinforced by laws that barred female suffrage. However, black husbands and fathers, unlike their white counterparts, perceived the preservation and physical welfare of their families (including protection from terrorists) to be distinct political issues, along with predictable measures like land reform and debt relief. In political activity, freedmen extended their role as family protector outside the boundaries of the household. One searches in vain for any mention of women delegates in accounts of formal black political conventions held during this period—local and state gatherings during which men formulated and articulated their vision of a just postwar society. Freedwomen sometimes spoke up forcefully at meetings devoted to specific community issues, but they remained outside the formal political process.

It is true that freedmen monopolized formal positions of power within their own communities during Reconstruction. But that did not necessarily mean that women quietly deferred to them in all matters outside the home. For example, in some rural areas two sources of religious authority—one dominated by men, the other by women—coexisted uneasily. At times formal role designations only partially reflected the "influence" wielded by individuals outside their own households. In the process of institutionalizing clandestine religious practices formed during slavery and separating them from white congregations, freed people reserved church leadership positions for men. In other ways, individual congregations fashioned a distinctly inferior role for women; some even turned women out of the sanctuary "before the men began to talk" about matters of church policy.

These examples must be contrasted with equally dramatic cases of women who exercised considerable influence over their neighbors' spiritual lives, but outside of formal religious bodies and, indeed, of Protestant denominationalism altogether. Elderly women in the long line of African and Afro-American conjurers and herb doctors were often eagerly consulted by persons of both sexes. They included the African-born Maum Katie, "a great 'spiritual mother,' a fortune-teller, or rather prophetess, and a woman of tremendous influence over her children," as well as other women whose pronouncements and incantations were believed to be divinely inspired.

＊

[Freedwomen's assertion of authority within and outside the black community threatened whites' views of proper sex roles.] In their descriptions of southern society during the fifteen years after the war, northern and foreign observers conveyed the distinct impression that black women were particularly outspoken and aggressive (by implication relative to black men) in their willingness to confront white authority

figures, "Freedmen's Bureau officers not excluded," noted one shocked Georgia agent. First, large numbers of freedwomen might have in fact found a release for their anger by publicly denouncing their white tormentors, taking their grievances to a local bureau agent, or goading into action other blacks more reticent or fatalistic than themselves. In his study of northern planters in the postbellum South, Lawrence Powell suggests that "the freedwomen did not give in easily to pressures from the planters. Women hands seem to have been among the most militant fighters for their rights among the ex-slaves."

However, a somewhat different approach to the problem would suggest that Yankee journalists, officials, travelers, and planters were intrigued by exceptionally strong-willed freedwomen and so tended to highlight individual cases and exaggerate their importance. Defenders of the notion of early Victorian (white) womanhood could not help but be struck by black women who openly challenged conventional standards of female submissiveness. Freedwomen were described as "growling," "impertinent," "impudent," "vulgar" persons who "spoke up bold as brass" and, with their "loud and boisterous talking," demanded fair treatment for "we people [left] way back."

As a group and as individuals, black women paid dearly for their own assertiveness and for that of their sisters who dressed, spoke up, shouted, and acted like free women. One night in April 1867, Harriett Murray, a servant in the home of Dick Porter near Panola, Mississippi, was dragged from the house into the nearby woods by her employer and another white man. There "her hands were tied to the fork of a limb" and she was whipped "until the two men were tired out; two candles were burnt out in the time." Porter then took her down from the tree, stripped her of her clothing, and held her while the other man continued to beat her. The cause of the assault is unknown, although the advice given to the victim by a local magistrate—that she should accept $38 in pay from Porter and forget about the whipping—indicates that a wage dispute was involved. Neither assailant was arrested.

Lacking any alternatives, some freedwomen continued to toil as they had under slavery and thus remained susceptible to "punishment" for any number of "offenses." The amount and quality of work performed by a woman, and disagreements over the compensation due her, provoked the rage of white men who were slave masters in all but name. In Athens, Georgia, Margaret Martin left her place of work to visit a niece one day in the spring of 1868 and was "badly beaten and choked" by her employer when she returned. The defiant freedwoman Caroline appeared before a Greensboro, North Carolina, Freedmen's Bureau official and reported that Thomas Price had failed to pay for her services; and when she next appeared on Price's plantation, the white man "knocked her down and Beat her with his fist" and ordered his overseer to bring him "the strap"; "then he whipped her with it holding her head between his knees on the bare flesh by turning her clothes up. . . ." The overseer also administered "a hundred lashes or more" after Price told him to "ware her out." Lucretia Adams of Yorkville, South Carolina, endured a night of terror initiated by eight drunken white men (she recognized all her assailants, including Oliver and Charles Boehmgart and Bill and Newman Thomas). They "just talked as anybody would" and told her, "We heard you wouldn't work. We were sent for . . . to come here and whip you, to make the damned niggers work."

The incidents just described were exceptional only in that they were reported to northern officials. Like Harriett Murray, most women heeded the warnings issued by their attackers to remain silent or leave the area if they did not want to be killed. Local officials often refused to make arrests despite overwhelming evidence against a man or group of men; most shared the view—expressed candidly by a Mississippi deputy—that "there was neither money nor glory" in making such arrests.

Even if a man were held to await trial, post-emancipation southern justice was less than forthright, rivaling in fact mythical Wild West lawlessness for sheer outrageousness. In specific cases concerning freedwomen, a town mayor assisted in helping an accused rapist to make his escape; and a judge charged with beating a women presided over his own trial, declared himself innocent, jailed his victim, and then forced her husband to pay for her release. Cases for black women plaintiffs were argued by drunken lawyers, and jury members stood up in the midst of proceedings to expound on behalf of the defendant. In June of 1868 an Upperville, Virginia, white man accused of assaulting a black woman leaped up during the trial and began beating her ferociously; he was acquitted.

The social consequences of freedom—the coming together of families to work and live—were accompanied by changes in the way women worked, dressed, and thought about themselves. But if liberation from bondage brought tangible, immediate benefits to some women, for others it represented but a fervent hope that their children would some day live as truly free people. A mother's belief that the future might be better for her offspring gave proof of the passing of slavery. The cook who "said she should die very happy, feeling that her children can spend 'the balance of their days in freedom, though she had been in bonds'" thought of freedom in terms of her family's future welfare and not her own current material condition. Black women throughout the South joined with men to form local education committees, build schoolhouses, and hire teachers at a time when their neighborhoods' material resources were slim indeed.

These mothers tried to prepare their children for a new kind of life. Poor but proud women refused to let their sons and daughters accept clothing (donated by whites) they considered ill-fitting or immodest; it was considered "highly indecorous to have the feet and ankles show below the dress," for example. Northern teachers and Freedmen's Bureau officials often showed a lack of sensitivity toward these women who chose self-respect over convenience. Mary Ames, a Yankee teacher, recorded a revealing incident in her diary: "One girl brought back a dress she had taken home for 'Ma says it don't fit, and she don't want it.' It was rather large and short, but she was very dirty and ragged, and we told her she must keep it." In other instances, parents disciplined their children with the liberal use of the rod, but they reserved the right to decide how and whether it should be used. Two years after the war, a Georgia bureau agent sustained charges brought against Eliza James because she had "impudently" refused to punish her son at the behest of a white man "and said she would not whip her child for no poor white folks etc." For a white person to demand the punishment of a child smacked of slavery, and this freedwoman would not tolerate it.

The elderly Sea Island evening-school pupil "who was much bent with rheumatism" but said she was "mighty anxious to know something"; the Savannah laundress who fastened her textbook to the fence so she could read "while at work over the wash tub"; and the Greenville, South Carolina, dressmaker who attended classes in the morning and worked at her trade in the afternoon were three of the few freedwomen to receive some formal education soon after emancipation. (In 1870 more than eight out of ten southern blacks were illiterate.) For most women, the rigors of childbearing and rearing, household chores and outside employment, represented a continuum from slavery to freedom, unbroken by schooling or other opportunities to expand their horizons beyond the cabin in the cotton field.

The Alabama Freedmen's Bureau agents assigned to conduct a "Negro Census" for 1865 in the Athens-Huntsville area probably resented spending so much time and energy on what they considered bureaucratic nonsense. Before too long they became careless in recording the ages and previous occupations of people they interviewed. However, for a while initially, they dutifully noted the required information: each person's name, age, sex, address, former owner, slave occupation, and "present employment." The first few pages of the census include these bits of data on about three hundred people. More than the gory details of an "outrage" report, or the tedious wording of a labor contract, this remarkable document chronicles the quiet revolution wrought in the lives of black women after emancipation.

Consider the Jones family: Caroline, formerly a house servant, and her daughter, Savannah, both of whom had been owned by John Haws, were now reunited with husband William (previously owned by a white man named Crawford). Caroline reported no occupation but instead said she was "caring for her family." William continued to work in a railroad shop. Two months before the census interview they had celebrated their new life together with the birth of a son, James, who was listed as "Free born." Nearby, Nelson and Phoebe Humphrey and their five children came together from two plantations (Nelson from one and Phoebe and the children from another). Both former field hands, Nelson was doing "Miscellaneous: for other people" and Phoebe took in laundry. Joanna (aged fourteen), who used to work as a house servant, was now attending school, and her thirteen-year-old sister Elizabeth no longer worked in the fields; she probably helped her mother with the washing.

Not too far away two young women in the Hammond clan took up employment as laundresses so that Easter (sixty), a former domestic, would no longer have to work; she was listed as ill. The women, Nettie (thirty-three) and Ata (twenty-nine), had six children between them, but no husband was listed for either. In the same neighborhood resided a second Jones family, consisting of Gilbert (fifty) and Julia (forty-eight) and the children they had retrieved from two different slave masters. The father had found work as a blacksmith and son William (twenty-one) continued to labor as a field hand. Gilbert, Jr. (fourteen), stayed at home rather than working in the fields as he had before, and Amanda (eighteen), also a former hand but "subject to fits" was now able to "help her mother."

Freedwomen like Phoebe Humphrey and Julia Jones would have had no difficulty listing the blessings of freedom: a reunion at long last with their families, the opportunity to devote more time to household affairs, and children attending school. Although it would be difficult to argue that their work was any less arduous than that of their slave mothers, these women were now in a position to decide, together with their husbands, how and when various family members should contribute to the welfare of the household. Nettie and Ata Hammond probably had fewer alternatives when it came to supporting their children, but at least they were able to relieve the elderly Easter of her duties as a house servant.

Still, all black women continued to occupy two distinct statuses that shaped their daily lives. In their neighborhoods they commanded respect as wives, mothers and upholders of cultural tradition. In the eyes of whites busy laying the foundations for the "New South"— planters and federal officials—they were still workers who belonged to a despised caste, considered apart from white women no matter how downtrodden. Yet freedwomen perceived freedom to mean not a release from backbreaking labor, but rather the opportunity to labor on behalf of their own families and kin within the protected spheres of household and community.

Questions for Study and Review

1. In what ways were black and white southern women's experiences of the Civil War similar? In what ways were they different?

2. From where did the belief that every freedman would get forty acres and a mule emerge, and in what ways did the lack of such support shape postwar race relations?

3. To what extent did black women and men continue to share familial and communal authority as black men gained the franchise, as marriage was legalized, and as contracts signed by husbands and fathers verified labor relations for the entire family?

4. Some historians have called the Civil Rights movement of the 1960s the Second Reconstruction. Why was a Second Reconstruction needed, and how did black women's roles change between the two periods?

Suggested Readings

Herbert Gutman, *The Black Family in Slavery and Freedom, 1750–1925* (1976).

Ira Berlin, Joseph P. Reidy, and Leslie Rowland, eds., *Freedom: A Documentary History of Emancipation, 1861–1867, Series II: The Black Military Experience* (1982).

Darlene Clark Hine, "Lifting the Veil, Shattering the Silence: Black Women's History in Slavery and Freedom," in *The State of Afro-American History, Past, Present and Future* (1986).

Suzanne Lebsock, "Radical Reconstruction and the Property Rights of Southern Women," *Journal of Southern History* (May 1977).

A Statistical Portrait

Ruth Milkman

To recapture the historical experience of women, scholars have pursued a host of new methods and turned to a variety of sources. Some famous or elite women left letters, diaries, and family papers, which historians have used to recreate these women's relations with their fathers and husbands as well as with female kin and friends. These documents also provide information about women's activities in churches, schools, and voluntary organizations as well as intimations of their attitudes toward children. A smaller number of poor, working-class, and minority women also wrote about their lives or had their spoken testimony transcribed by others. Yet uncovering and understanding the daily lives and thoughts of these nonelite and less well known women, and their male kin and neighbors, requires investigation of more than the conventional literary sources. Examinations of physical artifacts such as housing or dress, the use of visual and aural documents in the form of photographs or recordings, the gathering of oral histories, and the analysis of quantitative data all provide new means of illuminating the past. The use of statistical information is especially important for reconstructing the objective boundaries of people's lives. Such data might include the relative numbers of women and men in a community, the average number of children borne by an adult woman, the likelihood of a woman working for wages, the types of jobs she might hold and her average earnings, the life expectancy of women and men, and how each of these varied by region, race, class, and ethnic background as well as over time.

For most women, the size and makeup of their household, the amount and type of domestic labor they performed, and their access to paid employment set the framework of their lives. These factors shaped their relationships with relatives, neighbors, and the larger community and powerfully affected the opportunities open to them for education, recreation, and participation in public activities or institutions. For most of our nation's history, women of all regions, races, classes, and ethnic backgrounds shared certain experiences. More than 90 percent of all women did housework, were married or lived in marriage-like relations, and bore children at some point in their lives. Yet more often it was not these broad similarities but rather the differences among women that were important in shaping the contours of individual, family, and community history. Thus, it is critical to locate women in place as well as in time and to chart change over time both for women as women and in relation to men.

In the colonial period, for instance, men often outnumbered women by large margins, limiting opportunities for creating stable family lives. Life expectancy was relatively short by modern standards, a factor which also shortened the length of marriages and reduced the number of children that might be born to any given couple. Still, fertility rates were high as these early Americans sought to increase the new nation's population. One benefit of a larger population was a larger labor force, yet at least into the nineteenth century, Americans relied on immigration and enslavement, along with the natural increase supplied by births, to provide factory and field hands. Native-born white, African American, and immigrant women differed in their life expectancy, the size of their families, and the likelihood that they would work for someone other than their own family. Yet overall, from the first colonial settlements to the end of Reconstruction, fertility rates declined and women's participation in the labor force increased, setting the stage for more dramatic changes in the next century.

In the tables, figures, and graphs that follow, Ruth Milkman provides quantitative portraits of women from a range of families and communities and across the expanse of American history. Though limited by the amount, types, and quality of data collected in past centuries, these statistical snapshots allow us to view our ancestors with a new clarity and to compare their experiences—their life expectancy, the size of their families, the racial and sexual balance in their communities, their opportunities for paid work, and their participation in various occupations—with our own.

The articles in this volume describe women in specific times and places and engaged in a variety of activities—childbirth and childrearing, slave labor, factory or farm work, wartime service, or political or religious pursuits. Consulting the graphs and tables provided here as you read the articles will help you place the women you read about within the larger context of the American experience. For example, the figures indicate that in the early 1800s fewer than 10 percent of all women in the United States over the age of ten were gainfully employed. Thus, you can gain some sense of both the excitement and the fear felt by the thousands of farm daughters who entered the Lowell mills at that time. Similarly, the statistical information here will help you grasp better the different relationships among slave, free black, and immigrant women and men in mid-nineteenth century families. You will see, for example, that in the first group, there were roughly equal numbers of women and men; in the second, there were substantially more women than men; while among immigrants, there were far more men than women.

Examining the relatively short life expectancy and high rates of fertility among nineteenth-century women will help you appreciate the importance of changes in childbirth practices. At the same time, you can begin to imagine what dramatic changes in individual and family life occurred as the average woman bore fewer and fewer children over the course of the century, with a woman of the Reconstruction era bearing perhaps only half the number of children borne by her Revolutionary-era grandmother.

These statistical portraits throw into sharp relief the outlines of women's lives across the first two and one-half centuries of our nation's history. Tracing the common as well as the quite different experiences of women of various ethnic backgrounds, classes, and races across both time and place, the charts, graphs, and tables included here set the contours of our own lives in a larger context and help us understand the conditions and the constraints under which earlier Americans carved out their individual, familial, communal, and national identities.

Suggested Readings

W. Elliott Brownlee and Mary M. Brownlee, *Women in the American Economy* (1976).

Richard A. Easterlin, "Population Change and Farm Settlement in the Northern United States," *Journal of Economic History* 36 (1976).

Michael Gordon, ed., *The American Family in Social-Historical Perspective* (3rd ed., 1986).

Joni Seager and Ann Olson, *Women in the World: An International Atlas* (1986).

Helen L. Sumner, *History of Women in Industry in the United States* (1910).

U.S. Bureau of the Census, *Historical Statistics of the United States, Colonial Times to 1970* (1976).

U.S. Bureau of the Census, *Negro Population, 1790–1915* (1918).

U.S. Department of Labor, *History of Wages in the United States from Colonial Times to 1928* (1934).

U.S. Department of Labor, Women's Bureau Bulletin 198, *Time of Change: 1983 Handbook on Women Workers* (1983).

Robert V. Wells, "Women's Lives Transformed: Demographic and Family Patterns in America, 1600–1970," in Carol Berkin and Mary Beth Norton, eds., *Women of America, A History* (1979).

In the early colonial period, there was a shortage of females relative to males in the population of what later became the United States. The sex ratios gradually became more equal in the first part of the eighteenth century, although achieving this balance took longer in some colonies than in others. The first table below shows the sex ratios among white settlers from selected population censuses taken in various colonies prior to the American Revolution. The second table shows the sex ratios among blacks for the same period.

Sex Ratios in the White Population of Selected Colonies, 1624–1776

DATE	COLONY	WHITE MALE POPULATION	WHITE FEMALE POPULATION	FEMALES PER 100 MALES
1624–5	Virginia*	873	222	25
1698	New York*	5,066	4,677	92
1704	Maryland*	11,026	7,163	65
1726	New Jersey	15,737	14,124	90
1755	Rhode Island	17,860	17,979	101
1764–5	Massachusetts	106,611	110,089	103
1771	Vermont	2,503	2,147	86
1774	Connecticut	96,182	94,296	98

Sex Ratios in the Black Population of Selected Colonies, 1624–1776

DATE	COLONY	BLACK MALE POPULATION	BLACK FEMALE POPULATION	FEMALES PER 100 MALES
1624–5	Virginia*	11	10	91
1703	New York	1,174	1,084	92
1726	New Jersey	1,435	1,146	80
1755	Maryland*	10,947	8,007	73
1755	Rhode Island	2,387	2,310	97
1764–5	Massachusetts	2,824	2,067	73
1774	Connecticut	2,883	2,218	77

Source: U.S. Bureau of the Census, *Historical Statistics of the United States, Colonial Times to 1970* (Washington: GPO, 1975), 1169–71.

---

* These figures include adults only. Children were counted separately and not distinguished by gender.

In the nineteenth century, sex ratios in the native-born white population were fairly stable, with a slight male surplus. In contrast, there was a slight surplus of women among free blacks during slavery and among blacks generally after emancipation, and a substantial surplus of men among foreign-born whites in the second half of the century.

Population of the United States by Sex, Race, and Nativity

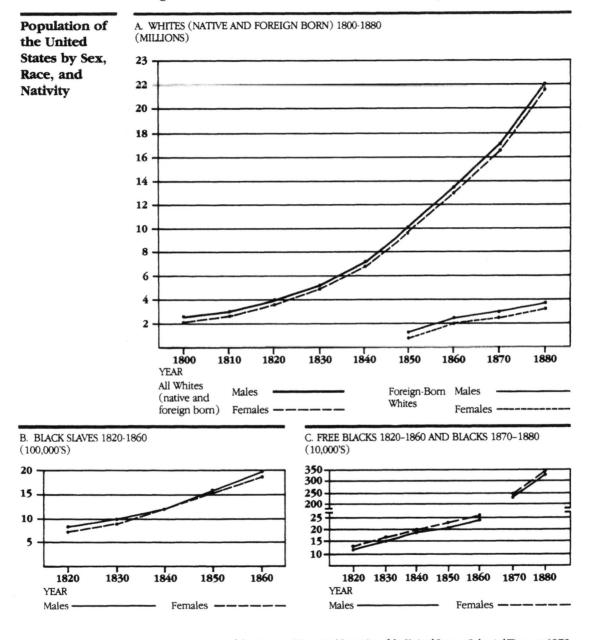

A. WHITES (NATIVE AND FOREIGN BORN) 1800-1880 (MILLIONS)

All Whites (native and foreign born)   Males ————   Females ——————

Foreign-Born Whites   Males ————   Females ——————

B. BLACK SLAVES 1820-1860 (100,000'S)

Males ————   Females ——————

C. FREE BLACKS 1820-1860 AND BLACKS 1870-1880 (10,000'S)

Males ————   Females ——————

Source: U.S. Bureau of the Census, *Historical Statistics of the United States, Colonial Times to 1970* (Washington: GPO, 1975), 14, 18.

Life expectancy was very low in the nineteenth century, by today's standards. Those who survived the first twenty years of life, however, were likely to be quite long-lived. Life expectancy was slightly higher for women than for men in the nineteenth century, and for both sexes it increased somewhat over time. The bar chart below summarizes the fragmentary data available for this period on life expectancy, which are from Massachusetts only. No data are available by race or national origin, but twentieth-century sources suggest that life expectancy for blacks and the foreign-born was considerably poorer than that for native-born whites, and there is good reason to think this was the case in the nineteenth century (and earlier) as well.

Life Expectancy at Specified Ages, by Sex, for Massachusetts, 1850–1882

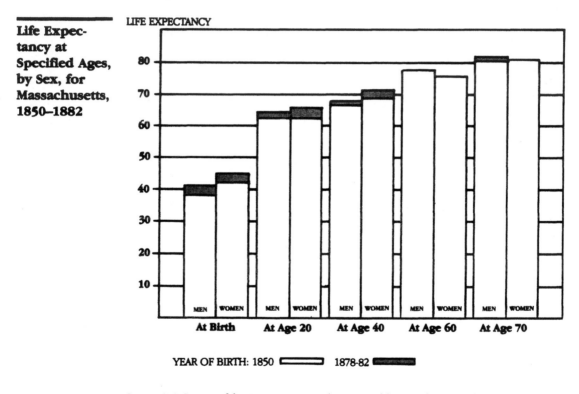

Source: U.S. Bureau of the Census, *Historical Statistics of the United States, Colonial Times to 1970* (Washington: GPO, 1975), 56.

Women typically married at around age twenty in the nineteenth century, and much of their lives thereafter was spent bearing and rearing children. In 1800, the average white woman bore seven children. Of course, given the high infant and child mortality rates, not all of these children survived into adulthood. Fertility rates fell significantly over the course of the nineteenth century for whites, as the table below shows. Data for black women for this period are fragmentary, but their fertility rates declined later, probably starting around 1880, than those of white women.

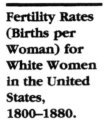

Fertility Rates (Births per Woman) for White Women in the United States, 1800–1880.

BIRTHS PER WOMAN

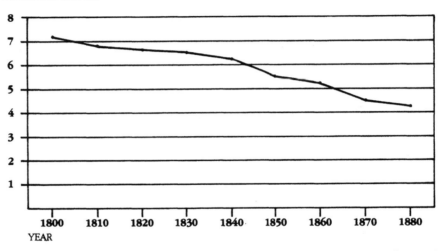

YEAR

Source: Ansley J. Coale and Melvin Zelnik, *New Estimates of Fertility and Population in the United States* (Princeton: Princeton University Press, 1963), 36.

The extent of women's involvement in wage labor increased slowly in the nineteenth century. (No figures are available prior to 1800.) The figures here do not include the bulk of the female population who labored at home without receiving a wage. And for 1800 to 1860, these figures include only free women, both black and white. An estimated 90 percent of female slaves aged ten and over were in the labor supply in this period, although very few were paid wages.*

Women's Participation in the United States Labor Force, 1800–1880

PERCENTAGE OF ALL WOMEN WHO ARE EMPLOYED

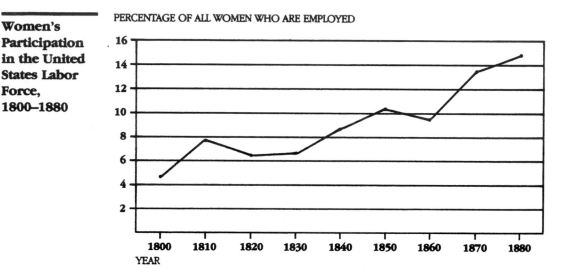

Source: W. Elliott Brownlee and Mary M. Brownlee, *Women in the American Economy* (New Haven: Yale University Press, 1976), 3.

* Stanley Lebergott, *Manpower in Economic Growth* (New York: McGraw-Hill, 1964), 59.

Before 1850, there are no national records of the distribution of women workers among the various occupations making up the wage labor market. In 1850, the U.S. Census Bureau began collecting such statistics for manufacturing industries only. The charts below show the distribution of women factory workers in 1850 and 1880 for major industry groups. Women workers in the clothing and textile industries were the overwhelming proportion of the female factory work force in this period; the textile and clothing industries relied on women for half of their overall work force. Women's representation was also substantial in the paper and printing, tobacco and cigars, and food industries. The number of women in each of these groups increased between 1850 and 1880, but only in food did they form a greater percentage of the work force by 1880. Keep in mind, however, that the largest number of women before 1880 were still employed in domestic service and agriculture.

Numbers of Women Employed and Percent Women Formed of Total Wage Earners in Manufacturing, by Industry Group, 1850 and 1880

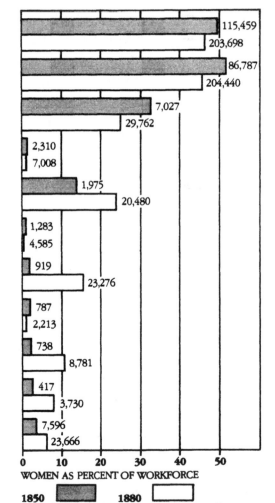

INDUSTRY GROUP

Clothing Industries — 115,459 / 203,698
Textile Industries — 86,787 / 204,440
Paper and Printing — 7,027 / 29,762
Lumber and Lumber Products — 2,310 / 7,008
Tobacco and Cigars — 1,975 / 20,480
Iron, Steel and Their Products — 1,283 / 4,585
Food and Kindred Products — 919 / 23,276
Clay, Glass, and Stone Products — 787 / 2,213
Metals and Metal Products Other Than Iron and Steel — 738 / 8,781
Chemicals and Allied Products — 417 / 3,730
Other Manufacturing Industries — 7,596 / 23,666

WOMEN AS PERCENT OF WORKFORCE

1850 ▨   1880 ☐

Source: Helen L. Sumner, *History of Women in Industry in the United States* (U.S. Senate Document No. 645, 1910), 250.

The 1880 census collected information about women's occupations both within manufacturing and in other fields of employment. The following charts show the distribution of women by major occupational group, revealing that domestic service was the most common form of employment for women, with nearly twice as many female domestics as factory workers by 1880. There were substantial variations in women's employment, depending on whether they were native-born or immigrant women. Figures in the pie chart refer to the percentage of all women employed in each occupational group.

Occupational Distribution of Women over Age Ten in Paid Labor Force, for Native- and Foreign-born Women, 1880

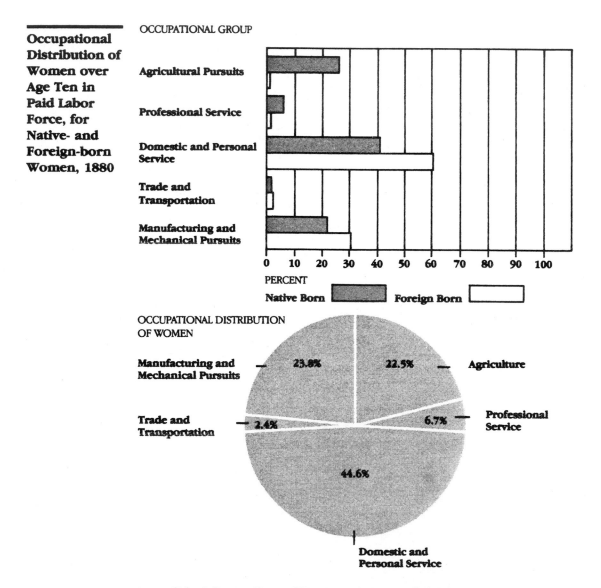

Source: Helen L. Sumner, *History of Women in Industry in the United States* (U.S. Senate Document No. 645, 1910), 246.

Patterns of women's employment in the late nineteenth century also varied considerably in different regions of the nation. The following charts provide a regional breakdown for 1880, which reveals that manufacturing employment was especially important in the North and West, whereas in the South agriculture was the major source of women's gainful employment. This pattern partly reflects the large number of black women in the South employed in agriculture. Domestic service was an important source of employment in all regions.

Women's Employment in 1880, by Occupational Group and Geographical Region

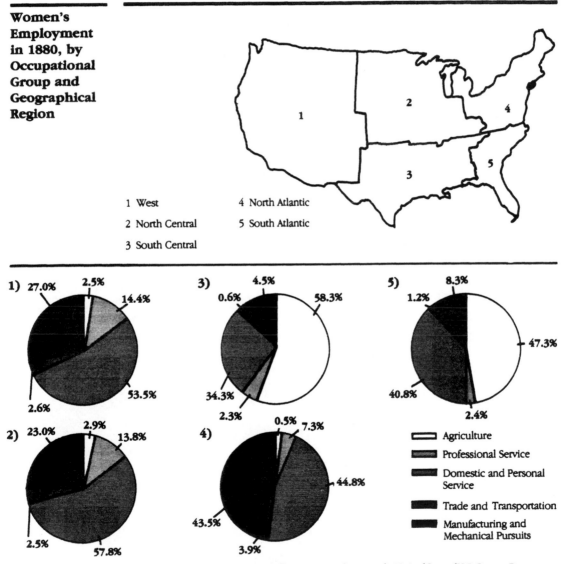

1 West   4 North Atlantic

2 North Central   5 South Atlantic

3 South Central

Source: Helen L. Sumner, *History of Women in Industry in the United States* (U.S. Senate Document No. 645, 1910), 246.

Credits

Appendix, "A Statistical Portrait" by Ruth Milkman. Copyright © 1989 by Ruth Milkman. Reprinted by permission of the author.

Photographs: Unless otherwise acknowledged, all photos are the property of Scott, Foresman and Company.

xvi Cook Collection/Valentine Museum, Richmond, Virginia   **2** Library of Congress   **8** Engraving by Theodore De Bry, From De Bry's *Florida Volume*, 1590, Courtesy of The Newberry Library, Chicago   **13** Drawing by Sidney E. King   **25** Painting, *Examination of a Witch*, by T. H. Matteson, 1853. The Essex Institute, Salem, Ma.   **50** Brady Collection/The National Archives   **58, 63** Library of Congress   **65** Library of Congress   **82** Massachusetts Historical Society   **98** Library of Congress   **106** The New-York Historical Society, New York City   **112** Warshaw Collection/Smithsonian Institution   **114** Museum of American Textile History, Andover, Mass.   **130** The New-York Historical Society, New York City   **141** Women's History Archive, Sophia Smith Collection, Smith College, Northampton, Ma.   **161** Green Corn Dance painting by Joseph Henry Sharp, from Thomas Gilcrease Institute of American History & Art, Tulsa   **174** November, 1853/*Harper's Weekly*   **186** The Kansas State Historical Society, Topeka   **192** North Carolina Department of Cultural Resources, Division of Archives & History   **198** Mrs. Katherine McCook Knox   **200** NYT Pictures   **204** Library of Congress   **209** Chicago Historical Society   **219** Folks All Home © 1875, Lightfoot Collection, Photo by O. Pierre Havens.